BOLLINGEN SERIES XXXVII

ERWIN R. GOODENOUGH

JEWISH SYMBOLS

in the

Greco-Roman Period

VOLUME NINE

SYMBOLISM IN THE DURA SYNAGOGUE

(*The first of three volumes*)

TEXT, *i*

BOLLINGEN SERIES XXXVII

PANTHEON BOOKS

THIS BOOK IS VOLUME NINE OF THE THIRTY-SEVENTH PUBLICATION
IN A SERIES SPONSORED AND PUBLISHED BY
BOLLINGEN FOUNDATION

Library of Congress Catalog Card No. 52–10031

Manufactured in the United States of America
by Kingsport Press, Inc., Kingsport, Tenn.

TO

THE MEMORY OF

SAMUEL THE PRESBYTER

SAMUEL SON OF SAPHARAH

ABRAM THE TREASURER

JOSEPH SON OF ABBA

UZZI, ARSACES, SILAS, SALMANES

..... THE PROSELYTE

WHO BUILT THE SYNAGOGUE AT DURA

AND DISCLOSED NEW-OLD DEPTHS IN

JUDAISM

PREFACE TO VOLUMES IX, X, AND XI

THE THREE VOLUMES here presented complete the publication and interpretation of *Jewish Symbols in the Greco-Roman Period*. A final volume of summary and over-all conclusions must close the series, but with these eleven volumes the reader has the data before him.

In discussing the synagogue at Dura Europos I have kept closely to my task, that of presenting what has seemed to be the symbolic material in it, and of trying to see what that material meant to the Jews of the synagogue. Dura has given a new kind of data altogether, for here Jews, while using many of the pagan and Jewish symbols discussed in the former volumes, were at the same time painting interpretations of their Bible. These two cannot be separated: a single person or group put together the pagan symbols and the biblical scenes, put, indeed, many new pagan symbols into the biblical scenes themselves. Such integration of paganism and Judaism in the whole decoration of the room, even within the biblical paintings, demands integration in the interpretation.

Professor Carl H. Kraeling, in his impressive volume *The Synagogue* (New Haven, 1956), began with quite other assumptions, and, naturally, reached quite different interpretations, as have others of my predecessors. It has seemed useless to make this study a running controversy, and I have not done so. My great number of references to Kraeling's work show that there are many disagreements, but also many matters about which we agree. Even those who judge that I have succeeded in interpreting the decorations more acceptably than he, however, will still find his work indispensable. I have felt no obligation to discuss systematically the archeological data, the condition of the paintings, their place in the history of art, and many other aspects of the paintings which Kraeling properly considered; I have gone into them only as they seemed to affect the problem of interpretation. It was necessary, however, to republish the paintings in detail, partly because the reader could not otherwise have followed my remarks, and partly because Kraeling's cutting of the larger pictures into segments obscured their value as compositions, the basis of any interpretation.

Mr. F. Anderegg made fresh photographs of the synagogue paintings for the color plates in Volume XI, and in doing so had most cordial and helpful cooperation from the Director of Antiquities and the entire staff at the great Archeological Museum in Damascus, where the paintings are now exhibited in a replica of the original building. All readers will join the author in thanking them for making the paintings available in such reliable reproduction. I have also reproduced in black and white the copies H. Gute made of the paintings as they were being uncovered. He worked *in situ* the second year of the excavation of the synagogue, and with no thesis for interpretation tried, simply by careful study of the brush strokes, to see what had originally been painted on the walls. Each evening, he said, the entire staff gathered to study his work of the day to compare it with the original, and he corrected any inaccuracies pointed out. Obviously, much appears in these paintings that cannot be seen in photographs at all, and I suspect that they give the most reliable report we shall ever have of what was originally represented. His originals, now fading, can be seen in the Yale University Art Gallery. I reproduce them here with the kind permission of the Dura Editorial Committee and the Gallery, and of Mr. Gute himself.

Permission to publish the synagogue paintings, as well as many architectural drawings and text figures, has been only a part of the extraordinary cooperation I have received from the Dura Committee, especially its Chairman, Professor Frank Brown, and the Editor, Dr. Ann Perkins. They supplied me with photographs of anything from Dura I wanted to use, and freely allowed me to publish them, as has the Yale University Art Gallery. Material from Dura not otherwise acknowledged I owe to the Committee and the Gallery. Less obvious is what I owe to the patience of these two scholars in explaining the details of which they were masters. They have probably not saved me from all errors, but they have enabled me to avoid many.

I do not repeat the long list of people and institutions mentioned in earlier volumes as having helped me, though they have continued to do so. To this list I must add Father Antonio Ferrua, S.J., who kindly allowed me to work with photographs of the frescoes in the new Catacomb Via Latina before their publication and to reproduce several of them. Professor Amedeo Maiuri of Naples, and the staffs of the Deutsches Archäologisches Institut, the Vatican Library, the Bibliothèque Nationale and the Louvre, the British Museum, the Archeological Museums in Damascus, Beirut, and Istanbul, and the Index of Christian Art at Princeton have all helped in obtaining for me many of the photographs here published. Members of the Department of Archeology in Israel have been especially kind in allowing me to publish pieces from Sheikh Ibreiq (Beth She'arim) before their collected publication of them appeared. I regret I cannot list here all the acknowledgments given for individual photographs throughout the book. I have been much helped by criticisms and suggestions from Professor Morton Smith of Columbia, Professor Judah Goldin, Professor and Mrs. Lawrence Richardson of Yale, and my research assistant Dr. B. Philip Lozinski.

These volumes are being published in the year after my retirement from Yale University. Above all, then, I give it thanks for the thirty-nine years in which I enjoyed its magnificent library and its dedication to creative scholarship.

ERWIN R. GOODENOUGH

Cambridge, Massachusetts
May 1, 1963

Contents

VOLUME IX

PART XV. THE PAINTINGS OF THE SOUTH, EAST, AND NORTH WALLS

The illustrations for Volumes IX and X form the contents of Volume XI.

ABBREVIATIONS

AAL, M.   *Atti della R. Accademia dei Lincei, Memorie della Classe di Scienze Morali, Storiche e Filologiche.*

AAL, N.   *Atti della R. Accademia dei Lincei, Notizie degli scavi di antichità della Classe di Scienze Morali, Storiche e Filologiche.*

AJA.   *American Journal of Archaeology.*

Amelung, *Sculp. Vatican.*   Walter Amelung, *Die Sculpturen des Vaticanischen Museums,* Berlin, 1903–1936.

ARF.   *See* Beazley.

ARW.   *Archiv für Religionswissenschaft.*

ASAE.   *Annales du Service des Antiquités de l'Egypte.*

ASE.   Archaeological Survey of Egypt.

Ashburnham Pentateuch.   Oskar von Gebhardt, *The Miniatures of the Ashburnham Pentateuch,* London, 1884.

AZ.   *Archäologische Zeitung.*

BAC.   *Bullettino di archeologia cristiana.*

BASOR.   *Bulletin of the American School of Oriental Research.*

BCA.   *Bullettino della Commissione Archeologica Comunale di Roma.*

BCH.   *Bulletin de correspondance hellénique.*

BD.   Book of the Dead. Unless otherwise stated, as transl. by E. A. W. Budge, *The Book of the Dead: An English Translation,* 2d ed., London, 1923.

Beazley, *ARF.*   J. D. Beazley, *Attic Red-Figured Vase-Painters,* Oxford, 1942.

Beyer and Lietzmann, *Torlonia.*   H. W. Beyer and Hans Lietzmann, *Jüdische Denkmäler,* I: *Die jüdische Katakombe der Villa Torlonia in Rom,* Berlin and Leipzig, 1930 (Studien zur spätantiken Kunstgeschichte, IV).

Bieber, *Kleidung.*   Margarete Bieber, *Griechische Kleidung,* Berlin and Leipzig, 1928.

Bieber, *Tracht.*   Margarete Bieber, *Entwicklungsgeschichte der griechischen Tracht,* Berlin, 1934.

BJPES.   *Bulletin of the Jewish Palestine Exploration Society.*

Bonner, *Amulets.*   Campbell Bonner, *Studies in Magical Amulets, Chiefly Graeco-Egyptian,* Ann Arbor, 1950.

Bousset, *Religion.*   Wilhelm Bousset and H. Gressman, *Die Religion des Judentums im späthellenistischen Zeitalter,* 3d ed., Tübingen, 1926 (Handbuch zum Neuen Testament, XXI).

BT.   Babylonian Talmud, with references to the various treatises. ET refers to the Engl. transl. made by various scholars under the general editorship of I. Epstein, London, Soncino Press, 1935 et seq. Similarly, GT refers to the German transl. of Lazarus Goldschmidt, pub. with the Hebrew text, Berlin, 1897; rev. ed. (German transl. only), Berlin, 1929.

Butler, *Architecture, 1899.*   Howard C. Butler, *Architecture and Other Arts,* New York, 1903 (Publications of the American Archaeological Expedition to Syria in 1899–1900, II).

Butler, *Architecture, 1904–1905.*   *Syria: Publications of the Princeton University Archaeological Expeditions to Syria in 1904–1905 and 1909.* Div. II, *Architecture,* by Howard C. Butler: Sec. *A,* "Southern Syria"; Sec. *B,* "Northern Syria," Leyden, 1919–1920.

By Light, Light.   *See* Goodenough.

CBM.   A Catalogue of the Greek Coins in the British Museum, London, 1873–1937.

Charles, *Apoc. and Pseud.*   R. H. Charles, *The Apocrypha and Pseudepigrapha of the Old Testament in English, with Introductions and Critical and Explanatory Notes to the Several Books,* Oxford, 1913.

Christensen, *Types.*   A. Christensen, *Les Types du premier homme et du premier roi,* Stockholm, 1917–1934 (Archives d'études orientales, XIV).

CIJ.   *See* Frey.

CL.   *Dictionnaire d'archéologie chrétienne et de liturgie,* ed. by Fernand Cabrol and H. Leclercq, Paris, 1907 et seq.

Cohn-Wiener.   Ernst Cohn-Wiener, *Die jüdische Kunst, ihre Geschichte von den Anfängen bis zur Gegenwart,* Berlin and Leipzig, 1929.

Coll. de Clercq.   *Collection de Clercq: Catalogue méthodique et raisonné: Antiquités Assyriennes,* Paris, 1888.

Const. Octateuch.   M. Uspenskii, "Konstantinopol'skii Seral'skii kodeks Vos'miknizhiia," *Izviestiia, Russkii Arkheologicheskii Institut v Konstantinopolie,* XII (1901), 1–255, and album of plates.

Cook, *Zeus.*   Arthur B. Cook, *Zeus: A Study in Ancient Religion,* Cambridge, 1914 et seq.

CSEL.   *Corpus scriptorum ecclesiasticorum Latinorum,* Vienna, 1866 et seq.

Cumont, *Fouilles.*   Franz Cumont, *Fouilles de Doura-Europos (1922–1923),* Paris, 1926 (Haut-Commissariat de la République Française en Syrie et au Liban, Services des Antiquités et des Beaux-Arts, Bibliothèque archéologique et historique, IX).

Cumont, *Lux.*   Franz Cumont, *Lux Perpetua,* Paris, 1949.

Cumont, *Symbolisme.*   Franz Cumont, *Recherches sur le symbolisme funéraire des Romains,* Paris, 1942 (Bibliothèque archéologique et historique, XXXV).

Cumont, *TMM.*   Franz Cumont, *Textes et monuments figurés relatifs aux mystères de Mithra,* Brussels, 1896, 1899.

Curtius.   Ludwig Curtius, *Die Wandmalerei Pompejis*, Leipzig, 1929.

CVA. Corpus vasorum antiquorum, Union Académique Internationale.

Danby, *Mishnah.*   Herbert Danby, *The Mishnah*, transl. from the Hebrew with introduction and brief explanatory notes, Oxford, 1933.

Daniélou, *Symboles.*   Jean Daniélou, *Les Symboles chrétiens primitifs*, Paris, 1961.

DS.   *Dictionnaire des antiquités grecques et romaines d'après les textes et les monuments*, ed. by C. Daremberg and E. Saglio, Paris, 1873 et seq.

Du Mesnil, *Deux Synagogues.*   Comte Robert du Mesnil du Buisson, "Les Deux Synagogues successives à Doura-Europos," *RB*, XLV (1936), 72–90, 1936.

Du Mesnil, *Peintures.*   Comte Robert du Mesnil du Buisson, *Les Peintures de la synagogue de Doura-Europos, 245–256 après J.-C.*, Rome, 1939.

Edgar, *Coffins.*   C. C. Edgar, *Graeco-Egyptian Coffins, Masks and Portraits*, Cairo, 1905 (Service des Antiquités de l'Egypte: Catalogue général des antiquités égyptiennes du Musée du Caire, XX).

Edgar, *Sculpture.*   C. C. Edgar, *Greek Sculpture*, Cairo, 1903 (Service des Antiquités de l'Egypte: Catalogue général des antiquités égyptiennes du Musée du Caire, IX).

EES.   T. Schreiber et al., *Expedition Ernst von Sieglin, Ausgrabungen in Alexandria*, Leipzig, 1908.

Eisler, *Orpheus.*   Robert Eisler, *Orpheus the Fisher: Comparative Studies in Orphic and Early Christian Cult Symbolism*, London, 1921.

EJ.   *Encyclopaedia Judaica: Das Judentum in Geschichte und Gegenwart*, Berlin, 1928 et seq.

ET.   English translation.

Farnell, *Cults.*   Lewis R. Farnell, *The Cults of the Greek States*, Oxford, 1896 et seq.

Ferrua, *Via Latina.*   Antonio Ferrua, S.I., *Le Pitture della nuova catacomba di Via Latina*, Città del Vaticano, 1960 (Monumenti di antichità cristiana, Series II, Volume VIII).

FR.   A Furtwängler and K. Reichhold, *Griechische Vasenmalerei*, Munich, 1904 et seq.

Frey, *CIJ.*   Jean-Baptiste Frey, *Corpus inscriptionum Judaicarum, Recueil des inscriptions juives qui vont du IIIᵉ siècle avant Jésus-Christ au VIIᵉ siècle de notre ère.* I, *Europe*, Rome, 1936; II, *Asie-Afrique*, Rome, 1952.

FT.   French translation.

Garrucci, *Arte cristiana.*   Raffaele Garrucci, *Storia dell'arte cristiana nei primi otto secoli della Chiesa*, Prato, 1872–1880. References unless otherwise stated are to the Jewish material in Vol. VI, 1880.

Gauckler.   *See Mosaïques.*

GCS.   *Die griechischen christlichen Schriftsteller der ersten drei Jahrhunderte*, ed. by the Kirchenväter-Commission der königlich preussischen Akademie der Wissenschaften.

Ginzberg, *Legends.*   Louis Ginzberg, *The Legends of the Jews*, Philadelphia, 1909 et seq.

Goodenough, *By Light, Light.*   Erwin R. Goodenough, *By Light, Light: The Mystic Gospel of Hellenistic Judaism*, New Haven, 1935.

Goodenough, *Introduction.*   Erwin R. Goodenough, *An Introduction to Philo Judaeus*, New Haven, 1940.

Grabar, "Le Thème."   A. Grabar, "Le Thème religieux des fresques de la synagogue de Doura," *RHR*, CXXIII (1941), 143–192; CXXIV (1941), 5–35.

GT.   German translation.

Hartman, *Gayomart.*   S. S. Hartman, *Gayomart, Etude sur le syncretisme dans l'ancien Iran*, Diss., Uppsala, 1953.

HDB.   James Hastings, *A Dictionary of the Bible*, New York, 1898–1904.

Hempel, "Problem."   Heinz-Ludwig Hempel, "Zum Problem der Anfänge der AT-Illustration," *ZAW*, LXVIII (1957), 103–131.

HERE.   James Hastings, *Encyclopedia of Religion and Ethics*, New York and Edinburgh, 1908 et seq.

HTR.   *Harvard Theological Review.*

HUCA.   *Hebrew Union College Annual.*

ICC.   *International Critical Commentary.*

IEJ.   *Israel Exploration Journal.*

IG.   *Inscriptiones Graecæ.*

JAOS.   *Journal of the American Oriental Society.*

JBL.   *Journal of Biblical Literature.*

JDAI.   *Jahrbuch des Deutschen Archäologischen Instituts.*

JE.   *Jewish Encyclopedia: A Descriptive Record of the History, Religion, Literature, and Customs of the Jewish People from the Earliest Times to the Present Day*, ed. by Isidore Singer, New York, 1901 et seq.

JEA.   *Journal of Egyptian Archeology.*

JHS.   *Journal of Hellenic Studies.*

JÖAI.   *Jahreshefte des Österreichischen Archäologischen Instituts in Wien.*

JRS.   *Journal of Roman Studies.*

JT.   *Jerusalem Talmud*, with references to the various treatises. FT refers to the French transl. of Moïse Schwab, Paris, 1871 et seq.

Kraeling, *Prelim.*   Carl H. Kraeling, "The Synagogue," in Rostovtzeff, *Dura-Europos*, VI, 337–383, 391 f.

Kraeling, *Synagogue.*   Carl H. Kraeling, *The Synagogue*, New Haven, 1956 (The Excavations at Dura-Europos, Conducted by Yale University and the French Academy of Inscriptions and Letters. Final Report, VIII, ed. by A. R. Bellinger, F. E. Brown, A. Perkins, and C. B. Welles).

Krauss, *Synag. Altert.*   Samuel Krauss, *Synagogale Altertümer*, Berlin and Vienna, 1922.

KW.   Heinrich Kohl and Carl Watzinger, *Antike Synagogen in Galilaea*, Leipzig, 1916 (Wissenschaftliche Veröffentlichung der Deutschen Orient-Gesellschaft, XXIX).

Lehmann, *Baltimore.*   Karl Lehmann-Hartleben and E. C. Olsen, *Dionysiac Sarcophagi in Baltimore*, Baltimore, 1942.

Leisegang, *Index.*   Hans Leisegang, *Indices ad Philonis Alexandrini opera*, Berlin, 1926 (L. Cohn and P. Wendland, *Philonis Alexandrini opera quae supersunt*, VII).

Leveen, "Wall-Paintings."   Jacob Leveen, "The Wall-Paintings at Dura-Europos," in his *The Hebrew Bible in Art*, London, 1944, 22–65.

Levi, *Antioch.*   Doro Levi, *Antioch Mosaic Pavements,* Princeton, 1947.

LS.   Henry Liddell and Robert Scott, *A Greek-English Lexicon,* new ed. of H. S. Jones, Oxford, 1925 et seq.

Maiuri, *Roman Painting.*   Amedeo Maiuri, *The Great Centuries of Painting,* Lausanne, 1953.

Marrou, *MA.*   Henri Irénée Marrou, *Mousikos anēr: Etude sur les scènes de la vie intellectuelle figurant sur les monuments funéraires romains,* Grenoble, 1937.

MDAI, Ath.   *Mitteilungen des Deutschen Archäologischen Instituts, Athenische Abteilung.*

MDAI, Röm.   *Mitteilungen des Deutschen Archäologischen Instituts, Römische Abteilung.*

Mém., AIB.   *Mémoires présentés par divers savants,* Académie des Inscriptions et Belles-Lettres.

Mém. Inst.   *Mémoires publiés par les membres de l'Institut Français d'Archéologie Orientale du Caire.*

Mém. Miss.   *Mémoires publiés par les membres de la Mission Archéologique Française au Caire.*

Menolog. Basil. II.   *Il Menologio di Basilio II.* Cod. Vaticano Greco 1613, Turin, 1907 (Codices e Vaticanis selecti phototypice expressi, VIII).

Mercer, *Pyramid Texts.*   Samuel A. B. Mercer, *The Pyramid Texts in Translation and Commentary,* New York, 1952.

MGWJ.   *Monatsschrift für Geschichte und Wissenschaft des Judentums.*

Migne.   *See PG, PL.*

Mon. ined.   *Monumenti inediti pubblicati dall'Instituto di Corrispondenza Archeologica,* Rome, 1829–1885. Continued by publications of the Deutsches Archäologisches Institut, in Rome.

Mon. Piot.   *Monuments et Mémoires,* Académie des Inscriptions et Belles-Lettres (Fondation Eugène Piot).

Morey, *Early Christian Art.*   Charles Rufus Morey, *Early Christian Art,* Princeton, 1942.

Mosaïques.   Académie des Inscriptions et Belles-Lettres, *Inventoire des mosaïques de la Gaule et de l'Afrique,* Paris, 1909–1925. 3 vols. in 2; Atlas in 6 fasc.

MR.   *Midrash Rabbah,* with references to the individual treatises. ET refers to the Engl. transl. made by various scholars under the general editorship of I. Epstein, London, Soncino Press, 1939 et seq.

MSJ.   *Mélanges de l'Université Saint-Joseph,* Beirut.

MW.   C. O. Müller and F. Wieseler, *Denkmäler der alten Kunst,* I, 1854; II, 1856.

Naményi, *L'Esprit.*   Ernest Naményi, *L'Esprit de l'art juif,* 1957 (Bibliothèque juive).

Nilsson, *Griech. Rel.*   Martin P. Nilsson, *Geschichte der griechischen Religion,* Munich, 1941–1950 (Walter Otto, Handbuch der Altertumswissenschaft, V, ii).

Nordström, "Water Miracles."   Carl Otto-Nordström, "The Water Miracles of Moses in Jewish Legend and Byzantine Art," *Orientalia Suecana,* VII (1958), 77–109.

Omont, *Miniatures.*   Henri A. Omont, *Miniatures des plus anciens manuscrits grecs de la Bibliothèque Nationale du VIᵉ au XIVᵉ siècle,* Paris, 1929.

PEF, *QS.*   Palestine Exploration Fund, *Quarterly Statement.* After 1938 called *Palestine Exploration Quarterly (PEQ).*

PEQ.   *See* PEF, *QS.*

PES.   *Syria, Publications of the Princeton University Archaeological Expeditions to Syria in 1904–1905 and 1909,* Leyden, 1914 et seq.

Pfuhl, *Malerei.*   Ernst Pfuhl, *Malerei und Zeichnung der Griechen,* Munich, 1923.

PG.   J.-P. Migne, *Patrologia Graeca.*

PL.   J.-P. Migne, *Patrologia Latina.*

Pope, *Persian Art.*   Arthur U. Pope and P. Ackerman, eds., *A Survey of Persian Art from Prehistoric Times to the Present,* London and New York, 1938–1939.

PRE.   *Pirke de rabbi Eliezer (The Chapters of Rabbi Eliezer the Great) According to the Text of the Manuscript Belonging to Abraham Epstein of Vienna,* transl. and annot. by Gerald Friedlander, London, 1916.

PW.   *Paulys Real-Encyclopädie der classischen Altertumswissenschaft,* ed. by G. Wissowa, Stuttgart, 1894 et seq.

QDAP.   *Quarterly of the Department of Antiquities in Palestine.*

RA.   *Revue archéologique.*

RB.   *Revue biblique.*

Reinach, *Peintures.*   Solomon Reinach, *Répertoire de peintures grecques et romaines,* Paris, 1922.

Reinach, *Pierres.*   Solomon Reinach, *Pierres gravées des collections Marlborough et d'Orléans, des recueils d'Eckhel, Gori, Lévesque de Gravelle, Mariette, Millin, Stosch,* Paris, 1895.

Reinach, *Reliefs.*   Solomon Reinach, *Répertoire des reliefs grecs et romains,* Paris, 1909–1912.

Reinach, *Statuaire.*   Solomon Reinach, *Répertoire de la statuaire grecque et romaine,* Paris, 1910.

Reinach, *Vases.*   Solomon Reinach, *Peintures de vases antiques,* Paris, 1891.

REJ.   *Revue des études juives.*

RgVV.   Religionsgeschichtliche Versuche und Vorarbeiten.

RHR.   *Revue de l'histoire des religions.*

Riedin, *Cosmas Indicopleustes.*   E. K. Riedin, *Khristianskaia Topografiia Kosmy Indicoplora po Grecheskim i russkim Spiskam,* Moscow, 1916, pt. I only.

Robert, *Sarkophag-Reliefs.*   Carl Robert, *Die antiken Sarkophag-Reliefs, im Auftrage des Kaiserlich Deutschen Archäologischen Instituts,* Berlin, 1890 et seq.

Roscher, *Lex. Myth.*   *Ausführliches Lexikon der griechischen und römischen Mythologie,* ed. by W. H. Roscher, Leipzig, 1884 et seq.

Rostovtzeff, *Dura-Europos.*   *The Excavations at Dura-Europos, Conducted by Yale University and the French Academy of Inscriptions and Letters,* ed. by M. I. Rostovtzeff et al. Preliminary Reports, New Haven, 1928 et seq.

Rostovtzeff, *South Russia.*   M. I. Rostovtzeff, *Ancient Decorative Paintings in South Russia* (in Russian), St. Petersburg, 1913.

RQ.   *Römische Quartalschrift für christliche Alterthumskunde und für Kirchengeschichte.*

RSV.   The Bible: Revised Standard Version.

SBE.   F. M. Müller, ed., Sacred Books of the East, Oxford.

Scholem, *Jewish Mysticism.*   Gershom G. Scholem, *Major Trends in Jewish Mysticism,* Jerusalem, 1941

(Hilda Strook Lectures, delivered at the Jewish Institute of Religion, New York, 1938).

Schürer, *Jüd. Volk.* Emil Schürer, *Geschichte des jüdischen Volkes im Zeitalter Jesu Christi*, 4th ed., Leipzig, 1901. ET refers to his *A History of the Jewish People in the Time of Jesus Christ*, transl. J. Macpherson, S. Taylor, and P. Christie, New York, 1891.

Smith, *GRA.* William Smith, William Wayte, and G. E. Marindin, *A Dictionary of Greek and Roman Antiquities*, 3d ed., London, 1890–1891.

Smyrna Octateuch. D. C. Hesseling, *Miniatures de l'Octateuque grec de Smyrne*, Leyden, 1909 (Codices Graeci et Latini photographice depicti, supplementum VI). (Burned in 1923. Cf. Weitzmann, *Roll and Codex*, 128 n.)

Sonne, "Paintings." I. Sonne, "The Paintings of the Dura Synagogue," *HUCA*, XX (1947), 255–362.

Strzygowski, *Kopt.* Josef Strzygowski, *Koptische Kunst: Catalogue général des antiquités égyptiennes du Musée du Caire*, Vienna, 1904 (Service des Antiquités de l'Egypte, XVIII).

Sukenik, *el-Ḥammeh.* E. L. Sukenik, *The Ancient Synagogue of el-Ḥammeh (Hammeth-by-Gadara)*, an Account of the Excavations Conducted on Behalf of the Hebrew University, Jerusalem, Jerusalem, 1935.

Swindler, *Painting.* Mary Hamilton Swindler, *Ancient Painting, from the Earliest Times to the Period of Christian Art*, New Haven, 1929.

Synagogue. See Kraeling, *Synagogue.*

Textiles. R. Pfister and Louisa Bellinger, *The Textiles*, New Haven, 1945 (The Excavations at Dura-Europos, Final Report, ed. by M. I. Rostovtzeff, A. R. Bellinger, F. E. Brown, N. P. Toll, and C. B. Welles, IV, ii).

Torlonia. See Beyer and Lietzmann.

TU. Texte und Untersuchungen zur Geschichte der Altchristlichen Literatur, Leipzig, 1882–1952.

Vienna Genesis. W. von Hartel and F. Wickhoff, *Die Wiener Genesis*, Vienna and Prague, 1895.

Ward, *Seal Cylinders.* William Hayes Ward, *The Seal Cylinders of Western Asia*, Washington, 1910.

Weitzmann, *Joshua.* Kurt Weitzmann, *The Joshua Roll*, Princeton, 1948.

Weitzmann, *Roll and Codex.* Kurt Weitzmann, *Illustrations in Roll and Codex: A Study of the Origin and Method of Text Illustration*, Princeton, 1947 (Studies in Manuscript Illumination, II).

Widengren, "Juifs et Iraniens." G. Widengren. "Quelques rapports entre Juifs et Iraniens à l'époque des Parthes," *Volume du Congrès, Strasbourg, 1956*, 1957, 197–240 (Vetus Testamentum, Supplements, IV).

Wilpert, *Mosaiken und Malereien.* Josef Wilpert, *Die römischen Mosaiken und Malereien der kirchlichen Bauten vom IV. bis XIII. Jahrhundert*, 2d ed., Freiburg im Breisgau, 1917.

Wilpert, *Pitture.* Josef Wilpert, *Roma sotterranea: Le Pitture delle catacombe romane*, Rome, 1903.

Wilpert, *Sarcofagi.* Josef Wilpert, *I sarcofagi cristiani antichi*, Rome, 1929–1932.

Zaehner, *Zurvan.* R. C. Zaehner, *Zurvan, A Zoroastrian Dilemma*, Oxford, 1955.

ZAW. Zeitschrift für die alttestamentliche Wissenschaft.

ZDMG. Zeitschrift der Deutschen Morgenländischen Gesellschaft.

ZNW. Zeitschrift für die neutestamentliche Wissenschaft.

Zohar. The Zohar. ET refers to the Engl. transl. of Harry Sperling and Maurice Simon, London, Soncino Press, 1931 et seq. FT refers to the French transl. of J. de Pauly, rev. by E. Lafuma-Giraud, Paris, 1906 et seq.

EXTANT TREATISES ATTRIBUTED TO PHILO

The English titles, except as noted hereafter, are those of F. H. Colson and G. H. Whitaker, with Supplements by Ralph Marcus, in the Loeb edition of the works of Philo. Roman numerals in parentheses refer to the number of the volume of that series in which the given treatise appears. I have furnished English titles for the Armenian works not in the Loeb edition.

Abr. De Abrahamo. On Abraham (*VI*).

Aet. De aeternitate mundi. On the Eternity of the World (*IX*).

Agr. De agricultura. On Husbandry (*III*).

Animal. Alexander, sive de eo quod rationem habeant bruta animalia. Alexander, or That Dumb Animals Have Reason. (Accessible only in Armenian and in Aucher's Latin transl.)

Antiq. Liber antiquitatum biblicarum. (Pseudo Philo, ed. by Guido Kisch, 1949, transl. M. R. James, 1917: *The Biblical Antiquities of Philo.*)

Cher. De cherubim. On the Cherubim, and the Flaming Sword, and Cain the First Man Created out of Man (*II*).

Conf. De confusione linguarum. On the Confusion of Tongues (*IV*).

Cong. De congressu eruditionis gratia. On Mating with the Preliminary Studies (*IV*).

Cont. De vita contemplativa. On the Contemplative Life (*IX*).

Decal. De decalogo. On the Decalogue (*VII*).

Deo. De deo. On God. (Accessible only in Armenian and in Aucher's Latin transl.)

Det. Quod deterius potiori insidiari soleat. That the Worse Is Wont to Attack the Better (*II*).

Ebr.   *De ebrietate*. On Drunkenness (*III*)

Flac.   *In Flaccum*. Against Flaccus (*IX*).

Fug.   *De fuga et inventione*. On Flight and Finding (*V*).

Gig.   *De gigantibus*. On the Giants (*II*).

Heres.   *Quis rerum divinarum heres*. Who Is the Heir of Divine Things (*IV*).

Hyp.   *Apologia pro Iudaeis*. Hypothetica (*IX*).

Immut.   *Quod deus sit immutabilis*. On the Unchangeableness of God (*III*).

Jona.   *De Jona*. On Jonah. (Accessible only in Armenian and in Aucher's Latin transl.)

Jos.   *De Josepho*. On Joseph (*VI*).

LA.   *Legum allegoria*. Allegorical Interpretation of Genesis (*I*).

Legat.   *Legatio ad Gaium*. Legation to Gaius (*X*, forthcoming).

Migr.   *De migratione Abrahami*. On the Migration of Abraham (*IV*).

Mos.   *De vita Mosis*. Moses (*VI*).

Mund.   *De mundo*. On the World.

Mut.   *De mutatione nominum*. On the Change of Names (*V*).

Opif.   *De opificio mundi*. On the Account of the World's Creation Given by Moses (*I*).

Plant.   *De plantatione*. Concerning Noah's Work as a Planter (*III*).

Post.   *De posteritate Caini*. On the Posterity of Cain and His Exile (*II*).

Praem.   *De praemiis et poenis*. On Rewards and Punishments (*VIII*).

Prob.   *Quod omnis probus liber sit*. That Every Virtuous Man Is Free (*IX*).

Provid.   *De providentia*. On Providence (*IX*).

QE.   *Quaestiones et solutiones in Exodum*. Questions and Answers on Exodus. (Supplement II to the Loeb edition, transl. Ralph Marcus.)

QG.   *Quaestiones et solutiones in Genesim*. Questions and Answers on Genesis. (Supplement I to the Loeb edition, transl. Ralph Marcus.)

Sacr.   *De sacrificiis Abelis et Caini*. On the Birth of Abel and the Sacrifices Offered by Him and His Brother Cain (*II*).

Samp.   *Sine praeparatione de Sampsone* [*sermo*]. On Samson. (Accessible only in Armenian and in Aucher's Latin transl.)

Sobr.   *De sobrietate*. On the Prayers and Curses Uttered by Noah When He Became Sober (*III*).

Som.   *De somniis*. On Dreams, That They Are God-Sent (*V*).

Spec.   *De specialibus legibus*. On the Special Laws (*VII*, *VIII*).

Virt.   *De virtutibus*. On Virtues Which, together with Others, Were Described by Moses; or on Courage, Piety, Humanity, and Repentance (*VIII*).

PART XIII

THE SYNAGOGUE

CHAPTER ONE

Introductory Problems

EW ARCHEOLOGISTS have had so amazing an experience as that of five young people when in November 1932 they saw the painted walls of a third-century synagogue emerge from the sands of Dura Europos, fig. 2. Their names should be freshly recorded: Clark Hopkins, Director; M. le Cte. du Mesnil du Buisson, Vice-Director; Miss Margaret Crosby; Frank E. Brown; and Van W. Knox. Others joined them when the magnitude of the discovery showed the need. The original group had gone out carefully coached by Franz Cumont, René Dussaud, and, above all, Michael Rostovtzeff, who, with his usual flair for the best place to dig, had spotted the great mound of sand on the desert side of the city, fig. 1.[1] Here, it turned out, a whole row of buildings had been preserved, including not only the synagogue but also the earliest known Christian meeting room or baptistry, and a magnificent Mithraeum.

About A.D. 256 the citizens of Dura, with a little Roman garrison, had been cut off from all help and faced inevitable extinction at the hands of an advancing Persian host. To strengthen the most exposed wall of the city the desperate people tore the roofs from the buildings in the street behind it and constructed a great ramp by filling the whole with quantities of earth. It did no good. The Persians tunneled under, and Dura was never heard of again until, in 1921, a British captain warring against the Arabs camped on the site, and in the course of "digging some trenches in the ruins" discovered the painting of the "Palmyrene gods." J. H. Breasted, who was near by, came and took photographs; he reported the discovery to the members of the French Academy of Inscriptions, who excavated the site for two years.[2] They did not touch the ramp behind the wall, however, and there the decorations of the synagogue, freshly painted just before being buried, remained in the dry earth. They came out eventually with the colors almost as clear as when the *morituri* had buried them.

When Jews first came to Dura we do not know. The painted synagogue was clearly built upon an earlier one, which in turn had been made by remodeling a typical dwelling of the city. Kraeling estimated that the first synagogue dated from the end of the second

1. The site of the synagogue before excavation.

2. The best accounts of the discovery are by J. H. Breasted, *Oriental Forerunners of Byzantine Painting*, 1924, 52–61 (University of Chicago Oriental Institute Publications, I); Cumont, *Fouilles*, pp. I–X.

to the beginning of the third centuries, approximately fifty years before it was demolished to make the second synagogue in A.D. 245.[3] The earlier synagogue had had a ceiling painted to imitate coffers, with a gilded plaster rosette in each coffer, fig. 354, and on the walls painted panels to imitate marble, fig. 353. An inscription on one of the ceiling tiles of the second synagogue established its date firmly,[4] but not the date of the murals. The ceiling this time was made of real painted tiles, fig. 352; some decoration, as on the reveals of the doorways, fig. 52, and the panel over the Torah niche, plate III, was probably done at once. Then, apparently, a great vine was painted over the niche to the ceiling, figs. 73 f. and 76—a device several times repainted, and finally divided to go with the extraordinary painted panels within grapevine borders with which the walls were entirely covered. This last was done very shortly before the fall of the city in 256, for paint droppings are still to be seen on the floor. We cannot suppose much more than a five-year interval. Plate I and figs. 317 f. show the general effect of the paintings, and figs. 319–322 indicate the scheme of vine borders in which they were put. These last will also be conveniently put to use as we continue, for I shall follow Kraeling in referring to the paintings by the numbers he put upon them in these diagrams.

The illustrations show also how the building was cut back to buttress the city wall, as just mentioned. Kraeling [5] has carefully reconstructed the steps taken in this emergency. At first sand was brought in from the desert to fill Wall Street to the level of the tops of the houses; but this put such great pressure on the walls of the houses that they began to buckle and had themselves to be braced. Apparently, embankments of earth and carefully packed mud were built from the inside against the threatened wall, and this was further strengthened by sand and by rubble from walls destroyed for the purpose. The portions of the walls of the synagogue which projected above the growing ramp were knocked off, to add their weight to the buttress. Accordingly, of the north and south walls less than half remains, while of the east wall at the back we now have only the dado and part of the bottom register of paintings. The west wall, however, was preserved almost intact, and since this was the wall toward which worship was directed, it seems to have been the most important of all. Enough of the whole is left to make the paintings one of the most important discoveries of all time for the history of religion.

A. *RELATION TO SURVIVING JEWISH LITERARY TRADITIONS*

AFTER THE FIRST WAVE of incredulity at the new discovery had passed, discussion began about what the paintings can tell us; though considering the importance of the material, they have received relatively little attention. The synagogue had quite as radical implications for our knowledge of Judaism as the Dead Sea Scrolls, if not far deeper; but whereas hundreds of people were prepared to read the Scrolls, no one alive knew how to read the language of the murals. In their remarks about the Dura Synagogue

3. H. Pearson in Rostovtzeff, *Dura-Europos*, VI, 311; Kraeling, *Synagogue*, 4–33.

4. See C. Torrey in Kraeling, *Synagogue*, 261–266.

5. *Synagogue*, 4 f.

scholars have thus far united only in feeling that explanation of the paintings must begin by orienting the paintings with their own conceptions of Judaism. Few scholars, that is, began with the paintings themselves: practically all began with notions from this or that body of Jewish literature, with which they insisted the paintings agreed. One scholar, for example, has said specifically that in interpreting archeological monuments we must "proceed from those elements which fit recognizable types and have reasonably certain meanings . . . that is, from the normal and obvious." So he recommends doing what Kraeling has done: explaining the relation of the paintings first to the Old Testament, next to the "great bulk of Jewish literary material of approximately their own time and area," and then to the contemporary pagan art of Dura. Other matters can safely be left, he says, to "special studies." [6]

Just what a special study may be he does not explain. But I see little to commend the assumption that we may consider the evidence offered by the place of the paintings in the history of iconography and symbolism only after we have safely chained them to a Jewish literary tradition of the same "time and area." For by that first move we shall actually have closed the door against seriously considering the evidence of the art itself, or of other types of Judaism. The history of art, as has often been recognized—conspicuously by the great Henri Focillon—is the history of the human spirit in terms of forms. Monumental texts, he rightly says, have the same value as written texts, and often a much higher value. "There exist whole segments (*pans*) of civilization for which their forms are the only, or almost the only, sources of information to reach us." [7]

Jewish art seems to have opened such a *pan* in Jewish history. The literary remains of Judaism in the Greco-Roman period had led us to suppose that Jews at that time used no images. Although for centuries archeologists had been finding a great number of Jewish images from the period, the Dura synagogue, and the other remains of Jewish art collected in the first three volumes of the present study, came as a total surprise to those historians who had used only literary evidence. In alluding to that collection I by no means forget the large number of predecessors I drew upon who did know some or all of this art, even before the discovery of Dura. Their labors, however, were not such that the art remains of Judaism had taken an important place in any general history of Jews in the period alongside the literary remains. Indeed very few even of those who themselves discovered and published the various monuments had considered for a moment that their discoveries were really opening up a new *pan* in that history. Jewish history, based upon Jewish writings, has been largely written on the assumption that the basic motif of all Jews of this period was total rejection of pagan religion. Even the monumental

6. Kraeling said essentially the same thing, *Synagogue*, 340: "There is great danger of letting our eyes be blinded to, or by, the novelty of the material, and thus of losing perspective either upon the paintings themselves or upon the picture of ancient Judaism as it has been developed from the study of other types of evidence by the scholars of the last hundred years."

7. H. Focillon, "Lettre à Josef Strzygowski," *Civilisations. Orient-Occident, génie du Nord-Latinité*, 1935, 133 f. (Institut International de Cooperation Intellectuelle. Correspondence IV). Quoted by Naményi, *L'Esprit*, 1.

study of Tcherikover [8] is devoted to the thesis that hellenization affected only a few great families corrupted by their riches, while the mass of Jews everywhere rejected any taint, and remained what G. F. Moore called "normative" Jews. By rejecting paganism, it has been supposed, Jews strengthened themselves as a group, a group distinguished by their worship of the one true God. Along with the peculiar cycle of sabbaths and festivals, the in-group marriage, and peculiar food went, it was thought, an abhorrence of images, especially those associated with pagan worship. Some Jews added mysticism to this normative Judaism, others messianism and eschatological concern, but however much such extremists as even Philo may have borrowed from pagan religions and metaphysical attitudes, they expressed the basic detestation of pagan worship and images quite as strongly as any rabbi. Paul might have drawn from either Philo or Gamaliel when he wrote of the pagans: "Claiming to be wise they became fools, and exchanged the glory of the immortal God for images resembling mortal man or birds or animals or reptiles." [9]

Suddenly, however, the new discoveries presented us with a Judaism that had no such feeling about pagan art or images—to the point that at Dura the god Ares, for example, could supervise the Exodus from Egypt, Victories bring their crowns on the acroteria of the Temple, and the three Nymphs guard the infant Moses while Aphrodite-Anahita takes him out of the little ark. Helios riding in the zodiac had occupied the center of Palestinian synagogues. All of them directly violate what had seemed the basic attitude of Judaism. True, nothing suggests that Jews ever worshiped these figures, any more than that they worshiped the Moses or Aaron or Abraham that accompanies them. We cannot on that account dismiss the fact that nothing in the literary remains of Judaism suggests anything but the most occasional and grudging tolerance of such art. Why would any loyal Jew (and all these were loyal Jews) have wanted to borrow the art forms of paganism, and represent them in their places of burial and worship, at Dura represent them alongside, and even integrally within, their paintings of Old Testament scenes? If the literary evidence gives us no way of explaining such a desire for pagan art forms, we must see that the monumental evidence has taken us into a new *pan* of Judaism, for which the art remains themselves are our only direct evidence. Because here, clearly, is a widespread Judaism that did want them.

How are we to deal with such a phenomenon? It was suggested in earlier volumes of this series that we should trace the history of the symbolic forms used by Jews to see whether out of their history we might recover some constants of meaning. Meaning we saw in a symbol's "value" rather than its "explanations," and Volumes V–VIII have been testing a hypothesis proposed in Volume IV, that a live symbol when borrowed by a new religion is borrowed for its value and given explanations (if at all) in terms of the traditions of the new religion. Debate on whether that demonstration was successful will

8. V. Tcherikover, *Hellenistic Civilization and the Jews*, 1959. See my review in *Jewish Social Studies*, XXII (1960), 105–108. And see H. Wolfson as quoted above, I, 56 f. Tcherikover speaks very well of the present work on p. 523, n. 2, but I cannot

agree that I am "anxious to emphasize the Hellenization of the Jews." I am "anxious" only to let the evidence, all of it, speak for itself.

9. Rom. I, 22 f. See Philo, *Decal.* 66–81, and my *Introduction*, 108 f.

apparently continue for a long time. The present volume must, of course, be written on the assumption that the hypothesis is acceptable. That is, we assume that Jews were borrowing the symbols of pagans not for ornament but to say something. What the symbols had said for pagans in terms of pagan religions the Jews wanted them to say in terms of Judaism. The rabbis clearly had no conceptions in their Judaism to express which they needed a figure of Helios, the eagle, Cupid, or Victory. This must not blind us to the fact that, in contrast, we are here dealing with Jews who felt that they needed precisely these figures to express values they found in, or projected into, their Judaism. On no other basis does it seem possible to explain the wide use of these symbols, the kinds of symbols selected from paganism, and the places they were used.[10]

It will be the thesis, or hypothesis, of this volume that the same method should be used in interpreting the paintings of Dura. The first premise is that we must get to verbal statements about the meaning of the art only after, and out of, a study of the monumental remains themselves, rather than begin by imposing verbal statements from some or other types of Jewish literature upon them. In my previous discussion I have tried to evaluate the pagan symbols found in synagogues and Jewish graves. The discussion takes on a new dimension when we see at Dura basically the same borrowed symbols accompanying an assembly of paintings obviously inspired by Old Testament incidents.

All of my predecessors who have discussed the Dura synagogue have regarded it as their first duty to explain that the pagan motifs in its ceiling and dado had no importance whatever, were "purely decorative." [11] The most elaborate of those attempts is Kraeling's; [12] he has presented a summation of all other arguments, with many additions of his own. One cannot disagree with him without reason, and as we expound the pagan motifs of the ceiling, the dado, and the reredos we shall have to take his ideas seriously. Many of the pagan motifs in the synagogue have already been discussed, and the new ones must be examined historically.

Pagan motifs in Jewish synagogues and graves have already led us to suspect that Jews used them to express faith in heaven, in the love of God, in coming victory, and, for some, in mysticism. I believe that, as we continue, the new symbols which Dura adds to the old vocabulary will seem to point to similar meaning. All these symbols—the vine, or birds in the vine, or the harnessed felines—had promised such hopes impartially in many pagan religions as they migrated from one religion to another. To early Christians the same symbols apparently expressed the same hopes, *hopes that ceased to be pagan when they lost their associations with pagan gods and myths.* They would indicate the Christian aspect of the hope explicitly as they were represented along with symbols from the Old Testament or life of Christ. The biblical scenes of Christianity in no sense detracted from the

10. Morton Smith, "The Image of God," *Bulletin of the John Rylands Library*, XL (1958), 473–512, has shown traces of hellenization in the rabbis themselves. He follows Saul Lieberman, and adds many scattered details. But the details remain scattered, and the rabbis give us no such collected and extensive hellenization as the Jewish art, at Dura and elsewhere, presents. See my "The Rabbis and Jewish Art in the Greco-Roman Period," *HUCA*, XXXII (1961), 269–279 (Julian Morgenstern Festschrift).

11. For these see below, pp. 48–64.

12. Kraeling, *Synagogue*, 39–54, 65–70.

symbolic power of the borrowed pagan emblems, or changed their values. The biblical scenes only spelled out how the Christians were reinterpreting the universal symbolic language, declaring Christian explanations for the pagan values now claimed by Christianity, presented in Christianity. The natural hypothesis is that at Dura, Jews were doing the same thing in the name of Judaism: that the biblical scenes they selected to present in such a setting would declare in Jewish terms the values and hopes which pagans had set forth by these symbols before the Jews used them, and for which Christians were already beginning eagerly to borrow them. For, let me repeat, I am confident that the representations in the synagogue, pagan and Jewish alike, express the Judaism of the people who designed the whole scheme. We must treat as a unit the decorations in the synagogue, along, indeed, with the plan of the building itself.

If we regard it as our first task to associate the biblical scenes with one or another body of Jewish literature, we at once rule out the possibility of such association with pagan devices, since, as was just said, we know no Jewish literature that shows any need of pagan symbols to express itself. In point of fact, all early attempts at explanation actually looked for elements in the paintings that would suggest the sort of Judaism each of us had come to know best by previous study. Some saw eschatological and apologetic cycles represented, and looked to this type of literature for proof texts. Others felt that if Dura was Jewish, it must be explained out of the Talmud and Midrash. Nearly twenty-five years ago I made a preliminary announcement that the paintings were inspired by hellenized Judaism of the kind I had learned from Philo.[13] None of these bodies of literature can be ruled out, a priori; much illumination will prove to come from all of them. The art, however, may be presenting us with a *novum* altogether, or such a mixture of elements as to constitute a virtual *novum*. The paintings may go back to any of these three great kinds of Jewish literature. But we obviously need some objective approach in appraising them.

B. DURA AND BABYLONIAN JEWS

WHAT SEEMED at first such an objective view was suggested years ago by Kraeling in a paper read to the New Haven Oriental Club. While I do not recall that he formulated the idea directly in his monumental *Synagogue*, clearly it still operates powerfully in his thinking and is commended in Smith's review just quoted. He suggested in his paper that we appeal to time and geography. He said that since Dura was on the Euphrates, only about 250 miles north of Nehardea, which was at that time the seat of the great Babylonian Jewish Academy, we should take their Judaism, as expressed in Babylonian Talmud and Midrash as well as in the Targumim, to be what presumably lies behind the art of Dura. This has always sounded to me like a treacherous criterion of judgment.

Nehardea and the towns about it had become a little island of Jews where Jewish traditions seem almost entirely to have taken over. How far this was true we do not know, for in A.D. 220, when the first synagogue of Dura was in operation, the great scholar Rav returned to Babylonia from his training in the Palestinian Academy and went through

13. *By Light, Light,* 209 f., 222, 242, 262.

the Jewish settlements of Babylonia establishing schools where his fellow Jews, whom he found painfully ignorant of the Law, could be trained. But these little Jewish communities of Babylonia had no importance as military or trading posts for either Greeks or Romans, and so were never permanently occupied or influenced from the West. Indeed when the Persians conquered all southern Mesopotamia and ruled it in place of the Parthians, the first Persian king persecuted the Jews of the region, but his successor relaxed this and allowed them to live peacefully according to their own legal traditions. In A.D. 258, two years after the destruction of Dura, the Palmyreans conquered Babylonia and destroyed a few Jewish cities, including Nehardea; but this, too, proved only temporary, and the Jews there soon continued to live their own lives with essentially no control from gentile civilizations. As a consequence, legalistic or halachic Judaism had a freer hand to develop there than at any other time or place in Jewish history, with the possible exception, much later, of similar Jewish centers in Eastern Europe. The fully developed halachic Judaism which we associate with the Babylonian Academy and life, and which produced the Babylonian Talmud, was probably still quite unformed when the Dura synagogue was decorated; so if there was any significant relation between the Judaism of Nehardea and Dura, Naményi [14] seems to me right in saying that Dura would have represented Babylonian Judaism before the halachic reform.

We may question, however, that the Judaism of Dura ever resembled at all closely the Judaism of the Babylonian communities. For in contrast to Babylonian Jews, the Jews in Dura constituted a small minority within a pagan city, where they lived cheek by jowl among first Greek, then Parthian, then Roman soldiers and merchants. Their little synagogue, when they had one at all, was engulfed and dwarfed by the houses and temples of the goyim throughout the city, fig. 310. Their surroundings, therefore, resembled much more those of Jews in Ephesus, Corinth, or Antioch than those of Jews of Nehardea. The bilingual inscriptions will show us that Greek was commonly spoken by the Dura Jews, and the art they used has itself an undoubted hellenistic base, with highly important Parthian or Persian accretions. In physical setting, then, the Jews of Dura, an outpost of Greco-Roman civilization, had much more in common with the Jews at other centers of that civilization than with the Jews in the natural ghetto of Babylonia. So far as actual distance goes, Dura lay closer to Nehardea than to Antioch or Damascus, but was closer to Palmyra than to Nehardea. The distance from Dura to the Babylonian center was really almost as great as that from Jerusalem to Alexandria. In culture and atmosphere Dura was utterly remote from Jewish Babylonia.

Obviously, then, we cannot insist that the art of Dura, or the Jews of Dura, must be confined to the terms of Babylonian Jewry, any more than we can assume that the two groups had nothing in common. Lacking any writings from the Jews of Dura, we must be equally open to the idea that the Jews of Dura thought quite like the Jews of Nehardea, or quite differently from them, much more like Jews in Ephesus or Alexandria. Or they may have thought in terms of a mixture of ideas from both sources, or in a way suggested by none of our literary sources. We have, indeed, no Jewish literature so full of Iranian

14. *L'Esprit*, 14.

elements as are the synagogue paintings. Let me repeat, we have only the monuments themselves from which to judge the opinions of the men who made them.

C. THE PAHLAVI INSCRIPTIONS

ANOTHER BODY of evidence in the synagogue cannot be ignored or explained away any longer—the Pahlavi inscriptions painted boldly on any handy patch of light color on several of the lower biblical paintings. One seeing the paintings as they stand in Damascus is struck by this prominent writing. Yet only those who have tried to decipher the inscriptions have taken them seriously: in interpreting the paintings themselves no one has considered them. They have been studied especially by two scholars, B. Geiger and F. Altheim.

According to Geiger,[15] the inscriptional dipinti for the most part record that on specified dates certain officials came to the synagogue and approved the paintings. With one possible exception to be considered shortly, all express most friendly sentiments. The visitors record their "praise" of a painting,[16] or their having visited the building and "seen" a given picture.[17] No hint of disapproval appears. Their being allowed to paint their comments, record their visas, on the paintings themselves show that they had an authority recognized, or at least tolerated, by the Jews in the synagogue. The visitors are called by Pahlavi titles, usually *dipīr*, which means "scribe" to Geiger but is twice expanded to mean, he thinks, "scribe of the building," though what, or what kind of, building was indicated he does not know. On one occasion it is recorded that the *dipīr* was accompanied by "Kantak, the *zandak* of the Jews," a title which Geiger despairs of identifying. However the title might have been translated into Greek or Hebrew, Geiger suggests that the zandak was a Jewish inspector.[18] The "scribe of the building" would

---

15. In Kraeling, *Synagogue*, 283–317.

16. Geiger, Inscription 43, pp. 301–303.

17. Ibid., Inscriptions 45–48, 54, pp. 305–309, 314. While this book was in the press, Geo Widengren remarked to me that he could be certain about nothing whatever in these Pahlavi inscriptions but the dates!

18. H. H. Schaeder, *Iranische Beiträge*, I, 1930, 274–296 (Schriften der Königsberger Gelehrten Gesellschaft, Geisteswissen. Klasse, VI, 5), takes the word to mean "heretic," or "wrong allegorizer" or "interpreter," and quotes a Sassanian royal decree of Shapur II, about a century later than the synagogue, in which the term is used in such a grouping as "Magi, Zandik, Jews and Christians," none of whom are to be prosecuted. Cf. L. Massignon in *Encyclopaedia of Islam*, IV, 1934, 1228 f. The zandiks in most of Schaeder's material seem to have been commentators, who were in some way unorthodox. Geiger, pp. 299 f., however,

quotes from S. Lieberman a case where in the *Aggadath Esther* the word is used of Jewish officials or dignitaries. The situation seems to be as follows. Through all later use of the term in languages of the Near East the word was a reproachful one for bad interpreters, or heretics. In the royal decree it was used simply as the name of a religious group, alongside Magi, Jews, Christians, etc. This might well imply that the term was not pejorative at all. In the Dura graffito it is used of an official in an honorific sense, as well as in the *Aggadath Esther*. If further investigation shows that Geiger's reading of the word in the inscription is correct and that it is actually the same word throughout these various appearances, one can at least suggest that the word became the name for a sect, the zandiks, from the fact that the sect's officials (or chief official) were popularly called the zandiks. We have analogy in that "papists" are people under the Pope, "Episcopalians" those under a bishop. If

very likely have been some sort of building inspector, or supervisor of decorations. If Geiger is right, I should guess that the shorter word *dipīr* was an abbreviation of the longer title, and that every *dipīr* was an inspector of some sort.

Altheim,[19] on the contrary, objects that these are painters' signatures, and that "by me was seen" should be read "by me was painted" in every case. Altheim has no clear suggestion of the meaning of the letters which Geiger reads as *dipīr*, but he is confident that "he was really a painter."

Faced with two such basically different interpretations (the differences go into a great number of less important details), we who have no linguistic competence must either ignore the inscriptions altogether or take another approach to the more probable choice between suggested meanings.

First, we must notice that all fifteen of the inscriptions are written upon the lowest register of biblical scenes. Three inscriptions lack names altogether and will seem to be interpretative. Of these, two appear on the north wall and one on the lower left corner of the west wall.[20] Twelve inscriptions contain names, presumably of those who made the graffiti. In this, at least, Geiger and Altheim agree. But all twelve are crowded into a single corner, eight of them upon a single painting, that of Esther on the west wall. Two (along with an inscription without a name) stand on the scene next to it where Elijah revives the widow's son, and the other two are on the two adjoining scenes on the south wall, SC3 and 4. In these the name Hormazd appears three times, twice on a single painting. Of course there may have been three men of this name, but the chances are that in this case there would have been at least a patronymic to distinguish them. If Hormazd was signing as painter, he would presumably not have signed twice on the same painting: but if he were making visits as an inspector, he might well have recorded three occasions on which he came. Several inscriptions have two or three names, so that we have fourteen names altogether by Geiger's reading and nearly that number, at least, by Altheim's. Perhaps fourteen different painters (sixteen if we count the three Hormazds) actually took part in the painting. We cannot dismiss this suggestion, but in that case it would seem more likely that the names would have been spread through the individual paintings, as are the Hebrew and Greek inscriptions upon a number of paintings.

Furthermore, while in the classical period Greek painters often signed their vases, the painting and mosaics of the hellenistic period in very few cases have names. A signa-

this was true we should further ask whether the word did not become a word for "heretics" or the like as the group fell into disrepute and their ideas were rejected by others whom they especially offended. We have in the Dura inscription evidence that a group of Iranized Jews used the title, and hence go on to ask whether these are not to be identified with the zandiks of Shapur's edict. Was it not men who reserved the name "Jews" for themselves who rejected the zandiks, and who made the word proverbial in that sense in Near Eastern

languages? We have gone a long way beyond (not against) our slender bits of evidence, and the suggestions can only be left as questions for experts and future discoveries to answer.

19. Most recently: F. Altheim and R. Stiehl, "Inscriptions of the Synagogue of Dura-Europos," *East and West*, IX (1958), 7–28. References to earlier studies can be found here.

20. That is, by Geiger's numbering, Inscriptions 52 and 53 on the Ezekiel scene in NC1, and 55 in WC1.

ture appears below only a single painting in Pompeii (not on it), and a few mosaics have names inconspicuously within them. But, in general, art from hellenistic times to the Renaissance is anonymous. This is as true for the East as for the West. That the artists of the synagogue should have finished their task by sprawling their names over the figures they had painted is possible but defies every antecedent probability.

Both Geiger and Altheim may be wrong, of course; the inscriptions may mean something quite different; but from general historical grounds I can only judge that while Geiger *may* be wrong, I simply cannot believe Altheim can be right. We may then discuss the possible implications on the basis of Geiger's readings.

If the *dipīrs* recorded their inspection and approval of the paintings, who were they? Obviously they were Pahlavi-speaking people, and hence we cannot associate them with the Roman governing group, who would have registered their opinions in Latin or (in the East) Greek. Geiger supposes that they were "Iranian visitors sent to Dura by the Sasanian king before the fall of the city as members of his retinue of ambassadors." This conclusion is strengthened in his mind by the fact that the Pahlavi inscription near Mordecai riding in triumph with the humiliated Haman reads "Judgment is near." He thought it a threat made by the Sassanian ambassadors that Dura would soon be destroyed.

Such a suggestion seems to me quite untenable, in view of the generally friendly tone of these dipinti. It quite surpasses my power of imagination that in the very brief interval between the decoration of the synagogue and its destruction Sassanian ambassadors had authority to inspect paintings in private shrines, and write alternately praise for the Jewish paintings and threats of doom for the city of Dura. These visitors were clearly people of recognized authority, and no Sassanian ambassador had any authority whatever in Dura so long as the Romans were holding the city against them.

The inscription which Geiger took to be a threat, however, goes excellently as an interpretation of the accompanying incident in which we shall see reason to think that the triumph of Mordecai prefigured a coming humiliation of the gentiles before the Jews by the intervention of God.[21] This inscription, that is, may well have been a titulus which declares the purport of the scene: "Judgment is near" may have meant that Mordecai's triumph was a type of the glory to come to Jews in the Messianic Age, as Purim has meant to many Jews ever since that time.

We then go on to notice that other inscriptions are best taken as titles or interpretations of the scenes they accompany. Two such were painted on the scene where Elijah restores the dead child to life: "Living the child(?) that had been dead," [22] and "praise to God, praise! For life, life eternally he gives (. . .?)." [23] Geiger has so many queries and reconstructions in these two that I have no confidence in details, but, in my own ignorance of the language I assume that he has generally given us the meaning of the inscriptions.

---

21. See below, pp. 185 f. Geiger, p. 300.

22. Geiger, Inscription 49, p. 309. The word "child" is quite undetermined in the inscription: Geiger supplies it from the scene. The same inscription is oddly repeated, with the addition of the name of the inspecting scribe, on the robe of Elijah in the adjoining scene, SC4, where he makes his sacrifice.

23. Ibid., Inscription 55, pp. 314 f. It is written above Elijah's right thigh.

As he translated them, we have interpretative tituli, in this case ones which declare that the painting indicates the hope of immortality in God.

On the scene of Ezekiel and the restoration of the dead bones, NC1, are two more inscriptions:

> This make ye known, that joyous ye are, and to God's voice listen; the peace upon us [will be].[24]

and:

> Many are coming, thou go otherwise! They go(?), and do not go otherwise! To God give thanks.[25]

Geiger's notes again show his uncertainty about many of the words in these two inscriptions. I should guess, however, that like the others, these also are interpretative tituli, since they can hardly record an official visit.[26]

Our Sassanian ambassadors seem to have understood the scenes extremely well. The inscriptions, then, according to Geiger, record the visit of Pahlavi-speaking inspectors of buildings and their decoration, men welcome to record their names and approval, or *visa*, upon the paintings, and who know Judaism and its hopes.

Another inscription,[27] recording a visit in which the zandak of the Jews was one of the inspectors, explains that in visiting the synagogue they had come to the "edifice of the God-of-the-gods of the Jews." This phrase comes directly from Psalm cxxxvi, 2, and Geiger says that only a Jew could have called the synagogue by any such biblical title. It goes exactly with the "threat" in the same painting, for it asserts the supremacy of the Jewish God above all others, a supremacy which the triumph of Mordecai and, we shall see, the four figures in the center of that painting might well have been intended to exhibit.

Here, then, we have Pahlavi inscriptions recording the visit of inspectors to the synagogue and their approval of the paintings. The inscriptions also in several cases constitute interpretative tituli for the paintings, tituli which show sympathy with Jewish traditions and hopes. To describe the building, they quote one of the most militant phrases of the Psalms, that the Jewish God is God of the gods, a phrase that must have had force indeed in pagan Dura. Had these inscriptions been written in Hebrew, Aramaic, Latin, or Greek, and had the names of the visitors been familiar in any of those languages, we should at once have supposed that the visitors were Jewish officials come from some recognized center of Judaism to approve the paintings and the Jewish sentiment the paintings expressed. It is most reasonable to suppose that, during the great period of Parthian supremacy, in some centers Jews took over the Parthian-Hellenistic civilization to the point

---

24. Ibid., Inscription 52.

25. Ibid., Inscription 53. Altheim and Stiehl in *East and West*, IX (1958), 10, translate:
> I shall come to many, go thou away, Inya!
> Servants do not fetch, Inya!
> Thanks shall I know.

26. Though they were so interpreted by Altheim, as quoted by Geiger, p. 313. Their relation to the painting can be suggested only after we have studied the painting in detail. See below, X, 194.

27. Geiger, Inscription 44, pp. 303–305. It is written on Haman's right leg in the Esther painting.

that they had Pahlavi names. Kantak the zandak of the Jews is himself most reasonably considered a Jew. The only explanation of the other inspectors which fits the data is that they were Jews also. No other interpretation accounts for the tenor of the inscriptions, or their being thus prominently painted upon the biblical scenes. Such a conclusion is opposed only by the fact that no center of Pahlavi-hellenistic Judaism is mentioned in Jewish writings to my knowledge. But we do know at least one place where such a center may have been. For the friend of Augustine, Orosius [28] tells how Artaxerxes III (362–339 B.C.) on his return from a campaign in Egypt "forced many of the Jews to migrate and ordered them to make their home in Hyrcania near the Caspian Sea. They have remained there even to the present day and have greatly increased their numbers." In this general region archeological investigations have revealed great Iranian settlements,[29] along with some later Jewish remains.[30] That an Iranian-hellenistic-Jewish center ever existed can hardly be the basis of an argument.[31] But lack of evidence for such a center must not keep us from taking all the three elements in the paintings seriously. We must begin with the evidence itself in this utterly unique monument.

D. PROCEDURE

THIS CONCLUSION leads us out into a new world, or a lost old one, which we must deal with cautiously, but one which it seems to me the mingling of hellenistic and Persian elements in the paintings themselves would have forced us to assume. For we must begin studying the paintings in their setting of pagan borrowings, with the Pahlavi inscriptions adding to the impression that we are dealing with a fresh problem in the history of Judaism, religion, and art alike. The art, I repeat, along with the architecture and inscriptions, must be approached as nearly as possible as a problem in its own right. As we shall see, the recognizable Old Testament scenes with their labels, along with the donors' and builders' and visitors' inscriptions, make it indisputable that the building was a synagogue, and we must suppose that the Jews who built it based their thinking on the Torah, as did both Philo and the rabbis, and, indeed, all Jews we know. Since the paintings represent scenes not only from the books of Moses but also from the books of the prophets and later history, we may at once conclude that Jewish interests here were not so concentrated upon the Pentateuch as were Philo's. But for the nuances of their Judaism we return to the archeological remains as our only source of light, the archeological remains as a whole, not as expurgated by our preconceptions.

28. *Apology*, III, 7. The translation is that of I. W. Raymond: Orosius, *The Seven Books of History against the Pagans: The Apology*, 1936, 118. Eusebius says the same in his *Chronicon*, ed. A. Schoene, 1875, II, 112 (Armenian version).

29. For the bibliography see *JAOS*, LXXVI (1956), 240 f.; G. Frumkin, "Archéologie soviétique," *Asiatische Studien*, XI (1957–58), 76–94; B. P. Lozinski, *The Original Homeland of the Par-*

thians, The Hague, 1959, 14–16, 53.

30. S. P. Tolstov, *Drevnii Khorezm*, 1948, 191 f.; French summary by R. Ghirshman in *Artibus Asiae*, XVI (1953), 233.

31. Kraeling, *Synagogue*, 390–392, similarly concludes, in a well-reasoned section, that the Jewish art of the paintings had an origin and considerable history in Palmyra, or other places in upper Mesopotamia and eastern Syria.

1. *Architecture*

WE MUST start, indeed, with the structure of the synagogue itself, where we shall discover that although it was made by remodeling a house, and still retained some features of domestic architecture, the original building was changed to resemble as far as possible the inner shrines of the pagan temples of the city, even to focusing the main room in a niche. Scholars have hitherto minimized this resemblance, and especially stressed the fact that in all the inner shrines of the pagans which focused in a niche, the niche was used for the cult statue or relief of the deity of the group.

Into this we shall go at greater length when we have the details in mind. Here I shall anticipate only to say that I see no contrast between the Jews and pagans in their use of the niche. When the Jews put their cult objects, especially the Torah scroll, into their niche, they put there the cultic means of obtaining the presence of Deity which is precisely what a pagan aimed to get from the cult image in his own niche. When the Jew opened the shrine, pulled back the curtains, and directed his "adoration" toward the scrolls, he was not of course "praying to" the scrolls. But he was, as he still is in that ritualistic act, praying to the Shekinah which the scrolls brought into the synagogue. All intelligent pagans would have denied any higher value than this to their cult figures. In brief, both pagan and Jewish shrines focused in a niche containing the symbolic means of bringing the real presence of deity into the room. The synagogue was built for Jewish worship of the Jewish Shekinah, but conducted deliberately in a frame devised by pagans. Only a preconception that Jews *could* not have been so influenced by paganism would prevent such a conclusion. Analysis of the architectural details will then be a highly important beginning, not only for symbolism but for suggestions of cult practices.

We must go from this to analyze the nonbiblical representations, which appear in the pictorial graffiti scratched into the plaster before there was any painting, but more especially in the ceiling and in the dado, as the lowest band of ornament round the room has always erroneously been called.[32] These will turn out to be made of symbols found elsewhere in Dura, ones that in the former volumes of this series, as I have just said, have seemed to represent deep religious feeling for both pagans and Jews throughout the Greco-Roman world. We must study the pagan symbols first appearing in the Dura synagogue as we did the symbols in my previous volumes. Those who begin with the present volume will bear in mind, I hope, that this study of the synagogue is written for readers familiar with the earlier volumes of the series. Much of the symbolic vocabulary in the synagogue, particularly that of the ceiling tiles, can, indeed, be found in other buildings of Dura, but among pagans at Dura it has appeared only rarely in private dwellings: it usually is associated with shrines. In general the association of these symbols with religious feeling both at Dura and elsewhere, among Jews, pagans, and later Christians alike, will harmonize very well with the impression made upon us by the architecture. Here, then, is Judaism, obviously loyal Judaism, but the Judaism of Jews who needed the symbols of

---

32. See below, pp. 59–64.

their neighbors to express at least some of the things which Judaism had come to mean to them.

2. Pagan Symbols

THE ARCHITECTURE and pagan symbols in the synagogue suggest strongly also that the Jews of Dura thought much as did the Jews throughout the Roman world (including Palestine) who used such borrowed symbols. It is from this point of view that we must approach the biblical paintings. For the first time in our study, as I have said, we find, at Dura, Jews using pagan symbols along with biblical scenes, and so giving a clue to how they interpreted their Bibles. In volume after volume we have suspected that Jews of that period, in adopting the pagan symbols, appropriated much of the religiosity of their neighbors, i.e. what seemed best to them in it. We have therefore supposed throughout that since they kept their loyalty to Judaism, they must somehow have interpreted their Judaism, or their Jewish Bibles, to include the values of the borrowed symbols. No evidence has appeared that they accepted polytheism or idolatry, or indeed any gods on a level with Yahweh or equivalent to him, or in any way worthy of worship. I see no hint of such a thing here at Dura. But new interpretations of the Bible, whether we call them allegories or midrashim, must have gone with the borrowed symbols of paganism.

It is obviously my belief that suggestions of such allegory can be found in the biblical paintings of Dura, but we cannot begin on that assumption any more than with an assumption of similarity to Babylonian Judaism from geographical propinquity. All we can say at this point is that the presence of the biblical paintings in the pagan-styled building with its pagan decorations establishes a possibility that the biblical paintings, through allegorized biblical incidents, expressed in Jewish terms ideas similar to those expressed by the pagan symbols. Yet although pagan forms stand thus alongside and within biblical scenes in the building, we must still begin with minds as free from prejudice as possible to examine the paintings themselves. We can do this only as we find a vantage point outside the problem of Jewish meanings. The only such vantage point I know is still in the history of art, in the history of the symbolic conventions used in the paintings, and in the way in which the decorations on the walls were planned to go together.

As to the over-all design, or arrangement of the paintings, this can be studied only in the west wall, plate I; the other walls are too fragmentary to disclose a general plan, if one existed. In the west wall the history and structure of a developing plan is quite apparent, however, and becomes an important guide in interpretation. No expert who has studied the paintings has the slightest idea that we have here a totally new creation by local Jews. In spite of the many differences from anything we know elsewhere, the biblical scenes at Dura show many details like those in the illuminations of early Greek manuscripts of the Old Testament, in some of the early frescoes in the catacombs, as well as in early Christian mosaics, so that we must presume a common art tradition behind them all. The Christian designs have for a number of years been thought to have originated with Alexandrian Jews perhaps a century before Christianity, and to have come over into Christianity in the Hexateuchs and other manuscripts of selections from the Septuagint,[33] or from architectural originals. In the illuminations of biblical and ritualistic manuscripts of medieval Jews no comparable similarity has appeared. Hence we may presume that since the early Christian illuminations of Old Testament manuscripts were essentially Greek in art form, just as the biblical texts they illuminated were in Greek, the artists who began making such illustrations not only were Jews but were in some sense hellenized Jews. We may also presume about the Jewish paintings at Dura that they derived ultimately not from Aramaic and Hebrew-speaking Babylonia but from the Greek-speaking West. Kraeling and others have used the Christian illuminations for reference in identifying Dura scenes, but that the Christian art itself may also have an ideological base in hellenized Judaism does not enter at all into their evaluation of it. Even if, however, the hellenized Jews who first began such Old Testament painting had all been hellenized exactly as was Philo (a position I should not dream of defending), and even though the paintings were all designed to illustrate ideas central to Philo's thinking (equally indefensible), it could just as little be assumed a priori that these ideas, and these only, carried through to Dura and inspired the synagogue paintings. All that this part of the art tradition tells us is that since the Jews who began it spoke Greek and used Greek art forms to illustrate their Bibles and books of ritual, the art began with Jews hellenized at least to that extent. But this at once takes us a step toward concluding that the paintings in the synagogue harmonize in some way with the hellenized architecture and symbols. We cannot on that account, I repeat, transport the hellenistic Judaism of Philo, the one we know best, in full details to Dura.

With the hellenistic features others as thoroughly Persian are elaborately combined —especially the dress of many of the figures, but also such details, we shall see, as the horse and figure of Mordecai, plate VI; the army beside the sleeping Saul, plate XVII; and the pair of gods lying shattered before the Ark of the Covenant in place of Dagon, plate XIII. These details are so completely integrated with what I may call the hellenistic base that such integration has seemed to everyone to antedate the examples we have at Dura. It may well have taken place in centers of the Persian-speaking but hellenized Jews who have been suggested to us by the Pahlavi inscriptions. But for the meaning of the mixture we can only hope that the art, since that is all we have, will at least partially answer the questions which it presents: is the eastern dress used in some symbolic way or, in other words, are the artists trying to say one thing when they represent a character in Greek dress and to mark with some other meaning those in Persian dress? We shall clearly be forced to investigate whether it seems likely that dress played a symbolic part in the original Alexandrian paintings.

It is useless to discuss a biblical painting without identifying the scene it was designed, at least basically, to represent. But suddenly we find that some of the scenes at Dura represent no biblical incidents, or combination of incidents, at all. Twice a stone temple is represented, once a temple with Aaron and the implements and animals of temple cult, plate X, and once a temple as a pure abstraction, plate XI, only masonry

33. J. Hempel in *ZAW*, LI (1933), 284–294; Morey, *Early Christian Art*, 76 f.; Hempel, "Problem," 103–131.

not even set on the ground. The second of these certainly was suggested by nothing in biblical description; the first shows Aaron with a stone temple utterly unlike the portable tent the Bible describes him as using. To complicate matters, both temples are formal and utterly unrealistic presentations of Greek temples, with winged Victories at the acroteria. Except for the menorah and Ark of the Covenant beside Aaron, all details of both temples are either Greek or Persian. Even the animals wear Greek garlands as they advance for the Jewish sacrifice. The artist may be trying to present the ideals and values of ancient Jewish temple worship; he is certainly not illustrating any biblical texts or descriptions. We cannot begin, then, with forcing even biblical texts upon these temples. Some of the paintings clearly correspond to texts—as, for example, the scene of Moses at the burning bush, plate v. But if some correspond to no texts at all, we must presume that the artists, even when they show a recognizable scene, have more in mind than to put up pictures merely as illustrations. And we suspect strongly that if some of the scenes point thus to symbolic intention rather than to specific illustrations, symbolic intention may also have guided the members of the congregation, or the artist, in selecting what scenes from the Bible to represent.

Here lies my basic disagreement with Kraeling. Is the didactic element in this art quite secondary to the narrative element, or are the scenes selected throughout for their didactic value, and the narrative or illustrating elements freely altered for didactic purposes? Kraeling [34] insists upon the former alternative, but I cannot see how one can avoid the latter; and although many of my interpretations differ from those of my predecessors, almost all commentators on the paintings have in fact assumed that various ideas, eschatological, messianic, or what not, guided the artist in selecting and arranging the biblical scenes. Our antecedent ideas of what might have guided the artist's selection and arrangement must be made secondary to studying the tradition of art and the plan and arrangement of scenes as whole. Then comes the highly important matter of identifying the individual scenes, along with recognizing how each scene differs from biblical descriptions. With all this in mind we can consult other literary sources of all kinds, and the history of conventions in Old Testament illustration, to try finally to understand what the artist was saying.

3. Order of Considering the Paintings

As to the order in which the paintings are to be considered, we notice at once that the artists never tried to represent biblical narratives or events as such. A succession of incidents, comparable to that which Giotto used at Padua in painting the walls of the Serovegni Chapel and made conventional for later painters, does not appear here at all. While several incidents of Elijah and Ezekiel were represented in sequence, incidents of Moses' career were put at various parts of the west wall with no apparent reference to one another, while incidents from the career of Elijah are painted quite out of order. To begin with any one scene or register will always be arbitrary. The only straightforward course, with any hope of objectivity, seems to lie in continuing to follow the architects and

34. *Synagogue*, 179, 202.

designers in their work. For it is well known that the paintings were not all done at once. We must then follow the development of designs for painting the walls. Experts who have studied the walls have united in the judgment that in the second synagogue the first mural, fig. 66, was a relatively small presentation of a menorah, lulab, and ethrog, along with an architectural façade (which I take to be a shrine), and the sacrifice of Isaac, which, as I shall argue presently,[35] seems to me to represent the shofar. Such interpretation must be justified, but in any case it is with these first paintings that we must begin.

The next painting to be put on the wall, all agree, was a large one put above that shrine, the central painting of the room, fig. 323. This painting (I shall call it the reredos) went through a series of modifications, which will all seem to point to the development of an idea in the mind of the artist, or of the people in the synagogue who repeatedly asked for these modifications. That we cannot be sure of the exact order of all these changes does not detract from the great importance of the changes we can identify. The successive changes in the reredos suggest that the artist and congregation were trying to express an idea in the painting, one which presumably would have harmonized with the ideas that seemed to motivate the architecture and the pagan designs.

We can then follow the plan of paintings on the west wall, paintings which clearly were designed to go with the reredos, and which, since so much care went into the symbolic design of the reredos, presumably expanded its meaning. These paintings have clearly an artistic balance which must have been planned. Four portraits were designed, two on each side, to flank the reredos, or be an essential part of it, figs. 93, 102, 324–326. On either side of these, in the middle row, the two temples already mentioned were painted in a balance that at once suggests a balance of meaning, but by their different details one of contrast not identity. Each of these temples is accompanied by a scene that may well emphasize the meaning of the temple it accompanies, plate 1. On the bottom register are two outer scenes concerning a baby, one baby restored to life by Elijah, the other the baby Moses saved from the Nile to be the ideal king. Between these and the reredos are two scenes, each of which refers to royalty: in one the pagan king is put at the service of Jews under Esther; in the other Samuel anoints the ideal Jewish king, David, plate 1. Again, that is, there is a definite balance of meaning. On the top register we cannot trace a similar balance because opposite the great narrative of Moses leading the People out from Egypt was a scene now almost entirely destroyed. In it king Solomon was enthroned with women before him—perhaps the Queen of Sheba, perhaps the two harlots with their disputed baby, perhaps something quite different. But if balance cannot be discussed in the top register, the principle of balance is well attested on the parts of the wall where pictures are preserved, so that it will be most instructive to see whether the idea derived from study of architecture, pagan designs, and the reredos seems further illuminated by this balance of scenes. The wall as it appears in the Damascus Museum adds to this what the reproductions cannot convey, that the colors of the backgrounds of the different paintings are likewise balanced. We shall see a similar balance in the dado, in both the designs and colors of the backgrounds. Also, the felines on one side are as distinctly female as those

35. See below, pp. 75 f.

on the other are male. This greatly strengthens the impression that the artist was doing everything possible to bring out the parallelism and contrast of the paintings on the two sides of the reredos.

4. *Methods of Interpretation*

IN INTERPRETING the individual pictures we shall often find ourselves forced into circular reasoning. Some scenes, as has been said, cannot be identified as being based upon any biblical incident at all. Most of the others, even though they can be so identified, include elements quite strange to any biblical text. To explain these we shall of course turn to the interpretative embellishments of Jewish traditional midrash, including the midrashim of Philo Judaeus. But we shall also have to watch, as has been suggested, the symbolic conventions of the art itself. Here the problem is acute. Shall we interpret the individual scenes in terms of an assumed language of symbols in the art—for example, that of the robes—or shall we begin by expounding that language in itself, and then read the paintings in terms of it? In either case our reasoning must be circular. Within the limitations of the synagogue itself we can show the symbolic meaning of the pictures only in terms of the symbolic code, and show the existence of the code only out of its consistent use in the paintings. But we cannot escape this circle by declaring it unscientific or poor logic, and concluding that we must deny to the painters a symbolic vocabulary or intent altogether. In essence such a declaration means that what is difficult to recover cannot have existed, and that a simple explanation is always preferred to a more complicated one, as being presumably nearer the truth. If we have learned anything from modern psychiatric study, it is that a simple explanation of human motives is apt to be the simplicity of closed eyes and minds. Actually circular reasoning often has most profitable results. It offers the only hope of deciphering a lost language, for example, or of breaking a code. We can only study the material we have, get a suggestion that a given word or sign means this or that, and then try it out on the rest of the material. Usually the guess is wrong, and will not work out. But as a few guesses do seem to lead us to meaning, we then build more guesses around these, until the language can be restored. When at the end the scholar presents the results of such study, however, all the wasted efforts, the wrong guesses, or most of them, are ignored—he simply says: here is the code; try it for yourself on other texts. Such confidence supposes that there is a mass of other texts, as in Egyptian, where the code can be tested, and a new scholar can try it out for himself with undeciphered inscriptions. I hope sincerely that more art like that of the Dura synagogue will appear in Jewish remains, so that the results of this volume can thus be tested and, of course, corrected. In the absence of such additional data I must here argue the value of my suggestions much more closely, and stay within the circle of reasoning to which the single building confines me. One can escape circularity somewhat, however, as one moves from painting to painting in the building. Will the symbolic implications of dress and arrangement that seemed significant in one scene prove to be so in others? We should expect that many scenes were represented in the synagogue through a desire to enrich the symbolism as a whole. The central reredos should announce the central theme for all the paintings, since it originally stood in the synagogue alone, and always remained central. New facets of meaning would be presented in the elaboration and change of that painting, yes, but probably only facets of the same meaning. If this is true, we do in some measure escape circularity.

The most important of the symbolic devices in the paintings, I have said, seems to be the dress of the characters. This one symbol, unfortunately, will not always work. When I go on in a later chapter to discuss it, it will be obvious that I do not understand it fully. Four chief types of dress appear: first, there are many figures wearing the ordinary eastern dress of caftan and trousers; secondly, the kings all wear this in a more ornate form (and yet the angels on the ladder of Jacob's dream wear the ordinary eastern dress); thirdly, many men and children wear only the simple chiton or tunic of Greek dress; fourthly, many great figures wear over this the Greek himation, cloak, or shawl, usually with distinctive marks upon its corners. This last Kraeling identified as the dress of private citizens, in contrast to that of kings and priests, but his theory seems to me not to carry through. The full Greek dress, however, can be investigated outside the circle of the Dura figures. We must accordingly look in Greco-Roman and early Christian art to see where this costume appears, who wears it, and under what conditions. If from such investigation it seems that this dress indicates a special character for the wearer, and if in the Dura paintings it appears that the dress is reserved for individuals who might have been thought in Jewish terms to have a similar character, we shall thereby have some objectivity in interpreting the value of those wearing it in the synagogue. Since even the very crudely drawn Abraham in the sacrifice of Isaac—part of the earliest painting in the building—wore this robe, we may well stop for such review before beginning upon the biblical paintings at all. Thereafter we must study the other scenes in the order indicated. I warn the reader in advance that at places the "code" I shall suggest will not seem entirely satisfactory. I shall suggest the code nonetheless, even though it obviously needs modifying in ways I cannot see. In this connection it is fair to remind the reader that although the early suggestions for reading the languages of ancient Egypt and Mesopotamia had to be drastically modified by later scholars, it would have served the cause of learning very poorly had the earlier ones timidly refused to publish the best they knew for others to use and correct.

E. *THE "PHILOSOPHER" OF THE SYNAGOGUE*

THE READER must further be warned that increasingly these paintings seem to me to witness a master hand, one who need not have been a painter at all, but may have been one of the men named on the tiles, "those who stood in charge of this work: Abram the Treasurer and Samuel son of Sapharah," or the "priest Samuel son of Yedaya" himself, who was elder of the group (perhaps also archon) when the building was erected.[36] It may have been Uzzi, who "made the repository of the Torah shrine." [37] Or perhaps

36. See Torrey in Kraeling, *Synagogue*, Inscription 1, pp. 261–266.

37. Ibid., Inscription 2, p. 269.

it was Orobazus, another Iranian-named Jew, apparently, whose name appears on five tiles.[38] It may have been any of a number of others thus named. The plan of decoration may have been the result of several of these serving together as a committee. I suspect that the decoration of an ancient building was rarely planned by the technicians themselves.[39]

The most important description of ancient workshops I know is that given in an account of the martyrdom of the Christian Claudius.[40] The document speaks of the Emperor Diocletian as coming to a great workshop in Pannonia where 622 workmen were employed as stonecutters under five "philosophers." The latter seem to have made the designs and supervised their execution. Diocletian first ordered a large figure of Helios in the chariot, with accompanying symbols, and this the best cutters—of whom Claudius, a Christian, was chief—carved without objections, though they kept stopping to cross themselves as they worked. When the image was completed, Diocletian had a temple made for it, with marble pillars cut to specified size in the same workshop. He then gave more orders. First he demanded *Conchas ex lapide porphyritico cum sigillis et herba acantu,* which probably means fountain basins with little figures of some sort, and acanthus leaves, but may mean little niche-shrines containing figures. He also ordered foliated capitals, Victories, Cupids, eagles, deer, and lions spouting water. None of these offered any problem to Claudius and his friends, and their work delighted the Emperor. But when he asked for a statue of Asclepius they refused to make it, on the ground that a human image was forbidden; they quoted Psalm cxxxv, 18, from the famous passage prohibiting the making of idols. The end result was that others were put frantically to work on the order. They made the image in thirty-one days, but Diocletian had the Christian recalcitrants executed. The significance of this document from the viewpoint of prohibited images I have discussed elsewhere.[41] Here it is relevant to note that the skilled craftsmen who did the carving were directed closely by the five "philosophers," men who would probably now be called designers. They probably also controlled symbolic development and expression. We recall that Strabo tells us

> The philosophers attend upon their kings, and act as instructors in the worship of the gods, in the same manner as the Magi attend the Persian kings.[42]

"Philosopher" would then seem to be the name currently applied to a master of symbols and ceremonies, one who understood meanings beyond the range of the ordinary craftsmen, or even beyond the king himself until tutored. We recall that for Philo the word "philosopher" meant a man who had gone into the deeper retreats of Jewish allegory, or had himself had the vision of God.[43]

It seems obvious to me, as I hope to make it to the reader, that such a creative

38. C. B. Welles, ibid., Inscriptions 26–28, p. 279.

39. Weitzmann, *Joshua,* 87, says the same about the planning of illuminations for a manuscript.

40. Published in the *Sitzungsberichte* of the Vienna Academy, X (1853), 115–126.

41. See my "Communications," *Judaism,* VIII (1958), 178.

42. Strabo, xv, i, 68.

43. See the great number of passages in Leisegang, *Index,* s. vv. *philosophia, philosophos.*

religious thinker designed the decorations of the Dura synagogue. The painters had to execute at least two, and probably several, designs upon the reredos before the "philosopher" was satisfied. And we shall see that the other paintings were so planned to fit the walls that they seem very likely to have been planned at Dura itself. If this were the case, the visit of the Pahlavi-speaking inspectors who were pleased with the designs and their symbolism again makes sense. Who the "philosophers" in the Dura synagogue were we cannot say, but we must approach the paintings with the possibility of such a thoughtful mind, or group of thoughtful minds, clearly before us.

F. THE GOUGED EYES

M U C H A S I feel the inevitability of assuming that symbolic designers were creatively at work in the synagogue, one little detail makes me doubt that we can speak of the Judaism of the Jews of Dura as though it were a unit, and to be reconstructed from the paintings. The biblical paintings, I believe confidently, pleased the priestly Elder Samuel and the other designers of the synagogue much more than they did some of the less influential Jews. The Jews who did not like the paintings seem to have been impotent to stop their being put up on the walls, but we appear to have clear evidence of their dissent. For on figure after figure of the lower registers the eyes have carefully been scratched out.[44] This at once suggests an incident recorded in the Talmud: Rab Judah had a figure on a seal which others had made for him, but Rabbi Samuel demanded that he annul it by putting out the eyes of the image.[45] The idea seems not to have been peculiar to Jews. Morton Smith has called my attention to a statement in a sermon of Macarius: "Even though an engraver in making an image of the king makes all the parts beautifully, he has wholly spoiled the work if he has left out a little of the eye, or spoiled it, or drawn it imperfectly." [46] It seems quite likely, then, that the eyeless figures in the synagogue attest secret visits by members who did not care or dare to demolish the building or ruthlessly to disfigure it, but who reached up with knives, and by taking out the eyes annulled the threat of such creations. In the gloom of the place their act may long have gone undetected, so that it would have been difficult to establish their guilt. But only such protest seems to me to account for these slight but deeply significant defacements. Perhaps those people represented a very considerable part of the congregation, or perhaps a single recalcitrant member gouged out all the eyes. But we must beware of thinking that the pictures reflect

44. The eyes of Mordecai and Haman are gone in plate XVI, of the woman presenting the baby in plate VIII, and of the first two, and probably the fourth, figures from the left in the Ezekiel panel, as well as of Ezekiel being arrested at the end, plate XXI. The eyes of Moses and of the small figure below him at the right in plate XII have also been dug out. This latter painting was in the second register. Kraeling, *Prelim.*, 309, had no evidence whatever for saying that "it was a fact" that the workmen who finally braced the wall with mud brick during the siege of the city were the ones who did this gouging.

45. See above, II, 215.

46. *Homilies*, XIII, 4. See E. Klostermann and H. Berthold, *Neue Homilien des Makarius/Symeon*, I, *Aus Typus III*, 1961, 69, lines 15–19. (TU, LXXII). See also E. Urbach, "The Rabbinical Laws of Idolatry," *IEJ*, IX (1959), 230 f.

a type of Judaism common to the group. On the other hand, the scratched-out eyes tell us that these pictures could hardly have been meaningless ornament to anyone in the congregation. Even those who mutilated them felt their power. The pictures attest a type of Judaism, perhaps one of the types we know from literature, perhaps a mixture of those types, perhaps a new type altogether.

It is the task of this volume to try to decipher that Judaism, in its essential features. The suggestions of predecessors to this study present a problem in composition. To recite all the various interpretations for each scene with my reasons for agreement, disagreement, or modification would be a labor of pedantry rather than scholarship. Rostovtzeff, du Mesnil, Sonne, and Kraeling seem to me to have made by far the most important suggestions, but even with them I shall not attempt to come to grips in detail. Without such elaborate controversy my references to the interpretations of other scholars (which I make *a piacere*) must seem spotty and unsystematic. I can only assure the reader that I have carefully considered all the important studies of the paintings that I know, and make my own suggestions with those studies well in mind.

CHAPTER TWO

Evidence from Structural Form and the Pictorial Graffiti

APART FROM THE ACTUAL PAINTINGS, the synagogue has evidence to show something of the character of the Judaism observed in it. In the first place, the form of the two buildings was itself basically copied from the temple architecture of Dura; and in the second, before there was opportunity to do much painting, some members of the congregation had scratched little formal representations into the plaster of the walls. Both these elements must be noticed as part of the integral testimony of the synagogue.

A. THE STRUCTURAL FORM

A DWELLING at Dura was twice adapted to become the synagogue. It was in the block marked L7 in fig. 310,[1] just about at the center of the long wall facing the desert. A lane, which we follow the archeologists in calling Wall Street, separated this row of buildings from the wall. Block L7 in its final form is shown in figs. 311 and 312, with the synagogue complex in the middle of the block; the complex is isolated in figs. 313 and 314.[2] Most of our attention will be given to the building in the second stage, but first we must consider the earlier synagogue.

1. The First Synagogue

ALL THAT WAS ACTUALLY FOUND of the structure of the earlier synagogue is shown in heavy black on fig. 315, and from this Henry Pearson reconstructed the ground sketch of fig. 316. He had formerly drawn it[3] in a way that showed Room 5 entered from Room 6, making these two a separate compartment, while he later made the compartment consist of Rooms 4 and 5, without any connection with Room 6. This difference will seem important as we continue, although decision between the two is quite arbitrary, since it can be seen on fig. 315 that no trace remains of the walls at this point.

---

1. Figs. 310–316 are from drawings made by Pearson. From Kraeling, *Synagogue*, plans I–III, V, VI, VIII.

2. See also above, III, fig. 595.

3. As published in Rostovtzeff, *Dura-Europos*, VI, plate IXB; see also du Mesnil, *Peintures*, plate V.

The building was about 70 feet deep and 50 feet wide in its outside measurements. However the house may originally have been entered, a passageway from the street, marked 3 on fig. 316, now led into the central part of the building, where there was an open court, Room 1. Four rooms, nos. 4, 5, 6, and 7, surrounded this court, and of these, like the courtyard itself, Room 7 had a direct entrance into the large Room 2 where the congregation met. The meeting room seems to have been created by removing a partition between two rooms of the original house.[4] What resulted was a synagogue of the "broad-house" type,[5] which Kraeling believes was the most primitive form.[6] The plan shows a niche for the Torah in the middle of the west wall, but this is purely supposititious, for of that wall nothing was left, as fig. 315 shows. It was entirely destroyed and reconstructed when the building was again altered to make the second synagogue. The earlier meeting room measured on the inside approximately 35 feet long by 16 feet wide.[7] It is estimated that the room was about 16 feet high. Benches ran round the four walls.

In the center of the room a patch of fine white plaster on the floor covered a hole approximately a yard square. Kraeling seems right in assuming that something had once stood there. Perhaps it was an earlier form of Torah shrine later replaced by a niche behind it in the west wall; perhaps it was the site of a lectern from which the scrolls were read. A lectern of some sort has always been essential in a synagogue,[8] but could of course have been made of wood. It seems difficult, however, to dissociate this square hole in the floor from the square object, a plaster block—slightly smaller to be in proportion with the smaller room but similarly placed—which stood opposite the door in Room 4. This room also had a bench round its four sides, so that the general similarity of the two rooms is definitely marked. The square object in the center of Room 4, about two feet on a side and eleven inches high, had a hollowed top blackened by fire. It might have been used for a brazier,[9] but it much more suggests an altar, and I strongly suspect it was an incense altar, since we have reason to believe that incense was used in the synagogues at the time.[10] That incense is not used in synagogue services now cannot be cited to show that it never was burned in synagogues. An object of such definite altar type must be allowed to speak for itself.

The same sort of object may also have stood in the square hole of the larger meeting room, no. 2. In that case it would have had a larger base, and may have been so high that it had to be removed when the second floor was laid less than two feet above the first floor.

4. For Pearson's guess at the plan of the original house before it was made into a synagogue at all see Kraeling, *Synagogue*, 26, fig. 8.

5. See above, I, 225–238.

6. Kraeling, *Synagogue*, 26–33, carefully analyzes the evidence for this rebuilding. I do not agree with him on this one point, but the matter is too speculative to warrant further debate; see above, I, 210. See also Pearson's analysis in Rostovtzeff, *Dura-Europos*, VI, 333 f.; and above, I, 227 f.

7. The room was irregular, and according to Kraeling, p. 29, measured 10.65–10.85 m. on the long sides, 4.6–5.3 m. on the short sides.

8. Kraeling's conclusion, p. 33, "Babylonia rather than Palestine should be regarded as the pioneer in, and the most significant contributor to, the development of the synagogue as a formal structure," goes far beyond the evidence, but may, of course, be correct.

9. Kraeling, *Synagogue*, 28, suggests that a lamp may have stood on it, but his description of it makes this quite unlikely.

10. See above, IV, 195–208.

That some square object stood in Room 2 is certain, as well as that an object, presumably an incense altar, stood in Room 4. It is therefore very possible that an incense altar stood in the large meeting room. The great similarity of Rooms 4 and 2, even to the benches and the "altar" in the floor, suggest a similar usage, and my own guess is that the smaller room was used for services during the time when the synagogue room at the back had been dismantled, so that the second synagogue could be built on its site. Kraeling [11] alluded to the talmudic law for tearing down one synagogue to build another, but did not indicate its relevance to the data we are discussing. The law is first attributed to R. Hisda, who a generation or two after the destruction of Dura laid down the principle: "A synagogue should not be demolished before another has been built to take its place." [12] One rabbi commented on this: "There is a difference if there is another synagogue." Throughout the passage, the Talmud assumes that worship must continue during the construction of a new synagogue. The law as stated by R. Hisda very likely only formulated an older custom. Quite possibly, then, Room 4 in the Dura building was turned into a temporary synagogue with its "altar" so that worship could be continued while the large room was being rebuilt. The two would accordingly never have been used simultaneously for formal worship. This temporary use of Room 4 would account for the absence of any trace of decorations in it such as seem to have enhanced the sanctity of Rooms 2 and 7.

How the rooms were originally used before Room 4 was temporarily made the room of worship cannot be guessed, especially since we do not know how they were connected. That some of them served as guest rooms, at least at night, seems to me probable; [13] but for any notion of the way worship may have been conducted in these rooms we must limit ourselves to Rooms 2 and 7, rooms set apart from the others by being directly connected, by the threshold of the connecting door having been deeply worn by much use, and because they were the only rooms in the group with decorated walls and ceilings. The decorations will be considered in the following chapter; here we must continue to study the implications of the ground plan itself. But for the moment we turn to the ground plan of the later synagogue.

2. *The Second Synagogue*

WHEN THE SYNAGOGUE was enlarged, presumably because the Jewish community had become more numerous and affluent, the complex of rooms was almost doubled in size. Fig. 311 shows the building as it came to include the rooms marked H1–H9, of House H, which lay in front of the first synagogue. The two sections marked "House of Assembly" and "Forecourt" on this plan occupy approximately the entire space of the complex of rooms used in the earlier synagogue. The new synagogue complex can be quickly distinguished as a whole in the middle background of fig. 312; the entrance on the street in front is marked by a cluster of four people in that drawing. The entrance can be seen at the lower right of fig. 313, and this plan will now be the most convenient for following the description of the complex. It will first be noted on fig. 311, however, that

11. *Synagogue*, 26, n. 116.

12. *BT, Baba Bathra*, 3b (ET, I, 9).

13. See above, I, 179, 182.

the doorway opened into an alley, marked 71. This passageway also led at its end to the entrance of a separate dwelling, whose rooms are numbered as belonging to House C. It seems likely that House C was the residence of some high official in the congregation, though of course that need not have been the case.[14] The new rooms of the synagogue complex Pearson has numbered with a preceding H, and Kraeling discusses the whole as House H. This house, approximately 85 by 59 feet, was itself larger than the original synagogue complex. To make the new unit, the old passageway from Wall Street was closed and the space thus gained was used to broaden the assembly room.

In describing these rooms Kraeling (my only source of information) sees in Rooms 1, 3, 4, and 5 in fig. 313 a single unit, one that leads directly to the forecourt of the synagogue. He plausibly thinks that Room 3, by analogy with other houses, was itself an open court. Room 4 behind it seems to him a diwan, what we should call the living room of the master of a house, and Room 5 probably served as a bedroom or back storage room. This block of rooms seems to him to have been so separate from the others as to make House H as a whole what he calls a "duplex," although Room 5 also opens off into the little Room 6, into which Room 7 from the other suite also opened. The second suite was entered through Room 2, which served as what we might call its vestibule, as Room 1 served for the other part of the "duplex." In the other part of House H, Kraeling sees Room 9 as again an open court, Room 8 behind it as a diwan, and Room 7 the usual back room off the diwan. This in turn, instead of being a closed room, also, as we said, opened into the little anomalous Room 6. Actually, we have no idea how these rooms were used except that the first suite obviously served as an entry to the court and synagogue at the back, and may well have also housed traveling Jews.[15] A place of so little privacy would hardly have served as the house of anyone. Kraeling suspects that the archon-elder Samuel, son of Idaeus, lived in the second suite, but several other prominent men are named in the inscriptions, and it is useless to guess which one might have lived there.

Fig. 313 shows the doorway at the back of Room 4 opening into the forecourt, an area which was designed like a sacred temenos. On stepping into the court, one faced three walls before which was an ambulatory with a roof upheld by massive columns. Directly behind the central opening between the four columns across the main axis stood the central entrance to the synagogue proper. The court was a little over 43' 6" by 34' 1"; the columns Kraeling estimated at nearly twenty feet high. One or two lavers seem to have been provided in the court. To enter so large a court within the packed building of the

14. In a letter to Kraeling, Pearson made the same suggestion on the ground that in rebuilding and expanding the synagogue the partition walls to House C had to be slightly moved, so that Room C29, especially, was made a little smaller. Permission for such a change may have been bought, but its being granted at all suggests a friendly attitude.

15. Ancient Jewish communities had a sense of obligation to provide hospitality for traveling Jews.

The material is well collected by S. Klein, "Das Fremdenhaus der Synagoge," *MGWJ*, LXXVI (1932), 545–557, 603 f.; see also the Tosephta to *BT*, *Pesahim*, 101a (ET, 536): "[The statement of the *Pesahim*] can be explained by supposing that it does not really mean a 'synagogue,' but was the term to refer to rooms adjacent to a synagogue, from which the kiddush could be heard." Cf. Kraeling, *Synagogue*, 11, notes 32, 34, 36; and above, I, 179, 182, 213, 239 f.; II, 75–78, 90.

ancient city must have made a deep impression. It is still most impressive to enter the court from this door as the whole unit is restored in the Damascus Museum.

Kraeling thought it unnecessary to go beyond the range of hellenistic house architecture to explain the origin of this forecourt.[16] He gives two parallels, the House of the Large Atrium [17] and the complex containing the Christian Chapel.[18] The House with the Christian Chapel is as dubious an example of domestic architecture as the synagogue itself,[19] but a number of other houses could be added to Kraeling's list.[20] Even so, on the whole the colonnade rarely appears in the courtyards of Dura houses, and none is shown on Pearson's plan of a "typical private house." [21]

3. The Inner Shrines of Pagan Temples

IN CONTRAST, the temples of the city, especially those built in the century of the later synagogue, used this basic plan almost invariably. That is, in the Dura temples of the later period a row of columns was so placed as to make an approach to a holy place through openings between them, usually through the central opening of the three. A glance at the entrances to the Temple of the Palmyrene Gods, fig. 3,[22] that of the Temple of Adonis, fig. 5,[23] of Zeus Theos, fig. 7,[24] as well as the Mithraeum, fig. 4,[25] shows the colonnades used in a way very much like the Jewish sanctuary in Dura. One entered the courtyard of the Temple of the Palmyrene Gods through such a colonnade, and after going through the central opening of the three the worshiper came directly to the main entrance of the temple proper, the pronaos with the naos behind it. On entering that door, he saw on a straight axis before him a niche very much like the niche in the synagogue. The Temple of the Gaddé, fig. 6,[26] shows a variant use of columns. The worshiper entered the court at the left through columns, and the court was flanked by three entrances between columns at right and left, while again he entered the pronaos through columns, or looked between these toward the sacred image in the naos behind it, Room 3.

The vaulted niche of the synagogue recalled to Brown the "late additions to the

16. *Synagogue*, 13, 22. He recognizes the similarity of at least certain elements between the Synagogue and the pagan temples of Dura, but thinks it unwise to "exaggerate" the extent of this relationship, partly because of the traditional attitude of Judaism to pagan worship and idolatry, and partly because of the differences between the pagan sanctuaries of Dura and the synagogue both in outward form and function. This seems to me to beg the question of what the similarities here investigated have been.

17. Rostovtzeff, *Dura-Europos*, IV, plate IV.

18. Ibid., V, plate XXXIX.

19. And the position of the columns was not at all certain: ibid., V, 243 f.

20. As those in blocks B2, J1, M7, N2 in the plan at the back of ibid., VII/VIII.

21. Ibid., V, plate VI.

22. From a drawing by R. Deigert, ibid., V., plate IV. The four columns dramatically frame the three entrances to the sanctuary, Rooms A and B, and one entered the court itself through a similar colonnade before Room Q.

23. From Frank Brown, ibid., VII/VIII, fig. 42 at p. 150. The columns here are not lined up with the two inner sanctuaries, which are at either end of the complex, but, standing alone as they do, suggest all the more that they had symbolic value.

24. From Brown, ibid., fig. 48 at p. 194.

25. From Pearson, ibid., VII/VIII, fig. 34 at p. 72. The Temples of Artemis and Atargatis at Dura, built on the Babylonian model, had no such columns: see ibid., III, plates IV–VI, and pp. 18–24.

26. From Rostovtzeff, *Dura-Europos*, VII/VIII, fig. 67 at p. 254.

Temples of Atargatis and of the Palmyrene Gods." [27] In a temple the niche in the naos seems to have contained the most sacred symbol of the cult, such as the cult image or, as in the Mithraeum, the cult scene of Mithra killing the bull. In the later synagogue, apparently, the niche was put directly at the end of the axis through the central opening between the columns as in the temples, but it was adapted for the use of Jews by making it the repository of the scrolls of the Torah, in whose direction Jews probably made their devotions, as they still do. The synagogue was altered, then, partly to enlarge it and partly to make it have more specifically the form of a place of worship as established during the previous century in the various temples of Dura. The convention of such a form for both pagan and Jewish places of worship was by no means limited to Dura, and one cannot say where it originated.

With this in mind the plan of the earlier synagogue takes on new possibilities. Fig. 316 shows that there was no space in that building for the complete presentation of the temenos as in the later synagogue, but it is now notable that while there was a basin for water, blocking the corner at the end of the entrance passageway, columns again framed three entrances to the court on both the north and east sides. Of these entrances the most important were those between the columns at the north and those from the passageway, and as one came through these one faced (not directly, to be sure) the arched entrance to Room 7. I strongly suspect that this arch was blocked by a curtain or a wooden screen, carved perhaps like the stone screens of the Capernaum synagogue.[28]

4. *Suggestions of Cult Usage*

I T W I L L B E R E C A L L E D that the niche Pearson indicated in Room 2 of this earlier synagogue was purely supposititious. Since the plan of the later synagogue was found so closely to resemble the temene of pagan temples, we look at these again in attempting to understand Rooms 2 and 7 of the earlier synagogue. It appears at once that a side room, presumably for cult objects, was often used in temple construction at Dura, as for example Room C in fig. 3.[29] While the columns seem a Greek, or Greco-Egyptian, contribution, Bellinger has shown that the side room off the naos is a direct heritage from Babylonian architecture,[30] and so presumably a very old feature of temple structure at Dura. A comparison of these plans shows that although neither the earlier nor the later synagogue had a pronaos, Room 7 in the earlier synagogue very much resembles the little side rooms off the naos of pagan temples. Room 7 in the synagogue is at the front, while Room C in fig. 3, and corresponding rooms in the other temples, are at the side, but the difference in position in the cramped little synagogue can well be explained by the need of the full width of the space available to make the meeting room large enough for the Jewish con-

27. Ibid., 256. Earlier temples had no such arrangement at all, as the Temple of Aphlad, ibid., V, 98, plate I; the Temple of Azzanathkona, ibid., V, 131–200, plate III.

28. See above, I, 181–182.

29. See also the rooms at the side of the Mithraeum, fig. 4.

30. Rostovtzeff, *Dura-Europos*, III, 18–24. But the design goes back to a far earlier period than Bellinger suggests, for it has been found in temples of the Uruk period, early in the third millennium B.C. See H. J. Lenzen, "Die Tempel der Schicht Archaisch IV in Uruk," *Zeitschrift für Assyriologie*, XLIX (1949), 1–20; see esp. plates 1 and 2.

gregation. If cultic emblems of various kinds were brought out of the side room for use in the services, or if part of the service was conducted with special secrecy in such rooms, the arrangement of the synagogue would have been quite as serviceable for such purposes as that in the temple.[31]

The suggestion that Room 7 may have had cultic relation with Room 2 has support from two points of view.

First, the well-worn threshold of the little door that joined Room 7 with Room 2 indicates a frequency of going back and forth unthinkable if the room was used for women, but quite intelligible if processions from one room to the other were a regular part of the ritual. A glance at the plans of oriental synagogues strengthens this feeling. Kohl and Watzinger [32] give a number of such plans, from which it is at once clear that if women were accommodated in the synagogues at all, they did not stroll in with the men and sit in full view of them. Rather they had a separate entrance from the outside to a room entirely screened off from the room where the men worshiped. The heavy wear of the sill shows that Room 7 in the early synagogue could not thus have been blocked off.

Secondly, the plans of other ancient synagogues support the idea that the little room at the side had a cultic relation to the main assembly room. At Hammam Lif in Tunisia we saw a large complex of rooms,[33] so many that speculation about the use of all of them was impossible. A main axis was entered through a doorway framed by two columns, which took one into a court paved at first with gravel, Room 1, and then with mosaic, Room 2, according to the utterly inadequate reports of the amateur excavators. Beyond this was Room 3, something like the pronaoi of the Dura temples, a rectangular room set broadside on the main axis and paved with mosaic in a pattern of lozenges. Near the far door of this room was a mosaic inscription that said: "Asterius, son of the archisynagogus Rusticus [and his wife] Margarita, [daughter of] Riddeus, paved this part [of the synagogue] with mosaic." [34] It is notable that chamber 12 opened off this "pronaos" at the left, as in several of the Dura temples.[35] The "pronaos" opened directly upon the inner shrine, Room 4, which, unlike the naoi of the temples, had no facing aedicula and was oriented lengthwise on the main axis. At the left side, however, was a niche, which one would at first suppose had been used for an aedicula for the Torah; but it is on the west wall, and so worshipers facing it would have been oriented directly away from Jerusalem. Quite possibly, then, it represented the "Seat of Moses," where presumably the archisynagogus sat, since worship in synagogues of the period was in general so carefully oriented toward Jerusalem that we should by no means quickly assume that the Jews

---

31. In his very kind review of the first four volumes of this work, *IEJ*, VI (1956), 194–199, M. Avi-Yonah reproved me for regarding halachic Judaism as too "monolithic." I agree that this is wrong: the rabbis differed greatly from one another on many points. But how easy it is to slip into monolithic assumptions appears when he himself dismisses my suggestion in those volumes that Jews at this time may have conducted some kinds of rites in separate rooms or behind the screens of Galilean synagogues by saying: "There is no such thing in synagogue worship," p. 197, n. 12. This is monolithic Judaism indeed.

32. KW, plate xviii; cf. p. 140.

33. See above, III, fig. 886; cf. II, 89–93.

34. See above, III, fig. 895; II, 90.

35. See, for example, the Temple of Zeus Theos, fig. 7.

here worshiped with their backs to the Holy City. Seated there, the archisynagogus would have faced Jerusalem.[36]

He would also have faced four doors that pierced the long wall opposite him. One of these openings gave on to a passageway, Room 8, leading to a side entrance. Each of the other three doors led into a small chamber, Rooms 5, 6, 7. In two of these, patches of undescribed mosaic were found, and in the center of Room 7 can be seen a square where the mosaic inscription already published was found [37] reading, in Latin, "Instruments of thy servant the Naronitan," and "Instruments of thy servant from Naro." Gauckler [38] interpreted at least Room 7, accordingly, as one that "served for the deposit of instruments of the cult and rolls of the Law."

All of this seems reasonable enough. The Torah and the other cult instruments may well have been kept in this room at Hammam Lif, as well as in Rooms 5 and 6; and part of the service may have been the bringing of these instruments out, as processions of the Torah still play a great part in synagogue ceremonial.[39] We notice that Room 7 at Hammam Lif, with this inscription, had a door also into the corridor. Whatever the usage of the rooms, the parallelism of this room with Room 7 of the earlier synagogue at Dura still stands, for that room at Dura also had two doors, one into the large meeting room and one to the main court. Perhaps the separate apartment at Hammam Lif, Rooms 9 and 10, that opened off this court, housed the hazzan.

On the Hammam Lif plan, Room 11 at the left looks like what would have been appropriate for a women's room, since it had its separate entrance and was entirely screened from the meeting room. How the other rooms, 12–17, were used I shall not try to guess, though it seems likely that the two lavers in Room 16 had ritualistic function.

If the building at Delos, as some have thought and I still believe, was a synagogue (above, II, 71–75; III, figs. 874–876), we would have an earlier presentation of this same functional plan. The building is dated late in the first century before, or early in the first century after, Christ. Here in the inner room, A, with its benches and the throne for the archisynagogus, the left wall was pierced by three doors to an inner chamber, also with benches, as in Room 7 at Dura, and also with an outside entrance. It is conspicuous that the throne at Delos was also against the west wall, so that its incumbent worshiped toward the east. I have suggested that the quite distinct Room C at Delos might have been used like Room 11 at Hammam Lif, by the women. Again the architectural plan is perfect for Room B to have functioned as an inner chamber where certain especially arcane rites could be performed before people seated on its benches, and from which the "instruments"

36. P. Gauckler, *Mosaïques*, II, 169, no. 505, calls this niche a *mihrab*, without noting its wrong orientation. The similarity of arrangement to the later mosques was noted above, IV, 139 f. See also E. Lambert, "La Synagogue de Doura-Europos et les origines de la Mosquée," *Semitica*, III (1950), 67–72; reprinted in his *Etudes médierales*, 1956, 59–64. It is a matter of great curiosity how scholars will explain the strange aedicula in the newly dis-covered synagogue in Ostia, Italy.

37. See above, III, fig. 892; see II, 91, for suggested interpretations.

38. Loc. cit. He also says that the rest of the pavement of this room was destroyed or scattered.

39. E. Renan's suggestion has already been noted (above, II, 90 f.) that the Old and New Testaments were called *instrumenta duo* in early Christian parlance.

could be brought out into the assembly room through one or all of the three doors.

At Smyrna a Jewish inscription was found celebrating the fact that Irenopoeus, son of Jacob (both father and son were presbyters) gave money for the (presumably mosaic) pavement of the *eisotikon* and the *scamnocancelli*. When I published this in a former volume [40] I took the eisotikon to be an inner chamber of a synagogue which was equipped with benches—the scamnocancelli—presumably like the inner room with benches that we just saw at Delos, and like the similar Room 7 at Dura; [41] and I see no reason to change my opinion. My colleague C. B. Welles says that the word *eisotikon* can in itself be pressed to mean no more than "inner" space as contrasted with an outer court, but that it could have meant an inner room equipped with benches as I am taking it. The word must be a varient of *esōtikos*, which, in the one place I can find it used, means the "immediate family," the "inner family circle." [42] Applied to a room or part of a building, as at Smyrna, it would most naturally mean an inner room. We contrast *exōtikos*, which means "foreign" or, in Porphyry's religious writing, "uninitiated." [43] Like "esoteric" as opposed to "exoteric," the esotikon, as we shall call it, seems to have been an inner room, presumably designed for an inner circle. The inference cannot be made with assurance, of course, but it is much strengthened by the actual existence in synagogues of inner rooms with or without benches. Far from calling these the women's rooms, accordingly, I shall call them the esotika.

The synagogues of Palestine had at first a similar esotikon in the space reserved behind the screen. Into this we need not go again in detail, but the plan of the synagogue at Capernaum can be consulted.[44] Here Jews solved the basic problem in another way, the problem of combining the basilica, as a place of meeting, with the temple as a shrine of the deity. The large colonnaded room of the typical basilica served as a meeting room, while the part shut off by the screen housed the "instruments," and functioned as the esotikon.[45] Only in Capernaum is a screen of stone preserved,[46] but quite possibly, in many of the others, screens of wood may have been used, since in them there is no trace of a niche for the Torah shrine.[47] The other end of the screened-off esotikon at Capernaum, it will be recalled, had the central door of the main façade of the synagogue. This perplexed me very much in the earlier discussion, but although still mysterious, it now seems to have as its parallels the other entrance to the esotikon both at Dura and at Hammam

40. See above, II, 80 f.; see now Frey, *CIJ*, II, 739. Frey recalls that KW, 141, took the *eisotikon* to be the mosaic of the central nave, and the *scamnocancelli* to be the balustrade that separated the seats of the presbyters in that nave from the rest of the synagogue.

41. If the building at Miletus discussed above, II, 78, was a synagogue, its various rooms may have some analogy to this structure, but nothing indicates with any probability that it was a synagogue.

42. See a Thracian inscription published by G. Seure, *RA*, Ser. IV, Vol. XX (1912), 258.

43. Porphyry, *De abstinentia*, IV, 6 (ed. A. Nauck, *Porphyrii Opuscula*, 1886, 237, line 16): The Egyptian priests, he says, who kept themselves ceremonially pure, could not associate with any *tōn exōtikōn tēs thrēskeias*. LS properly translates this the "uninitiated."

44. See above, III, fig. 451; cf. I, 181–184.

45. Above, I, 190–192.

46. Though one has been suspected at Chorazin; see above, I, 196 f.

47. Above, III, figs. 503–507, 519 f., 529; I, 199–205, 208.

Lif. How the doors were used I cannot guess, but it may well be that the officiants went directly into the esotikon from the outside, and came only properly robed into the room of assembly. At Chorazin the screen may well have been omitted, since the plan shows a little room opening off from the side of the synagogue, which may have been the esotikon in the more usual form.[48] Here there is no outside entrance: the officiants may have had a screen to cover them as they came in by the side door only a few feet from the entrance to this chamber.[49]

It would be most convenient if the three forms we have been seeing could be dated, but I can only say that the esotikon as a separate room off the assembly room seems the earliest. It appeared as a screened-off portion of the main room, and then as an aedicula or Torah shrine in the main room. No one who has carefully studied this material would dare suggest a precise chronology, since the older fashion seems often to have been used long after the new fashion was adopted elsewhere. But the sequence in Dura has great importance in showing that the custom of a separate room or screened-off part of the synagogue as a place for the "instruments" and as a place (since benches were there) for some important and secret rites was the older, because it afterward gave way to the new convention by which the esotikon became the curtained niche we call the Torah shrine.

Krauss[50] discussed this matter (before the discovery of Dura) and suspected that such a room existed, and with such use. He has even indicated a talmudic reference to it of great interest, which stipulates that the congregation is not to leave the room of prayer until the Torah scrolls have been picked up and put away in their place. If, the passage continues, there is a second door, the people need not wait until the scrolls have actually been carried through the door proper for them, but may leave by the other door as soon as the scrolls have been lifted up to be returned to their place.[51] The point clearly is that if the room has only one door, the congregation must decently wait to allow the Torah to go out first, but that when a special door leads to the place where the scrolls are kept, the congregation may take the picking up of the scroll as a signal that the service is ended, and go home by their own exit. Clearly the scrolls were carried out of the assembly room, often by the door used by the congregation, but preferably through a second door. Whether there was one door or two, we must assume another room where these "instruments" were kept.[52] The similar door in the second synagogue in Dura that opened out into the courtyard was probably an architectural survival from the second door of the earlier room of assembly, but may have been used also for processions of some sort, per-

---

48. Above, III, fig. 484; cf. I, 192 f.

49. The esotikon seems to me indicated at the north end of the synagogue room at Sheikh Ibreiq (Beth She'arim), though the excavators in a preliminary and very sketchy report call it the *bema*, and say the Torah shrine was at the other end. Their diagram leaves almost any conclusion possible. See above, I, 208; III, fig. 535.

50. *Synag. Altert.*, 328, 373, 375.

51. *BT, Sota,* 39b (ET, 194 f). The English translation is here not correct: Krauss, p. 375, and L. Goldschmidt in GT have rendered it properly, as my colleague Leon Nemoy assures me.

52. We have already quoted Renan's remark that in Christian parlance *instrumentum* meant the Bible: the Old and New Testament. See above, p. 32, n. 39.

haps to take the scrolls to one of the rooms in front, where they were kept locked up when not in use.

Another rather early rabbinic passage seems relevant to our discussion, one to which Elbogen [53] has called attention, and which Leon Nemoy has translated for me as follows:

> The elders sat facing the people with their backs toward the *kodesh* (holy place). When the ark (*tebah*) was set down it faced the people, and its back was toward the *kodesh*. When the priests raised their hands [in blessing] they, too, faced the people, and had their backs toward the *kodesh*. But the precentor of the synagogue faced the *kodesh*, and so did the people all face the *kodesh*.[54]

The picture we get from this passage corresponds best to such an arrangement as the one most clearly seen at Capernaum. All becomes clear if the esotikon behind the screen is, in Hebrew, the *kodesh*. In that case the elders sat on chairs or a bench facing the congregation and with their backs to the screen. The *tebah* containing the scrolls was brought out (from the kodesh) for the service and put between the elders and the assembly, with its opening presumably toward the people, since its "back" was toward the elders. The Cohens, in blessing the people, stood with their backs to the kodesh, facing the people; the precentors faced just the other way, i.e. toward the kodesh like the congregation. Since it is stated that the elders were between the kodesh and the ark, I should guess that the precentor and Cohens stood between the ark and the people. What is most important is the reference to the tebah with the scrolls brought out for the service.

This passage, then, becomes explicable in terms of a movable ark, brought out for the service but then put away. In the synagogue that inspired the passage in the Tosefta, the kodesh could not have been a side room as at Dura, but when ground plans for synagogues differ as radically as do those discovered, we must expect that descriptions of procedure also will not always fit.

A passage in Ezekiel throws some light on the word. The prophet speaks of *kodeshim*, holy chambers:

> The north chambers and the south chambers opposite the yard are the holy chambers, where the priests who approach the Lord shall eat the most holy offerings; there they shall put the most holy offering—the cereal offering, the sin offering, and the guilt offering, for the place is holy. When the priests enter the holy place, they shall not go out of it into the outer court without laying there the garments in which they minister, for these are holy; they shall put on other garments before they go near to that which is for the people.[55]

The Tosefta seems to carry over to the synagogue this term from the Temple, presumably for a holy chamber. The word would seem in the synagogue to be the Hebrew equivalent of the esotikon; it could be applied to a separate chamber or to the space

53. I. Elbogen, *Der jüdische Gottesdienst in seiner geschichtlichen Entwicklung*, 1913, 470.

54. *Tosefta Megillah*, IV, 21 (ed. M. S. Zackermandel, 1881 or 1937, 227, line 12).

55. Ezek. XLII, 13 f.

behind a screen in the main room. The important thing, according to both the rabbinical passages, is that there be a holy chamber in the synagogue, with, if possible, its own door to the assembly room, where the scrolls could be kept in a portable ark and from which they could be brought out for the services.

One is tempted to suppose that, after the analogy of the rooms off naoi in the temples, and the holy chambers mentioned by Ezekiel, this room had other "instruments," such as the officiating robes of the synagogue officials. The benches we have seen in these rooms may even be taken to indicate that, as Ezekiel tells us, the priests in the temple ate the various food offerings in their "holy chambers," so there may have been consumed in the esotika some sort of sacred meals such as we have often suspected were eaten by an inner group of Jews.[56] I hasten to add that the last suggestion carries us, if not beyond possibilities, at least well beyond any direct evidence. But it seems to me highly likely that the kodesh was also a robing room for those who led the prayers. If the rolls were kept permanently in the niche of the later synagogue, I should suppose that one of the front rooms would have functioned as a vestry for robing.

From this analysis of the ground plans of the two synagogues we have found a mixture of hellenistic-Roman and Jewish approaches to the making of a sanctuary. The older idea, reflected in the first synagogue at Dura, was to use the portico as entrance to mark the enclosure beyond as a sacred temenos, though there is no architectural remain of anything cultic permanently opposite the entrance except what I take to have been an incense altar. The holy instruments, primarily the scrolls, were kept in a special holy inner room, and brought out, presumably to stand before the altar during services. This older Semitic usage, which continued to the end in many of the Dura temples, was felt by Jews to be inadequate. In a temenos proper the divine token should be opposite the door of the shrine itself. In remodeling, accordingly, the Shekinah or real Presence was brought to precisely this axis and put into a new little kodesh, the *aron hakodesh* or holy ark behind curtains. The new plan soon became the universal and fixed plan for Jews, as it did for western Christians in their churches—the plan that from the moment of entering the building the worshiper had before him a sanctuary with the real Presence. It would indeed be a large conclusion that the change was made by the Jews of Dura for the first time. A similar change was taking place in Palestine, we saw in discussing Palestinian synagogues in Volume I.[57] But that the new idea had been adopted by the Jews of Dura by the first half of the third century can be assumed with confidence.

It may seem bold that I have applied the Greek words *temenos* and *eisotikon* to the inner shrine of the two synagogue complexes, but for this I have excellent precedent in Philo, who, though he usually speaks of the synagogues of Alexandria as places of prayer (*proseuchē* or *proseuktērion*), he once calls them "sacred enclosures" (*hieroi periboloi*) and

56. See above, VI, 216–222.

57. C. Roth in *Judaism*, III (1954), 182, reviewing earlier volumes of this study, mentioned a "later development, when the architectural Torah-shrine introduced from Babylonia (the later Se-phardi *Hechal*) took the place of the removable Ark (the Ashkenazi Aron) of earlier Palestinian tradition." Since no "Babylonian" synagogue except Dura exists, it is hard to take this suggestion seriously.

once *temenē*, both words used of the inner temple precincts.[58] One of the reviewers of an earlier volume of this series protested correctly against my statement: "Now no Jew would . . . bow or show other form of reverence to a synagogue."[59] He added: "It is customary to bow towards the Ark on entering, without any suggestion that 'a real Presence' is ensconced in the building."[60] That I have just translated Shekinah as real Presence is something I will stand by. I was certainly wrong in saying that Jews do not do obeisance to this Presence in their synagogues. Not only do the more strict Jews bow to it on entering, but Rabbi E. Fischoff, who heartily approved translating Shekinah "real Presence," has told me how, on the Day of Atonement, at the prayer "We bow down and prostrate ourselves and give thanks before the King of Kings, the Holy One, blessed be he" all bow to the scrolls and the precentor prostrates himself on the floor before them and has to be lifted up by a man on either side. If it be argued that the prostration is toward the Shekinah, the real Presence, that abides in the scrolls, and not toward the scrolls themselves, I have no objection. It quite suffices for my argument that where the scrolls are, there is the Shekinah or Presence of God in all reality, and that certain prayers must be made in its direction. The protests of Chrysostom,[61] that the Jews were wrong in thinking that the presence of the scrolls made the synagogue a holy place to be venerated, in itself establishes at least a likelihood that Jews did make such a claim. The Jews of Dura who put the scrolls in a Torah shrine opposite the entrance of their second synagogue were thereby declaring that as over against the false idols of the pagans, they came into the real Presence of God in entering their temene. This came to seem to Jews, and later to Christians of the West, a better way to make a "sacred place," as Jews called their synagogues,[62] than to keep the Presence in an inner room, to be brought out to the congregation as Jews apparently did in their earlier worship, and as eastern Christians still do with the *sacra*. In the West the procession of the scrolls-Shekinah through the congregation, like the carrying of the Host through the crowd of worshipers in Christian churches, seems a survival of the older custom.

The decorations of Rooms 2 and 7 further confirm our feeling that ritualistically they formed a unit, and give some indication of the spirit of the worship.

B. THE PICTORIAL GRAFFITI

KRAELING[63] RECORDS that in addition to the epigraphic materials a number of graffiti representing objects were scratched onto the walls. Most of them, he says (without distinguishing which), were scratched into the plaster before it was painted, and now, under the paint, they are hard to discern. He is by no means sure that he has recognized them all, for he often found it extremely difficult to know what was mere random scratching and what an actual figure. Five which he published are so unformed that I do not

---

58. For references see above, II, 86 f.

59. See above, I, 184.

60. Roth, 181.

61. *Adversus Judaeos*, I, 5 (at end); VI, 6 f. (Migne, *PG*, XLVIII, 851, 913 f.)

62. See above, I, 201 f.

63. *Synagogue*, 318–320.

reproduce them.[64] He calls them a lyre, an eye, a tent(?), a human figure or demon(?), and a Torah shrine(?). He might well have questioned the first two of these also. Other figures, however, though for the most part very crudely drawn, are extremely interesting.

The first of these had been scratched on the bench of the early synagogue, text fig. 1,[65] and shows a clearly recognizable object of the sort used on Jewish coins of the Bar Kokba revolt, and similar to the Ark of the Covenant as shown three times in the paintings.[66] The form is that often used in the period for Torah shrines,[67] and which of the two the man had in mind when he scratched the little design cannot be said. But whichever it was, we begin the graffiti with a form which had symbolic reference. It is the only strictly "Jewish" form among them, but raises the question whether others may not have had meaning beyond the mere scratches of a doodler.

A design appeared on the fragment of a door jamb found in the forecourt, text fig. 2.[68] Kraeling called it a plant or tree, but it is clearly the lilaceous plant which appeared over and again on Jewish ossuaries of Palestine.[69] The motif is not uncommon on pagan bowls and jewelry of the region, and in tombs,[70] which would suggest that it presents the flowers of the Elysian Fields, and hence symbols of immortality appropriate for funerary objects. In any case, they have appeared too often on ossuaries to be taken casually: they probably had active symbolic power in Jewish thinking.

A vase without handles, text fig. 3,[71] was scratched into the wall where the reredos painting was soon to be put, at the bottom of the space and behind the upper panel of the Torah niche. But it was exactly in this space, covering the graffito, we shall see, that the great vine symbols were soon to be painted, a symbolism that sooner or later called for at least three craters. When the graffito was made, the niche below it must have already been constructed and, possibly, been used in ritual. One wonders whether to the people at Dura the Torah so essentially suggested wine symbols that the vase was really a premonition of what would come, a substitute for it when no great painting was available. At least we see that the man who made it thought highly of the vase form.

On the east wall, with no reference whatever to the scene later painted on it (so far as we know: the painting is too fragmentary to judge [72]) an arrogant eagle was scratched, text fig. 4.[73] The eagle, we have found, was one of the most important and widely used symbols for Jews at this period, one which suggested not only royalty but immortality and mysticism.[74] Not far away on the same wall a well-drawn horse was outlined in flying

---

64. Ibid., nos. 64, 65, 67, 69, 72. An additional sketch, painted rather than scratched is reproduced and discussed below, p. 225.

65. Ibid., no. 71.

66. See below, X, 84.

67. Du Mesnil, *Peintures*, 8, has an interesting collection. But see above, III, the Jewish examples listed in Index 1, s.v. Torah shrine.

68. Kraeling, no. 70.

69. See above, I, 124 f.; III, figs. 176–183, 189, 192.

70. See the Nabatean bowls, above, III, fig. 182; Rostovtzeff, *South Russia*, plates LXXIV, LXXVI, LXXVIII–LXXXI. And see the exergue of the Sassanian plate, below, XI, fig. 262.

71. Kraeling, no. 58.

72. See below, X, 160–162.

73. Kraeling, no. 66.

74. See above, VIII, 121–142.

gallop, text fig. 5.[75] The eagle and the horse might well have been done by the same person, so far as skill in drawing shows. Quite another hand drew also on this wall two of the amorphous objects which I do not reproduce.[76] In the fifth one on this wall, text fig. 6,[77] we can at last recognize an extremely crude human bust, but what the lines below it represent, if they go with the man at all, cannot be guessed. They show, however, a direct interest in representing the human figure which must antedate the later painting —an interest, we therefore see, not limited to people of culture and artistic ability, or models.

75. Kraeling, no. 63.

76. Ibid., nos. 64 f.
77. Ibid., no. 62.

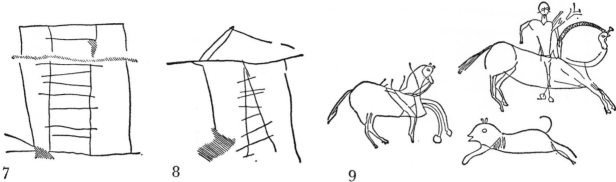

7　　　　　　　　8　　　　　　　　9

Under one of the figures of the leopard in the dado on the north wall one can see traces of two other graffiti. The first, text fig. 7,[78] has been called a wall with a ladder, and it reminded Kraeling of the similar design he and C. Hopkins published from a private house in another part of the city,[79] which has three tiers of divisions like the single one of this design. The two on the left have eight, the one at the right nine, divisions. Various largely unintelligible words are written in the spaces, but the fourth space from the bottom of the central tier reads *tauta samas*, which led Kraeling reasonably to assume, since *samas* is the Semitic word for "sun," that the whole was a most imperfect diagram of the eight planetary steps of Mithraic mysticism.[80] Of the column with nine divisions he says nothing, but presumably it had some relation to the ladder with eight. We can conclude about the graffito of the "ladder" in the synagogue, then, which also has nine steps, only that there is some likelihood that it too had a mystic association.[81]

The second graffito under the leopard, text fig. 8,[82] Kraeling took to be either a tent or a Torah shrine. Like him, I should have to leave both possibilities open, but because of the peaked roof I am rather inclined to class this form with the tents of figs. 331 and 348. Unlike these, the tent of the graffito, if such it be, has front curtains which spread slightly to show what they are, but are carefully tied by cross ropes. Since not only the tents but similarly closed or veiled fronts appear as part of the symbolic representation in the paintings,[83] I take it that this, like the others, was a symbol of some sort, though without context I would not dare to suggest its symbolic value.

The last of these graffiti was made in the left part of the scene in which Elijah and a strange companion come to the widow, fig. 340. It shows a hunting scene with two horsemen and a single running lion, text fig. 9.[84] Since the paint had almost entirely gone from that part of the painting, Gute represented it lightly but clearly in his painting. There is every reason to suppose that such scenes also had symbolic value in this region at the time. Rostovtzeff has collected them,[85] and shown that they were very commonly put up by people who scratched on the walls of Dura.[86] From their appearance in

78. Ibid., no. 61.

79. In Rostovtzeff, *Dura-Europos*, V, 93–97.

80. See below, X, 46–49.

81. On the symbolism of the ladder in general, see above, VIII, 148–157.

82. Kraeling, no. 60.

83. See below, figs. 332 and 333.

84. Kraeling, no. 68.

85. "L'Art gréco-iranien," *Revue des arts asiatiques*, VII (1931–32), 202–222. See also Kraeling, *Synagogue*, 280, no. 34.

86. Rostovtzeff, 205, fig. 1; 209, fig. 3; 211, fig. 4; 213, fig. 5; and plates LXIVa; LXVIIa.

so many places where they could not possibly have been tributes to kings, as in private houses and tombs, the assumption must be that these royal hunts had some definite meaning. I have shown reason to connect that meaning with immortality.[87] Again I would not guess too closely at what the Jew in Dura had in mind when he scratched his version of the design.

The importance of the pictorial graffiti seems to be that they suggest a strong symbolic motivation on the part of the Jews in Dura quite apart from the later formal paintings. No Jew of Dura, or anyone in his senses since, could suppose they were scratched in for "decoration." They were either just childish doodling or a crude but earnest attempt at getting symbols on the walls. Just as we saw the Jews in Rome and Beth She'arim hallowing their dead with such crude representations and felt that the very crudity reflected a symbolic sincerity, so I feel that these little forms had far greater significance than I can define. In that case the symbolism of the later painters could have been heartily welcomed by at least many in the congregation.

87. See above, VII, 28–86.

CHAPTER THREE

Painting in the First Synagogue

T WO ROOMS of the early synagogue would seem marked as especially important by their walls alone having been covered with painting, and by the character of the designs put upon them. Kraeling [1] points out that the walls and the ceiling of a room were rarely painted at Dura; indeed for parallels he can refer only to the cellas of the Temples of Bel, of Zeus Theos, of Adonis, and of Mithra, to which we may add the Christian Chapel. If only five rooms at Dura in addition to those in the two synagogues were completely painted, and all these were inner shrines, *naoi*, of temples or of Christian worship, it becomes highly probable that such painting, or the things painted, had religious significance, were not "merely ornamental."

In the assembly room of the earlier synagogue, Room 2 on fig. 316, the walls were divided into three zones, as in fig. 353, of which the top zone was apparently left blank. The lowest zone, about three feet high, was painted to look like a facing of yellow marble, grained in green. The painting of the central zone represented a series of marble panels of various colors overlaid upon the wall, technically known as incrustations. Each panel showed a border of colored marble surrounding what might be a plain rectangular slate, or four triangular pieces that together made the rectangle, some with a round-centered lozenge in the rectangle.

On the ceiling of Room 2 was represented a pattern of panels or coffers, fig. 354; a gilded plaster rosette was affixed in the center of each coffer and perhaps also in the round disks that marked the intersections of the "beams." Such rosettes on coffered ceilings were commonly used in the period, but seem to me far from being conventional or commonplace. The design as a whole is to be found occasionally in ordinary rooms, of which I show two ceiling patterns from the Palace of the *Dux Ripae* at Dura itself, figs. 8 [2] and 9.[3] Here it appears that in spite of the varieties of coffers represented, the "round object" (i.e. a circle surrounding a smaller circle), the round-centered lozenge, and rosettes are the elements of the vocabulary. It is now quite out of date to suppose that the use,

---

1. *Synagogue*, 66.

2. From Rostovtzeff, *Dura-Europos*, IX, iii, plate VII, 2.

3. From ibid., plate VIII, 2; cf. plates VI–IX. See also the ceiling of the House of the Roman Scribes, ibid., VI, 283–288.

even common use, of a design in a private house in itself demonstrates that the design had no symbolic value. Kraeling not only makes this assumption,[4] but even suggests as further proof of the design's lack of meaning that it was often used in temples and tombs at the time.[5] Of the instances to which he refers, I reproduce two from the great temple at Palmyra, the soffits of two doorways, figs. 10 [6] and 11.[7] The latter of these shows clearly that the design indicates the starry heaven, and its symbolism is made specific by the eagles, zodiac, and the gods within. The whole distinctly recalls the "dome of heaven" [8] design which Lehmann expounded and which has proved repeatedly important for our symbolic vocabulary.[9] For Lehmann has shown many instances of ceiling decorations of the Roman period, pagan and Christian, in which a central plaque is encircled by other plaques, and he has clearly demonstrated both that this design represented the heavens and that in the central plaque would be put the god or symbol through which the devotee hoped especially for immortality. In fig. 11 the zodiac and planetary gods of the week [10] are set in the larger environment of rosettes. In studying rosettes themselves we have seen that they often allude to stars.[11] The coffered ceiling with rosettes also had importance in Palmyrene tombs, where the ceiling could represent merely the coffers and rosettes of various shapes, or could show the deceased or the gods in heaven, fig. 12.[12] In a temple of the sun god, e.g. the temple at Palmyra, or in the graves of his devotees the symbolic importance of the sky as what in religious language is called heavens is too obvious to be inadvertent. Astral immortality had quite taken over the ancient world, as we have already had occasion to recall.[13] So it becomes significant that the walls and ceiling of a tomb at Brestovic in Bulgaria of about the same period were decorated in the same way as the Dura room we are discussing, fig. 14,[14] and that the square divisions of the ceiling of another ancient tomb in South Russia were filled with solar rosettes, fig. 13.[15] Still more significantly for our purposes the Roman Jews similarly ornamented soffits of the arches in arcosolia in the Catacomb Torlonia, fig. 15.[16] That the Jews here were using more than formal ornament appears at once from the fact that the rosettes in this soffit are drawn

4. *Synagogue*, 53 f., "fundamentally conventional"; "The basic fact . . . is that the decoration of the [second] synagogue's ceiling was in large measure a 'commercial' job."

5. For round-centered lozenges on the walls of tombs of South Russia see E. H. Minns, *Scythians and Greeks*, 1913, 315, 318.

6. From Robert Wood, *The Ruins of Palmyra*, 1753, plate VIIID.

7. Ibid., plate XIXA; cf. plates XD, G; XIIIC, E. See also the pattern of carved rosettes from the ceiling of the "Court of the Altar" in the great temple at Baalbek; G. Hoyningen-Huene and D. Robinson, *Baalbek, Palmyra*, 1946, plate 36.

8. "The Dome of Heaven," *The Art Bulletin*, XXVII (1945), 1–27.

9. See above, I, 267; II, 21, 36, 67; V, 12, 19; VI, 149.

10. That the figures within the zodiac are the gods of the week, Saturn in the center, appears from a similar design on a mosaic from Bir-Chana, Tunisia: Gauckler, *Mosaïques*, II, 151, no. 447. At Palmyra, Mars and Mercury seem interchanged according to the engraving.

11. See above, VII, 179–198.

12. From Wood, plate LVA; cf. plates XXXVIIB; XLIC, D; XLIIA–C.

13. See above, VIII, 177–184.

14. From A. Frova, *Pittura romana in Bulgaria*, 1943, fig. 26; cf. M. Valtrovich in *Starinar*, N.S., I (1906), plate 5.

15. From Rostovtzeff, *South Russia*, plate LXXXII, 4; cf. 3.

16. From Frova, fig. 27; cf. Beyer and Lietzmann, *Torlonia*, plate 9a.

definitely as stars (i.e. rays from a center) or as suns (i.e. rays from a central circle). We shall see the same distinction of sun and stars in one of the paintings of the second synagogue at Dura.[17] But in the same Jewish catacomb at Rome the suns and stars could appear formalized as rosettes, fig. 16.[18] We must accordingly ask whether the formal example shows that the design had lost all symbolic value for the Jews, or the more realistic representation of sun and stars make it probable that the design had meaning even when represented only formally? The question cannot be answered definitely, of course, but the "heavenly" designs of Lehmann's type are used on almost every other bit of decorated ceiling in the catacomb, so that it is much the greater probability that the whole tomb was decorated to show, and to ensure, the soul's going to "heaven" at death. Even the designs on the walls of this Jewish catacomb seem to indicate the same hope.[19] We have seen that the Jews of the time appear to have been deeply affected by current astronomical ideas of immortality.[20] Whether the heavenly bodies were represented as formal rosettes, accordingly, or in what seemed to people of the time to be the more realistic presentation, has relatively little importance.

We cannot stop to trace the history of the starry heavens as a symbol of immortality,[21] but that it was very old and had for centuries the same implications can be seen at once in a few Egyptian examples. In a room dating somewhere between the XXth and XXVIth Dynasties, that is roughly in the first half of the first millennium B.C., "many fragments of a starred roof painted with red and blue were found." [22] In the tomb of Abba, of the second half of the seventh century B.C., the first room had a painted starry ceiling, across which ran a band with Abba's name and titles.[23] Ceiling designs of rosettes very much like those we have seen from the Roman period were also used in the Theban Tombs of Egypt in the fifteenth century B.C., as in fig. 17.[24] The ceiling in the vestibule of the tomb of Neferhotpou at Thebes, of the end of the fourteenth century B.C., also has such a design, fig. 19,[25] with Neferhotpou's name and title repeatedly worked into openings of the design. The implication is clear in all these that the person has gone with his name to the upper heavens, or hopes to do so. Another device for saying the same thing, from about the beginning of the tenth century, was to paint the starry heavens within the coffin, so that the corpse was put directly among the stars, fig. 18.[26] We shall see the donor's name

17. See below, p. 115.

18. Courtesy of the Pontificia Commissione di Archeologia Sacra, Rome. See Beyer and Lietzmann, *Torlonia*, plate 14a.

19. See above, II, 35–41; IV, 128, 211.

20. See esp., VIII, 167–218.

21. Interesting material on "Sky Ceilings" is presented by W. R. Lethaby, *Architecture, Nature, and Magic*, 1956, 110 f.

22. W. M. Flinders Petrie, *Tanis*, Part I, 1885, 16 (The Egyptian Exploration Fund, II). See also above, VII, figs. 162, 165.

23. V. Scheil, "Le Tombeau d'Aba," 1894, 625 (*Mém.* Miss., V, iv). The inscription is fragmentary,

but this much Professor R. A. Parker of Brown University has kindly assured me can be said.

24. From N. de G. Davies, *Five Theban Tombs*, 1913, plate XIII; cf. p. 4 (ASE, XXI).

25. From *Mém.* Miss., V, iii, plate VI. The tomb is dated by reference in one of the inscriptions to Neferhotpou's having been invested in the reign of Haremhebi: see the description of the tomb by G. Bénédite, p. 496. The priest's title was "Father of the god," as Professor Parker told me.

26. From E. Chassinat, *La Seconde Trouvaille de Deir el-Bahari (Sarcophages)*, Le Caire, 1909, plate I, no. 6002; cf. pp. 3–8 (Catalogue Général des Antiquités Egyptiennes).

in the ceiling of the second synagogue at Dura, apparently with the same implication.[27]

The design clearly had a long history that began with the Egyptian craving to rise from the lower darkness to the bright region of the sun and stars. We shall see that in going over to the hellenistic world it does not seem to have lost its symbolic life.

Before seeing more of these designs, however, we must have in mind the correlate ceiling of Room 7.[28] Kraeling says that the fragments of painted plaster from Room 7 are fewer and less revealing than those from Room 2. The south wall, he reports confidently, was divided into two sections by a red line. The lower section formed a relatively narrow wainscoting, and was unpainted. In the upper section upon a yellow background leaves, fruit, and flowers had been painted in some sort of continuous design which cannot be reconstructed. Kraeling [29] notes that this "floral style" of ornament appears in the eastern Mediterranean in hellenistic times, particularly in tombs. His parallels are all in tombs. To these again the Jewish Catacomb Torlonia [30] could be added, and the highly mystical scene of birds among flowers, peacocks, and the sprouting vase in the mosaic floor of the Hamman Lif synagogue.[31] Kraeling follows Rostovtzeff in thinking that the design came from Egypt, eventually, perhaps, from carpets with flower patterns hung on the tents of nomadic tribes. Since the flowery patterns usually appear on ceilings, this suggestion is not impressive. Ordinarily the flowery patterns are backgrounds for birds of heavenly reference, and such seems likely to be their reference here.

The ceiling of Room 7, fig. 354, was divided into small painted square fields in each of which was depicted in bright colors a separate motif of fruit or flowers. The reconstructed design shows pomegranates, citrus fruits, and four-petaled roses. From analogy with similar ceilings, probably other motifs were also represented, such as birds and grapes.

This sort of ceiling design often appears in antiquity, especially from the later years of the Empire. We may begin with fig. 20,[32] a mystic tomb of the fourth century A.D., in Silistra, ancient Durostorum, in Bulgaria, whose decoration will repeatedly seem important to us. The tomb was in the form of a small room whose walls and vaulted ceiling were entirely painted. The vault was covered with such coffers as those in Room 2 of the synagogue, with rosettes still represented by the dots at the round junctions of "beams." In the coffers themselves were put designs more varied than can be restored for Room 7 at Dura, but clearly of the same general type.[33] Here again are the flowers and fruit, but also the birds, grapes, tree of life, ducks, and peacocks, of the symbolic vocabulary we have established in the previous volumes and shall see on the ceiling of the later synagogue. With these several times appear also an adorant with raised hands and a figure hunting a boar or lioness. Mystic scenes in the wall below [34] make it highly likely that here we have another "heaven" with its saving symbols among the stars.

27. See below, pp. 56 f.

28. For the decorations of Room 7 see Kraeling, *Synagogue*, 31.

29. *Synagogue*, 36.

30. See above, II, 39; III, fig. 813.

31. Above, II, 96; III, figs. 887 f., 901. See also the use of such a flowery setting for heaven in the

Catacomb of S. Callisto, Rome: Swindler, *Painting*, fig. 634; cf. fig, 635. I very much suspect eschatological reference also in fig. 637.

32. From Frova, fig. 18.

33. For the decorations of Room 7 see Kraeling, *Synagogue*, 36–38.

34. See Frova, figs. 1–15.

The basic motif of this decoration seems to me again to have been worked out in Egypt. We have already noted that the plan of such a heavenly ceiling apparently originated there. With these earlier ones go the ceilings of the graves at Anfushi, near Alexandria, where appeared the earliest examples known to me of this design with hellenistic adaptation. In one room the ceiling is decorated with painted coffers of the sort we have discussed. But another ceiling is divided into squares with a figure represented in each, "apparently scenes or individual figures from Greek mythology." [35] We shall have occasion to return to this design in discussing the ceiling of the second synagogue.[36] Notably, here were ceilings in adjoining rooms quite similar to those in Rooms 2 and 7 of the synagogue. No evidence exists to prove either that such designs had symbolic implications or that they had become meaningless ornament. Clearly to me the probability is greater that they were often used at the time not because they had so little meaning but because they had so much, and that in the synagogue they mark the heavenly hopes of the worshipers in these two rooms.[37] That the same basic idea was developed more fully for the ceiling in the assembly room of the second synagogue, along with little plaques containing donors' names within wreaths, illegible from the floor, seems to me to make the symbolic intent of the paintings in the two rooms of the earlier synagogue all the more probable.

Of the complex of chambers in the earlier synagogue, Rooms 2 and 7 alone seemed important enough to be decorated, and this fits in with the plan of the two rooms and the unmistakable evidence that there was much passing back and forth from one room to the other. Most naturally, therefore, we have concluded that these two rooms functioned together as a cultic unit, and that the smaller room served at least as a robing room and storage place for the cult instruments. The benches in the smaller room suggested some sort of ritual for a group smaller than the main congregation, a special and selected group.

What sort of rites might have been celebrated in the smaller room to the exclusion

35. A. Schiff, *Alexandrinische Dipinti*, I, Leipzig, 1905, 25 (Diss., Rostock University). R. Pagenstecher, *Nekropolis*, 1919, 118 f., and Rostovtzeff, *South Russia*, plate XXV, 2, illustrate these rooms, but the ceilings were not properly reproduced. Pagenstecher, 116 f., reports that photographs of these ceilings were made at the excavation and reserved for publication by a scholar who then lost them. The ceilings have now so degenerated that photography is impossible, and so he can report only that the square openings were painted with scenes of Greek mythology, and that nothing whatever can be added to this statement. The photographs published reveal female heads such as we have discussed above, VII, 202–229, and shall see again in the second synagogue. A general study of ancient ceilings seems to me highly desirable. To Lehmann's design of the heavenly dome must not only be added the one we are discussing but peculiar ceilings in South Russia with birds and human figures floating against a background of flowers, leaves, and untied leafy garlands ready for those who ascend to the heaven the design seemingly represents. See Rostovtzeff, *South Russia*, plates LVI f., LXII, LXXXI.

36. See below, p. 48.

37. An important study for the history of symbolism would be to collect these various ceiling designs and see how they were taken over for mosaic floors in late antiquity. I suspect that from such a study we would have further evidence that the passing of ceiling designs to the floor implied not the loss of their symbolic value, but their mystic appropriation for daily living and protection; that this would prove a variant way of expressing what Paul meant when he said "Our citizenship is in heaven": Phil. III, 20.

of the rest of the congregation? That the rites and instruments had something to do with making the worshipers ready to go to heaven seems indicated by the decorations, but more than that the evidence of the earlier synagogue does not even suggest.

In the paintings of the second synagogue we shall see that the implications of the earlier symbolism were writ larger as the painting went from stage to stage.

CHAPTER FOUR

The Ceiling Tiles and Dado of the Second Synagogue

THE PAINTED TILES of the ceiling of the second synagogue must have been part of the original structure of the room. Their designs in no case, except those with the donors' inscriptions, showed direct reference to Judaism. When the walls were painted, the lowest tier, usually called the dado, was devoted also to purely pagan forms. These two, accordingly, can be considered together, though I suspect that the dado represents a definitely later stage in the plans for decorating the room.

A. THE CEILING TILES

BUILDERS OF THE LATER SYNAGOGUE elaborated the decorative ideas of the earlier synagogue in making its ceiling. Here a new technique was used, that of putting ceiling tiles in rows held up by wooden beams, apparently the technique imitated in painting on the ceiling of the earlier Room 7, fig. 354. Such imitation of tiles seems also represented on the ceiling of the Stabian Baths at Pompeii, fig. 21,[1] while a side wall at Pompeii carries out the effect exactly, along with the female heads of the Dura ceiling, fig. 22.[2] The synagogue ceiling as reconstructed at the National Museum, Damascus, appears in fig. 352.[3] I am convinced, however, that the reconstruction is at fault, and that the tiles were held also in a series of crossbeams such as the painting of Room 7 suggests. This sort of ceiling was taken for granted, and well discussed by Margaret Crosby[4] when she published the similar ceiling tiles in the House of the Roman Scribes in the same block with the synagogue. She refers to many ceilings with such tiles from

1. Courtesy of the Vatican Library. Cf. Swindler, *Painting*, fig. 619; Curtius, 415, fig. 226.

2. From Rostovtzeff in *Yale Classical Studies*, V (1935), fig. 32a. It is a tricliniam mural at the Casa dell' Artiste, Pompeii. See also the same heads in mosaic panels from a house in Sousse, Tunisia: L. Foucher, *Inventaire des mosaïques*, 1960 (Feuille 57

de l'Atlas Archéologiques, Sousse, Institut National d'Archéologie et Arts, Tunis), plate XIX.

3. Courtesy of my former pupil, Professor Leander E. Keck of Vanderbilt University. For defense of the reconstruction see Kraeling, *Synagogue*, 53, n. 105.

4. In Rostovtzeff, *Dura-Europos*, VI, 283–288.

all over the ancient world, and in every case the tiles are held up in the same way. Examination of the synagogue tiles preserved in the Yale University Art Gallery and at Damascus strengthens this impression. The edges of the original tiles are so often untrue that if they had been laid together without some kind of covering for all four sides, they would have made a very unsightly ceiling, as can be seen in fig. 23. On most of the tiles the paint is eroded along the edges in such a way as to suggest that they rested upon a support, across as well as lengthwise, or at least that there was some sort of cross-stripping for finish. That is, the effect was almost certainly, as Frank Brown said to me, that of the coffered ceilings in which such tiles always have appeared.

It seems just as inevitable that the little plaster rosettes "found on the floor of the chamber" [5] had been affixed originally at the intersections of these beams. I have been unable to ascertain exactly where in the rubble they were found, but think it likely that they had a place in this ceiling similar to that of the rosettes in the earlier synagogue.[6] With rosettes put, presumably, at the intersections of the beams or hoists holding up the tiles, the basic feature of the starry heaven of the earlier Room 2 would have been combined with the symbols on tiles as painted in the earlier Room 7.[7] Where the plaster rosettes were put, I repeat, we cannot be sure. It is certain, however, that worship in the second synagogue was conducted under a ceiling filled with emblems painted on square tiles. The effect was to perpetuate the starry heaven of the earlier room, and we shall see that, as Kraeling pointed out, the design also put the room under the trellis of a vine.[8]

The surface measurements and thickness of these tiles as contrasted with tiles from other buildings at Dura [9] show that the tiles themselves were made to order so as to fit the dimensions of the synagogue room. We know that some of the tiles, specifically those which, we shall see, bore inscriptions honoring the donors, had been painted to order, and it is dangerous to assume that pagan craftsmen were allowed to paint on the others anything they pleased.

The designs selected for the tiles have to a considerable extent been analyzed in earlier volumes of this series. Kraeling classifies the designs—with a few exceptions to which we shall come at the end—as being personifications, flowers, fruit, grain, animals, and astrological symbols. The "personifications" are not masks but female heads, Kraeling believes, and he correctly sees in them "a late rendering of the ubiquitous Demeter-Persephone of the eastern Mediterranean"; that is, she is the mother goddess as a fertility

---

5. The field notes available to me say nothing of these, and Clark Hopkins, who led the expedition, wrote me he could not recall where they were found. Kraeling, *Synagogue*, 63, emphatically asserts that they had been put into the reredos, the painting over the Torah shrine, in the holes of all sizes that had been dug quite at random in that painting. We shall discuss this again when we describe the reredos: see below, p. 83, n. 23.

6. See above, pp. 42–46.

7. The two appear together in the ceiling of the Stabian Baths of Pompeii, fig. 21.

8. See below, pp. 57 f.

9. For example the tiles, otherwise very similar, from the House of the Large Atrium. I cannot say in which room of that house they were found, since in Rostovtzeff, *Dura-Europos*, IV, 31, they seem to have been in quite a different place from that reported, ibid., 43. In any case, all the rooms in this house were definitely smaller than the assembly room of the later synagogue.

goddess, figs. 24 and 25.[10] Her emblems were traditionally flower, fruit, and grain, so that since most of the tiles contained either this goddess's head or her emblems, she is elaborately represented on the tiles. The goddess appears in exactly the same way at Dura on a tile from the House of the Large Atrium, while another tile from there shows three pomegranates, another a Capricorn, another the two fish of Pisces.[11] To the goddess we shall return when we discuss the female masks in the dado. She will seem to be in heaven and to represent man's hope of reaching there, like the great figures in the coffers of the ceiling of the temple of Bacchus at Baalbek, fig. 120,[12] where such female divinities, or persons being apotheosized, are carved.

In the synagogue, as on the tiles of this house, tiles with the goddess' head are accompanied by the tiles with fruit grouped in threes. Fig. 26 [13] shows a tile with three heads of grain between leaves; fig. 27,[14] with three pomegranates; fig. 28,[15] with what are reasonably taken to be three oranges; fig. 29,[16] with three pine cones; fig. 30,[17] with three bunches of grapes; fig. 31,[18] with a conventionalized flower in a wreath; fig. 32,[19] the same flower alone. Three of these flowers appeared in a group on five tiles, Kraeling reported,[20] but all were too fragmentary to reproduce. The same tendency to group the fruit, flowers, and grain in threes we saw commonly in Jewish representations of grapes elsewhere,[21] and also of grain [22] and fruit.[23] Fruit in threes occupied many panels in the ceiling of Room 7 in the earlier synagogue, fig. 354. It is accordingly notable that although grapes, pomegranates, oranges, and cones are found on the tiles at one other house in Dura, these are usually single bunches of grapes, or groups of four of the other fruit.[24] A group of three pomegranates, however, was found painted on the wall of the pronaos in the Temple of Artemis-Nania.[25] Baur [26] follows Cumont in saying that the earliest literary "reference to a group of three pomegranates is in Eriphus,[27] a poet of the Middle Comedy of the fourth century B.C., who states that the pomegranate tree was planted by Aphrodite in Cyprus,

10. See also above, VII, figs. 236–238, and Kraeling, *Synagogue*, plate VIII. Kraeling, p. 50, says that the "personifications" are not otherwise attested in Jewish art. One has definitely appeared at Yafa, see above, III, fig. 993, and symbolically they seem to me to go with masks, as treated above in VII, 202–229. Four tiles with this lady have not been published anywhere because they are poorly preserved, but they are almost exactly like those shown here or in places indicated in this note. Christians had little use for this lady, but I have seen her in the Catacomb Panfilo at Rome.

11. See Rostovtzeff, *Dura-Europos*, IV, plates VI f.

12. From R. Wood, *The Ruins of Baalbec*, 1757, plate XXLX.

13. Cf. Kraeling, *Synagogue*, plate XIV, 1; cf. 47.

14. Ibid., plates XII, 4, XIII, 1; cf. 46.

15. Ibid., plate XIII, 3; cf. 47.

16. Ibid., plates XIII, 4, XIV, 2; cf. 47.

17. Ibid., plate XIII, 2; cf. 46.

18. Ibid., plate XII, 2; p. 45, no. 10.

19. Ibid., plate XII, 1; p. 45, no. 11, Type A.

20. Ibid., 45, no. 11, Type B.

21. Especially on coins, above, III, figs. 694–697, but also in tombs, III, fig. 31. And see the three grapes, ibid., fig. 633.

22. On coins, above, III, figs. 682, 686.

23. Three pomegranates in synagogues, above, III, figs. 563, 635.

24. Kraeling, *Synagogue*, 51.

25. Cumont, *Fouilles*, I, 176, fig. 9. This building was for a time called the "Priest's House," Rostovtzeff, *Dura-Europos*, III, plate IV, but was later recognized to be a temple: F. Brown, ibid., VI, plate XIII.

26. Ibid., IV, 43.

27. In Athenaeus, *Deipnosophists*, III, 84B, C (ed. C. B. Gulick, Loeb Series, 1927, I, 362).

and in that connection he refers to three pomegranates." Baur thinks this statement is "evidently based on some picture," but nothing in the text remotely suggests it to me. What seems more significant in view of the other fruit in threes is that Heracles took three golden apples from the Hesperides,[28] and it is generally recognized that this was the act that finally brought him to immortality with the Olympians.[29] The grouping of three fruit cones, heads of grain, and bunches of grapes cannot be taken to be originally Jewish, then, but was a device that appealed to Jews to the point that, especially at Dura, it appears in Jewish art in a proportion otherwise unknown. If the three golden apples (oranges) of the Hesperides did have connection with immortality, this might explain the frequent use of three-fold fruit by Jews, though we cannot by any means take this for granted.

In any case, we see that in associating these symbols of fruit and grain with the heads of Demeter-Persephone-(Astarte), those who planned the decorations of the second synagogue only brought into more specific expression the symbolism of flowers and fruit of Room 7 of the earlier synagogue.[30]

Kraeling took the female heads to represent three distinct types, but said that the differences in form were not references to different deities, and with this we fully agreed in the earlier discussion.[31] In the syncretism of the later Empire symbolic elements from various mystery cults were combined as freely as are the names of deities in the prayer of Apuleius or in the *Orphic Hymns*.[32] Actually the female heads or masks are apt to appear in what seems a Dionysiac setting, not, we saw, because they referred to the theater, but because the great Female was so universally accepted as a mystic objective. In the synagogue we have the heads especially with Mother Goddess symbols in the ceiling, and with Dionysiac symbols in the dado. Neither of these remotely suggest to me that the Jews at Dura worshiped Dionysus or the Great Mother; but the invasion of a synagogue by such representations can hardly be taken to show that the Jews bought ready-painted tiles manufactured as what Kraeling calls a "commercial job," [33] or had them painted with no consideration of what they represented, merely for their decorative value. For they were all, I am sure, painted to order, as the tiles bearing inscriptions certainly were painted, and the large number of faces of the goddess, and her attributes, would have been specifically approved and selected by the Jewish buyers. When we shall have seen the great care exercised in getting a correct design for the painting above the Torah shrine, the reredos, we shall be increasingly reluctant to believe that the goddess came so conspicuously into the synagogue by inadvertence or mere convention.

28. Apollodorus, *Library*, II, v, 11 (ed. J. G. Frazer, Loeb Series, 1921, I, 230). This seems important to me, though there is no tradition of the three apples in representing the scene: A. Furt-wängler in Roscher, *Lex. Myth.*, I, 2227–2229.

29. Diodorus Siculus, *Historical Library*, IV, xxvi, 4 (ed. C. H. Oldfather, Loeb Series, 1935, II, 426).

30. Kraeling, *Synagogue*, 361 f., saw that Per-

sephone and the fruits belonged together—to him only conventionally, as a part of the "current repertoire of design" for ceilings.

31. See above, VII, 203 f.

32. Above, VI, 107–113.

33. *Synagogue*, 54. H. Strauss was also carried away with such an idea for Jewish designs in general: see *Judaism*, VII (1958), 81–85; and my reply (with his answer), ibid., 177–180.

Kraeling [34] thinks it highly important, as do I, that donors' portraits were not included in the designs. Wisdom xiv, 15, specifically points out the danger of making portraits, since they become honored as gods, and *mustēria* and *teletaia* are offered them. The Jews at Dura had apparently the same reservation. The fact remains, however, that the reservation oddly did not extend to heads of the traditional goddess and her attributes. That the Jews were so careful at one point suggests that they had limits for what ornament they would allow. It is entirely subjective on our part to say that the limit permitted them to use only conventional ornament, and that since they used these heads and attributes of the great goddess, the whole must have been entirely conventional. Kraeling correctly says it is dangerous to suppose that these tiles mean "that the Jews of Dura had abandoned the basic premises and allegiances common to Judaism as a whole." [35] But to discover what basic premises and allegiances were "common," and how far the Jews of Dura went from them, is the end of our search, not the question we beg at the outset. [36]

The other tiles strengthen the suspicion that the ceiling was designed to present familiar mystic motifs in a Jewish connotation. In fig. 29 we saw a tile with three pine cones in a setting of vine tendrils. [37]

The pine cone especially recalls the head of the bacchic thyrsus, and set in the tendrils does so even more specifically. We know of other instances where Jews used pine cones, once on a sarcophagus fragment at Rome, [38] once as a cluster of three in a vine on a sarcophagus in Palestine, [39] and we shall see the cluster of three, along with groupings of three fruit, in the reveal of the arch of the Torah shrine in the Dura synagogue. [40] This latter seems to me of especial importance, and we shall return to it. [41] The cones were definitely part of the mystic lingua franca of the day, whatever it was they expressed.

Figs. 33, 34, and 36 [42] show each a specimen of designs of birds eating the fruit within a wreath. In the first, a bird appears to be a "dove" (Miss Crosby was safer in calling it merely a "gray bird") [43] with three pomegranates; in the second, a peacock(?) with a bunch of grapes; in the third, a peacock with three yellow fruits, probably oranges. A single tile with a "bird with a perky tail" was reported. [44] Since all these, according to Kraeling, are within wreaths, the symbolism of the fruit is at once seen to be made more specific. Birds have appeared to be a vivid part of the symbolic vocabulary of the period, and birds eating fruit to have represented the soul in heaven with the divine sustenation. [45] The bird eating grapes was especially favored by Jews at the time, [46] and went into Christianity as a eucharistic symbol, or as a symbol of the soul saved by the grace which the

34. Loc. cit.

35. Kraeling, *Synagogue*, 54.

36. See above, IV, 17.

37. Kraeling, *Synagogue*, 48, called these sesame pods or blooms, but I see in them no resemblance whatever to any illustrations of pods or blooms I can discover.

38. See above, III, fig. 802.

39. Ibid., fig. 235.

40. See below, p. 66.

41. Below, p. 67.

42. For the numbers of each of these preserved see Kraeling, *Synagogue*, 41–51.

43. Kraeling, ibid., 45, Type A, compares it to a crow. He says that one tile seems to show two birds, another only one pomegranate.

44. Ibid., Type B.

45. See above, VIII, 22–70.

46. Ibid., 22–27.

Eucharist supremely offered.[47] That the bird itself seems on two of the designs to be a peacock heightens the poignancy of the symbol, since that bird had quite detached itself from Hera and become a symbol of immortality among pagans, Jews, and Christians alike.[48] When this design is put into a wreath, symbolic reference is again suggested, since wreaths were so commonly used on synagogues and graves by Jews and Christians, as well as pagans, to intensify the symbolic value for immortality of the person or object shown within it.[49]

With these should be mentioned the design in fig. 35 where a "round object" stands within a wreath, as it appeared on Palestinian synagogues.[50] The "round object" could have many references, but we saw clear evidence that as over against grapes it represented bread, the concomitant of wine. This it clearly meant in Christianity, and there is good reason to suppose that it meant the same in Judaism. As before, the wreath surrounding the "round object" presumably sanctified it. We shall see that object again in the reredos design of this synagogue balancing a crater of wine, so that it would seem that in the ceiling it referred to some sort of "Bread of Heaven." [51]

Several tiles have designs of running gazelles, figs. 37, 38, or deer, figs. 39, 40, which seem to be variant presentations, alone or in pairs, of an animal fleeing from some beast of prey or hunter. Behind the back of each of them rises a tree, usually with two main sprays of foliage. These not only "provide a suggestion of a sylvan background"; [52] they carry on the tradition of an animal identified with a tree which we have seen so often.[53] Kraeling noticed that black "scrolls" grow out from the trunks of these trees below the animals' feet, what seemed to be vine tendrils when shown with the fruit.[54] The scrolls are so consistently present on these animal tiles that they seem an inherent part of the design. They may still bring in the value of the vine, but no interpretation can be insisted upon for them. The fleeing victim, we saw above, might be the hare, the deer, or many others, and it might be running free, or be under the claws of the lion or other ferocious animal. It usually seemed to represent, we concluded, the soul pursued or caught by death or the god, symbolizing victory in defeat.[55]

Another series of animate creatures recall the marine thiasos. Two of them are also signs of the zodiac: Pisces, fig. 41, and Capricorn, fig. 42. The marine thiasos itself probably had astral reference, for when Poseidon appears in it he often has the halo of Helios.

47. Ibid., 37 f.

48. Ibid., 52–58.

49. Above, VII, 148–171.

50. Above, III, figs. 464, 468, 493, 495 f., 500; cf. the device on a sarcophagus, ibid., 556.

51. Exod. XVI, 4; cf. John VI, 31–41. John's interpretation of this is very similar to Philo's, for whom manna, the "bread from heaven," is the divine Logos: see W. Bauer, *Johannes*, 1912, 67, note to John VI, 31 (Handbuch zum Neuen Testament, II, ii); above, V, 91; and B. Gärtner, *John 6 and the Jewish Passover*, 1959 (Coniectanea Neotestamentica, XVII).

52. Kraeling, *Synagogue*, 44. He gives an excellent review of pertinent literature, especially from the East.

53. See above, VII, figs. 110, 117, 123, 129; pp. 89, 97 f. For the convention in very early Mesopotamia see Lenzen in *Zeitschrift für Assyrologie*, XLIX (1949), 11, figs. 14–16. For it in Christianity see B. Bagatti, "Il Significato dei mosaici della scuola di Madaba (Transgiordania)," *Rivista di archeologia cristiana*, XXXIII (1957), 143.

54. Above, VII, 46.

55. This especially came out with the hunted hare; see above, VIII, 91–93.

So it is conspicuous that only the two pisciform signs of the zodiac are represented.[56] With these, then, go the other animals chiefly represented on the tiles: the dolphin, fig. 43, and a peculiar fish-tailed creature with the head and bill of a bird, probably of a duck, fig. 44. This last—which, like the dolphins, fig. 43, should have been painted within wavy lines for the sea—stands or floats across the background of a plant which again has ivy scrolls as well as leaves. Realism here at last has completely broken down, and the fish-duck must be regarded either as a product of such uncontrolled fancy as people of the Middle Ages used or as having some symbolic intent. To reject the former is far from meaning that we can assuredly determine the latter, but the duck has appeared so definitely a part of the symbolic vocabulary that its presentation as a member of the marine thiasos with vegetable background seems again to look to eschatological hope.[57]

The last of the animal designs also has marine association. It shows a centaur with flowing chlamys holding out a fish toward the observer, fig. 45. We discussed this figure above, and found that it could not be identified with Sagittarius, since with that sign the distinctive feature is not the centaur but the bow and arrow which he usually shoots.[58] The centaur, which appears elsewhere on a Jewish synagogue,[59] seemed a token of salvation. Its emblem here is the fish.

The animal figures, then, primarily present the values of the marine thiasos, the convention strangely but almost everywhere used for representing the Dionysiac riot at this period, one that became especially favored for sarcophagi both pagan and Christian. That we have little clue to why this happened by no means indicates that so strange a convention was merely conventional. The whole seems to me, here and elsewhere, to refer to hope of life after death—to refer, that is, to heaven.

Two other tiles by no means weaken the impression that the motifs of the ceiling as a whole had dynamic reference, if not inherent dynamic power. On these tiles are painted two versions of the magical eyes so popular at the time for amulets. One of these eyes, fig. 46,[60] is being attacked by snakes and three daggers, above which du Mesnil was certain he could identify the letters *IAŌ*. A beetle or scorpion advances to attack the eye from below, while lines down from the eye apparently indicate two streams of tears. This can quickly be identified with the "much-suffering eye" of magic. Labeled Iao, it certainly is not itself the "evil eye," but is a good eye, suffering and hence potent against the evil eye. The eye of Horus, from which this descends, not only had "magical" power but has long

56. I follow convention in saying that the two fish are "signs from the zodiac." There is good reason to suppose that the two fish as an amulet antedated their use in the zodiac, and that the zodiac never absorbed them completely. See the Jamdat Nasr amulet in E. Heinrich, *Kleinfunde aus den archaischen Tempelschichten in Urak*, 1936, plate 13*i* (Ausgrabungen der Deutschen Forschungsgemeinschaft in Uruk-Warka, I); and the Gawra amulet in A. J. Tobler, *Excavations at Tepe Gawra*, 1950, II, 160, plate CLXX, 177 (University of Pennsylvania, Museum Monographs). It seems highly likely that all the signs of the zodiac were familiar forms in men's minds before they found them outlined in the constellations.

57. On the duck see above, VIII, 46–50.

58. See above, VIII, 169.

59. Above, I, 185, 194–196.

60. From du Mesnil, *Peintures*, 136, fig. 96, 1. The paint on this tile faded quickly and no photograph was made in time. Fortunately du Mesnil made this quick sketch of the design when first discovered. See above, III, fig. 1065, and II, 238.

been recognized as having power to convey immortality. Bonner [61] did not like an earlier suggestion that linked the beasts attacking the eye with those attacking the bull of Mithra, but the suggestion seems to me of value. Here the eye of Horus has become the eye of Iao, but I doubt that for Jews it had lost its power in the transition. Rather, as Morton Smith pointed out to me, it is an oft-repeated rabbinic saying that when Israel suffers, God suffers with them. Hope for man through a God that suffers was expressed everywhere and in many forms in the ancient world. In Egyptian tradition Set tore the eye of Horus into sixty-four pieces, but it was later restored by Thoth, and Horus himself "gave it to thee that thou mayest become glorious thereby, that thou mayest become mighty before the spirits." [62] Bonner mentions a tombstone from Auzia (now Aumale) in Algeria, fig. 49,[63] which includes several of what we have seen were tokens of immortality. Above the standing man and wife the same couple appears on the eschatological banqueting couch flanked by subdued and couchant lions. Below them stand their children. The boy holds a rabbit; the girl has a dove in one hand and a bunch of grapes in the other, which the father touches with his staff. Between the two children at the bottom is the much-suffering eye, with what looks like an eyebrow above it, turned up at the ends like a boat. Bonner thought this design of the eye had been put on the tombstone to protect it: I can agree with this while feeling that the eye was also another symbol of the family's hope for immortality.

The second Dura tile with an eye on it, fig. 47,[64] shows an eye not attacked at all. It stands between what appear to be light symbols, and above it is a peculiar object again turned up at the ends and with little spiky projections on the lower edge. When we see the banquet bolster below the eye, the similarities with the Algerian tombstone become impressive. In an earlier volume I guessed that the object over this Dura eye was a boat, the little projections the familiar row of oars. This now seems all the more likely because of what resembles a boat over the eye on the tombstone, for on the stone the eschatological banquet is also presented.[65] The boat is itself a familiar eschatological symbol.[66] Here we have what I suppose was meant to be the "sound eye," the restored eye but, like the suffering eye, shown with the eschatological associations of banquet and ships. Both this and the suffering eye, therefore, I must consider immortality symbols and fetishes.

In spite of the diversity of the motifs, then, analysis of the tiles indicates that with all the designs was associated a single symbolic value, that of immortality.

The ceiling of the second synagogue was designed as a trellis, but the trellis is also the heavens, filled with a collection of heavenly symbols. We saw above that in what seemed the original heavenly ceiling in Egypt, certainly in very early ones, it was customary to insert the names of those who hoped for immortality, insert them presumably

61. Bonner, *Amulets*, 98, n. 10; cf. 97–100.

62. For expansion and documentation of this see above, II, 238–241, and n. 209.

63. Courtesy of M. Leglay of the Service des Antiquités de l'Algérie. Cf. *RA*, Ser. II, Vol. VII (1863), plate VIII; cf. pp. 293–298. In this study Detlefson calls the eye "Mithraic," with, so far as

I can see, no justification. Leglay writes me that he also sees no connection of the stone with Mithraism.

64. From du Mesnil, *Peintures*, 136, fig. 96, no. 2. This eye is discussed with the other in II, 238–241.

65. On the bolster, see above, II, 46–50; III f.

66. On the boat, see above, VIII, 157–165.

as a fetishistic device to help them into immortality. It is accordingly no surprise to discover that the only tiles we have not yet described present donor's inscriptions, those in Greek with the names inside the wreath, those in Aramaic more crudely executed. Since the room was 18 feet high and these inscribed tiles were made with such small writing, few people in the poorly lighted room could have read these names upon the ceiling.

The two inscriptions in Aramaic are essentially a single one that covered two tiles. A third tile had a few lines graffito along with a few dipinti, each a rather free rendering, apparently from memory, of the first lines of the same inscription.[67] This third tile had been painted over with a floral design which flaked off during its transportation to New Haven and thus revealed the inscription under it,[68] an interesting fact because it shows that the tiles were painted directly for the synagogue and did not come from a common stock of ready-made tiles. As translated by Torrey,[69] the inscription reads:

> [*Tile A*] This house was built in the year 556, this corresponding to the second year of Philip Julius Caesar; in the eldership of the priest Samuel son of Yeda'ya, the Archon. Now those who stood in charge of this work were: Abram the Treasurer, and Samuel son of Sapharah, and . . . . . the proselyte. With a willing spirit they [began to build] in this fifty-sixth year; and they sent . . . . and they made haste . . . . and they labored in . . . . a blessing from the elders and from all the children of . . . . Peace to them, and to their wives and children all.
>
> [*Tile B*] And like all those who labored [were their brethren . . . .], all of them, who with their money . . . . and in the eager desire of their souls . . . . Their reward, all whatever . . . . that the world which is to come . . . . assured to them . . . . on every sabbath . . . . spreading out [their hands] in it (in prayer).

It is a great pity that the writing on the second tile is so badly preserved. Abraham the Treasurer, Samuel the son of Sapharah, and a proselyte whose name is lost supervised the building of the synagogue, if they did not largely pay for it ("money"). The "reward" for them and for their wives and children, will be "Peace," the *shalom* so often on funerary inscriptions obviously with reference to the future life.[70] The "reward" had some relevance to "the world which is to come." The last two lines suggest that the congregation would thereafter pray for these benefactors by spreading out their hands for them on the sabbath.[71] That so funerary an inscription should be put up while these men and their families were alive does not change the fact that it is thoroughly funerary in form.

The Greek inscriptions on ceiling tiles have less funerary flavor. Three of them read:

Samuel, son of Idaeus, elder of the Jews, built it.

67. The Aramaic inscriptions are edited and translated by C. Torrey in Kraeling, *Synagogue*, 261–268.

68. Ibid., 262, n. 3.

69. Ibid., 263 f.

70. See above, II, 124–137.

71. Torrey admits that this is conjecture, but it seems a reasonable one.

Samuel, son of Sapharas: may he be remembered! He built this [building] thus [as you see].

Abram and Arsaces(?) and Silas and Salmanes assisted.[72]

Samuel son of Sapharas thus reappears in Greek, and Samuel, son of Idaeus, was presumably the man mentioned in Aramaic, "In the eldership of the priest Samuel, son of Yeda'ya, the Archon." The phrase "may he be remembered" has often occured in funerary inscriptions with eschatological reference,[73] but in the Greek inscriptions in the synagogue the funerary atmosphere was conveyed by putting each of them within a wreath.

Whether the rosettes on the floor came from the ceiling (as I believe) or not, the designs of the ceiling unite in being a representation of heaven, with the psychopomps and symbolic influences that would bring the devout to it. The men most responsible for the building anticipated their ascent by having their names put directly into the heavenly setting. In form, the ceiling put heaven with its symbols as a trellis over the heads of the worshipers.

Kraeling [74] called to our attention not only that the ceiling itself suggested a trellis, but that when the walls were finally decorated, those who planned the murals definitely enhanced this effect by having a pilaster painted in each corner with a vine running up to its top at the ceiling, fig. 48.[75] He rightly feels that, however crudely executed here, the design is the common one of the time for a flat pilaster: a pair of vine-stems run up the surface, opening to make plaques where ordinarily a symbol was put. Fig. 50 [76] shows the magnificent examples on pilasters of the Severan Basilica at Leptis Magna in North Africa, made only about seventy-five years before the painted ones at Dura. The design itself was a favorite of Jews in mosaics and friezes.[77] Kraeling says that pilasters and ceiling together make the whole room into a bower under a trellis.[78] We saw above, however, that from early times in Dionysiac symbolism the satyrs or sileni, or later the cupids, climbed up in the vine, or climbed a ladder to a vine on a trellis or arbor, to bring down to men the divine fruit, which was crushed to make wine for the faithful.[79] That the trellis

72. C. B. Welles in Kraeling, *Synagogue*, 277 f.

73. See esp. the inscription at Jericho, above, I, 261; II, 129. Cf. those at el-Hammeh in Sukenik, *el-Ḥammeh*, 41, 48, 56; at Naaran, in Frey, *CIJ*, II, nos. 1197–1205; at Isfiya, ibid., no. 885; at Chorazin, above, I, 198. See also I, 266. The eschatological reference, when fully spelled out, was "may he be remembered with the Patriarchs."

74. *Synagogue*, 53, 66, 68 f. Kraeling's discussion of these is interesting. He concludes that the pilasters are part of an original design which later painters of the biblical scenes could not disregard, though they cut them off at the bottom to make more room for the new paintings. Originally, he suggests, the pilasters ran down to a dado painted to resemble marble plaques.

75. Ibid., 252, fig. 70. Photographs do not show this design at all clearly.

76. Courtesy of the Superintendent of Monuments and Excavations in Libia.

77. See above, III, figs. 632, 887, 910 f.; cf. VIII, fig. 27, for the design in mosaic; III, figs. 473 f., 488–497, 537, 575 f., 610, 616, carved horizontally on fringes. While these volumes were in the press M. Avi-Yonah published the magnificent synagogue floor at Ma'on: *Hebrew University, Louis M. Rabinowitz Fund, Bulletin III* (1960), 25–35, from which I have taken fig. 327. I can only say that this much strengthens my sense of the ideological importance of the vine for Jews at this time.

78. See also *Synagogue*, 37 f.

79. See above, VI, 46–51, and figs. 213, 217–226.

should have been combined with the starry heaven and with other forms representing heaven discussed in the first part of this chapter was most natural in that age of syncretism.

Actually a simple device in the final painting re-emphasized this sense of the grape arbor. The biblical scenes were all represented as separated from one another by a conventionalized running vine with grapes, a design which has already appeared more realistically represented on Jewish synagogues [80] and sarcophagi.[81] It is made of a single stem that undulates rhythmically from the top to the bottom of a frieze, while grapes or leaves appear in the alternating spaces thus created. Only three dots represent the bunches of grapes in the narrow Dura borders, but their effect, which I do not doubt was intentional, is that the biblical scenes look out at us from the interstices of a vine that encompasses the room, as one will visualize at once from the drawing in figs. 319–322. The vine stem has actually become a continuous running ribbon.

A more elaborate version of the same design was found among the mosaics of Antioch, fig. 51.[82] It was used under a design of confronting peacocks, with a basket of grapes between them and an elaborate vine in whose interstices are grapes. A cock eats grapes at the right, and a gazelle leaps at the left—the whole, one of the commonest designs of immortality in pagan and Christian antiquity. The border below with its running ribbon has the grapes in bunches of three actually growing from the ribbons. The origin of the design of ribbon and grapes I do not know, but it clearly is a variant representation of the grapevine at Dura as well as in Antioch. This vine is only suggested in the synagogue ceiling by the trellis itself, but there its value is enriched and expanded by the various heavenly symbols of the Female Principle and her salvation, including, of course, grapes. The whole design is couched in the mystic lingua franca which we can only partially read. The inscriptions of the Elder Samuel and his friends were safely ensconced at the center of this ceiling—that is, at the apex of a mystic cosmos. Since this is the setting elaborately provided for the biblical scenes and for the worship of the congregation, one must always entertain the possibility that it has relevance for interpreting both.

Entirely in keeping with the spirit of the vine and trellis, the bottom row of painting beneath the biblical scenes is a dado devoted to Dionysiac symbols. Before turning to the dado, however, it should be mentioned that on each of the reveals of the smaller door, a tier of "round objects" was painted, fig. 52,[83] as well as on the painted pilaster in the northeast corner.[84] Since the upper part of both the door and the pilaster was destroyed, we have no way to determine the original number of these "round objects." [85] Such a tier was important in the region to represent the planetary deities, or the sun god, and we know

---

80. Kraeling, *Synagogue*, 69, seems wrong in calling this "a twisted ribbon pattern, a fact which marks the completion of its transition from the architectural into the decorative sphere." See above, III, figs. 549 f.

81. Above, III, figs. 232, 235, 238 f.

82. Courtesy of the Worcester Art Museum. Cf. Levi, *Antioch*, 195.

83. See also above, III, fig. 546; VII, 198; and Kraeling, *Synagogue*, 253.

84. Kraeling, *Synagogue*, plan x.

85. I suspect that the tier of six shown in fig. 52 is more nearly right than the nine of Kraeling's drawing. There were rarely more than seven of them in the *sēmeion:* cf. VII, 201.

two other cases, both on the stone doors of tombs,[86] in which Jews adopted them. There is accordingly good reason to suppose that they had symbolic implications at Dura, though no specific account can be given of them.

B. THE DADO

TREATMENT OF THE DADO can be rather summary here. Kraeling's carefully detailed descriptions and diagrams [87] can be used to supplement our figs. 317 f. and plate I, where the general effect appears. In brief we can say that when the synagogue was completed, a dado was painted round the entire room, broken only by the Torah shrine on the west wall and the two doors on the east. The dado was divided up into well-arranged plaques. Twelve of them were painted to imitate inlaid blocks of marble; six show each a "leopard cub" in a circle within an inlaid marble plaque as in fig. 53; ten represent harnessed felines, usually with a paw on the head of a victim as in fig. 54; [88] and fourteen show, again in a circle, a mask or head of some sort, ten of them female as in fig. 55, four of them male as in fig. 56.[89] Several of the female masks have a peculiar bell on their heads as in fig. 55, which I followed my predecessors in calling a calathos. This seems to me now, however, to be actually a flower, and to go with the other flowers which prompted archeologists to call her "Flora." They appear as lilies in fig. 57,[90] a wall painting in South Russia. We have all known from the first that they looked very little like the calathos. It was used several times to mark a maenad in the Casa del Criptoportica at Pompeii, fig. 59,[91] and on the heads in the plaques of the Pompeian wall painting illustrated in fig. 22. In a mosaic at the Villa de Soueidié, Baalbek, a cupid personalizing "Harvest" (*Theros*) brings a handful of wheat to "Earth" (*Gē*) as a goddess, fig. 58.[92] She wears an elaborate headdress of flowers and calathos, and further justifies Kraeling in identifying the female head on the ceiling with the "ubiquitous Demeter-Persephone of the eastern Mediterranean." [93] There seems to me little doubt that this is the figure in both the ceiling and dado of the synagogue.

Kraeling believes that the dado as we now have it took the place of one originally planned but never executed, one that, as in the earlier synagogue, would have consisted only of plaques painted to imitate slabs of stone. He may be right, but in that case the complete change of conception by which, still using a few such panels, the painters put in their place the row of felines and masks, needs explanation, since the plain marble would

---

86. See above, III, fig. 44; VII, fig. 226 (with pp. 200 f.).

87. Kraeling, *Synagogue*, 240–250; cf. 64–66.

88. See above, VII, figs. 23, 26.

89. Cf. above, VII, figs. 239–242; Kraeling, *Synagogue*, 247–249, and plates XXXVIII f.

90. From Rostovtzeff, *South Russia*, 1913, II, plate VII, 2.

91. From V. Spinazzola, *Le Arti decorative in*

Pompei e nel Museo Nazionale di Napoli, 1943, I, 493, fig. 558; see also figs. 559–565. Lilies, often on Jewish ossuaries, seemed especially significant to M. Smith in *Bulletin of the John Rylands Library*, XL (1958), 458 f.

92. Courtesy of M. Chéhab, Director General of Antiquities, Libania. See his *Mosaïques du Liban*, 1958, plate XIV; cf. p. 33 (Bulletin du Musée de Beyrouth, XIV and XV).

93. See above, p. 49.

seem much more in harmony with traditional conceptions of Judaism than these strikingly pagan substitutions. The plain "marble" or "porphyry" had sufficed to give dignity to the earlier synagogue. Why the change for the later synagogue?

Only two answers are possible; one, given by Kraeling, is that the new artist who planned the paintings for the walls wanted figured representations to conform to the decorations in the ceiling above and "was merely following the developing fashions of his day and age in the introduction of animals and masks." [94] For this the evidence comes largely from tombs and temples (dubious usage to consider merely conventional) and from similar masks (no felines) in the Antioch mosaics, which themselves can hardly be taken assuredly to have no implications beyond the decorative.

Awareness of the unity of decorative motifs in the Dura synagogue, and of their harmony with symbols borrowed by Jews from pagans elsewhere, increases the sense that these masks and felines might possibly have had symbolic implications.

Felines of the sort painted in the dado have been discussed in a previous volume, [95] and shown to have definite meaning in the vocabulary of this symbolism. For it should be noted that not animals in general are presented in the dado, but only felines—lions, tigers, panthers, and leopards—animals which were especially associated with the Great Mother and Dionysus. Most of these felines, indeed all but what Kraeling calls leopard cubs, wear a harness, and he is rightly impressed with their invariably "subdued and almost tame demeanor," although the standing animals have a foot upon the skull of the victim. [96] The feline wearing a harness, even more than one not thus accoutered, had mystic implications, [97] since the Great Mother and Dionysus had the nature of the lion (or other felines). For men, that nature was tamed, a transformation witnessed, Ovid tells us, by the Mother's lion-drawn chariot. When we saw the harness become a mere stem of ivy, [98] it seemed clear that the familiar felines pulling the chariot of Dionysus had the same meaning. A single instance of a gladiatorial combat with harnessed lions has led scholars generally to forget that this is indeed a single example, and that the harnessed lion of religious art (like the harnessed griffin!) was not a pet "from a private zoo" but a figure of that tamed wildness which we have over and again found to be one of the deepest conceptions of religion. [99] For comparison, I show fig. 60, [100] a female leopard with a blue collar, recently found in a Dionysiac mosaic near the Cathedral at Cologne.

The idea that the harnessed feline may still have conveyed such an association in the synagogue will seem strengthened when we see shortly that Orpheus tames the animals, pre-eminently the lion, in the great reredos painting. [101] Felines appear once more in the synagogue, for a pair of them have their fore paws on either side of a crater also in the reredos, figs. 74, 76. That felines should appear in a bower of vines surmounted by the trellis of the ceiling, where the symbols of fertility appear with the Female Principle; that they

94. *Synagogue*, 244.
95. See above, VII, 29–86.
96. *Synagogue*, 245.
97. See above, VII, 72–77.
98. Ibid., fig. 94.

99. See above, VII, 135–171.
100. Courtesy of the Römisch-Germanisches Museum, Cologne.
101. See below, pp. 89–104.

should be harnessed to show, like Orpheus, the taming of the ferocity of Divinity; and that felines should be identified as wine symbols by being at the crater in the reredos—all this suggests that the appearance of felines as the only animals in the dado can with little likelihood be called a "cliché," if only for the reason that such a row of felines, so far as I know, has appeared nowhere else from antiquity.

It is again entirely appropriate, symbolically, that the felines are associated in the dado with male and female masks or heads.[102] These masks of the dado we have had occasion to discuss in connection with the masks that appeared in other Jewish and pagan remains.[103] The evidence seemed to indicate that masks, especially those in a pagan religious setting, had, at least originally, some cult reference. They appeared frequently in what can most naturally be explained as cult scenes, or, in Pompeian wall paintings, at the top of steps, along with Dionysiac accouterments, interestingly enough set as in Dura in a bower of leaves and fruit.[104] The evidence I have thoroughly illustrated. It never reaches what I would call proof, but whatever may or may not have been implied by the distinctions of mask forms, I shall assume that masks had become a meaningful part of the mystic lingua franca of the day, and were used for their mystic implication by Jews. A striking new instance of Jewish appropriation of the symbol has recently come to light in the cemetery of Sheikh Ibreiq in Israel, fig. 61.[105] Here a lintel has a female mask with hair that suggests, possibly, Hathor,[106] but the mask has definitely been used for its funerary significance. A menorah was scratched in beside it, perhaps later, obviously by another hand, to Judaize the lintel, and, perhaps by the same hand, "Of Socrates" was also added. The new example only confirms our feeling of the living value of the symbol for Jews at the time. In the synagogue four male and ten female masks (or heads) appear in the dado, which makes us recall again the large number of female heads on the ceiling tiles. There can be no question that the artist wanted not heads or masks in general in the synagogue, but pre-eminently female ones, and that to him the male masks play a quite subordinate role.

In discussing the figure previously I did not make sufficient point of the fact that most of the so-called masks of pagan representations are drawn not as what we would call masks, but as full heads. Fig. 266 of Volume VII, for example, has always been taken to be an actor buying masks in a shop, but quite clearly the "masks" are not such at all, but heads which, if drawn in proportion, could not possibly have been put over the "actor's" head. A mask without an elastic back and yet large enough to be put on over the head and allow freedom for speaking would have to be in the absurd proportions of the one worn by a cupid on a sarcophagus, shown in fig. 254 of the same volume. The mystic initiation in

102. The only other association I can recall of a female mask with a harnessed feline is from Hadrian's Villa: see above, VII, fig. 270.

103. See above, VII, 202–223, esp. 215 f. This entire section should for many reasons have stood here.

104. The paintings from Pompeii reproduced above, VII, figs. 243–246, especially stress the connection of the masks with the bower.

105. Courtesy of the Department of Archeology, The Hebrew University, Jerusalem. Cf. N. Avigad, "Excavations at Beth She'arim, 1955," *IEJ*, VII (1957), 76, and plate XVIIB.

106. A similar treatment of hair appears on the mask shown above, VII, fig. 268.

the Villa dei Misteri at Pompeii, fig. 62,[107] shows, actually, the use that explains most of these forms: the initiate sees reflected in water a mask held up behind him. Often the heads or masks are being thus held up,[108] though not usually to initiates. But they are accompanied by mirrors,[109] or sit on altars, either approached by steps [110] or without steps,[111] or they are with cult implements, and with felines and their victims.[112] Sometimes masks and heads appear together so that we know both were used,[113] but in the majority of cases the artist has represented full heads, objects that were not possibly designed to be worn, and so could have had no relation to the theater. What their place was in Dionysiac mysteries, why they were so often represented with felines, I cannot say, but the "masks" and heads of the synagogue dado, usually the female head, along with the felines, by no means reflect formal decoration from the arena and theater. They seem to come out of the heart of mystic symbolism, no less by the very fact that so often in ceiling and dado they were heads, not masks.

Still another bit of light comes from the rich material collected by R. B. Onians,[114] which shows that the head was considered to be the seat of the soul, and reveals how widely and variously heads of the gods were used to conjure the presence of divine power. For pagans the heads were the gods themselves in their most potent form.

Who, then, was this Female, and what could she have meant to the Jews of Dura that they so repeatedly represented her, her fruits, her harnessed felines at the bottom and on the ceiling of the synagogue? Here is a deliberately selected mystic vocabulary, but what is it saying? We are faced with a situation such as my colleagues in linguistics describe when they hear people speaking a jargon which they cannot understand but which they know, from the way it is used, is actually a meaningful language. They have techniques for coming to that meaning, techniques that have as yet no counterpart in the study of symbols. Associated with the Judaism of the biblical paintings, the goddess and her attributes must in the synagogue be talking of some sort of Judaism. This we cannot doubt for a moment. But they had no place in the Judaism we have hitherto associated with the rabbis. If Gamaliel had no objection to urinating before a statue of Aphrodite in a bath, that does not mean he would have wanted the head of her eastern counterpart repeatedly represented in his synagogue. I do not believe she could possibly have become conventional enough for him.

In discussing [115] what her role might have been, here and elsewhere in Jewish symbolism, I was forced to draw heavily upon Philo Judaeus, the only writer of the hellenized Jews whose works we have *in extenso*. In him we found a great deal of mysticism in terms of a Female Principle, whom he called usually Sophia or Virtue; by having spiritual

---

107. Photo Alinari. K. Lehmann's brilliant posthumous study of these paintings has just appeared: "Ignorance and Search in the Villa of the Mysteries," *JRS*, LII (1962), 62–68.

108. As in VII, figs. 250–252, 257 f.

109. Ibid., figs. 255, 262, 267: I cannot assert that some of these may not be cymbals, but would resist an assertion to the contrary.

110. Ibid., figs. 243–247, and possibly 263.

111. Ibid., figs. 268, 270–273, 282.

112. Ibid., figs. 274–277.

113. Ibid., figs. 262, 267.

114. *The Origins of European Thought about the Body, the Mind, the Soul, the World, Time, and Fate,* 1951, 131–144, 164–166.

115. See above, VII, 217–223.

intercourse with her one came into the larger life of the spirit. The whole was very much the sort of mysticism that Greek mystery religions had made out of the original relations with the fertility goddess, the identical goddess represented in Greco-Roman form in the synagogue and originally as Astarte and others, and perhaps also as Isis, worshiped with ritualistic physical intercourse throughout the East. The immaterial-mystical substitute for this goddess obviously appealed to Jews, and was Judaized, by Philo at least, by identifying the Female Principle, as Sophia or Virtue, with the wives of the various Patriarchs. How much of that sort of elaborate allegory we may associate with the Jews at Dura will always be a question of dispute. Two points, however, are indisputable, one that the goddess and her attributes appear over and over again in the synagogue, in what we shall increasingly see is a mystic setting, and the other that the mystical version of her appeal had so impressed at least Philo that he went to tortuous lengths to bring her into Judaism for mystical stimulus in the persons of Sarah, Rebecca, and the others.

Another feature of the dado which should be mentioned is the elaborate symmetry of its design. A glance at plate 1 will show that the representations on either side the central niche are planned for balance within themselves, and with each other as wholes. Each side has seven panels. On the north (right) side, reading from left to right, we have (1) a harnessed lion facing right, (2) a female head, (3) "marble," (4) a leopard cub, (5) "marble," (6) a male mask, (7) a harnessed lion facing left. This is exactly reproduced in the dado at the south (left) side of the niche, even to the colors of the "marble" panels and the places of the male and female heads, except that the harnessed lions have become harnessed tigresses. The designs in the dado on the other walls are similarly balanced within themselves, and the north wall has the same arrangement as the south wall. Kraeling [116] has carefully listed these subjects and brought out the balancing. At Damascus the effect is still more striking when one sees that even the colors of the "marble" are put in balance.

In all this the most impressive feature is the frequent balancing of the sexes. On the west wall females (tigresses) balance males (lions), and on the north wall a pair of male and female leopards face each other with a mask between them. The south wall does not have this contrast, but the sexes are so frequently in balance that they would seem to be intentionally and meaningfully so. The most striking contrast, that between the female side of the west dado and the male right side, may suggest what that meaning might have been. For in mystic symbolism, which will increasingly impress us as we continue to examine the paintings, the female symbolizes an approach quite inferior to the male. It will be pointed out that the same contrast of a lower and higher sort of mysticism seems presented in the paintings on either side of the west wall, with the lower mysticism above the "female" side of the dado, the higher mysticism above the male. I can only allude to the matter here, for to draw any such conclusions from the dado itself would be totally unwarranted. We shall return to it at the end.

The pagan decorations of the second synagogue, if I may call them such in contrast to the biblical paintings, present themselves as a surprisingly consistent body of motifs.

116. *Synagogue,* 240–244.

The running deer with a tree behind him, the harnessed feline, and the various beasts from the marine thiasos, along with the "much suffering eye" and the "sound eye," seemed potent symbols of hope quite in harmony with what men sought from the great Female and her fruits. That she should have suggestions of a male counterpart or consort by no means alters the symbolism, for all is properly set in the great vine and trellis of Dionysus. In themselves the pagan borrowings unite in speaking of a mystic hope of salvation. None of these symbols has the prominence of the biblical paintings. But the Jewish paintings in such a setting must now be investigated with the greatest care. Are the biblical scenes so presented that they suggest a synthesis in which Judaism and the Jewish Book have been made into the true mystery—that is, the true way to rise from death to life, from the mortal to immortality?

CHAPTER FIVE

The Torah Shrine

O PPOSITE THE CENTRAL DOOR of the synagogue stood an aedicula, plate III, as in the pagan naoi, and we naturally assume that this architectural device had been Judaized so that it contained not the cult image of the god but the central object of Jewish ritual and prayer, the Torah,[1] whether permanently or only during services.

A. THE NICHE

T HE AEDICULA was built as a semicircular niche, protruding from the wall and approached by four steps. The first three steps were of equal height, and a column stood at both ends of the third step. Above this step the fourth, considerably higher, had as its top the floor of the niche. Apparently the *aron* or box that held the scrolls was laid upon this higher level by men who themselves ascended only the first three steps. The columns and their pedestals together measured slightly less than 4′ 8″, but the arch lifted the central part of the opening to nearly 6′ 2″, so that there was plenty of head room for an ordinary man of those times.[2] Apparently to mark it as belonging to the inner part of the aedicula, the riser of the fourth step was painted, to resemble insets of marble so arranged as to construct a round-centered lozenge.

Three bands were painted in the rounded back of the niche. The lowest of these bands presented five of the now familiar panels painted to represent incrusted marble. The pieces of "marble" in the central panel were again arranged to make a round-centered lozenge, as in the accompanying drawing, text fig. 10.[3] That is, the design used conspicuously on the walls of the first synagogue, a design which we saw was especially favored for tombs at the time, reappears for the inner part of the aedicula. I still cannot assert that it had significance here.[4] Marble graining appears apparently for its decorative

---

1. This parallelism was recognized also by Naményi, *L'Esprit*, 51.

2. For dimensions and construction see Kraeling, *Synagogue*, 16. We may all change our minds about the way in which this aedicula might have been used, when full information is available about the similar aedicula approached by three steps in

the recently discovered synagogue at Ostia, Italy.

3. From ibid., 55.

4. But one wonders at Kraeling's calling it, with complete finality, "entirely conventional": *Synagogue*, 54. Kraeling gives here a detailed description of the technique of rendering these panels.

10

value, as on the surface of the columns of the aedicula, which also had marble graining. We have seen panels of painted incrustation in the dado. Kraeling concludes from the conspicuous use of these incrustations, as well as from other features, that the painting of the aedicula belonged in inspiration rather with the paintings in the earlier synagogue than with those that covered the walls of the second building.[5] The two upper bands in the aedicula were painted in plain colors—the lower, yellow, the upper, blue.

In the arch at the top an elaborate scallop shell was introduced, heavily superimposed upon the semidome rather than structurally integrated with the surface. It was painted a light blue, with its thick curled front a dark green. The mid-third century, when the shell was put there, marked the very peak of its symbolic vitality. It was used on graves and sarcophagi, on sacred objects of all kinds, to indicate the divine character of the object under it or to give an object sanctity. I see no reason for supposing that when put thus in exaggerated prominence in the aedicula it did not equally mark the sanctity of the scrolls beneath it, as it seemed to do on a great number of the Torah shrines in Palestine and Rome at the time.[6] Indeed, the whole form was abstracted as a symbol for a Jewish sarcophagus recently found at Sheikh Ibreiq (Beth She'arim), fig. 64.[7] It seems incredible that the person who put this design on the sarcophagus did so without symbolic intent. The form seems itself a symbol both on the sarcophagus and on the Torah shrine.

On the soffit of the arch between the columns was painted a design, plate II, that Kraeling thought likewise merely conventional because it had similarly been represented fifteen years earlier on the face of the arch over the baptismal font of the Christian Chapel, fig. 65.[8] He calls the design "a continuous fruit garland . . . crossed diagonally with pairs of yellow ribbons that divide the garland into seven fields." [9] The fruit are, in succession, three pomegranates, a bunch of grapes, three oranges, a bunch of grapes, three cedar cones, three oranges, one pomegranate.[10] The grapes appear now in single bunches rather than triple, but otherwise the fruits represented on the ceiling in groups of threes persist; they do so, notably, on a surface that corresponds to a ceiling and to the starry

---

5. *Synagogue*, 56. But since the device appears in the dado, we cannot stress the point.

6. On the shell in Judaism and its pagan and Christian parallels see above, VIII, 95–105.

7. Courtesy of the Department of Archeology, The Hebrew University, Jerusalem. See N. Avigad in *IEJ*, VII (1957), 244. A Hebrew inscription is crudely painted across this design: "This sarcophagus . . . the daughter of Rabbi Joshua.

(May) the memory of the just be blessed."

8. See above, III, fig. 601.

9. *Synagogue*, 55; P. Baur in Rostovtzeff, *Dura-Europos*, V, 255, calls it a "winding fillet" as it appears in the Christian chapel.

10. On the Christian counterpart are twice a bunch of grapes, twice a group of three pomegranates, and once some ears of grain.

soffits seen at Palmyra and the Jewish Catacomb Torlonia at Rome. I should guess, however, that Kraeling is wrong in calling the whole a "fruit garland," for in garlands the fruit is always intertwined in leaves and stems. Here the fruits are just painted in the spaces between the yellow ribbons. What else could the design here and the very similar one in the Christian Chapel then represent?

If we begin with a semicircular object bound with strands of ribbon we think at once of the banqueting bolster so conspicuous on the Sabazius scenes at Rome,[11] on two Jewish gold glasses,[12] and abundantly in Christian *Fractio Panis* scenes.[13] The ribbons round the bolster can be seen especially clearly on one of the Jewish gold glasses with a fish meal.[14] They will appear again on the reredos painting of the synagogue, fig. 76, and on the bed of Elijah, fig. 335. This bolster, if such it be, I have never seen thus with fruit except in the synagogue and in the Christian Chapel, but its appearance on the baptistry in one case, on the Torah shrine in the other, and only there, makes its symbolic implication highly likely. In Christian and in Sabazius scenes the bolster was always used for the eschatological banquet, a promise of immortality.[15] The bolster in other Jewish representations was set at a fish meal, with which the eschatological banquet was often associated.[16] But wine (grapes) had equally strong eschatological associations,[17] and the bolsters of both the Christian and the Jewish presentation at Dura seem to speak in terms of the fruits and tokens of the fertility cults that had become part of the lingua franca of contemporary symbolism. So above the Torah stood not only the sanctifying and life-giving shell but the symbol of eschatological fulfillment in the messianic hope, the banqueting bolster and the mystic tokens of food and drink. That the celestial banquet should be associated with the seven appears not only in the Christian Chapel of Dura but repeatedly in early Christian representations of the heavenly banquet in the catacombs, fig. 153, or in multiplication (eucharistic) scenes, fig. 154.

All of these representations on the aedicula Kraeling grouped together as its conventional decoration. Except for the panels of incrustation, however, and possibly even with them, these decorations belong in our symbolic vocabulary and could have been used quite properly for Jewish hopes.

B. *THE UPPER PANEL*

ABOVE THIS PART of the aedicula stands a rectangular panel, its bottom edge rounded upward to fit the arch of the aedicula below it, fig. 66.[18] On it is painted ornament of quite a different kind, primary symbols of Jewish cult we have met everywhere in the

11. See above, III, figs. 839–843. These two bolsters do not have the ribbons, and they are often omitted in Christian art.

12. Above, III, figs. 973 f.; cf. II, 111 f.

13. Above, II, 46–48; Wilpert, *Pitture*, II, plates 15, no. 2; 41, no. 3; 57; 133, no. 1; 184. See also M. von Berchem et E. Clouzot, *Mosaïques chrétiennes*

du IVme au Xme siècle, Geneva, 1924, 132, fig. 75.

14. Above, III, fig. 973; cf. V, 10.

15. In the Christian Chapel at Dura the vaulted ceiling behind the bolster is again a heavenly one —white stars on a blue background.

16. See above V, 40–53.

17. Above, VI, 163–198.

18. See also plate III, and above, III, fig. 602.

Jewish remains, the menorah, the lulab and ethrog, and a façade. The fourth chief symbol, the shofar, is not shown: in its place is the scene of Abraham offering Isaac, the Akedah.

1. *The Façade*

THE CENTRAL OBJECT, the façade, seems to me to be also the center of interest in this design, while the other representations are fitted as best the artist could do on either side of it. That the menorah, ethrog, lulab, and Akedah as shofar should stand here is entirely in the mood of Judaism everywhere in the period. We have already seen [19] the deep importance of these objects for Jews at this time, as symbols of hope here and hereafter. A new example has just been found on the end of a lead sarcophagus at Sheikh Ibreiq (Beth She'arim). The designs on the sarcophagus are so important that I include all its faces in fig. 69.[20] Here the façade, represented only by the arch, contains the other sacred cult symbols, including, here, the incense shovel. It seems at first purely tautological to put a picture of the façade directly above the actual façade of the aedicula at Dura. If, as I surmise without any direct evidence, menorahs, or a menorah, also stood on the floor beside the shrine, the depicting of a menorah above the shrine would at first seem likewise superfluous. It must be recalled, however, that we saw apparently the same repetition at Beth Alpha, where the cult instruments were on the floor in mosaic directly before what must have been the actual shrine and its accompanying objects, and that there also the Torah shrine was represented in the center of all the instruments. Such a cluster of the instruments about the shrine must have inspired the decorations of Roman gold glass,[21] although their tiny spaces were usually divided into two registers to get enough length for all the instruments. The design appeared also in the arcosolia at the Jewish Catacomb Torlonia in Rome,[22] where the assumption would be that it had eschatological reference or value. On two gold glasses [23] the row of instruments, with the shrine in the center, appears in the upper register, with the eschatological fish meal before the bolster in the lower registers. It becomes clear that such a cluster of Jewish cult objects with the Torah shrine at the center was a fixed compendium of Jewish symbols, and that it so often appeared in eschatological association that it seemed to represent the final hope of Jewish faith. Artists could arrange these symbols according to their sense of design in the space available. We saw above that as pagans represented themselves on their tombstones in ritualistic acts or in drunken riots or at the eschatological banquets, or being born on a shell like Aphrodite —in any case representing themselves in the happy hereafter in terms of an eternal celebration of their cult—so Jews in this period used their cult objects in the full panoply or in abbreviation on their graves and synagogues to indicate their hopes of heaven. These instruments shown together above the actual shrine could thus well have indicated heaven itself, as they seem to have done in Jewish funerary art.

19. See above, IV, 63–212.

20. Courtesy of the Department of Archeology, The Hebrew University, Jerusalem. See Avigad in *IEJ*, IX (1959), 215–218.

21. See above, III, figs. 964–972.

22. Ibid., fig. 817; cf. figs. 811 f.

23. Ibid., figs. 973 f.

Quite naturally in such a group the Law holds central place, since it held that place for rabbinic and more hellenized Jews alike. All else that was Jewish stemmed from the Jewish Law. I see no reason to suppose that the central façade, uniquely as it is here presented, means anything but the Torah shrine. Indeed, as presented we have a four-column façade with a central element, all in yellow, perhaps to indicate, as Kraeling supposes, gold. It has often been recalled that the façade with its enclosure much resembles the façades upon coins of the Bar Kokba revolt of the Hadrianic period, in which case it has been customary to suppose that the façade represented the lost Temple of Jewry.[24] The round-topped object within the façade as represented on the coins always has two bosses on its face, and seems to me to be also the Torah shrine, not the old Ark of Covenant which had been lost for centuries, so that the façade itself seems a sanctifying frame over the portable Torah shrine rather than a reference to the Temple. We have discussed at some length the significance of such a façade covering a holy object.[25] I show here fig. 67,[26] the end of a lead sarcophagus from Palestine. Its motifs include the head we discussed in the previous chapter, the figure of a naked man on a pedestal—i.e. a cult image, and an animal beneath him—all in the central opening. The whole was a convention for presenting sacred objects. Graffiti in the Palestinian cemetery of Sheikh Ibreiq quite confirm the impression that the object within the shrine above the Dura niche and on the coins is the Torah shrine.[27] In the graffiti the inner element within a shrine is the aron proper, with a menorah at either side. There the idea of the shrine for the portable box is kept, though the shrine has no columns and cannot conceivably be taken to refer to the Temple. The round-topped object within the Dura façade seems also the Torah shrine proper, with its two doors under the shell. It recalls the Torah shrine as everywhere represented; but it recalls especially the front of the shrine on wheels in the frieze of the synagogue at Capernaum, with its shell and columns.[28]

The two bosses on the front of the shrine of the coins correspond to the two "round objects" on the doors at Dura, a feature which may have been intended also on each door of the little Capernaum shrine. That such "round objects" on the doors had significance seems definitely attested by another little shrine carved on a lintel at Capernaum,[29] for here the "round objects" are transferred to the gable.[30] The "round objects" appear with

24. Ibid., fig. 692; cf. I, 277. Du Mesnil, *Peintures*, plate XII, published six of them; cf. Kraeling, *Synagogue*, 60.

25. See above, IV, 99–142.

26. Courtesy of the Palestine Archaeological Museum, Jerusalem, Jordan. It was found at Na'lieh, and is probably to be dated in the third century.

27. See above, III, figs. 58–61.

28. Ibid., fig. 472. The Ark of the Covenant, as represented at Dura, takes much the same form, fig. 332. I should guess that the form was first used by Jews for the Torah box, and then came to represent the Ark of the Covenant, rather than that it began as a form for the older Ark, since the form is traditional for a chest, but does not remotely correspond to biblical descriptions of the Ark.

29. Ibid., III, fig. 471.

30. On the door of a Palestinian tomb, III, fig. 44, and on a lamp, III, fig. 282, the shrine with shell is depicted with a round-centered lozenge under it. On the lamp "round objects" are above the shell, and little bosses, apparently for the doors, under the lozenge.

the façade in a great many places where the façade frames a vase with grapes on lamps.[31] We notice, then, on the overlapping flange of the two doors a column of seven "round objects" which Kraeling calls "bosses or nails." [32] To make the matter still more confused, five little circles run up each of the two columns of the shrine proper, and a row of eleven "round objects" seem to crown the entablature.[33] When we see that the branches of the menorah likewise are made of shafts of these "round objects," and recall fig. 52, where a column of six of them are painted on the reveal of the smaller door of the synagogue, the form begins to take on much significance.

We have wrestled with this form at least twice already, and with little satisfaction. It has appeared to represent sometimes bread,[34] sometimes a celestial luminary, especially the sun [35] (often as an alternative for the rosette); and now it has been suggested to me that the objects may sometimes represent jewels in their metal setting. They have appeared on menorahs [36] and Torah shrines [37] in Palestine and Rome. The little circles on the two columns may well stand for jewels, but the larger the representation, the less it seems possible to interpret the "round objects" in this way. They may well have had some reference in these places to the heavenly luminaries as divine symbols.[38] It would seem dangerous to conclude that on the shrine, or on the menorah (where also a rosette stands conspicuously in a way unique in this art) the "round objects" suggest literal astral worship. But that the Jews in this environment should have taken for their God the sanctifying symbols of the heavens goes well with their commonly using "Heaven" as a direct name for God.[39] One more detail should be mentioned about this shrine, namely the peculiar treatment of the columns. Of the capitals I have been able to make nothing whatever,[40] but the four outer columns with their fluting upon only one part of the shaft recall the divisions of the spiral shafts of early Christianity. The two smaller columns of the shrine within the façade are made spiral by the bands that seem to run up them. These distinct bands of fluting and the spiral effect on the columns both recall the much more elaborate spiral columns with bands of fluting and with vines, which as Ward Perkins pointed out were Dionysiac motifs "taken over and baptized by Christian architects." [41] But that faint echoes

---

31. Ibid., III, figs. 286 f. Cf. the "round objects" on lamps in III, figs. 261, 263, 273–275, 277, 280, 299, 300, 303, 305, 335, 342.

32. *Synagogue*, 60.

33. Kraeling, ibid., calls them semicircular antifixes, but they are so represented that the dot in the center could appear in each of them. Jews were fond of such rows upon their ossuaries. See above, III, figs. 178, 214, and the lamp, ibid., fig. 374.

34. See above, V, 54, 62–76, 83.

35. Ibid., 65 f.

36. Above, III, figs. 334–337 (on 335 the lights of the menorah are also "round objects"), 345, 349(?), 440, 571(?), 646, 651 f., 817, 925 f., 928, 932(?), 942, 948, 966 f., 974(?).

37. Ibid., figs. 471, 646 (over the gable), 817, 964, 966.

38. Such a conclusion will seem forced to readers who do not have in mind the material presented above, VIII, 167–218.

39. For references see K. Kohler in *JE*, VI, 298. We recall also Helios in the Palestinian synagogues and on the amulets: see above, I, 217, 248, 255, 258; II, 258–261.

40. I see no reason to disagree with Kraeling's description of them as "Egyptianizing," but know nothing quite like them in Egypt.

41. J. B. Ward Perkins, "The Shrine of St. Peter and Its Twelve Spiral Columns," *JRS*, XLII (1952), 28 f.; cf. J. M. C. Toynbee and Perkins in *Papers of the British School at Rome*, XVIII (1950),

of the convention still carried any symbolic implication in the synagogue it would be dangerous to conclude.

2. The Lulab, Ethrog, and Menorah

OF THE LULAB and ethrog nothing need especially be said except to recall that they had become symbols of immortality.[42] The menorah needs little more comment also. It, too, symbolized the hope of future life,[43] but here it is marked as a subsidiary symbol by the orientation of the burning lamps at the top. Strictly, the three outer lamps on each side should be oriented to burn toward the central one to represent the six other planets, as the ancients understood them, oriented toward the sun at their center. Here, however, all seven lamps are turned to honor the shrine in the middle of the panel, a detail that shows how the whole design had a unified intent.

3. The Sacrifice of Isaac

WE TURN to the scene of the sacrifice of Isaac with renewed presumptions of its symbolic importance. Here various details are unique.[44] The first is that Abraham, who wears what we shall continue to call the Robe,[45] is drawn knife in hand with his back turned to the observer, so that his head is only a mass of black hair. This could be taken as a crude way of showing that he is facing the altar on which Isaac lies, if Isaac too were not presented lying on his side and with only the black hair of the back of his head toward the observer. With this goes a peculiar tent in the upper right corner,[46] in whose open door stands a figure, also presented a tergo. The position of Abraham cannot be separated from that of the other two, for all three are looking at something. Only two things in the painting can be holding their attention. One, the less likely, is the Torah shrine in the center of the design; the other is the hand of God at the top of the scene of the Akedah. The ram at the bottom, tied to the tree,[47] which as always with animals at Dura is much

---

23–29; idem, *The Shrine of St. Peter*, 1956, 204 f., 247–251; above, VI, 159–161.

42. See above, IV, 145–166.

43. Ibid., 65–98.

44. The scene does not correspond exactly to any of the types of representation distinguished by A. M. Smith, "The Iconography of the Sacrifice of Isaac in Early Christian Art," *AJA*, Ser. II, Vol. XXVI (1922), 159–173. It is closest to his "Asiatic-Hellenistic Type," pp. 163 f., because it shows Isaac on the altar. Two new representations of the incident occur in the new Catacomb Via Latina, though again neither of them resembles the Dura design. See Ferrua, *Via Latina*, 55 and plate XCIX; 72 and plate LXVII.

45. See below, pp. 124–126.

46. I quite agree with Kraeling, *Synagogue*, 57 f., that the object is a tent. See his discussion of other interpretations. But as will appear, I do not follow his interpretation of the tent and its figure.

47. Kraeling, ibid., suggests that the incident follows the Targum Onkelos, since the Targum translated the Hebrew word for "thicket" by an Aramaic word for "tree." He does not mention that the LXX, using *phuton* at the passage, likewise translated the Hebrew by "tree." R. Meyer in *Theologische Literaturzeitung*, LXXIV (1949), 30–34, made much of the fact that the ram, here and at Beth Alpha, is tied to the bush, not caught in it by his horns according to Scripture. He sees in this the Pharisaic doctrine of determinism. D. Lerch, *Isaaks Opferung christlich gedeuted*, 1950, 8, n. 1 (Beiträge zur historischen Theologie, XII), thought Meyer's conclusion beyond the evidence, and I agree. The ram is also tied to the tree in the scene in el-Bagawat discussed below, pp. 73–75.

better drawn than the human figures, seems relatively detached. We are quite prepared
that the ram should be thus secondary in the sacrificial group, for although in the deepest
rabbinic interpretations of the incident the ram of course played its part, it had only a
subordinate role. Except for the ram, every figure is apparently oriented toward the divine
hand, and by this orientation the mood of the scene is indicated. A stone on which this
sacrifice appears was published by Naményi,[48] fig. 68.[49] Here Abraham turns his head
toward the hand, and Isaac lies again on his side on the altar. I quite agree with Naményi
that we should consider this stone a Jewish piece.

In that case it becomes increasingly important to identify the third little figure standing in the tent. Kraeling suggested that it is one of the two young men who were left behind with the asses when Abraham and Isaac went on alone to the place of sacrifice. The
suggestion seems to me quite unlikely, because there is only one figure, and that one is
associated not with asses but with a tent, in contrast to the scene at Beth Alpha where the
two men hold an ass.[50] The artist had room at Beth Alpha for only one ass, apparently,
but he had to show that there were two men with it. In a former volume[51] I suggested
that the figure in the tent at Dura was that of Sarah, and this still seems to me what the
artist intended. Jewish tradition commonly associated Sarah with a tent. She was in a
tent at Mamre when the "three men" appeared to Abraham,[52] and after her death, when
Isaac married Rebecca, he took her into "his mother Sarah's tent" to consummate the
marriage,[53] and so "was comforted after his mother," which the Septuagint seems to me
to translate correctly as "for (peri)" his mother.[54] Philo[55] also makes a considerable point
of Sarah's tent (which in the Septuagint becomes a "house"). A person in a tent, therefore, would at once be taken in this story to be Sarah. One legend connects both Sarah
and her tent with the Akedah. The legend tells that when Abraham and Isaac returned to
Sarah in her tent, and she heard how near Isaac had come to being killed, she cried out six
times—"corresponding to six blasts" of the shofar—and died.[56]

Two objections can be raised to this identification of the figure in the tent. One is
that Sarah wears a very different garment from that in which women are ordinarily
represented in the synagogue.[57] She wears what would at first seem to be the chiton
striped with clavi, a dress which in the other paintings is worn only by men.[58] But in
Christian art the chiton with its clavi soon became the dalmatic as the sleeves were wid-

48. L'Esprit, frontispiece; cf. his pp. 40 f. Naményi thinks that this and the Dura scene are
contemporary, the oldest Akedah scenes known.

49. Courtesy of the Cabinet des Médailles de la
Bibliothèque Nationale, where the stone is no.
1330. It is of banded sardonyx, two cm. in di-
ameter. See above, II, 224; III, fig. 1040.

50. See above, III, fig. 638.

51. Above, IV, 189.

52. Gen. XVIII, 2.

53. The LXX ēgapēsen autēn here is one of the
many places where the root, in spite of modern

theologians, directly means sexual intercourse.

54. Gen. XXIV, 67.

55. QG IV, 145 f., where it appears that Isaac
was consoled for his mother because in Rebecca
his mother returned to him (that is, Virtue) now
not old but in youthful beauty, and the symbol of
all this is that Isaac consummated his marriage in
Sarah's "house."

56. MR, Levit., XX, 2 (ET, 253 f.).

57. See figs. 329, 335, 338, 340.

58. See below, pp. 124 f.

ened, and as such is quite familiar as a woman's garment.[59] In the newly discovered fresco in the Roman Catacomb Via Latina, fig. 70,[60] Jesus, according to Ferrua, is depicted with the Samaritan woman. Both have the full-sleeved chiton or dalmatic: Christ wears an himation over it, the woman only the dalmatic.[61] Egyptian mummy portraits show many women wearing the chiton with its clavi.[62] Fig. 72 [63] shows the dress complete, and notably the woman in it has short hair. If this figure were drawn from the back, it would look quite like the figures we are discussing. Sarah, then, if it be she in the tent, is properly dressed in this garment.

The second objection to its being Sarah in the tent is that in the biblical account she was left behind in her own tent, and I know no rabbinic source that tells of her being at the sacrifice. Christian representations also usually omit her, but one very important painting in an Egyptian tomb-chapel dated in the first half of the fourth century, fig. 71,[64] puts the possibility beyond dispute. Here Sarah is definitely represented in the dalmatic, and named beside Abraham and Isaac. The three persons are not oriented toward the hand of God above them, as in the synagogue painting, but in addition to the dress the two drawings have several points in common. First, the tree to which the ram is tied is of a different type from that in the synagogue, but is again a tree, and the ram is tied to it.[65] Secondly, the altar has triangles on it, in this case three of them, to correspond to the one triangle on the synagogue altar. Kraeling thought this one represented the faggots that Isaac had carried to the scene, and that suggestion is fortified by the fact that in the Christian painting the faggots are burning. The knives (why two additional ones are in the air I do not know) have much the shape of the knife Abraham holds at Dura. Sarah could, then, indisputably be represented at the sacrifice.

With these two objections removed, the suggestion that the figure in the tent of the Dura representation is Sarah seems quite the most likely. Abraham, Isaac, and Sarah alike face the hand of God; in the Egyptian painting the three stand as a unit facing the audience. So far as the scene itself goes, the three in both cases seem to have great importance as a group, and the very fact that Sarah has no scriptural warrant for being at the scene suggests that those who put her there did so from a desire to interpret the Akedah rather than merely represent it. The interpretation would seem to involve making the three together a unit quite beyond what the scriptural narrative literally suggests.

59. Below, p. 158.

60. Courtesy of the Pontificia Commissione di Archeologia Sacra, Rome.

61. For a brief history of the dalmatic see R. Sinker in William Smith and S. Cheetham, *Dictionary of Christian Antiquities*, I, 523–525.

62. See below, p. 145. This will appear in any collection of such portraits. See, for example, P. Buberl, *Die griechisch-ägyptischen Mumienbildnisse der Sammlung Th. Graf*, 1922, 19; plates 4, 9, 11, 18, 23, 26, 28, 31–34, 36, 39, 45. Women of course wear other sorts of clothing as they do at Dura, but this simple striped garment was very common for them.

63. Courtesy of the Metropolitan Museum of Art, New York. It is the portrait of a woman painted on linen, second century after Christ, from Fayum. See A. Reinach, "Les Portraits gréco-égyptiens," *RA*, Ser. V, Vol. II (1915), 16, fig. 13; cf. p. 18.

64. From A. Fakhry, *The Necropolis of el-Bagawāt in Kharga Oasis*, 1951, 72, and plates xx f. (Service des Antiquités de l'Egypte: The Egyptian Deserts). Cf. p. 88, fig. 72.

65. See above, p. 71, n. 47.

We look then for an interpretation of this family in which Sarah has such a place in the trio, and, so far as I know, we find it only in Philo. Here the historical importance of the Patriarchs and their wives is not lost, but in allegory, and for "initiates," they represent the saving gifts and meditation of God. Thus Sarah and Rebecca in Philo both represent Virtue or Sophia, and Isaac is both the son and the spouse of this divine Female.[66] For when he took Rebecca into his mother's tent to consummate his marriage, as we saw, she became the substitute for the mother.[67] He was also her son after God had himself sown the seed in Sarah, so that Abraham, like the Christian Joseph, was only the supposititious father of the son. Accordingly Philo calls Isaac "the son of God." [68] For, Philo argues, if God promised Abraham "I will give thee a child from her," the child must belong to God, must be not a human being (*anthrōpos*) but "joy, laughter, the unprojected son of God who gave him." Philo continues with other examples of God's begetting sons in human mothers, and returns to Isaac to show that when Sarah says "The Lord has made laughter for me" it is "the same as saying that 'he formed, he wrought, he begat, Isaac'. " Such teaching, Philo hastens to add, should never reach any but ears properly trained to understand it, his usual way of referring to the inner circle whom at other times he calls "initiates." When, now, in his relation with Rebecca in Sarah's tent the divine child begets by his own mother, as Virtue, we have the age-old pattern that the son is his own father, what Egyptians called "the bull of his own mother." In this way, we saw, the fullness of Godhead was best preserved in ancient mythological terms, the fullness that required the three —father, mother, and son—to represent its richness.

The paintings in both Dura and el-Bagawat present the father-mother-son as involved in the Akedah. We must all the more regret that we have no Philonic interpretation of the sacrifice. The treatise on Isaac has completely disappeared from the *Exposition* of Philo, and the sections of the *Questions on Genesis* where the incident would have been discussed are likewise lost. In Philo's passing references to the sacrifice Sarah is never mentioned by name, but of course Philo clearly thought that the story conveyed the deepest sort of mystic doctrine. The "place" which Abraham saw from far off before he reached it and set up the altar was God himself—that is, the whole is a story of the mystic ascent.[69] Like the rabbis Philo vacillates as to whether Isaac himself was really offered on the altar. In one passage he says that God stopped Abraham from offering Isaac as a "whole burnt offering" [70] and so was prevented from removing from men the "self-taught genus." [71] But in another passage Abraham seems actually to have offered his "beloved and only legitimate son," who is the "clearest image of the self-taught Sophia," [72] by which he means Sarah, who was an example, parallel to Hannah, of one who "received divine seed and became pregnant." [73] The extraordinary family indeed appears when the statement

66. See my *By Light, Light,* 153–166 for Philo's interpretation of the character of Isaac.

67. *QG* IV, 145.

68. *Mut.* 130–140. God is said to have begotten Isaac also in *Migr.* 141 f.

69. *Post.* 17; *Migr.* 139 f.; *Som.* I, 64–67.

70. He calls it ἡ τοῦ ἀγαπητοῦ καὶ μονοῦ παιδὸς ὁλοκαύτωσις: cf. Ps. L, 18 (LXX).

71. *Som.* I, 194 f.

72. *Immut.* 4.

73. *Ibid.* 5; cf. *LA* III, 209.

"Sarah nursed the child" is explained to mean that it was the child who gave milk to the mother, since he was quite above receiving sustenance from anyone else, even from Sophia. It is this child which, at the sacrifice on the mount, "is properly offered to the One who gave it according to the law established for thanksgiving (*eucharistia*)." [74] When we recall that Philo calls the offering in this connection the "necessary and fitting thank offering (*charisterion*)" [75] and that Abraham offers up Isaac, "the image of the self-taught Sophia," we begin to see that a representation of the Akedah, in which Sarah appears, suggests that behind it, whether in Jewish Dura or Christian el-Bagawat or in a much earlier time when the design originated, lay the sacrifice in which Abraham became "the priest forever after the order of Melchizedek." [76]

All mere allegory? By no means. To Philo the historical narrative had the great importance that it rooted his metaphysics as well as his hope of spiritual achievement in acts of God that not only revealed God's grace but effectively brought it to man. Philo's hope of salvation, like that of Christians, rested not upon mere speculation but on the character of historical persons whom God had himself begotten and given to men. May I point out that the modern Jew or Christian who does not take Philo seriously on this point and cannot believe that Philo himself took it seriously quite corresponds to the modern skeptic who regards all theories of atonement as mere theological allegories of the death of Jesus of Nazareth. To the Christian believer the phrase "mere allegory" for his theories of the "work of Christ" hardly represents his attitude, or the way he feels before a cross or a picture of the Holy Family. The phrase seems to me as little to represent either the spirit of Philo or what was implied when the Akedah was pictured as the supreme act of Abraham, Sarah, and their, or God's, beloved and only son. Whether the full sophistication, or spiritual depth, of Philo was present in Dura seems irrelevant. Our object is to understand the significance of the symbols and designs as originally intended, not to determine how far each Jew in Dura understood them. It seems definite that the figure is that of Sarah in her tent,[77] less definite that Philo's own pages lay behind the design. But it is highly probable that some interpretation making the three into a unit prompted the Jews in Dura to put Sarah and her tent on the mount of sacrifice, where she gazes with Abraham and Isaac at the hand of God.

In the earlier discussion of the shofar, it was pointed out that the representation of

74. *Migr.* 140–142.

75. The χαριστήριον or εὐχαριστήριον which it is ἀναγκαῖον and ἁρμόττον to offer recalls the liturgic: εὐχαριστήσωμεν τῷ κυρίῳ. καὶ πάντες ἄξιον καὶ δίκαιον of Christian tradition. See G. Dix, *The Treatise on the Apostolic Tradition of St. Hippolytus of Rome*, I, 1937, 51; cf. the prayer in the *Apostolic Constitutions*, VIII, 12 (in C. C. J. Bunsen, *Christianity and Mankind*, VI, 1954, 401), a prayer discussed as originally Jewish in my *By Light, Light*, 320–326.

76. For Abraham in this role see above, IV,

176, 184, n. 137. Cf. Philo, *Cher.* 31, where Abraham in the sacrifice takes the "fire and sword" (Gen. XXII, 6) and cuts off and burns his own mortal part.

77. The tent itself seems to look to a Hebrew text, since it became *oikos*, house, in the LXX, and is so represented in a mosaic at Santa Maria Maggiore: see above, III, fig. 1. The "tree" might, as we saw, have stemmed from either an Aramaic targum or the LXX. The ideology of the Jews at this time seems not to have had linguistic boundaries.

this scene could well take the place of the shofar along with other cult instruments. That evidence need not be repeated, but one passage will explain the matter. In the Tanhuma, Abraham and God converse, and the conversation ends:

Abraham: "And why, then, didst thou afflict me thus?"

God: "It was my wish that the world should become acquainted with thee, and should know that it is not without good reason that I have chosen thee from all the nations. Now it hath been witnessed unto men that thou fearest God."

Hereupon God opened the heavens, and Abraham heard the words, "By myself I swear!"

Abraham: "Thou swearest, and also I swear, I will not leave this altar until I have said what I have to say."

God: "Speak whatsoever thou hast to speak!"

Abraham: "Didst thou not promise me thou wouldst let one come forth out of mine own bowels, whose seed should fill the whole world?"

God: "Yes."

Abraham: "Whom didst thou mean?"

God: "Isaac."

Abraham: "Didst thou not promise me to make my seed as numerous as the sand of the sea-shore?"

God: "Yes."

Abraham: "Through which one of my children?"

God: "Through Isaac."

Abraham: "I might have reproached thee, and said, O Lord of the world, yesterday thou didst tell me, In Isaac shall thy seed be called, and now thou sayest, Take thy son, thine only son, even Isaac, and offer him for a burnt offering. But I refrained myself, and I said nothing. Thus mayest thou, when the children of Isaac commit trespasses and because of them fall upon evil times, be mindful of the offering of their father Isaac, and forgive their sins and deliver them from their suffering."

God: "Thou hast said what thou hadst to say, and I will now say what I have to say. Thy children will sin before me in time to come, and I will sit in judgment upon them on the New Year's Day. If they desire that I should grant them pardon, they shall blow the ram's horn on that day, and I, mindful of the ram that was substituted for Isaac as a sacrifice, will forgive them for their sins." [78]

It seems justifiable to conclude that when the artist put the scene of the Akedah thus with the other cult instruments in this little panel above the sacred niche, he intended it to take the place of the shofar, but the shofar as interpreted in terms of the Akedah. We must, I believe, go one step further and see that by implication the other cult instruments —the menorah, the lulab and ethrog, and above all the enshrined Torah—similarly are to be taken not as mere pictures of the instruments but as reminders of the potency of Jewish cult to take one to the Shekinah, the presence of God, if not in this life then in the

---

78. Ginzberg, *Legends*, I, 284 f.

next. Indeed I am myself convinced that here, as in the funerary representations of these instruments, they had come to mean that in the celestial regions Jewish cult would find its full and eternal expression, and man his perfect destiny. This the ceiling seems already to have said, and the reredos above these cult objects suggests that mystics may have much of this experience in the present life.

CHAPTER SIX

The Reredos

ARCHEOLOGISTS and experts in painting who have examined the decorations of the Dura synagogue agree that the first part of the wall to be painted was a panel that reached from the top of the aedicula we have been discussing to the ceiling, or at least to the top of the wall below the line of little windows, if, as I sometimes doubt, such windows were included. When this painting stood alone on the otherwise blank walls, it must have given an effect similar to that of the reredos in a Christian church, and lacking a better term I shall use it for the painting. See plates I and IV; figs. 73–77, and 323.

A. DISCOVERY OF THE PAINTING

THE REREDOS has unique importance, for not only did it stand out in great impressiveness when alone, but its successive alterations show that great attention was paid to the problem of what should be represented in it. Unfortunately it presents tantalizing difficulties. The plaster at this place was obviously painted and repainted many times. In such a case an underpainting can usually not be reconstructed without destroying the overpainting. We know of the underpaintings here by an unusual circumstance. The reredos was one of the first paintings to be uncovered, and the archeologists had briefly a very clear view of the overpainting. In the excitement of the moment they made no immediate attempt to photograph it. In two hours, to their consternation, the exposure to the glaring sun began to make the underpainting show through the overpainting. All the layers of paint were soon so blurred together that none could be clearly distinguished from the others. Much as we wish we had clear photographs of the painting before this occurred, had it not happened, no one, probably, would have suspected the history of the painting, so that we can well afford to have lost some of the details. As I saw the original at Damascus, it was so hopelessly confused that I could distinguish little in it. I shall describe it as the experts who have studied it with great care report what they have observed.

First du Mesnil, who was at Dura the season the paintings were discovered, made sketches of what he saw. These sketches were done rapidly, and have been questioned by later observers, but he was drawing at a stage when much may have been visible that later disappeared. His sketch of the reredos is shown in fig. 75, the upper part,[1] and in fig. 77, the lower.[2] That was in 1932–33. The following year, 1933–34, as we noted in the Preface, H. Gute, a painter, Went to Dura to copy the paintings. He worked with meticulous care and with no preconceptions as to what might have been represented. Each night he called in the archeologists Clark Hopkins and Frank Brown to compare what he had done with the original. His copy of the reredos is shown in fig. 323. The following season, 1934–35, the paintings were cleaned and taken down by H. Pearson, whose training was primarily in architecture. He drew figs. 73 and 76,[3] which represent his conception of the earliest design in the reredos. Kraeling studied the paintings that same season at Dura, but made his detailed notes more than a decade later, 1945–46, after the paintings had been set up in Damascus and considerably restored (how much we shall never know) by Pearson. Later Gute drew fig. 74 for me from his own painting, which shows his notion of the design before its final repainting.

B. THE EARLY DESIGNS

ALL OBSERVERS agree that the first design showed a great tree. Pearson believed that the tree originally had a heavy trunk as he represented it, fig. 73, and as it appears in Gute's painting, fig. 323. Gute thinks, however, that this heavy trunk was put on later, and that originally the tree grew out of a vase as he shows it in fig. 74, for he clearly saw the ear of such a vase painted upon one of the lions at the right. I strongly suspect that Gute is right and that originally the tree grew out of a vase which was later painted out to make room for the two devices put in at the bottom to flank the tree. Clearly the two lions and the vase at the bottom could not have stood on the painting at the same time, so that if the vase ever stood there, it presumably antedated the lions.

As to the tree itself, everyone is confused. Without doubt, at one time it had the stocky trunk and spreading top of a tree. Its branches, however, as all agree, end in tendrils that could belong only to a vine, and the leaves seem to be those of a grapevine. On the other hand, if a vine was intended, especially one growing from a crater, we are perplexed at the absence of grapes. Kraeling [4] thought on the whole that what was represented was the tree of life, certainly a reasonable suggestion and one that I accept without hesitation as part of the symbolic value of the design. The objects represented with it, however, and the way in which the painting was successively altered, make me feel that this does not exhaust the meaning of the tree for the members of the synagogue. I see no reason not to take the details just as they were presented—that is, as a confluence of tree with vine. In discussing the vine [5] and the tree,[6] we came out with a very similar meaning for both. The tree of life appeared in art more commonly as the palm tree bearing two clusters of fruit. The vine

---

1. From du Mesnil, *Peintures*, plate xx.
2. Ibid., plate xxiii.
3. See above, V, 103, and fig. 117. These two drawings of Pearson's are reproduced from original drawings at the Yale University Art Gallery.

See Kraeling, *Synagogue*, 62, and plate xvii.
4. *Synagogue*, 63. See also Leveen, "Wall-Paintings," 24–27.
5. See above, V and VI.
6. Above, VII, 87–134.

had as its greatest function giving the fluid of life in the grapes, but itself was the god in whose branches birds (souls) could take refuge. Kraeling recalls that the vine was often a figure for Israel and for the Torah,[7] which seems to me relevant but not enough to explain the great prominence of the vine in the synagogue. We shall see how the painters finally associated Israel with the tree-vine, as the tribes seem to be coming to future bliss or mystic completion through it. Kraeling's interpretation of the tree-vine as the tree of life has undoubtedly a place in this symbolism. He refers to a late Midrash (a treatise containing much early material) where the tree of life is described in Eden: "And by [8] the tree of life the souls of the righteous are going up and down to heaven and from heaven to the Garden of Eden, like a man going up and down a ladder." [9] It often appears in Jewish tradition that the tree of life is the source of the divine fluid of the cup,[10] so that we do not have to reject either the tree of life or the vine for the reredos painting. The details of the painting, however, do not allow us to forget that if the tree represented the tree-vine of Jewish hopes, it had not lost the values of the pagan tree from which its representation was derived.

I strongly believe that the earliest representation showed simply the tree-vine, growing out of the large crater. If this is true, then the plant was primarily a vine, for at that stage the heavy spreading trunk would not have appeared; a properly proportioned base-stem of a vine would have been what grew out of the crater. That is, I am convinced that the first design looked very much like fig. 73, but with the crater as in fig. 74, and nothing else. When we recall that the vine and other Dionysiac symbolism seem to have been from first to last in the minds of those who planned the whole room as a vine bower,[11] it is not at all surprising that the symbolism should have been made specific by a great vine over the Torah shrine. The suggestion of a continuity of ideas will be strengthened when we see that Dionysiac symbols were at one stage painted under this tree-vine. I must not, however, be understood as saying that the Dionysiac tree-vine of the reredos represented the classical Dionysus. The tree, as we shall see, is full of both Greek and Iranian motifs; and from the way it is presented it would presumably reflect the confluence of the two, such as appears in many connections on monuments of the region.[12]

In evaluating such a representation above a sacred aedicula it would be taken for granted in either a pagan or Christian shrine that the representation set forth the meaning or power of the contents of the aedicula. The simple tree or vine growing from a crater would seem to say that the power of the scrolls or Torah in the aedicula or Torah shrine was that of the vine of Dionysus. This did not mean that these Jews worshiped Dionysus, any more than that such a vine would refer to Dionysus himself in a Christian church. But if for both Christians and pagans the vine referred to the divine power made available to

7. *Synagogue*, 63; cf. above, VI, 182 f., 204.

8. Morton Smith, who has translated this passage for me, points out that the Hebrew preposition here means "from"; but he agrees that the context suggests that the tree itself serves as the ladder.

9. *Bet ha-Midrash* (ed. A. Jellinek, Jerusalem, 1938, II, 28).

10. See above, VI, 181, 188, 190 f. Daniélou, *Symboles*, 33–48, has added a new collection of material on the tree-vine since the above was sent to the printer.

11. Above, p. 57.

12. For the tree in the East see above, VII, 91–94.

take one to heaven, as seemed to be the case when we discussed the vine above, the chances are overwhelming that the vine meant here not Israel itself but the hope of Israel, the hope that Jews would come to salvation through the Jewish God who was to his people what the vine represented to others. "I am the Vine, ye are the branches" may originally have been a mystic description of the relation between God and Israel. At this stage, however, when only the tree-vine was represented, the tree might simply have represented Deity. Morton Smith has recently presented the case for the tree as the image of God in Judaism,[13] and if the design ever existed in this simple form, the tree may have been put over the Torah shrine with exactly that symbolism in mind. The World Tree as an image of God in Iranian thought must also come to mind in view of the Iranian king figure soon to be put at the top of this tree, if it was not originally there.[14]

The tree-vine alone, however, apparently did not seem enough, since the crater at the bottom was painted out, apparently to make room for the details to be added.[15] Hence the trunk had to be drawn down, and widened to give some sort of structure to its form. In the space thus made available at the sides of the trunk, designs were painted under the tree-vine, which, from their character, seem to have been planned to make its meaning more specific. At the right was put a pair of rampant felines with some object between them which Pearson drew as an incredible scroll of a type I have never seen elsewhere, fig. 76. Gute saw a small crater between the felines, fig. 74, and, rather uncertain, thought the scroll above the crater which joined the heads of the felines might have been a pair of confronting snakes. The snakes and the crater between the felines are less assured than the felines themselves; but I have great faith in Gute's powers of observation, and furthermore it seems entirely natural that the symbolism of the original crater would have been kept in this way, intensified by being put between the felines and snakes.[16] Felines at a vase, presented in many poses, not only are familiar in pagan painting,[17] but as a symbol especially attracted Jews. We have seen it on their synagogues in Palestine,[18] and a new

13. "The Image of God," *Bulletin of the John Rylands Library*, XL (1958), 473–512.

14. G. Widengren, "Stand und Aufgaben der iranischen Religionsgeschichte," *Numen*, I (1954), 19, 40 f. The connection of tree and royalty continued with the Mandaeans: B. Gärtner, *Die rätselhaften Termini Nazoräer und Iskariot*, 1957, 27 (Horae Sonderblomianae, IV).

15. Clearly the ear-handle of a crater and the feline upon which it appears could not have stood in the painting simultaneously. It is more reasonable to suppose that the crater was painted out for the more elaborate details than the reverse.

16. The triad of lion, crater, and snake is familiar, though discussions of its meaning seem to me rather subjective: see the latest mention, with earlier titles, in E. Will, *Le Relief cultuel gréco-romain*, 1955, 404–406 (Bibliothèque des Ecoles Françaises d'Athènes et de Rome, CLXXXIII).

17. See the wall painting in the grave of Pancratius in Rome (middle of the second century A.D.): F. Wirth, *Römische Wandmalerei*, 1934, 84, fig. 42; and the wall painting from the atrium of L. Caecilius Jucundus at Pompeii: A. Mau, *Geschichte der decorativen Wandmalerei in Pompeji*, 1882, plate XVIII. A panther comes out of a wine cup on a silver cantharus at the Bibliothèque Nationale: *Mémoires de la Société des Antiquaires de Normandie*, 1831–33 (pub. 1833), plate XIII. See also the panthers on the drinking horns on the same cantharus, above, VII, fig. 275; also ibid., figs. 59 f., 65 f., 68, 77, 97, and p. 68; K. Lehmann in Rostovtzeff, *Dura-Europos*, IX, i, 187–202, with plate XXII.

18. See above, III, 460, 509, 536.

representation, whose crudity only emphasizes its symbolic motivation, has been found in the great Jewish cemetery at Sheikh Ibreiq (Beth She'arim), fig. 78.[19] Putting the crater now with the lions, and perhaps the snakes, preserved the symbolism of the original tree-vine growing from the crater, and emphasized its Dionysiac value.

The reason, however, that the crater was moved over to be a special item was apparently that the group of which it was the center might be balanced by a table on the other side of the trunk. On top of the table Gute saw a peculiar crescent form, fig. 74, upon which Pearson descried four bands. The bands, if they were there, would identify the object as the banqueting bolster of which we have had much to say.[20] It was used particularly in a variety of pagan religions, in Christianity, and often in Judaism, to indicate the ceremonial religious meal which would find its eternal celebration in heaven. Between the legs of the table both observers saw what we call a "round object," a circle that at the center contained, according to Pearson, the usual smaller circle, but according to Gute, a cross. Symbolically there is nothing to choose between these, for a round object by a table might indicate a libation vessel, we have seen; but here it more probably, as often, indicated bread.[21] It certainly represented bread if Gute's cross in the center is correct. If the meal of ceremonial bread thus prominently stood at one side, it was entirely fitting that the potent wine of the crater and the felines should have balanced it on the other.

The original symbolism of the vine seems thus only to have been underscored by putting in the tokens of bread and wine. The change may have been made very soon after the first design was completed. In any other environment we should at once conclude from the table, bread, and crater that the people worshiping in the room had a sacrament of wine and bread, one which they not only took in this life but regarded as the sign and means of the immortality figured in the simpler original tree-vine. That some such rite was actually performed by Jews at the time seemed a likely conclusion after the discussion of fish, bread, and wine in Volumes V and VI.[22]

In view of the Christian adaptations of Old Testament ritual to make the table of the tabernacle into the table with the Eucharistic elements, fig. 245, and the pagan mystic table with bread and wine at the Basilica di Porta Maggiore at Rome, fig. 247, it would seem that the Jews at Dura may well have had some direct ritualistic association with the table and symbols of bread and wine they put under the tree-vine of the reredos. The design in each is different, but the idea seems identical. The fact that we cannot even guess at the theological explanations Jews would have given for a rite of bread and wine seems to me no reason for closing our eyes to the plain if symbolic language of the design itself.

19. Courtesy of the Department of Antiquities, Israel.

20. See above, II, 46–50, 111 f.; V, 10. At the top of the semicircle of the bolster a small object seems indicated, of which I, like Kraeling (*Synagogue*, 64), can make nothing.

21. Above, V, figs. 78, 80 f.

22. This conclusion followed upon the almost universal use of bread and wine in Jewish symbolism, the later usages of wine in Judaism, especially in connection with circumcision, marriage, the kiddush of Sabbath and Festivals, and the wine of funerary ritual, as well as the references to the sacred table by Philo. The reader will agree that the conclusions of the earlier volumes cannot be freshly defended at this point.

C. *THE THRONE GROUP*

Alterations of the original design continued, always in the direction of elaborating the same basic meaning—that the vine or tree offered mystical ascent and immortality. I should guess that the next two additions were inserted at the time the table with bread and felines with wine were painted in,[23] so that at one stage the design looked like fig. 74. These additions consist of two groups of figures, each of which we must consider seriously.

The first group to have been added, if it did not stand in the original design, seems to have consisted of the enthroned figure at the top in royal Eastern dress, with two smaller guards before him in Greek himation and chiton. The combination of a king with his two companions appears three other times in the synagogue, as we shall see. In one of these a throne is marked "Solomon," but the wall above it is broken so that the king himself is entirely lost. In the two other cases where the king's figure is preserved he wears the Persian belted caftan with trousers,[24] over an open topcoat with sleeves. In the reredos, however, the king has no coat; his caftan is striped at the border and on the front from the belt down, and there is a stripe down the front of one trouser leg (we are presumably to understand a stripe down the other also).[25] The dress of the three kings which still exists in the synagogue, then, while it varies in detail, has been thoroughly standardized. The royal figure obviously is an Iranian one, so that it is conspicuous that he spreads his knees exactly as do Parthian or Sassanian kings, fig. 79.[26]

23. The time of additions of this material is especially discussed by Kraeling, *Synagogue*, 218, n. 862. He lays considerable emphasis upon the filling up of holes for the rosettes, as he calls them. But if, as he says, the tree design was abandoned in later painting entirely, it is inconceivable that the rosettes taken from the tree painting would have been kept for several years lying on the synagogue floor. I still cannot be convinced that the rosettes ever stood in the reredos. If they did, they were certainly not "blossoms in the form of applied plaster rosettes," blossoms in the tree instead of grapes (Kraeling, 63), for the holes were made in the trunk, or below the branches in spaces beside the trunk, in a way to show that whatever the function of the holes, they were not made to hold blossoms in the tree. Could they have held some sort of votive or memorial fetishes? Since, as Kraeling said, they were put in at all stages of the painting, so that earlier holes were filled up and painted over in the later painting, we seem to have evidence of a continuous practice. Did the holes contain pegs with names written on papyrus, names commemorative like the names in the ceiling? One

can make such suggestions, but we must not be carried away by our own ingenuity when we have no direct evidence.

24. N. P. Kondakov, "Les Costumes orientaux à la cour byzantine," *Byzantion*, I (1924), 20–25; H. Seyrig, "Armes et costumes iraniens de Palmyre," *Syria*, XVIII (1937), 13–19.

25. Kraeling, *Synagogue*, 219, says that the king in the reredos wears a "long-sleeved red coat," and that his tunic has a yellow band down the front, but the coat appears in no photograph or drawing.

26. From E. Herzfeld, *Am Tor von Asien*, 1920, plate xxv; cf. p. 55 (where it is discussed as plate xxvi). It shows a Parthian king from Ras al-Ain, but perhaps a deity. The statue has now disappeared. See also Seyrig in *Syria*, XVIII (1937), 20 f., fig. 11; Widengren, "Juifs et Iraniens," 208. The Iranian king, we recall, is an image of God, so that from the first this *double entendre* is suggested. Certainly, the figure in the reredos does not represent the contemporary Sassanian monarch: see L. de Saussure in *Journal asiatique*, CCII (1923), 288. For representations of Iranian kings see further

Two companions stand or sit beside each of these four thrones, and from their being always present, clearly reflect a tradition of royalty. I can find no such tradition, however, outside Jewish and Christian art. One type of these companions appears in the Octateuch of Constantinople, fig. 80,[27] where Aaron casts his rod before Pharaoh. Moses and Aaron stand at the left, and three Egyptian "wise men and sorcerers" are shown on the other side of Pharaoh. The king himself sits between two men who hold shields and spears. These accurately reproduce the two *doruphoroi*, spear bearers, who, as we shall see, Philo often says flank a king, especially God as king. The two are often literally "spear bearers" in the Octateuch tradition of illumination, a tradition we shall have much occasion to parallel with the Dura paintings, and which Philo himself may well have known at Alexandria. For example, fig. 81 [28] shows Joseph presenting his father to Pharaoh, who sits between the spear bearers. Philo uses the term "spear bearers" only to indicate the most immediate attendants of the king; their spears have no part in their actual function as he discusses it. Consequently three other Greek words could be used better to express Philo's own meaning and to describe the companions of the kings at Dura: the common *paredros* [29] and the much less common *sunedroi* [30] and *sugkathedroi* [31]—all of which meant literally "those who sit beside," but which took on the meaning "counselors." *Sugkathedroi* is the word used for them at Dura, for it is inscribed beside them on the scene of Solomon.[32] I can find in no pagan literature or painting, however, any fixed convention that a human king should have two of these and two only, such as we find both in Philo and in the Christian and Jewish paintings. The inevitability of the two in the Jewish-Christian tradition of painting lay deeper than that of making a balanced presentation, however, for at the throne of Ahasuerus in Dura the two companions stand together at the left, fig. 336, while in the painting of the presentation of Joseph's father to Pharaoh in the Constantinople Octateuch, fig. 175,[33] the two are beside Pharaoh at the right. The tradition under Christian influence went over to the representation of secular rulers,[34] but it so constantly appears in representations of God,

Syria, XX (1939), 182, fig. 4; Cumont, *Fouilles*, plate xcix; *Berytus*, I (1934), plate xii; *Wallraf-Richartz-Jahrbuch*, XVI (1954), 29, fig. 11; and cf. *Syria*, XV (1934), 158, n. 2.

27. From *Const. Octateuch*, plate xx, 105; it is fol. 175ᵛ.

28. Ibid., plate xviii, fig. 83.

29. So far as I know Philo used *paredros* only of *Dikē* as the ruler, or the counselor of the Ruler of all things "whose right and duty it is with the surpassing keenness of her never-sleeping eyes to survey the secrets of the corner as though they were in bright sunlight": *Spec.* iv, 201; cf. *Mut.* 194; *Mos.* ii, 53; *Jos.* 48; *Decal.* 177.

30. *Legat.* 350.

31. For example, Ulpian the Grammarian (third century after Christ) says: "*Paredroi* are given to young [rulers], men now called *sugkathedroi*.

For since the ruler must pass judgment upon all the orphans and matters of inheritance, and may sometimes through his youth give inexperienced judgment, a Paredros is given him to advise him": H. Wolf, *Demosthenis et Aeschinis . . . Opera*, Frankfurt, 1604, 687 f. Here one such counselor seems enough.

32. Inscription 31, edited with comment by C. B. Welles, in Kraeling, *Synagogue*, 279.

33. This scene is discussed below, p. 198.

34. See, for example, the fourth-century diptychon of Probianus and the fifth-century diptychon of Lampadius in O. Wulff, *Altchristliche und byzantinische Kunst*, 1914, I, 191 f., figs. 192 f.; also the sixth-century representation of Christ before Pilate in the Codex Rossanensis: N. Kondakov, in *Histoire de l'art byzantin*, 1886, I, 118.

Christ, or Mary enthroned that its association with the divine throne in Christian tradition needs no documentation whatever. Since I can find no pagan royal tradition of the kind, I must suppose that the Christian royal tradition came from religious symbolism rather than the reverse. Indeed in Christian tradition divine royalty appears with two Throne Mates in the Gospels themselves. The sons of Zebedee wanted to sit at the right and left hand of Jesus in his kingdon,[35] and in the glory at the transfiguration Jesus appeared with Moses and Elijah at either side.[36] Christ is to be at the right hand of God in glory,[37] where the Holy Spirit soon balanced him in Christian tradition. If no pagan tradition of royal kings with Throne Mates appears in art, the balancing of God with such a pair seems a very deep religious tradition, one that frequently recurs in Syrian religions. By at least A.D. 200 Mithra, like many other gods, had come to present himself in a "Mithraic trinity," [38] and the convention of the three in Dura may well have had some of its roots there.

In Philo, however, we find this idea connected with metaphysics in terms of his quite Neoplatonic-gnostic conception of the two Powers of God or the Logos. The conception can be studied in detail in Chapter One of my *By Light, Light*, and it will be discussed below.[39] In brief, Philo believed that the absolute God was inaccessible to human comprehension. God manifested himself in a triple form. The primal manifestation of himself as unity was the Logos, but the Logos quickly lost this unity as it descended, and was revealed in two Powers (*doruphoroi, dunameis*), from which beams come down to the human soul. God

> speaks from between the Creative Power and the Royal Power. The mind understands this as follows: the Logos (speech) of God, which is in the middle [between the two Powers] leaves no word in nature, but fills all things and acts as mediator . . . First is the Being more primal than the One, the Monad, and the Beginning. Second is the Logos of the Being, the essence germinative of things that exist. From the Divine Logos, as from a fountainhead, the two Powers divide themselves off. The one is the Creative Power, with reference to which the Creator founded and ordered all things, and this power is called "God." The other is the Royal Power, with reference to which the Creator rules over the things that have come into being, and this Power is called Lord.[40]

Those two Powers are called God's Goodness and Sovereignty.[41] The description may be abbreviated, so that Philo seems to say that God and his two Powers make the Three, and the Three together the One, which comes out in his allegory of the vision of the Three Men who appeared to Abraham, and were collectively God:

> Most natural things to those who are able to see does [Scripture] present, [namely] that it is reasonable for One to be Three and for Three to be One, for they were One

---

35. Mark x, 37.

36. Ibid. ix, 2–8 and parallels.

37. Ibid. xiv, 62; cf. Acts vii, 56. See E. L. Allen in *HTR*, XLVI (1953), 163.

38. See F. Behn, *Das Mithraheiligtum zu Dieburg*, 1928, 14 f. (Römisch-germanische Forschungen, I); R. Dussaud, "Azizos et Monimos parédres du dieu solaire," *RA*, Ser. IV, Vol. I (1903), 128–133; Cumont, *TMM*, I, 1899, 203–213.

39. See below, X, 91–96.

40. *QE* ii, 68. The Greek of this is preserved in a fragment reprinted in the Loeb ed., 255 f.

41. *Cher.* 27.

by a higher principle.[42] But when counted with the chief Powers, the Creative and Kingly, he makes the appearance of Three to the human mind. For this cannot be so keen of sight that it can see him who is above the Powers that belong to him, [namely] God, distinct from anything else. For so soon as one sets eyes upon God, there also appear, together with his being, the ministering Powers, so that in place of One he makes the appearance of a Triad. . . . He cannot be seen in his oneness without something [else], the chief Powers that exist immediately with him [namely] the Creative, which is called "God," and the Kingly, which is called "Lord." [43]

Then after explaining that the eyes raised are the eyes of the soul Philo continues:

[Abraham] begins to see the sovereign, holy, and divine vision in such a way that the single appearance appears as a Triad, and the Triad as a unity.[44]

For in the highest experience and clearest vision the Triad disappears in the One, which makes itself appear without the assisting Powers; and accordingly Abraham

clearly forms an impression with more open eyes and more lucid vision, not roaming about nor wandering off with the Triad, and being attracted thereto by quantity and plurality, but running toward the One. And [the One] manifested himself without the Powers that belong to him, so that [Abraham] saw [God's] Oneness directly before him, as he had known it earlier in the likeness of a Triad.[45] But it is something great that he asks, [namely] that God shall not pass by nor remove to a distance and leave his soul desolate and empty. For the limit of happiness is the presence of God, which completely fills the whole soul with his whole incorporeal and eternal light. . . . [46]

So that truly and properly speaking, God alone is the measure of all things, both intelligible and sense-perceptible, and he in his Oneness is likened to a Triad because of the weakness of the beholders. For the eye of the soul, which is very lucid and bright, is dimmed before it falls upon and gazes at him who is in his Oneness without anyone else at all being seen. For just as the eyes of the body when they are weak, often come upon a double appearance from a single lamp, so also in the case of the soul's vision, it is not able to attain to the One as one but finds it natural to receive an impression of the Triad in accordance with the appearances that attend the One like ministers, [namely] the chief Powers.[47]

The king, for Philo, always has these two aspects of his rulership, the creative or merciful opposed to the legal or punitive, and indeed kingship gave form to Philo's con-

---

42. R. Marcus reconstructs the Greek as *kat' anōteron logon*, but translates the Armenian "one by a higher principle." The passage is quite ambiguous by itself and may here literally refer to the Logos as I took Aucher's Latin to do in *By Light, Light*, 33. Philo is saying that God, the Monad, is himself manifest in the Three, the Triad, not in the One plus the two Powers.

43. *QG* IV, 2.

44. Ibid.

45. Cf. *Abr.* 131 f.

46. *QG* IV, 4.

47. Ibid., 8. Since I do not read Armenian, I have taken Marcus' translation verbatim for these passages, though Aucher often understood the original differently from Marcus. The differences would have no bearing upon the general meaning of these passages, or upon my purpose in quoting them. I have kept Marcus' precise word "Triad," but remind the reader that *trias* became the Greek word for the Christian "Trinity."

ception of God as much as the conception of God reappeared in describing the king.[48] We now recall the many variations by which in various parts of the ancient world Deity was presented in a group of three. This has been long known, and D. Nielsen [49] has systematically gathered the material. I strongly suspect that as the idea went from religion to royalty in Christian art, it did the same in Philo's thinking. In any case, his God manifests himself as Three.

Clearly I have it in mind to suggest that the designs of this, and other paintings in the Dura synagogue, were ultimately inspired by a type of thought known to us chiefly through Philo Judaeus. Before going any farther, may I repeat what I have said so often—that hellenized Judaism of a mystic type must be documented primarily from the writings of Philo only because the writings of Philo alone survive to bear literary witness to it. No evidence whatever suggests that he created it, or that his thought inspired the Dura paintings directly, or that the Jews in Dura ever read his writings. In an iconological study, however, we must suppose that designs were made to illustrate ideas, ideas which themselves make the designs intelligible. Quite apart from the argument for symbolic intent in the designs on Jewish remains elsewhere (an argument presented in the first eight volumes of this study), it seems incredible that Jews painted the Old Testament scenes of the Dura synagogue with such pagan invasions as we are seeing they introduced, unless those who designed the paintings had set out to illustrate some rather definite ideas from their understanding of the Torah and Judaism. It would be altogether too repetitious to describe the paintings as such, and then to return to interpret the meaning, for we should have to reproduce in the second stage much of the description of the first. I avoid such repetition by interpreting each scene as I describe it, but in doing so I shall inevitably seem at first to read altogether too much into the scenes discussed. Only as I can make it appear that a consistent idea inspired the whole group of paintings, or a considerable part of them, can I hope to arouse in the reader any sense of probability that my interpretations may be on the right track. With some of the designs I shall fail to make such connection, not because they contradict my thesis but because we have no literature that illuminates them, or because, like the Akedah scene, nothing about the presentation indicates one sort of Jewish thinking rather than another (even here we found the extraneous Sarah in her tent at least suggesting a convention).

The great difficulty in looking for the "intention" of a poet or artist is that we may project meanings into his work that have meaning for us but may not have been in his mind at all. If a given framework of ideas, however, makes intelligible a whole series of paintings, it becomes less likely that the subjective element is guiding our thought than if we rest our conclusions on a single example. In interpreting the royal group at the top of the tree, then, I shall make suggestions of meaning I should not dare to do without the support of a large number of other scenes that have what seem to me to be similar implications. In this convention, while the Three Men of Abraham do not appear in the Dura paintings, the three are represented in two other scenes at Dura exactly as in Christian

48. See the chapter "Kingship" in my *The Politics of Philo Judaeus*, 1938, 86–120.

49. *Der dreieinige Gott*, 1922. Cf. above, VIII, 37 n.

paintings of the Abraham incident, paintings that we shall feel stem from a common ancestor with the Old Testament art of Dura.[50]

On the reredos of any other shrine of the time, we should expect to find represented the saving God of the shrine, or some symbol of his saving power. One needs to recall only the shrines of Mithra. In representing this king with his two companions in Greek dress it is my conviction that the Dura artist presented the Jewish God, not in his essence but as the great Three whereby Philo (and, presumably, many who thought like him) conceived God manifested himself to human minds and mystic vision. God himself is of course One, and cannot be represented; but to man he appears as the Three. So, I suspect, the reredos represents at its top the One God, who in himself is unity yet "is likened to a Triad because of the weakness of the beholder." [51] Philo adds,[52] however, that a person has to be much advanced in mysticism (be a *teleios*) to see even the Three. Ordinary mystics, I would infer, see only a blur of light. The Three at the top, then, would not be the One God himself, but the Logos and the two Powers, collectively God, but God as we apprehend him, not in his essence. That is, the Three of the reredos seem a device for representing Deity indirectly, as was also done by the Hand of God. I do not for a moment suppose that the Jews of this synagogue had broken down their monotheism any more than had Philo himself. They cleverly avoided representing their One God, by presenting him in the Triad.[53]

The dress of the two companions confirms me in this interpretation. They wear a Greek undergarment, or chiton, marked with stripes or clavi that run from the shoulders to the hem. Over this is thrown the large shawl, cloak, or himation normally going from the feet up over the left shoulder and under the right arm, its end held on the left arm. Near the ends of the himation as represented in the synagogue usually heavy marks appear, marks that seem always to end in a square prong. One can be seen clearly in fig. 323 across the knees of the companion on the right. This dress recurs in a great many places in the synagogue, and we will have to stop to consider its history as a symbol in itself in the following chapter. Here we may notice that of the three other throne scenes in the synagogue, the companions of the king do not wear this robe except in the mutilated painting of the enthroned Solomon, fig. 329. Here only the bottoms of the robe appear on the figures sitting in chairs at either side of the throne, but the pronged ornament shows very clearly on the himation at the right. The significance of the Solomon scene can never be adequately guessed from the fragment that remains,[54] but it is conspicuous that the companions of the two gentile kings, Ahasuerus and Pharaoh, wear the Eastern caftan and trousers. In Christian art the enthroned kings (even Pharaoh himself as in fig. 175), wear the Greek dress. Apparently in the art tradition known to the painters at Dura a king

50. See below, X, 91 and 157.

51. *QG* IV, 8.

52. Ibid., 30.

53. Naményi, *L'Esprit*, 22, says with confidence that "in Jewish art, throughout its history, every image of God was banished; his presence was suggested, occasionally, only by his hand." Leveen,

"Wall-Paintings," 31, proposed that the king of the reredos is Pharaoh with Moses and Aaron before him in the Greek dress. The first of these statements is highly questionable (see Helios in the synagogues, above, I, 250 f.), and the second pure fancy.

54. See below, X, 99–104.

existed only in the eastern form. But they seem to me to be saying something about the group when they represent in Persian dress the companions of gentile kings, yet give the Greek dress to the companions of those other kings.[55]

It must briefly be said here in anticipation that this Greek dress of striped chiton and marked himation will appear only on characters of especial sanctity—heavenly beings or the very great Patriarchs. At the throne in the reredos the companions seem to me to have the Greek robe instead of the Persian dress to mark them as heavenly beings—indeed to give special meaning to the group as the Three manifest. We must see whether this interpretation of the Three (in contrast to the still unpictured One [56]) fits into the scene as totally designed, just as we must wait to see whether putting a person into this Greek dress has any consistent meaning. I should emphasize, however, that the addition of the Three only spelled out the significance of the great tree-vine itself.[57] By both, as I have said, Deity was presented, not represented.

In suggesting this identification I am at least temporarily ignoring the assumptions of most of my predecessors, who unite in seeing in the king the Jewish Messiah. Except that the Messiah was to be a king, nothing in the painting indicates the Messiah at all. Nor is there any reason to identify the figure specifically with the "Son of Man," who in Enoch is often described as sitting on a throne with the elect ones before him,[58] though that tradition may well have contributed to the painting, and been in the mind which designed it. The king in the reredos must be considered in his context, that of the tree-vine, Dionysiac symbols, and Orpheus—the painting judged, that is, as a whole. We shall return to the king when we have discussed the Orpheus figure below him.

D. ORPHEUS

At about the time when the Three were added at the top of the vine or tree, another group of figures, Orpheus playing to the animals, was painted across its middle. Orpheus was represented at the left playing his lyre, with the typical eagle of the East in yellow behind his head.[59] Before him stands a huge lion. Above the lion's tail Gute drew

55. The combination of a monarch wearing an oriental costume along with a person in the Greek dress appears, so far as I know, only on the great Apulian "Persian" vase at Naples, dated by Furtwängler at the time of Alexander the Great: FR, plate 88; cf. Text, II, 142–155; see also Will, *Le Relief cultuel gréco-romain*, plate IV at p. 352. Here a king, labeled Darius, sits enthroned in his native costume (with robe, not trousers). Before him stands a man with an oriental long-sleeved undershirt beneath his chiton, high Persian shoes, and a Persian hat, with the label "Persian." But his chiton and himation are Greek, and the chiton has the clavi running down it; see fig. 111, and below, p. 134.

56. For a pagan representation of the unnamed God with two minor personalities, the Sun and Moon, see above, VIII, 134 f.

57. See above, pp. 85–89.

58. Enoch XLV, 3–6; XLVII, 3; LI, 2 f.; LV, 4; LXII, 2 f.; LXIX, 27, 29; cf. Dan. VII, 13 f. In Jewish mysticism these figures were probably not kept very distinct. J. Muilenberg, "Son of Man in Daniel and the Ethiopic Apocalypse of Enoch," *JBL*, LXXIX (1960), 197–209, has again pointed out that Son of Man is very likely an "apocalyptized and mythological Wisdom" figure.

59. Kraeling, *Synagogue*, 224, implies that the yellow eagle is a golden eagle, and so not a "living creature." The identification of yellow with gold by no means consistently works out, and does not seem to apply here.

a little duck, which Kraeling[60] says is now quite invisible. I suspect, however, that it was there, since du Mesnil saw it also, fig. 77. Comparison of these sketches will justify my despair of any confident assertions. Du Mesnil missed the eagle behind Orpheus' head which all other observers agree they could see, and which appears in the later photograph, fig. 323. On the other hand du Mesnil puts in a monkey and a dove which the others could find no trace of. He and Kraeling agree that Orpheus wore not only his typical hat but also the eastern caftan and trousers, with a Greek chlamys hanging down his back. Trousers on Orpheus are unusual: so far as I know they appear only once and then possibly are drawn from an eastern model, since a leopard and elephant stand among the animals.[61] The chlamys or a mantle, with or without other Greek garments, may be said to be the usual garb of Orpheus.[62] It is possible that the Dura figure actually looked much like the Orpheus in the Jerusalem mosaic reproduced in an earlier volume.[63] For here are the stripes of the chiton such as the other observers reported at Dura, and which may well have suggested trousers in the indistinct lines of the Dura rendering.[64]

Whether Orpheus wore the trousers makes little difference to us here, but the problem of what was represented will obviously confuse us throughout as we discuss the group. In the present condition of the painting it is probably useless to go back to study it again on the wall at Damascus; we must admit that many of these points we shall never know.

Kraeling, we have said, did not see the duck that all the others agree stood above the lion's tail. All say, however, that they could see no trace of the monkey and the dove du Mesnil also reported. For interpretation of the painting, disagreement here becomes more serious. It seems to me quite incredible that du Mesnil should have merely imagined this monkey, and all the detail which he included—especially since a monkey appears so commonly with Orpheus. Du Mesnil[65] called attention to the similarity of what he saw to the "dog of David" in the Chludov Psalter, fig. 82.[66] But the "dog" in the picture is clearly a

60. *Synagogue*, 224. I incline to believe that Gute would not have painted the duck so clearly in the reconstruction, fig. 323, if he had not had more reason to do so than Kraeling allows. Gute said to me that although he worked with the uncleaned paintings, and the dirt was in the way, he saw them with more of the original paint on them than those who saw them when cleaned.

61. H. Stern, *Recueil général des mosaïques de la Gaule*, I, *Gaule-Belgique*, i, 1957, 50, and plates XXIV f.: a mosaic at Blanzy-les-Fismes. Trousers are also drawn in an eighteenth-century copy of an Orpheus in the Christian cemetery of Domitilla, but that painting was soon destroyed: see it as most conveniently reproduced by H. Leclercq, CL, XII, ii, 2740, fig. 9237; Garrucci, *Arte cristiana*, II, plate XXV; cf. p. 29. Another Orpheus, however, painted after this same ancient model a century later in the same catacomb, seems to have had only

the chlamys thrown over the knees in the usual way of the seated Orpheus: O. Gruppe in Roscher, *Lex. Myth.*, III, i, 1203, fig. 17.

62. For a collection of Orpheus figures see Gruppe, loc. cit., esp. figs. 2–7, 16; Leclercq, loc. cit., 2739–2753; Reinach, *Peintures*, 201–209, 403 f.

63. See above, V, fig. 113. If he wore trousers his knees would be in the position of Iranian royalty: see above, p. 83 and fig. 79.

64. A glance at the mosaic of the Good Shepherd in the Mausoleum of Galla Placidia at Ravenna shows how easily this could have occurred: see R. Huch and W. Volbach, *Early Christian Mosaics*, 1946, plate IV.

65. *Peintures*, 49–51.

66. Courtesy Bibliothèque Nationale, Paris. Cf. Omont, *Miniatures*, plate I. It is ms. grec. 139, fol. 1; cf. Eisler, *Orpheus*, plate XXIX.

medieval corruption of an original monkey,[67] for one appears in a Vatican Psalter, fig. 83,[68] in exactly the pose of this and of du Mesnil's Dura monkey. The monkey was also put beside a pagan Orpheus in the second- or third-century mosaic at Palermo fig. 84,[69] on a mosaic at the Isle of Wight, fig. 86,[70] on a mosaic at Henchir-Tina in Tunis,[71] while a monkey actually sits on the lyre in the ivory pyxis of Bobbio, fig. 85.[72] Indeed Orpheus himself becomes a monkey on a mosaic from Sousse, Tunisia, at the Louvre, fig. 87.[73] Accordingly, since du Mesnil saw the monkey in so typical a pose, and since a monkey is so entirely to be expected with Orpheus, I see every reason to suppose that it had been there but had faded out by the following year when the next observers saw the painting. Especially does this seem a natural conclusion because I, like my predecessors, will conclude that the Jews here called the Orpheus "David," and the monkey is especially frequent in Orpheus-David representations. It would seem to have come into the synagogue in some way from an original Jewish tradition of David as Orpheus which continued in the medieval Christian psalters. In the Chludov Psalter, also, fig. 82, Orpheus-David sits in a tree. I suspect that it was Jewish tradition that preferred the eagle to the Muse with Orpheus.

Whether the dove that du Mesnil reported was also there cannot be concluded with even this relative conviction. A dovelike bird is commonly in the tree beside Orpheus,[74] and may well have been at Dura also. But the form of a little dove in the foliage could more easily be mistaken than that of the large monkey, as it could more easily be obscured, so that I have no idea whether it was ever in the Dura painting at all. The duck with Orpheus is not common, but water birds of various sorts do appear, and a variety of birds, here represented by the duck and perhaps the dove, would be quite appropriate.[75]

The eagle was not unusually painted beside Orpheus in these scenes. Callistratus specifically mentions the eagle in the painting of Orpheus he describes,[76] and one is to be seen at the right in fig. 85, while one sits upon Orpheus' cap on a deeply carved marble

67. On the monkey with Orpheus see J. Strzygowski in O. Kern, *Orpheus*, 1920, 60 f. The monkey has become a dog in the Psalter at the Biblioteca Barberini, no. III, 29: see A. Venturi, *Storia dell' arte italiana*, II, 457, fig. 311.

68. Courtesy of Vatican Museum, Rome, where it is Pal. Gr. 381 B, fol. 1ᵛ; cf. Kondakov in *Histoire de l'art byzantin*, 1891, II, 31.

69. Courtesy of the Soprintendenze alle Antichita, Palermo. Cf. A. Blanchet, *La Mosaïque*, 1928, plate VI; B. Pace, *Arte e civiltà della Sicilia antica*, 1938, II, 184–186. fig. 173.

70. From J. E. Price and F. G. H. Price in *Royal Institute of British Architects, Transactions*, 1880–81, plate at p. 134; cf. p. 133. The mosaic is dated in the fourth century (p. 158).

71. Gauckler, *Mosaïques*, II, plate 32a.

72. Courtesy of Ente Provinciale per il Turismo,

Piacenza, Italy. Cf. W. K. C. Guthrie, *Orpheus and Greek Religion*, 1935, plate 15 at p. 264.

73. Courtesy, Service des Archives Photographiques, Paris. See Reinach, *Peintures*, 427.

74. See, for example, Roscher, *Lex. Myth.*, III, i, 1191, fig. 14; 1199, fig. 16; 1203, fig. 17; and see above, V, fig. 113. Philostratus the Younger, *Imagines*, 6, and Callistratus, *Descriptions*, 7 (ed. A. Fairbanks, Loeb ed., 311, 402), mention especially the birds that are tamed by Orpheus. A dove is not only in a tree beside Orpheus, but one sits on his lyre on a Christian sarcophagus at Porto Torres: Garrucci, *Arte cristiana*, V, plate 307, no. 4. Cf. G. Bovini, *I sarcofagi paleocristiani*, 1949, 98 (Monumenti di antichita cristiana, II, 5).

75. See, for example, the carved gem of Berlin illustrated in CL, XII, ii, 2754, fig. 9248.

76. Loc. cit.

relief at the museum in Athens, fig. 89.[77] Fig. 88,[78] a mosaic of the "Roman period" at Istanbul from Cos, shows Orpheus again in a tree with animals, including the lion and eagle (in the same position behind Orpheus' head), and various sorts of birds. The eagle would seem to have the meaning with Orpheus which we saw that it frequently had in the East, when it symbolized divine inspiration, just as it continues to do in Christianity when connected with John the Evangelist, and when used on the lectern for the Bible in Christian churches.

The lion, the last of the animals with Orpheus in the reredos at Dura, appears even more constantly with him than almost any other animal. In a painting at Pompeii,[79] Orpheus sits between a lion and a lioness or some other feline; in a mosaic of Switzerland he sits directly upon the lion.[80] The figures of Orpheus already shown, except those in the Christian psalters, show a lion in every case.[81] As often, the lion of the Dura reredos is the quiet, tamed lion.

Orpheus in the tree or vine, with the animals and birds as reported, made an entirely fitting combination, and I cannot believe they were painted otherwise than as a group. Kraeling, however, has raised an important objection to this. He said [82] that the lion was painted into the vine first, and that "without the slightest doubt" it stood for the "Lion of Judah." He published a drawing of the vine with only the lion added to the vine at the center.[83] He explained that a lion was represented thus as a peaceful animal when it was a guardian or a servant of a deity, and that it was copied here from some such original without further meaning by the painter. He did not suggest that when a lion is put with Orpheus, he usually thus quietly faces its tamer.[84] The lion, he says, was painted directly on the vine, while Orpheus was painted upon a red wash that covered the vine. Since such a red cover-coat was used as a base for later additions, Kraeling supposes that Orpheus was definitely put in later than the lion. But how much later? I should guess that the lion was indeed put in before Orpheus, that he was painted immediately after the insertion of the royal group at the top, which likewise was painted directly over the vine. But apparently the technique was not working very well; perhaps the underpainting had already begun to show through in the group above; so that in finishing the Orpheus group a cover-coat was used as a foundation for Orpheus himself. This proved so successful that the other changes, whenever they were introduced, began with a similar cover-coat over the original

77. Courtesy of the Byzantine Museum, Athens. Cf. Strzygowski in *RQ*, IV (1890), plate VI; On pp. 104–106 Strzygowski expresses the opinion that this is a Christian, not a pagan, object, and calls the eagle the "Roman-Byzantine imperial eagle." Like the eagle at Dura, it is simply the eagle of the East, which had many interpretations. With Orpheus the royal eagle is certainly the least likely of all. The monkey here again sits on Orpheus' lyre.

78. Photo Saba. See Musée d'Istanbul, *Guide illustré des sculptures*, etc., 1935, 15, no. 1304. See a

second mosaic at the same museum from a Christian Church, above, V, fig. 113, where the eagle sits beside Orpheus.

79. See Roscher, *Lex. Myth.*, III, i, 1178, fig. 2.

80. Reinach, *Peintures*, 202, no. 3.

81. See ibid., 199–203, for further examples.

82. *Synagogue*, 218 f.

83. Ibid., plate XXXIII.

84. The peaceful attitude of animals with Orpheus, including the lion, is especially noted by Philostratus the Younger, *Imagines*, 6 (Loeb ed., 309 f.).

painting. Such a suggestion of the order of painting, while purely supposititious, would account for the fact that although Orpheus and the animals seem so coherent as a group, Orpheus himself was painted upon a cover-coat while the animals were not.

What seems to me basic is the integrity of the group, in whatever order or circumstances it was painted. For here is an Orpheus with the animals, certainly with the eagle and lion, probably also with the monkey and duck, possibly with the dove; these were designed as a group—if not from the first, certainly at the end. As with the group of Three, we pass on at once to the question of the Jewish identity of this Orpheus figure, for Orpheus *qua* Orpheus would be as unthinkable in the synagogue as in an early Christian chapel or grave.

With Orpheus *qua* Orpheus we must, however, begin. We recall that a strange loan-word in a new language, while usage in the second language may have modified the original meaning, is best explained in terms of its meaning in the first language. If Jews and Christians borrowed the figure of Orpheus with the animals, it may be presumed that there was something in the pagan Orpheus which prompted them to do so. We may, I believe, accept the statement of Ovid concerning what the figure represented to pagans:

> While men still roamed the woods, Orpheus, the holy one and prophet of the gods, made them shrink from bloodshed and brutal living; hence too the fable that he tamed tigers and ravening lions.[85]

Ovid goes on to tell how other singers have tamed men and introduced law and order in place of savagery. The figure of Orpheus playing to the animals presents, then, the power of divine song to quiet human savagery. In the same way Orpheus could represent for Christians the saving power of Christ, if not Christ himself. And for Jews he would most naturally have been associated with David, the singer who could quiet even the madness of King Saul, and who perpetuated his magic in the Psalter. It has long been agreed that in Christianity, also, Orpheus was used in two connections, as Christ the Good Shepherd, or as David. These two are not so distinct as might at first appear, for "David was a shepherd boy" and Christ was often an alter-David. The tradition of Orpheus as David in Christian psalters has already been recalled, and I see no reason to suppose that the Orpheus in the Dura vine or tree was any other than David.[86]

Kraeling also identifies the Orpheus figure with David, but only after separating from him all the birds and animals except the eagle, which, because of its yellow color, he pronounces the golden heraldic eagle of royalty. There is no more reason for this than with the Orpheus in the Istanbul mosaic, fig. 88. The synagogue artist wanted to put David at this point in the tree-vine, Kraeling argues, so took the Orpheus figure as a "cliché" of

85. *Art of Poetry*, 391–393: see the translation of H. R. Fairclough in the Loeb Series, 483. Ovid is by no means our only testimony to this value of Orpheus. See the rich collection of material by Jean Coman, "Orphée, civilisateur de l'humanité," *Zalmoxis*, I (1938), 130–176.

86. A fine collection of material on David was published by Helen M. Roe, "The 'David Cycle' in Early Irish Art," *Journal of the Royal Society of Antiquaries of Ireland*, LXXIX (1949), 39–59.

a singer, and made it royal by representing it with the eagle.[87] That the Orpheus figure as such had any meaningful connection with the design as a whole he does not suggest.

I must go on to ask questions Kraeling did not raise: primarily, why did the artist want to put David as the tamer just here? We have seen that the original vine or tree growing from a vase was changed to make more explicit the symbolic and ritualistic implications of the vase by inserting the banqueting table, and the crater with felines, beside the trunk. The supernal goal to which the tree led was spelled out by putting the great Three at the top. In that case it would be strange indeed if the people so carefully working out the symbolism of the reredos simply inserted into the middle of the tree odds and ends of figures that had no ideological relation to the whole design. Granted that Orpheus was thought to be David, what did David mean to the congregation, that with his animals he should have been put thus in the center of the tree?

In rabbinic literature David was of course the great king, but that capacity is not represented by Orpheus with the lyre. David for the rabbis was also a prophet,[88] and they said that the Psalms consist of compositions made in ecstasy as the Holy Spirit came upon him, and gave him revelations of the future history of Israel. Hence the passages in the Psalms dealing with Israel's salvation refer to the messianic salvation.[89] Whether Philo echoes this from rabbinic tradition or the rabbis adopted "Philonic" ideas, Philo also says that David sang his songs to God [90] and was a prophet.[91] But more, for Philo he was a disciple (*gnorimos*),[92] a companion (*hetairos*) of Moses [93]—words that Philo commonly uses in a mystical sense; hence he means the same when he says that David belonged to the inner mystic group (*thiasos*) of Moses.[94] Philo and the rabbis agree that his inspiration led to a divine frenzy of the joy of the Lord, but Philo goes beyond the rabbis when he says that this was inspired by "heavenly and divine love" (*erōs*). So it is not surprising that one of Philo's most mystical and profound passages about the One who reveals himself through the two Powers of Justice and Mercy is presented as an allegory of verses from the Psalms of David, especially from the verse "There is a cup in the hand of the Lord full of unmixed wine, mixed." [95] Quite as was to be expected, then, Philo called David a *thespios* man, which means one who is superhuman to the point of being divine. Philo quotes the Psalms more often than any books in the Bible except those of Moses, and it seems to me important that he quotes them only in his most deeply allegorical writings designed for those who understand his mystic language. I should guess he is drawing here upon the ritual of his synagogue, which then, as ever since in both Judaism and Christianity, has made constant

---

87. *Synagogue*, 224 f. The lion, he argues, having been put in earlier, as the Lion of Judah, had no relation to the Orpheus figure.

88. See the references in Ginzberg, *Legends*, VI, 249, n. 24.

89. See ibid., VI, 262, n. 81.

90. *Conf.* 149; cf. Acts XVI, 25.

91. *Agr.* 50; *Heres* 290.

92. *Conf.* 39.

93. *Som.* II, 245.

94. *Plant.* 39.

95. *Immut.* 74–81; Ps. LXXIV (LXXV), 8. The complete contradiction of the LXX translation made it possible for Philo to interpret the verse as meaning that the pure Monad represented the ultimate, inherent, character of Godhead, but that it presented itself in a plurality of God and his two Powers, the Three.

use of the devotional language of the Psalms. The Qumran sect also had a book of psalms for its devotions, one largely composed of the more mystical phrases of the Psalms of David.

In the economy of symbols, however, we cannot limit the explanation of a scene to *an* explanation. If, as I believe, the mystic musician was primary and his identification with David secondary, the Orpheus figure could also have referred to other singers, and indeed to the saving value of harmony and song in itself. Methodologically, such a further step is dangerous, for it can easily take one into a sort of allegory as far from anything in the artist's or donor's mind as Philo's allegories often are from the literal meaning of the biblical text. Kraeling demands economy of explanation,[96] and, stopping at the simplest possible interpretation, takes that very simplicity to witness its verity and sufficiency. Such a procedure belies the nature of all symbolic expression. The intricacies of this design, made up of the tree, table, cushion, and bread, the lions with the crater, and the Three at the top—to say nothing of Orpheus and the animals—all put over the niche for the Torah, seem projected from minds desiring to speak a symbolic language, not to express economically literal denotation. For the design as a whole patently denotes nothing historically or biblically objective, and it is the design as a whole we must always have in mind in evaluating its parts. Possibly there was some relation in symbolism through a common ancestor to the verses where the Christian Apocalyptist (Rev. v, 5–7; xxii, 16) calls the Redeemer before the heavenly Throne the "lion of the tribe of Judah" and the "Root of David."

When I discussed Orpheus in the vine in an earlier volume,[97] I pointed out, first, that although Dura has preserved the only Orpheus playing to animals in Jewish remains, the lyre or harp was a favorite symbol on the coins of the Bar Kokba revolt,[98] often shown with a bunch of grapes on the reverse. When the Dura artist combined Dionysiac symbols with Orpheus playing to animals in the tree-vine, he may well have been spelling out a familiar Jewish idea reflected also on these coins.

I find it strange, accordingly, that in discussing the scene, my predecessors have identified the singer with David (naturally, but arbitrarily) and then been content to search in Jewish literature for references to David the singer. These references are important, and we shall return to them. But one would more naturally begin by looking in Jewish literature for references to Orpheus himself, or for adaptations of Orphic literature. These I mentioned in an earlier volume of the series, but since the only scholar who alluded to the passage in reviewing that volume quite misunderstood what I was saying, I must here expand that discussion.[99]

Aristobulus, the hellenized precursor of Philo, quotes at considerable length an Orphic poem, in which, he admits, he has made some changes. Fortunately we are able to see exactly what he has done, since the same verses are preserved in apparently their

96. For example, in *Synagogue*, 213.
97. See above, V, 103–111.
98. Ibid., 105, and fig. 115.

99. H. Stern, "The Orpheus in the Synagogue of Dura-Europos," *Journal of the Warburg and Courtauld Institutes*, XXI (1958), 1–6. See my comments, ibid., XXII (1959), 372.

original pagan form as a quotation from the tract *Testamenta* of Orpheus.[100] This work of Orpheus, says the author of the Pseudo-Justinian *De monarchia* (II), introduced three hundred and sixty gods; but

> he [Orpheus] appears to repent of his error in that he wrote the following: [101]
>
> I speak to those who lawfully may hear:
> Depart and close the doors all ye profane.
> But thou, Musaeus, child of the bright moon,[102]
> Lend me thine ear; for I have truths to tell.
> Let not the former fancies of thy mind
> Deprive thee of the blessed number ten.[103]
> But look unto the Word divine, and fix
> In him your mind. The intelligible sphere
> Of your own heart set straight; tread well
> The Road; look only on creation's Lord.
> One he is, the Self-Begotten: all
> Begotten things arise from One; he
> Towers up above creation. No mortal eye
> May pierce to him, yet he himself sees all.
> He from his goodness gives to mortals evil,
> Sending both chilling wars and tearful griefs;
> And other than the great King there is none.
> Yet him I cannot see, for clouds forever
> Gird him round about; and mortal eyes
> Have only mortal eyeballs, weak, too weak
> To see great Zeus reigning over all.
> He sits established in the brazen heavens,
> Upon his golden throne; he plants his feet
> On the broad earth, and stretches his right hand

100. The material has been tentatively analyzed by L. Cerfaux, "Influence des Mystères sur le Judaisme alexandrin avant Philon," *Muséon*, XXXVII (1924), 28–88, esp. 36–48, where earlier literature is discussed. Cerfaux calls this *Le hiéros logos juif*, but that seems too sweeping. In the Jewish Mystery the *hieros logos* was always the Scriptures. Cerfaux' article has merely touched the whole problem, not probed it. His treatment of Philo shows no sense of the material that could be marshaled, and his conclusion is accordingly of little value. But he has incidentally suggested many interesting points, which I am glad to be able to use.

101. The author of the Pseudo-Justinian *Cohortatio ad gentiles*, XV, introduces the same lines by saying: "Orpheus, who was as one might say

your most elaborate polytheist, and the first teacher, latterly proclaimed to his son Musaeus, and the other legitimate auditors concerning the one and only God." A few of the lines are quoted by Clement of Alexandria, *Stromata*, V, xiv, 123.

102. I have inserted here two introductory lines from *Cohortatio ad gentiles*, XV.

103. To translate *philē aiōn* "blessed number 10" seems a bit strained until one looks at Iamblichus, *Theolougumena arithmeticae*, 59, where it is stated that the Pythagoreans called the *aiōn* the 10, as a symbol of cosmic perfection. In the same passage the idea occurs that God *perigenētai* the cosmos. The figures throughout seem to me Pythagorean. The phrase really means that one's preconceptions must not hold one back from *perfection*.

To all the ends of ocean, and around
Tremble the mountain ranges and the streams,
The depths, too, of the blue and hoary sea.[104]

This fragment is in itself a very interesting Orphic piece, one that seems genuinely pagan. It is the sort of paganism, however, that one can recognize as what must have been adapted by mystic Judaism. God is the great ruler of all, utterly beyond creation in his being, but permeating all creation with his powerful rulership. He is invisible to mortals. Yet a Road leads to him, the Road of the Divine Logos or of the *kosmos noētos.* The reward is the perfection of the "dear aeon"—possibly, as I have dared to translate it, the number ten, or seven.

Now it must be recalled that Aristobulus, in quoting these verses, admits that he has made some changes in them. He actually says that he has taken out from them "the name of Zeus which runs through the poems; for it is to God that their thought is sent up, and for that reason I have so expressed it." Aristobulus has certainly cut out the name of Zeus! He has completely altered the fragment into a call to the Mystery of Moses. The lines must be quoted in his new redaction, with the new matter italicized for convenience:

I speak to those who lawfully may hear:
Depart, and close the doors, all ye profane,
Who flee the ordinances of the just,
The law divine announced to all mankind.
But thou, Musaeus, child of the bright moon,
Lend me thine ear; for I have truths to tell.
Let not the former fancies of thy mind
Deprive thee of the blessed number ten.
But look unto the Word divine, and fix
In him your mind. Direct your heart
To the intelligible sphere, tread well
The Road; *and have regard to him alone*
Who is the immortal Framer of the world:
For thus of him our ancient story speaks:
One he is, *the Perfect in himself,*
All else by him *made perfect.* Though he
Is *ever present* in his works, he yet
Remains by mortal eyes unseen, *by Mind*
Alone discerned. He from his store of good
Ne'er [105] sends dire evil down to mortal men.
Both love and hatred wait upon his steps
And war and pestilence and tearful grief:

104. Many of these lines are taken from the translations of Gifford, and of Reith in M. Dods, G. Reith, and B. Pratten, *The Writings of Justin Martyr and Athenagoras,* 1867 (Ante-Nicene Christian Library, II).

105. That God can be the cause of evil was frequently denied by Philo. It is interesting to see how Aristobulus has corrected this passage to make it accord with hellenized Jewish thought by inserting the negative.

For there is none but him. All other things
'Twere easy to behold, could'st thou but first
Behold himself: here present upon earth,
The footsteps and the mighty hand of God
Whene'er I see, I'll show them thee, my Son.
But him I cannot see, so dense a cloud
In tenfold darkness wraps our feeble sight.
Him as he rules no mortal could behold
Save one, a Chaldee sprout unique [*mounogenēs*] *from heaven:*
For he was skilled to mark the sun's bright path,
And how in equal circle round the earth
The starry sphere on its own axis turns,
And how the winds career o'er sea and sky;
And how the might of force-born fire shines forth.
But God, *in contrast, on high* [106] heaven unmoved
Sits on his golden throne, and plants his feet
On the broad earth; his right hand he extends
O'er ocean's farthest bound; *the eternal hills*
Tremble in their deep heart, nor can endure
His mighty force. Himself a heavenly being
In all respects, he perfects earthly things,
And is himself beginning, mean, and end.
So runs the story of the men of old,
So tells that man from Water born,
Taught by the two-fold tablet of God's Law,
Nor dare I otherwise of God to speak:
In heart and limbs I tremble at the thought,
How he from heaven all things in order rules.
Draw near in thought, my son; but guard thy tongue
With care, and store this doctrine in thy heart.[107]

A number of points at once become clear from this fragment. Orpheus is regarded as having drawn his mystery entirely from Moses, and as having dared, at the end, to teach nothing contrary to what Moses has learned from God and transmitted in the Torah. The Orphic ideology has been slightly toned down, but ever so slightly, and the teaching it embodied is ascribed to Moses. Abraham as the Chaldean sprout, the one who saw God ruling, strikingly recalls Philo's treatment of Abraham. The Patriarchs, the "Men of Old," with Moses at the head, are the sole revealers of the mystic doctrine of the Logos-Road to God. The mystic element is not toned down; rather the presentation of the account as a secret to be revealed only to Museus and those worthy to be associated with him is intensified by the closing lines, lacking in the original.

In presenting this material formerly [108] I have given analyses I need not repeat. But

---

106. Aristobulus has taken out the *bronze* heaven.   108. *By Light, Light,* 279–298.
107. Eusebius, *Praeparatio evangelica,* XIII, xii, 5.

other main passages should be quoted to show how highly Jews prized this demonstrably Orphic material. The Sibylline Books of the Jews, for example, while generally quite orthodox in their emphasis upon the literal Law of Judaism, have the following passage, which I have shown to be full of phrases from the Orphic original:

> Ye men who have the form of God, moulded in his likeness, why do you vainly wander and follow not the straight Road as ye bear always in mind the immortal Creator? God is One, the sole ruler, ineffable, dwelling in the ether, self-sprung, invisible himself but seeing all things. No stone carver's hand did make him, nor does some model formed from gold or ivory by the varied skill of man represent him. But he, himself eternal, hath revealed himself as One who is and was before, yea and shall be hereafter. For who being mortal can gaze on God with his eyes? Or who could bear to hear even the mere Name of the mighty heavenly God who rules the world? He by his Logos created all things, the heaven and the sea, the tireless sun and the full moon, the twinkling stars, mighty mother Tethys, springs and rivers, unquenchable fire, days and nights. He is the God who fashioned the tetragram Adam, the first man fashioned, who completes in his name east and west, south and north. He too fashioned the form of mortal men and made the beasts and things that creep and fly.[109]

There can be no question at all that the Jewish Sibylline forger, if he did not have the same Orphic poem before him, was following a definite Orphic convention of description of God. He, like Aristobulus, is making Jewish changes and insertions. But the passage belongs to that type of Judaism represented by Aristobulus, a Judaism which was drawing heavily upon Orphic sources for its basic conceptions, and was patently revising Orphic texts to make Jewish mystic utterances. For both Aristobulus and the Sibyl the true Road was the looking to a superficially Judaized version of the God of the Orphic mystery. A Sibylline fragment that seems certainly Jewish is again worth quoting entire:

> Ye mortal men and fleshly, who are naught,
> How quickly are ye puffed up, seeing not
> The end of life. Do ye not tremble now
> And fear God, him who watches over you,
> The One who is most high, the One who knows,
> The all-observant witness of all things.
> All-nourishing Creator, who has put
> In all things his sweet Spirit and has made
> Him leader of all mortals? God is One;
> Who rules alone, supremely great, unborn.
> Almighty and invisible, himself
> Alone beholding all things, but not seen
> Is he himself by any mortal flesh.
> For what flesh is there able to behold
> With eyes the heavenly and true God divine,
> Who has his habitation in the sky?

109. *Sibylline Oracles*, III, 8–28; ed. J. Geffcken, 1902, 46–48 (*GCS*).

Not even before the bright rays of the sun
Can men stand still, men who are mortal born,
Existing but as veins and flesh on bones.
Him who alone is ruler of the world,
Who alone is forever and has been
From everlasting, reverence ye him,
The self-existent unbegotten One
Who rules all things through all time, dealing out
Unto all mortals in a common light
The judgment. And the merited reward
Of evil counseling shall ye receive.
For ceasing the true and eternal God
To glorify, and holy hecatombs
To offer him, ye made your sacrifice
Unto the demons that in Hades dwell.
And ye in self-conceit and madness walk,
And having left the true, straightforward path
Ye went away and roamed about through thorns
And thistles. O ye foolish mortals, cease
Roving in darkness and black night obscure,
And leave the darkness of night, and lay hold
Upon the Light. Lo he is clear to all
And cannot err; come, do not always chase
Darkness and gloom. Lo, the sweet-looking light
Of the sun shines with a surpassing glow.
Now, treasuring Wisdom in your hearts, know ye
That God is One, who sends forth rains and winds,
And mournful cares, and storms of snow, and ice.
But why do I thus speak them one by one?
He guides heaven, rules earth, himself exists.[110]

Again we are in the Orphic atmosphere of the other passages, and it is conspicuous that, unless we have documents mutually dependent, the ideas are definitely conventionalized. The familiar "himself invisible, he sees all things" reappears, again elaborated with reference to the weakness of human eyes of flesh. On this an interesting variant appears in the form of the question: How could human eyes see God when they cannot even gaze upon the sun? The implication that God is a light brighter than the sun is warranted by what follows.

New in emphasis is the fact that the Road is the Light of God, in contrast to the common light of the sun, a "darkness." But the Orphic Phanes,[111] discussed above, shows that the idea is still purely Orphic, while the whole plan of the poetic fragment is in general only a metrical variant of the Orphic original of Aristobulus. With this are two other new

110. Quoted in Terry's translation: M. S. Terry, *The Sibylline Oracles*, 1899, 257–259.

111. See *By Light, Light*, 284, n. 91.

elements, the "sweet spirit" and "Sophia." "God has put his sweet Spirit in all things and made it the leader of all mortals." One's instant reaction is to suggest "Stoic influence," and perhaps that explanation is the true one. But it has no certainty. The Stoics did not invent the word *pneuma* and I do not recall a case where the one God of all is said by Stoics to have put his Spirit into all things. God is himself the Spirit in Stoicism. Furthermore, the mystic suggestion that the Spirit is the Guide of mortals is not Stoic. The *pneuma* seems here a variant of the Orphic Phanes, since an early Christian text tells us that the Orphics made that identification directly.[112] One recalls further the Orphic couplet: "Men complete all things through the mighty help of the immortal God, through the wise impulse of the Spirit." [113]

From Ezekiel, the tragic poet of Judaism, we have also a few relevant lines. He describes an extraordinary vision which Moses had when he was an exile in Midian. He seemed to see on Sinai a great Throne reaching to heaven upon which was a man of noble countenance wearing a diadem and holding a scepter in his left hand. The Throne, except that it is now placed on Sinai, is exactly the divine Throne we have met in the Orphic fragment. We have not left the Orphic atmosphere at all, though Moses is being assimilated into the conception as not even Aristobulus had done. For, according to Ezekiel, God, the great king, with his right hand beckoned Moses to come and take his place on the throne, to make which possible the great King himself descended. Indeed the King even gave Moses his diadem and scepter. From this seat the entire cosmos was opened to Moses' view, the circle of earth, the regions under the earth, and the heavens above. The stars came in a great host to do obeisance at his knees. As he counted them he awoke.[114]

Here is unmistakably the divine kingship of Moses set forth, a kingship not only over men but over the entire cosmos. He is in the place of God! His father-in-law interprets the dream for him, explaining that it means he is to be a great king, the judge and guide of mortals, with vision of the past, present, and future.[115] Ezekiel has indeed shown us a mystic origin for Philo's kingship of Moses. The conception of God has come directly from Orphic sources,[116] and the conception is, as Cerfaux has pointed out, that of the astral mystery of Egypt. Moses' nature is taken up to associate itself with the nature of the stars. One recalls Philo's description of the ascent of Moses, in which Moses' supreme moment was when he was united with the heavenly beings and bodies in the great hymn of the cosmos to God.[117] It is quite to be expected that the symbolic representation of Moses with the heavenly bodies should reappear in the iconography.

Artapanus, likewise of the second century B.C., tells us still more of the elaboration of Moses in Orphic terms, and brings in for the first time specifically Egyptian motifs. He tells us that Moses was called by the Greeks Musaeus. He was the teacher of Orpheus, and

112. Clement of Rome, *Homilies*, VI, 5; O. Kern, *Orphicorum Fragmenta*, 1922, 134, fr. 56.

113. Didymus Alexandrinus, *De trinitate*, II, 27; Kern, fr. 340. The date is indeterminable.

114. Eusebius, *Praeparatio evangelica*, IX, XXIX (440A–C).

115. Ibid., 440C.

116. Cerfaux, in *Muséon*, XXXVII (1924), 55, has some interesting remarks upon the solar mysticism of the vision.

117. See *By Light, Light*, 196 f., and below, pp. 116–118.

when he had grown up he taught men many things. "For he invented ships, and machines for laying stones, and Egyptian arms, and contrivances for irrigation and for war; and he invented philosophy."

Hellenized Jews obviously admired the figure and teachings of Orpheus so much that they deliberately adapted passages from his poems for Jewish purposes, and even consciously identified various Jewish heroes with him. The Throne in the Dura reredos which appears as the Triad now makes sense as the Throne of God, which man cannot bear to see as One; Orpheus in the vine below such a King is quite to be expected. We cannot say that the figure on the Throne is God or Moses; or that the Orpheus figure represents Moses as David; or that the Jews at Dura thought that the King was God himself as the Triad; but this will present no difficulties to those who have freed themselves from modern conventions of thinking, and can accept the fluidity of ancient allegories and identifications. It is chiefly important to recognize that whatever the identifications intended by the painter, the Orpheus and King together would have indicated the sense of this mystic ascent, an idea in which all the fragments unite.

It seems relevant, finally, to recall Philo's idea that the properly functioning soul becomes an organ in whose mighty voice all music is united, though its sound can be perceived by God alone, who is the musician *noētos*—that is, the musician who exists in the world of forms, or is capable of hearing noetic music. This applies especially to Moses in his conversation with God on Sinai.[118] Similarly, when God spoke to his people from the Mount "he fashioned a sound in the air more marvellous than all [musical] instruments, harmonized into perfect harmonies . . . [which was] a speaking [or reasoning, *logikē*] soul . . . a flaming fire . . . that sounded out like breath (*pneuma*) through a trumpet." [119] It is easy to see that Philo is fancifully expressing here his doctrine of the Logos of God, and presenting it as a divine music heard at once everywhere.

The saving song which is at once the *pneuma* in a trumpet and the *pneuma* lyre of David reappears in Coptic Christian magical incantations which seem to me to be Christian adaptations of a Jewish original.[120] For in a series of charms David, or his magical counterpart Davithea, is addressed as "David, who sits above the cup or the church of the first-born." In another charm he "sings psalms in the church of the first-born of heaven," and "plays his lyre (*kitharē*) of ten strings behind the veil of the altar of joy." In still another, Davithea is

> the speach of the angel, the voice of the archangel, the vision (*ephorasia*) of the heavenly, the hymn of the Father. . . . He lies upon the bed of the tree of life and holds in his right hand the golden plectrum, in his left the *pneuma*-lyre as he assembles all the angels to hail the Father.

Kropp goes on to point out parallels in this literature and in the Didache and Clement of Alexandria, where the Eucharist is the blood of the Vine of David. We should hardly have

118. *Heres* 15–19.
119. *Decal.* 32–35.
120. In what follows I am digesting the inter-

pretation of the extraordinary material in A. M. Kropp, *Ausgewälte koptische Zaubertexte*, 1930, III, 33–39.

been justified in assuming from this literature that all of this is a gnostic-Christian adaptation of a mystic-Jewish conception of the harmony of God made available in the harmony offered by Judaism, especially in the mystic singing of David, but also in a tree of life that is the vine with a saving cup. But now such a possibility is definitely opened by this reredos painting, where it is presumably David who, as Orpheus, plays his music and tames birds and beasts in the great tree-vine that leads up to the Throne of the Three, but has the bread and wine at its base.

Those who know Judaism must be surprised that I have hitherto not alluded to the great tradition of the Throne in Jewish mysticism. This was because the method I am using demanded that I begin with the details represented, and nothing in Jewish Throne-mysticism that I know suggests either that the Throne should be a Triad or that Orpheus had any relation to it. In discussing the reredos more briefly in an earlier volume, however, I did show awareness that such a relation was possible, and quoted Scholem as saying, "The earliest Jewish mysticism is Throne-mysticism." [121] The statement is accurate only if one ignores Philo and the other sources for hellenistic Jewish mysticism; but when he goes on to say that the Throne-world is to the Jewish mystic what the pleroma, with all its various descriptions, is to hellenistic Christian, gnostic, and hermetic mystics,[122] he is entirely right. So far as we can gather, while the documents for this mysticism are from later citations, the mysticism itself actually flourished at its height during the second and third centuries—that is, precisely at the time when the painting was made. The famous Metatron may indeed personalize this Throne-mysticism.[123] Of this we cannot be sure, but of the Throne-mysticism itself there is no possible doubt.

Whence it came into Judaism, however, or how it arose has not been ascertained at all. The reredos suggests to me strongly that it may have been adopted by mystic Jews, mystic rabbinic Jews, from such hellenized speculation as I have been examining. Faced with the emphasis upon the Trinity by Christians, the presentation of the Throne as a Triad, would quickly have been abandoned, if, as seems likely, it originally existed in such mysticism. Its complete absence from the fourth- and fifth-century Jewish documents which Scholem chiefly quotes, accordingly, would by no means certify that it had not been in the original form of the rabbinic Throne-mysticism, just as it is in Philo's mysticism. We must never imagine that our utterly fragmentary and disconnected evidence will lead us adequately to understand what lay behind the Dura pictures. There, at least, the Throne is the Triad, and we must leave the possibility clearly open that this Throne-Triad may have had much more relation to the current Jewish Throne-mysticism than we can demonstrate. For here, with its Triad and Orpheus, it still presents its hellenized form.

---

121. See above, V, 108–110.

122. I quoted this passage in full, above, V, 109.

123. Scholem, *Jewish Mysticism*, 68 f., recalls that this derivation has been suggested, but he considers it impossible. S. Lieberman has written me, however, that *ho meta tou thronou* or the like would naturally have been contracted into the single word in Hebrew, and that he does not exclude the possibility that this occurred. But since we have no positive evidence that it did, the word, he thinks, remains a *vox mystica*.

In seeing all this possibly inherent in the design I feel myself only supplementing, not basically discarding, Kraeling's, Grabar's, and H. Stern's notion that the whole refers to Israel's eschatological and messianic hopes.[124] We have seen throughout this study that mysticism is in its true sense "realized eschatology." In the mystic experience one is caught up like Paul and the writers of the Apocalypses into the presence of God, or one experiences in this life the unity and fellowship with God into which the mass of men hope to come only after death. The difference between Jewish mysticism and Jewish messianic eschatology is essentially that in eschatology the cosmic as well as the personal transition is stressed, the destruction of the bad in all men along with the universal achievement of the good. Fig. 74, with its sacraments at the base, its great tree-ladder, the saving means of divine music and harmony—all leading to the Three at the top—present a scheme of salvation that need not await any "far off, divine event." It was to be consummated for everyone in the heavenly future, to be sure, but the design represented what those who painted it thought Judaism offered both here and hereafter to the faithful. The design, let me repeat, stood upon the Torah niche which contained the basic symbol of Judaism, the Torah itself. Out of this root all the rest of the tree grows.

E. THE FINAL DESIGN

THE DESIGN, however, did not yet satisfy those who were directing its execution. From the changes next made I can suppose only that when brought to this stage it seemed to them not sufficiently Jewish. As I have described it, and as Gute has drawn it for fig. 74, the design could have stood before a group worshiping Sabazius, Dionysus, or almost any other pagan deity where bread and wine were used to get a spiritual harmony that was the harmony of the tree of life, the cosmos, and led to the throne of God. The Torah beneath the painting, and the Jewish emblems over the niche, made the religion of the room definitely Jewish. But while everything in the painting above these could be given a Jewish explanation, the painting itself had not yet been made specifically so.

It is tempting to suppose that such a conscious purpose prompted all the further decoration of the synagogue, in which, as I think can be shown, the mystic value of Judaism was spelled out by interpretative scenes from the Scriptures. Whatever prompted the whole scheme of decoration, however, the latest alterations in the reredos clearly only Judaized it. For the tree-vine was left, with Orpheus and the animals in the middle, to lead man to the Three at the top. But the crater with felines and the table with bolster and bread beneath the tree-vine were now painted out with the red cover-coat, and the upper part of the vine at either side of the Three was also eliminated. All four walls were now to be divided into bands or registers of painting, and the reredos, which reached the top of the paintings, now actually was the width of two registers. The reredos was accordingly divided across the middle by the border ornament used to separate paintings on all the walls. The line came just above the lion and Orpheus, and just below the two

---

124. See above, p. 89, and V, 110, n. 75.

Throne Mates, so that the space between these, I should guess, determined the line of division between registers across the wall, just as the line of the top of the niche determined another division. Artistically the unity of the tree-vine was thereby lost, but since the vine and the Orpheus group were left below the division and the Three remained in the vine above it, the audience would still have felt the relation of the two scenes.[125]

In place of the wine and bread symbols of the old design two groups of figures were introduced, about whose identity no one, to my knowledge, has any doubt. The type of scene is familiar from paganism: it is that of a funerary banquet of a father on the couch, surrounded by his sons or followers. Fig. 90 shows the type on a relief from Smyrna.[126] The scene at Dura, however, like so many we shall see, adapts this type, or follows an earlier adaptation of it, to fit it to a biblical scene. For here a man in the same Greek robe as that worn above by the Throne Mates reclines upon a bed with a stool or table before it.[127] He sits half upright, leaning upon a cushion with his left elbow. Behind him stand twelve smaller figures in caftan and trousers. In spite of the black hair of the man on the couch, and the beardless young face, we may presume with all other observers that Jacob here lies on his deathbed blessing his twelve sons. Balancing this figure at the right of the tree trunk Jacob again appears in the same way upon the bed, this time with a man at the right bringing in two boys who stand directly in front of Jacob. The man seems to be Joseph in caftan and trousers again, but with a sword apparently to indicate his political power; so that Jacob can bless them he brings in his two sons, who wear Greek striped chitons.[128] The two scenes together quite confirm the identification of each. It is usually forgotten that by this extra blessing the twelve tribes were made actually thirteen. The odd tribe, Levi, got no division of land, and in the Wilderness the Levites marched with the Ark to guard it, while six tribes marched behind and six before them.

These two paintings clearly stem from a tradition of Old Testament illustration, for Christian art offers many parallels to them. For example, fig. 91 [129] shows Jacob in the same position, the boys again in Greek chitons. Joseph wears Greek dress but not the formal Greek chiton and himation, and his dress is replaced at Dura by the Iranian caftan and trousers. Fig. 92 [130] shows Jacob blessing, or prophesying to, the thirteen tribes, with Joseph in royal robe, fillet, and halo at the center. Jacob wears what is still recognizably the Greek robe of splendor, with the clavus very distinct over his shoulder, though

125. There seems to me good reason to suppose that this division may have been earlier, and that Orpheus, who with his animals fits so neatly beneath the line of division, was put in after that line had been drawn, so that Gute's drawing, fig. 74, should show the line. In any case, the changes were otherwise as indicated above.

126. Courtesy of the Rijksmuseum van Oudheden, Leiden, Holland. Cf. E. Pfuhl in *JDAI*, XX (1905), 136, fig. 27; 137, fig. 28, and the parallels cited in his notes.

127. In Christian art a stool appears twice in these scenes of blessing: *Vienna Genesis*, plates XLV f.;

British Museum, *A Guide to the Early Christian and Byzantine Antiquities*, comp. O. M. Dalton, 2d ed., 1921, 64, plate v.

128. Kraeling, *Synagogue*, 222, says that Joseph's right arm goes across to the farther boy's head, but I can see nothing in Gute's painting or the photograph to justify this. The two scenes appear most clearly in fig. 93.

129. From *Smyrna Octateuch*, fig. 144. See also the *Vienna Genesis*, loc. cit.; and the new example just published from the Catacomb Via Latina: see Ferrua, *Via Latina*, plate xxv.

130. From *Smyrna Octateuch*, fig. 146.

the form of the bed has become medieval. The thirteen heads of the tribes, who at Dura wear caftan and trousers, preserve the contrast to Jacob by wearing the medieval peasant's or shepherd's dress. In all these details the Christian version of the paintings has probably been altered as much from what must be presumed to be the Jewish original as is the Dura rendering. But too much is alike in the two to have come from anything but a common original.

With reference to the thirteen tribes established by the lower scene in this final design of the reredos, the thirteen tribes were inserted into the upper painting. They stand on either side of the Three, still in their caftan and trousers. The painting now seems to tell us of the ultimate glory of Israel, who from their blessing ascend the ladder of the tree-vine with the help of the divine music to take their places beside the Throne. The whole is more obviously the apocalyptic Judaism so abundantly preserved to us. The forms of presentation vary in the apocalyptic books, but all these documents look toward exactly this sort of eventuality.[131] It may be that the double scene of identification of the thirteen was inspired by the donor, who, if himself a Levite, wanted his tribe specifically represented in the final scene.

Again, however, bearing in mind the dangers of a single explanation, we recall that for Philo "Israel" meant both an individual, "He who sees God," and a people, the "race that sees God." The true Israel was a matter not of racial descent but of the mystic vision, so that a gentile who achieved it was reckoned a true Israelite, above an unperceptive Jew.[132] Philo speaks of the "race endowed with vision which is called Israel" as "journeying along the royal road" to God.[133] "He [Israel] that sees God, drawn to him by his surpassing beauty, has received the lot and share of the one seen." [134] The painting in its final form may well be described in the words of Philo when he discusses the Jewish people as a royal, priestly, and holy race.

> Its name indicates its power; for in the Hebrew language the race is called "Israel" which is to be translated as "he who sees God." Sight such as we have through the eyes is the fairest of all sense experiences, since by it alone we apprehend the fairest things that exist, the sun and moon and the whole heaven and universe. But sight as it is effected through the leading part of the soul, namely mind which is the eye of the intelligence, surpasses its other faculties.[135] A man may rest assured that he has reached the acme of happiness when he has come not only to apprehend through knowledge the various phenomena of nature, but even to see the Father and Creator of all things.[136] For nothing

131. The most familiar is the version of the tradition in the last chapters of the Christian Revelation to John. There, in xxii, 1–5, the Throne (cf. xx, 11; xxi, 5) is beside the tree of life, whose leaves are for the healing of the nations, and God's servants worship before him.

132. See my *By Light, Light,* 177–179, 353 f.

133. *Immut.* 144.

134. *Post.* 92; cf. *LA* iii, 186.

135. Philo's terminology in such connections leaves much to be desired. Here he says that

phronēsis is the sight of the *dianoia;* in a parallel passage, *Immut.* 45 f., it is *nous* that is the eye (*opsis*) of the *psuchē.* Translation becomes correspondingly difficult. In his note to the latter passage, III, 484, in the Loeb series, Colson traces the idea to Aristotle and to an earlier anonymous philosopher whom Aristotle quotes.

136. This reflects a Platonic ascent from *phronēsis* to *epistēmē;* the ultimate vision of God quite beyond *epistēmē* is a Neoplatonic addition.

is higher than God, and if any man has so extended the vision of his mind as to reach to God, he should pray to stand there, permanently. For the roads that lead upward are toilsome and slow, but a rushing descent, in which one seems not to go but to be swept down, is swift and easy. Many are the forces that would drag us down, but none of them can prevail when God suspends the soul from his Powers, and draws it to himself by a more powerful force.[137]

Philo, as often, has suddenly shifted his figure. From vision of God, which again includes the Powers, the mystic has come to be ascending a road to God. When he has reached the top, God gives him *monē* and *stasis*, "endurance" and "stance," which I have paraphrased rather weakly as ability to stand there permanently.

Quite in accord with this conception, the final stage of the painting has presented us with the tree of life which is the road to God. At the foot of the tree were originally the bread and wine by which man may rise to the divine harmony and to the Three, the Logos and Powers, the highest vision of the One possible for man. This scheme was later changed only to show that the path, the tree, the harmony are the special privilege of Israel; for, blessed at the bottom by a Patriarch wearing the white robe of a man of God on earth, Israel can go up to stand permanently beside the Throne with the Powers. In this final achievement the painting shows the triumph of Judaism. From the New Testament, from Early Christian usage, and from the change of robes which we shall see in other paintings in the synagogue, we should have expected that the thirteen tribes would have stood beside the throne in white garments such as the Patriarch wears below and the Throne Mates above. Their being in the Persian dress when glorified beside the throne will need explanation.

Such is the impression we get from the series of alterations made in the painting of the reredos tree-vine, and from casual bits of information in the midrashic tradition. The scene as a whole still perplexes us. What could have inspired this painting with all these details? Clearly nothing quoted from either Philo or the rabbis to this point does more than throw possible light on one or another detail. Fortunately one great allegory of Philo does much more than illuminate details, for in it almost every detail of the painting appears, as well as much that could not be put into a single design.[138] We cannot, of course, here go into all points of the allegory, although the reader would do well to stop and read it entire. But we must present at least an outline of the argument.

The allegory purports to be based upon the biblical statement that Noah planted a vineyard, but it at once goes on to the "plants set in the universe," and God their great Planter. The cosmos is itself the prime plant, and in it all living things are branches. Philo is clearly substituting the great tree or plant for the cosmic "animal" of the *Timaeus*,[139] and in its construction, according to Philo as to Plato, the Creator used up the total supply of the four elements.[140] This tree stands in empty space upon "the eternal Logos of the ever-

---

137. *Abr.* 57–59.
138. The allegory is in *Plant.* 1–72.
139. Plato, *Timaeus*, 30B–D. The change is por-

tentous, for the Gospel of John (xv, 1–8) also had a great Vine (the Logos), of which we are branches.

140. *Plant.* 2–8; cf. the same use of elements in *Timaeus*, 32C.

lasting God," [141] which also is the bond, permeating the tree and holding its elements together.[142]

For those not familiar with Philo's method this allegory of the tree in terms of the *Timaeus* is illuminating. Clearly Philo feels himself committed alike to the biblical text and to Plato's metaphysics, with Stoic elements freely added. The combination, the cosmic tree, will seem ridiculous to Platonists, and to biblical students a far cry from the tree of life of Genesis. But Philo, like religious spirits ever since, is content, for he has justified to himself his holding metaphysical ideas by stating them in biblical terms, however far-fetched.

The allegory becomes increasingly tortuous as Philo goes on to make not only all other trees but all animals, especially man, into branches of this cosmic tree-vine of Eden or Noah. Man has a distinct power of vision—physically by means of his eyes, which unlike other animals are cast up to the heavens, but also, more importantly, by means of his mind which enables him to see metaphysical reality, and so become aware of the vine as a whole and of its great Being at the top. Consequently his soul becomes filled with *erōs*, like the proper soul in the *Phaedrus*,[143] and grows wings so that he tries to go up the tree to Reality (*to on*), or the One without Beginning (*ho agenētos*).[144] This craving, *erōs*, is directed toward Wisdom (*sophia*), and one who "philosophizes genuinely" can achieve the goal.[145] Actually only Moses, "the keeper and guardian of the rites (*orgia*) of the Existent One," has ever soared to the top, and "been allotted to produce not [rational objects that are only] shadows [of the forms] but the actual archetypes of objects." [146] One like Bezalel who follows Moses' instructions—that is, one who has access to the forms not directly but through Moses' intervention and revelation—can reach only a secondary place, produce only imitations of the original forms. But that is a high place indeed. The reader will recall that Bezalel made the tabernacle and holy cultic objects according to Moses' instructions and models. Philo returns shortly to this unique place and achievement of Moses.

Meanwhile, Philo's allegory goes on to the trees of the Garden more specifically. He names several of them, but they are all, really, only the original two, the tree of knowledge of good and evil, and the tree of life,[147] for all of these trees are paths to life and immortality.[148] Especially, we suddenly are told, David exemplifies this, since he was a member of Moses' thiasos, who summons us to delight in the Lord—that is, to a frenzy described in Bacchic terms where man finds his gladness in God alone.[149] A digression points out that God does not need ferocious animals to guard his possessions, and he put none in the Garden. But earthly man does have such animals in his body, the passions, just as irra-

---

141. *Plant.* 8.

142. Ibid. 9 f.

143. Plato, *Phaedrus*, 255B–D.

144. *Plant.* 22.

145. Ibid. 23 f.

146. Ibid. 26 f. Philo almost makes Moses the original Logos that created the forms. In the next

sentence, however, God seems only to have shown them to Moses.

147. Ibid. 36.

148. Ibid. 37.

149. Ibid. 39. Philo denies the literal orgies, obviously to imply their concomitant in mystical "frenzy."

tional animals were put into Noah's ark, which symbolized the body.[150] Clearly these must be tamed in man, and Philo implies here what he so often says, that mystic achievement is possible only for a man in whom the wild animals of passion have been tamed. Man as he was originally created (in the first chapter of Genesis) had no body, and so was put directly into Eden, "stamped with the spirit which is after the image of God," and was himself the tree of life.[151] But the man who was created from the dust of the earth has a body, and must choose whether he will go up or down to life or death.[152] Moses prays that the "people endowed with sight" may be replanted in the place whence physical Adam, the earthly mind, was banished.[153] He prays for this to happen in the petition that we be "planted in the mountain of thy inheritance." [154] Moses wants us not to become "irrational and unruly in our natures," but to attain to a power to live according to nature.[155] So Philo can paraphrase Moses' prayer that we be "planted in the mountain of thy inheritance":

> Like children just beginning to learn, introduce us by the teachings of wisdom and the things shown to us, and do not leave us ignorant of the first elements, but plant us in the high and heavenly Logos.[156]

To be introduced into the sacred teaching and given sight of the sacred objects was the stock description of initiation into the mystery religions of the day. By initiation into the Jewish mystery, in whatever sense, according to Philo we become planted, engrafted, in the Logos, the tree of the universe, and so become slaves of the supreme One who is "Sovereign for ever and ever." [157] "Neverceasing slavery before thee is better not only than freedom, but than the greatest sovereignty." [158]

Ordinary people who make the mystic ascent, accordingly, can hope only that at the end they will be slaves at the throne of God. The four great ones, of whom Moses is the supreme exemplar, have a special place, but Philo explains that the "People Israel became the portion of the Lord," [159] as Moses said in his great Song before he died, a song that will seem of the greatest importance to us shortly.[160]

The connection of this allegory with the reredos painting seems so intimate and detailed that it is hard to believe it was not actual. By this I do not mean that the "philosopher" at Dura was necessarily working with Philo's text literally in hand or in mind. But such elaborate similarity indicates relationship, and the less one takes the painting to imply direct knowledge of Philo's writing, or close kinship to him, the more one is driven to acknowledge a very generalized tradition of the Philonic type of thinking among hellenized Jews. The painting and the allegory both present the tree-vine as the basic fact in the relation of God with man and the universe. The tree is the cosmos, built upon and infused with the Logos, in which all the elements are contained, and all plants and ani-

150. Ibid. 41–43.
151. Ibid. 44.
152. Ibid. 45.
153. Ibid. 46.
154. Ibid. 47; Exod. xv, 17 f.

155. *Plant.* 50, 53.
156. Ibid. 52.
157. Ibid. 53–58.
158. Ibid. 53.
159. Ibid. 59; Deut. xxxii, 9.
160. See below, pp. 116–118.

mals are branches. The idea is clearly that to which Jesus, the Logos in the Fourth Gospel, is made to allude when he says, "I am the true vine, you are the branches." At the top is God himself, and man has the unique power of perceiving this celestial reality beyond creation, so that he grows wings, and soars up to it. In the thiasos, when this occurs, David teaches men the divine frenzy by which they tame the wild animals of their passions and so become able to rise to be servants at God's throne. This, precisely, the painting told us when it showed the tribes of Israel first blessed by Jacob who wears the sacred robe, and then rising, still in servants' robes, to stand beside the throne at the top of the tree. The great mystagogues, we shall see, wear the white robe, as do the Throne Mates. But the mass of Israelites, while they may ascend to the throne, do so through the mediation of the Patriarchs, especially of David and Moses, and remain servants before the Throne.

The first painting showed merely the tree growing from the vase, just as the cosmic tree of Philo rested upon the Logos. Then Orpheus-David was put in to quell the passions, and the Throne was inserted at the top to mark the goal of ascent through the tree. Perhaps at the same time the "tokens of bread and wine" were put beneath the tree, but on this the allegory of Philo throws no light at all. To show the tokens was not sufficient for those in the synagogue planning the reredos, however, so the ascent of Israel to be slaves at the Throne took its place. I cannot believe, however, that the "tokens" had not, when put in, a very specific reference to a cult act. In any case the painting ended completely on the note of Philo's allegory, the unique achievement of true Israel—that is, of mystic Israel. I strongly suspect that the underpainting came through and blurred the overpainting because the first paint was not fully dry when the new paint was put over it. This would imply, if true, that the composition was worked out by concentrated trial and error for symbolic effect, and was not a series of casual and fanciful additions and embellishments.

F. THE FOUR PORTRAITS

ONE THING highly important in Philo's allegory, namely the unique mystagogue, Moses, does not appear in the painting of the tree-vine, unless, as we cannot assume, it is Moses who sits on the throne at the top. The central painting seems to represent the salvation of Israel as a People. Apparently to compensate this, the artist put up four portraits, two on either side of the reredos proper, so placed that they form an integral part of the central design. Kraeling calls them wing panels, plate v, fig. 93.

Each of these portrait panels presents a single full-length figure clothed in the white Greek robe. Not only does their position declare their importance, but also the fact that they are the only individual portraits in the room. In view of the care with which the symbolism of the central painting of the reredos was evolved, it must be presumed that the subjects of these portraits were selected with more than random attention.

All observers have agreed that the four constitute a series beginning at the upper right of fig. 93—that is, the hero in plate v and fig. 325. Of his identity no one has ever had any doubt. He stands in the Greek dress we have seen on the Throne Mates and on Jacob in the central painting. He has brown hair and beard, and his clavi are clearly drawn, as well as the marks on his himation which we shall follow Christian convention in calling the gams.[161] Three threads extend down from the corner of the himation. Beside his bare feet stand his high boots, and he gestures with his right hand toward a bush beside him, filled with red strokes through the green leaves. The right hand [162] of God above the bush in the upper left corner indicates divine intervention. At the level of his head a broad band runs across the scene, but is broken so that his head is framed in a square background. The device gives the hero a square halo of the type more distinctly to be recognized in the two lower panels. In presence of all these details we should not have needed the words "Moses, son of Levi" [163] in Aramaic at the right of the figure's shoulder to identify him as Moses at the burning bush. It is the only label on any of the four portraits. While it is familiar in the biblical account of his birth that Moses was "son of Levi" by both his father and mother, as Torrey points out its being mentioned here would seem designed to "emphasize the priestly origin of Moses," that is, his priestly character. Rabbinic writings frequently discuss his having been forbidden the priestly office, and accordingly, while they comment upon his temporary priestly functions, do not ordinarily use the term "priest" for him. Much is made of Moses as intercessor and mediator for his people, but in rabbinic writings Moses' powers of that sort were recalled almost entirely as he exercised them during his life. Yet in some places it would seem that Moses had a permanent ministry, at least of intercession. Ginzberg points out [164] that the souls of the pious are nearest to God, a little farther away are Mercy and Justice, but close to these stands Moses. Ginzberg notes [165] that the phrase "Moses the man of God" was occasionally interpreted to mean that Moses was half man and half God. Other interpretations of this phrase are also quoted by Ginzberg, but he especially notices that this one resembles Philo's statements about the character of Moses. Certainly Philo makes more of this conception than do the rabbis, as has appeared and will soon appear again.

Philo saw a special event indeed in God's appearance to Moses in the bush. It was the occasion on which God revealed himself to Moses as pure Being. So Philo interprets the Septuagint translation of "I am who I am." [166] The Greek, *egō eimi ho ōn*, means "I am he who exists," or "the existing one," a change which modern commentators have often considered a hellenistic reinterpretation by the Septuagint translators themselves long before Philo. To Philo, it meant that in this vision God revealed to Moses the difference between Being and Not-Being.[167] All things "after" God belong in the category of Not-Being in comparison to God as Being proper (*kata to einai*).[168] In commenting on this in another passage Philo leaves the personal masculine, and equates God with the purely abstract neuter, Being (*to on*).[169] As a result of this version, Moses very nearly becomes

161. See below, p. 162.

162. The impression that this is the left hand is removed by the carefully drawn fingernails, as in the hands with Ezekiel, figs. 348 f.

163. See Torrey in Kraeling, *Synagogue*, 271, inscription.

164. *Legends*, III, 107; see the references in VI, 44, n. 241.

165. Ibid., III, 481; cf. VI, 166, n. 965.

166. Exod. III, 14.

167. *Mos.* I, 75; see below, X, 95.

168. *Det.* 160; cf. *Mut.* 11.

169. *Som.* I, 230.

divinity himself: he is "given as a god to Pharaoh," [170] Philo goes on to say, which means that from the human point of view he will indeed be regarded a god "by all conception and seeming, though not in truth and Being." [171] We shall find it extremely important that this presentation of Moses should be the one to which the Migration of Israel leads.

Moses reappears on the top panel at the left, figs. 93 and 324. Since the upper part of the painting is destroyed, we cannot say with confidence that this panel had no label, but since the lower two panels are not inscribed, that is a natural assumption. Here Moses on Sinai—the mountain indicated sketchily by a white curving line behind him—steps forward in the white robe, marked with the same details and with his shoes again removed, to receive the Law from Heaven. The Tables of the Law would presumably have been extended to Moses by the right hand of God.[172] In the Ezekiel scene, figs. 348 f., five of the incidents are marked with the heavenly hand, all of them right hands, so that it was obviously of symbolic importance there, and here, to represent the right hand.

The design of Moses on Sinai seems to stem from an original that also lay ultimately behind fig. 94,[173] where the same tall shoes of the Dura rendering appear, and the burning bush has come to be a fire from a gadrooned brazier, or possibly the flaming object in the lower right corner. Moses here wears the Greek robe as he gets the Law on Sinai, but when he tends the sheep he has only the chiton. He has his hands covered to receive the Law, and similarly covers his hands in the lower left panel at Dura. Another product of the same tradition, fig. 95,[174] appears in the Chludov Psalter, from which we saw the monkey of Orpheus, fig. 82. In the Psalter, Moses' shoes have become sandals at the foot of the mount, but the mount is itself more like what probably lay behind the mount in the Dura panel, and the Law is the square table, and not the scroll of fig. 94. Again the bush is a real bush, shown before Moses and under the hand of God. I strongly suspect that like these Christian drawings the original showed the bush and Sinai in the same scene, and that the shoes appear off Moses' feet in the Dura scene because in making two scenes out of one the shoes were copied with both figures of Moses.[175]

170. Exod. VII, 1.

171. *Det.* 161 f.

172. In *MR, Deut.*, XI, 10 (ET, 185), it is said that Moses received the Law from the right hand of God. See fig. 63 and below, X, 106, n. 8.

173. From Cosmas Indicopleustes, *Christian Topography*, fol. 61ᵛ; ed. C. Stornajolo, 1908, plate 25 (Codices e Vaticanis selecti, X). Moses the shepherd stands under the hand of God with his sheep at the left, and the mountain is strangely represented as the flaming arc at the lower right. The hand comes here from a cloud in the convention we noticed at Beth Alpha, above, I, 246 f.; III, fig. 638. For appearances of the design in other manuscripts of this work see Riedin, *Cosmas Indicopleustes*, I, 200–203, 242–255. In these the bush becomes various kinds of burning altars.

174. From Omont, *Miniatures*, plate x. It is

from the Bibliothèque Nationale, Paris, ms. grec 139, fol. 422ᵛ.

175. The tradition of the covered hands in receiving the Law was adapted by Christians for representing Peter in the act of receiving the *nova lex* from Christ enthroned: see Hannah Jursch, "Tradition und Neuschöpfung im altchristlichen Bilderkreis," *Wissenschaftliche Zeitschrift der Friedrich-Schiller-Universität Jena, Gesellschafts- und Sprachwissenschaftliche Reihe*, IX (1950–60), 205, and figs. 27 and 31. This study, which reached me after the present volume had gone to press, is very rich in ideas and material. See also G. Sarfatti, "The Tables of the Covenant as a Symbol of Judaism" (in Hebrew), *Tarbiz*, XXIX (1960), 370–393, esp. figs. 3, 6, and 9. I suspect that these also represent the giving of the *nova lex*. But the figure seems to be Moses again on a seventh-century Christian tomb-

With the two upper panel portraits so firmly identified as Moses, we turn to the two lower portraits, and find that here all scholarly agreement vanishes. The panel at the right,[176] which like Kraeling we shall call the third, plate v, fig. 326, shows an extremely impressive figure. A man in the same robe stands holding a large open scroll before him, clearly reading it. Beside his right foot is a round-topped box covered with a cloth, a box that all agree is the ark of the scrolls, presumably the smaller portable ark that would have been kept in the room for the "instruments," or behind a screen, or, ultimately, in a Torah shrine such as the niche in the synagogue represented. The head is framed by a rectangle even more distinct than the similar rectangle behind the head of Moses at the bush. In trying to identify this figure, most scholars have looked in the Bible for references to a man reading the Law, and rather arbitrarily have chosen one or another such incident by which to identify the reader. Kraeling feels that Moses [177] or Ezra [178] are both possible, but he inclines to Ezra because he identifies the fourth portrait with Abraham, and feels it unlikely that there would be three portraits of Moses and a single one of another Jewish hero. His discussion of the four portraits, however, is based only upon scriptural texts and not upon the tradition of early Christian biblical illustrations, which clearly stem from the same prototypes as the Dura paintings. Here from three manuscripts a tradition definitely emerges that after Moses receives the Law on Sinai he next reads it to the people. Fig. 96 [179] shows one such sequence very clearly, though in it Moses is reading the Law from the stone tables, or a medieval codex.[180] In the Dura panels I see the same sequence of Moses reading the Law after getting it on Sinai, except that at Dura, Moses' audience is omitted, and Moses stands alone, so that he reads the Law to the living audience in the synagogue before him. The incident, of course, is familiar in rabbinic tradition, which Ginzberg [181] paraphrases as follows:

---

stone at Berlin: O. Wulff, *Altchristliche und mittelalterliche byzantinische und italienische Bildwerke*, III, ii, 1909, 19, no. 32; Wulff gives further instances and bibliography. I am by no means now so confident that in the archetype of these paintings the incidents of the bush and Sinai appeared in the same painting. For in the newly discovered catacomb in the Via Latina, Rome, Moses stoops to remove his shoes while he looks back over his shoulder to the hand of God above him presenting him with the Law. See Ferrua, *Via Latina*, 56, plate xxxiii, 2; 70, plate lxiv, 2.

176. For a detailed description of the painting and its technique, as well as for a record of various interpretations, see Kraeling, *Synagogue*, 232–235.

177. With reference to Exod. xxiv, 7.

178. Neh. viii.

179. Courtesy of the Bibliothèque Nationale, Paris, where it is Lat. 1, Bible of Charles the Bold, fol. 27ᵛ. See W. Köhler, *Die Schule von Tours*, 1930, plate 7 (Die karolingischen Miniaturen, I); other

manuscripts in A. Boinet, *La Miniature carolingienne*, 1913, plates xliv and cxxiiia; cf. *Const. Octateuch*, plate xxiii, fig. 134. A painting in the new Catacomb Via Latina shows a man on a rocky eminence speaking to a crowd of people below him. See Ferrua, *Via Latina*, 47, plate xiv. Ferrua calls the scene the Sermon on the Mount, and he may be right. But since so few new scenes from the New Testament appear in this catacomb as compared with the great number from the Old Testament, and since it resembles so much early Christian representations of Moses teaching the Law to the Israelites after his descent from Sinai, it seems more probable that that is what the painting depicts.

180. "It is another of the attributes of the tablets that, although they are fashioned out of the hardest stone, they can still be rolled up like a scroll": Ginzberg, *Legends*, III, 119, based upon *MR, Song of Songs*, v, 14, 1 (ET, 245).

181. *Legends*, III, 87; for references see ibid., VI, 33, n. 191.

God now instructed Moses to transmit to the people his words without adding to them or diminishing from them, in the precise order and in the same tongue, the Hebrew. Moses hereupon betook himself to the people to deliver his message, without first seeing his family. He first addressed the word of God to the elders, for he never forgot the honor due the elders. Then, in simple and well-arranged form, he repeated it to all the people, including the women.

The art type is preserved in the Catacomb Peter and Marcellinus in Rome, fig. 97,[182] an anomalous representation which Wilpert calls St. Peter with the Law. But this painting takes us to the common phenomenon of the philosopher reading or only holding the scroll, a matter to be treated at greater length in the following chapter.[183] Fig. 98 [184] shows vividly that the scroll when held up thus for reading could contain mystic philosophy, for here, in a Pompeian painting, a priest of Isis reads what we should suppose is the *hieros logos*, the secret teaching of the Mystery. We see such a reader in action again in a ritualistic procession of Isis on a relief at the Vatican, fig. 99,[185] while the same pose appears in the Dionysiac initiation scene of the Villa Item at Pompeii, fig. 101.[186] The figure at Dura seems to have come directly from the vocabulary of the mystic religions. The most likely presumption is that, after the two scenes of Moses above, the figure here is also Moses, this time presented as the mystic hierophant reading the *hieros logos* he graciously brought to Jews. That Moses reads the mystic text as a mystagogue means not that the Scriptures were literally kept secret, but that to these Jews in Dura, as to Philo, the true meaning of Scripture, the allegorical, was to be presented fully only to those "initiated." Inherently for Philo and, we presume, for many other hellenized Jews, the Old Testament was a mystical book.

We cannot identify the reader positively with Moses, however, because in the mosaic in the Basilica of S. Vitale, Ravenna, fig. 100,[187] Moses gets the Law on the mount at the right, and at the left Jeremiah reads it in this same mystic pose. I still believe, nevertheless,

182. From Wilpert, Pitture, plate 84; cf. 93, where it appears that the figure is seated. See Christ with roll and box, ibid., plate 168; also Christ with scroll on the Lipsanoteca of Brescia, above, IV, fig. 116.

183. See below, pp. 139 f., 146.

184. From O. Elia, *Le Pitture del tempio di Iside*, 1942, fig. 186; cf. p. 16 (Monumenti della pittura antica scoperti in Italia, III, ii). Photographs of the painting in its present condition lack many details: see C. Schneider in *Kyrios*, IV (1939–40), 192, fig. 3.

185. Photo Anderson. The procession shows an Isis priestess, the reader, a prophet holding the holy pitcher with covered hands, a servitor with the sistrum and ladle. See J. Liepoldt and S. Morenz, *Heilige Schriften*, 1953, 96 f., and plate 7. These scholars have an excellent discussion of secret scriptures in antiquity, pp. 88–114, with special reference to Jewish and Christian usages as compared with the pagan.

186. Photo Anderson; cf. Liepoldt and Morenz, plate 9, and loc. cit. The foregoing was finished for the press when I first secured K. Weitzmann's new study, *Ancient Book Illumination*, 1959 (Martin Classical Lectures, XVI). On pp. 116–127 he discusses biography and author portraits, and again identifies the man reading a scroll, whether standing or seated, with the ideal philosopher or poet. He shows a representation of Obadiah (his fig. 129 and p. 121) from Paris, Bibl. Nat. cod. gr. 1528, fol. 218ᵛ, which is quite like the Moses figure. Old Jewish tradition said that the Scriptures should be read standing: J. Neusner, *Life of Rabban Yohanan ben Zakkai*, Leiden, 1962, 38.

187. Photo Alinari.

that the mystic reader of the Law at Dura is more likely to be Moses in his philosophical and mystical importance than any other single figure we might select. If the following panel, the fourth, can with any probability be taken to show Moses also, such an identification of the third figure becomes more likely. The argument, actually, works both ways, as Kraeling feels: now that we see more evidence for associating the third figure with Moses than Kraeling considered, the fourth figure seems more apt to be Moses, though I can identify the fourth even less confidently than the third.

The fourth portrait panel, plate v, fig. 102, and the accompanying sketch, text fig. 11,[188] shows a man with white hair and beard, the head this time against a black rectangle, apparently to set off the white hair, though the black square may have another meaning. He again wears the special Greek costume with its markings on both chiton and himation, but this time the himation is pulled over both shoulders, and covers the man's hands. That he stands upon the ground appears clearly from the shadow line which the artist felt it necessary to put only on this portrait.[189]

11

Above his head an arc [190] indicates the heavens, with the sun, moon, and seven stars within it. The sun is drawn as a "round object" with laddered rays, to which, like Kraeling, I can find no parallel. The rays recall the symbolism of the ladder discussed above, and Philo's interpretation of the divine ladder that connects man with God, up and down which go the logoi of God.[191] The conception that God reveals himself in a Light-Stream which offers a means of ascent to God appears constantly in Philo's writings.[192] The unique presentation of the rays here, accordingly, may well indicate such an idea. The way of presenting the stars seems no less significant; for they are made of a central dot with eight rays, and a dot at the end of each ray. The stars as a central dot with rays is familiar enough, as on the ceiling of the apse in the Christian Chapel at Dura, in the Dura Mith-

188. From Kraeling, *Synagogue*, 236, fig. 61. See his interesting discussion there, esp. the parallels cited in his notes.

189. A trace of such line does appear with Moses at the bush.

190. Kraeling says that the arc is gray, and such an original contrast with the light pink of the rest of the background is most likely. I suspect that his gray was originally blue. All contrast has now faded out, as plate v shows. The text figure is reproduced from Kraeling, *Synagogue*, 236, fig. 61.

191. *Som.* 1, 144–156. The passage on the dream of Jacob will be discussed at greater length below, X, 169. On the ladder see above, VIII, 148–157.

192. See my *By Light, Light*, passim. For example, in *Praem.* 43, Philo says that the "truly admirable ones . . . advance from down to up by a sort of heavenly ladder."

raeum, and in the Octateuch art.[193] But to repeat the dot at the end of each ray has no parallel that I know. Symbolically it may be important that these dots give the stars the form we have seen having great importance in magic, a form in which rays go out from a central circle, and the central circle is repeated at the end of each ray. These could be presented crudely on charms,[194] or as elegant symbols on sarcophagi, where the circles both at the center and at the ends of the rays now become rosettes.[195] Both sun and stars, accordingly, appear at Dura in peculiar forms that associate them with mystic symbolism.

Many suggestions have been made for the identity of the hero in this panel, most of which Kraeling has adequately disposed of.[196] He himself prefers to call the person Abraham. This interpretation has great credibility for a reason he mentions but does not press, namely that in the early Christian tradition of biblical illustration, which we have already found so illuminating for these paintings, almost exactly this scene is used to represent Abraham called out to count the stars.[197] If the scene had been isolated, I should agree that this is the most likely identification, just as by itself I should have judged the third to be Jeremiah.[198] Set in with the other three panels, however, the third of which most probably represents Moses, as do the first two certainly, it would seem likely that the last portrait represents Moses also, now in old age and ascending to heaven. Iconographically this is quite possible, for a mosaic in Santa Maria Maggiore definitely makes the death of Moses (represented differently, to be sure) to be the sequel of his reading the Law to the People, fig. 103.[199]

The Dura portrait might at once be the aged Moses, and yet show him in relation with the heavenly bodies, since the tradition of his ascension appears so widely in Judaism. The tradition must be very old, for even in Deuteronomy he is reported to have begun one of his songs before he died:

> Give ear, O heavens, and I will speak:
> and let the earth hear the words of my mouth.[200]

In the following song he blesses each of the twelve tribes. But later tradition made much of this. The Rabbis (not unanimously, as Kraeling points out [201]) associated Moses with the cosmos on two occasions. He was devised before the beginning of the world to be the mediator of the Covenant [202] and so was shown the universe on the successive days of its creation, when each newly created part had shrunk back at the sight of Moses' supremacy. For God put all created things on one side of a scale, but Moses outweighed them on the

---

193. See *Const. Octateuch*, plates IX, fig. 16; X, figs. 17, 19 f., 22. See above, p. 44, and figs. 15–17.

194. As, for example, above, III, figs. 999 f., 1007.

195. See above, VI, fig. 237, pp. 64–66; VII, fig. 213.

196. *Synagogue*, 237.

197. He refers to the scene in the *Vienna Genesis*, plate VIII. See also cod. vat. gr. 746, fol. 70ʳ; cod.

vat. gr. 747, fol. 37ʳ; *Smyrna Octateuch*, plate XXI, fig. 56; *Const. Octateuch*, plate XIV, fig. 44.

198. See fig. 100 and above, p. 114.

199. Photo Alinari. The lower half shows the procession of the Ark, probably around Jericho.

200. Deut. XXXII, 1.

201. *Synagogue*, 237, n. 947.

202. Ass. Mos. I, 14; *proetheasato me ho theos*. See Charles' note to the passage in his *Apoc. and Pseud.*

other. Also, at the end of Moses' life, when God "was taking him to himself," he showed Moses the whole universe, past and present.[203] So Moses was the man of God, half man and half God.[204] Josephus called Moses the "divine man," the *theios anēr*.[205] He [206] tells how at Moses' death the hero was taken by a cloud into a ravine, but that people later dare say that on account of his supererogatory virtue he was taken *eis to theion*. This phrase may mean "to heaven," or "into divine nature." Josephus seemed to Bousset [207] to be trying to contradict a common rumor of Moses' assumption. He may have been contradicting the near-deification of Moses which Philo reflects. So, the rabbis taught, God said to Moses, "Thou that didst lead my children in this world, shalt also lead them in the future world." [208] When God bade the soul of Moses leave the body he said, "Soul, go forth, do not delay, and I will raise thee to the highest heavens and will place thee under the Throne of Glory next to the Cherubim, Seraphim, and other troops of angels." [209] From rabbinic and apocalyptic tradition, then, Moses would naturally be represented viewing the heavens.

In rabbinic sources, however, the conception has no central place. The idea was much more strikingly developed in hellenized Judaism. When we look in Philo for an old man who goes into the presence of God (the covered hands) in the company of the heavenly bodies, or for an incident in which the stars played an important part, we are led immediately to Moses. For according to Philo, when Moses had disposed of all his earthly affairs at the end of his life, one hundred and twenty years old, he began his final song of praise while still in the body.[210] In order to sing this song with absolute perfection, he gathered together a mighty company. Philo's description of what followed, his version of the real meaning of the psalms attributed to Moses in Deuteronomy XXII f., is too remarkable for paraphrase:

> He [Moses] gathered together a divine company, that is the elements of the universe and the most effective parts of the cosmos, namely earth and heaven, earth the hearth of mortals and heaven the home of the immortals. In the middle between these he composed hymns using every musical mode and every type of interval in order that men and ministering angels might hear, men as learners that he might teach them a similarly thankful attitude, and the angels as critics to watch how, as judged by their own technique, he made not a single false note. The angels would also be strengthened in their faith if a man clothed in his mortal body could have a power of song like the sun, moon, and the sacred choir of other stars, and could attune his soul to the divine instrument, namely the heavens and the whole cosmos. But Moses the hierophant, when he had taken

203. II Baruch LIX, 3–12.

204. Ginzberg, *Legends*, III, 481; VI, 166 f., notes 964 f.

205. Josephus, *Antiquities*, III, 180.

206. Ibid., IV, 326.

207. As Bousset, *Religion*, 121 f., said, it is presupposed in the transfiguration scene in Mark IX, 4 (with parallels), that Moses ascended like Elijah, since the two heroes appeared there together with Jesus. Some such tradition may also lie behind Jude 9. Presumably it was told in the lost ending of the Ass. Mos. Schürer, *Jüd. Volk*, III, 301–305, has assembled much of the material in Jewish and Christian sources.

208. Ginzberg, *Legends*, III, 481; VI, 167, n. 966.

209. *MR, Deut.*, XI, 10 (ET, 187).

210. *Virt.* 72.

his place in the aetherial chorus, mingled, along with his hymns of praise to God, true emotions of good will to the Nation. He reproved them for their past sins, gave them warnings and corrections for the present, and advice for the future based upon good hopes which were bound to be fulfilled.[211]

According to Philo, then, in Moses the "hierophant" the gulf between mortal and immortal, the cosmic and the human, has been bridged. In the presence of the sun, moon, and stars a man has sung the perfect song while yet in the body, and the faith of the angels themselves has been strengthened. Yet this great person, even as he was in the height of his grandeur, could not forget his loving-kindness to the people, and while he rebuked them for their sins, he gave them such instructions and advice that the future became full of hopes which must be fulfilled.

The wing panel we are considering can be understood as depicting the incident. Moses, now one hundred and twenty years old, is at the end of his life. He stands upon the earth (his shadow), but associates himself with the heavens and their bodies. That the sun should offer a ladder in its rays and that the stars should be the potencies of the circle reproducing itself quite agree with the mood of this conception of Moses' ascension through the heavens. There he sings the great song, which by Philo's account was the supreme moment of his career.

The series of portraits seem to progress, then, from the bush to Sinai, and thence from the reading of the Law to the assumption of Moses. The incidents selected represent exactly the incidents most stressed in the mystic account of Moses by Philo. Moses, Philo explained, had from the first been a special incarnation of the Logos, a loan from God to men. His early experiences did not, like those of Abraham, represent the renunciation of the body and the gradual winning through to the Logos. Instead, like Isaac, he had all of this from the beginning. So at the bush he was simply called to his specific task of saving the race, just as Jesus, by orthodox tradition, came into no new state at his baptism, but only received his commission. For Moses, too, the bush was the scene of his definite instructions and first realization of what his task was to be. He is the great mystagogue or hierophant in the robe even at the bush. He then went out to act as savior in the Migration, a function which was highly important for others but which did not represent a specific advance in his own experience. For Moses himself, the next great event after the bush was Sinai. When God called up Moses (to the Mount) this was

a second birth better than the first. For the first birth is mixed with a body and had corruptible parents, while the second birth was an unmixed and simple soul of the sovereign, being changed from a productive to an unproductive form,[212] which has no mother but only a father, who is [the Father] of all. Wherefore the "calling up," or, as we have said, the divine birth, happened to come about for him in accordance with

211. Ibid. 73–75.

212. I have kept Marcus' phrase here, since I do not control the Armenian. But I disagree with him in his note (p. 91h), and consider the Greek must have here *agenēton*, "unproduced," or "without beginning," or, from the context, *agennēton*, "unbegotten," since the mother is excluded, apparently to explain this very word.

the ever-virginal nature of the hebdomad. For he was called up on the seventh day, and differed in this from the Protoplast. For the Protoplast [created on the sixth day] was made out of earth and had a body. Accordingly the number six [was assigned] as proper for the earthborn, but the most sacred nature of the seven for the other.[213]

Moses, the second and superior Adam, became through this experience the Lawmaker for the Jews, or rather the author of the Mystic Torah, the *hieros logos* of what Philo calls the mystery. So at Dura, Moses is represented in the third scene as reading not the table of the Decalogue but the Torah as a whole. From this time until his assumption nothing of importance happened for Moses himself, since mystic Judaism, like all Judaism, ignored as far as possible Moses' disobedience at the rock of Meribah. The incidents selected, accordingly, not only are in chronological order but give exactly the events in Moses' career of greatest importance for mystic Judaism.

Philo compressed into a remarkable passage the significance of these four events. He had been praising the Patriarchs and explaining that among them Isaac was supreme, because while other men belong to what Philo called "species," Isaac had been "translated into the 'genus' which is indestructible and fully perfect." These men, Philo says, form a thiasos of which Isaac is admittedly a member.[214] Some, however, go beyond this, Philo continues, though his plural is anomalous, for only Moses is named, and only Moses could have been thus greater than Isaac, as, in the allegory of the tree-vine, he was superior to Bezalel:

> There are others whom God has advanced even higher, and enabled to soar up beyond all species and genera, and has caused to sit beside himself. Such is Moses to whom he says "Stand here with me." [215] So when Moses was about to die he did not "leave" to be "added" as did those others [Isaac and the other Patriarchs]. No room in him for adding or taking away. But he was translated "through the word" (*rhēma*) [216] of the Supreme Cause through whom also the entire universe was created. Thus you may learn that God ranks the Wise Man [217] on an equality with the universe, since it was by the same Word (Logos) [218] that he both created the universe and lifts up the Perfect Man from earthly things to himself. When [God] sent [Moses] as a loan to the earthly sphere and suffered him to dwell therein, he endowed him by no means with any such common virtue as that of a ruler or king, wherewith he would forcibly guide the soul's passions.[219]

213. *QE* II, 46. I have translated the Greek where it exists, and otherwise followed Marcus for the Armenian. See his valuable notes, ad. loc., and the Greek at his p. 251. It must be recalled that Paul assigned a similar double birth to Christ in Rom. I, 3 f. Paul says that Christ was "descended from David according to the flesh and designated Son of God in power according to the Spirit of holiness by his resurrection from the dead."

214. *Sacr.* 6 f.

215. Deut. v, 31. Philo has kept the biblical "stand," in quoting the text, but interprets it that

Moses "sits" beside God. The idea was to have a portentous history in Christianity.

216. Ibid. xxxiv, 5.

217. The perfect but mythical Sophos of the Stoics, whom Philo found actually to have existed in Moses.

218. Philo, as often, is taking the LXX *rhēma* to be allegorically a reference to the metaphysical Logos.

219. Philo often speaks about the royal virtue of self-rulership, following the tradition of the day. See my *Politics of Philo Judaeus*, 1938, 86–120. By

Rather [God] appointed him a god (*theos*) by making subject and slave to him the whole region of the body and its leader, the mind. For, says [Scripture], "I give thee as a god to Pharaoh." [220] But a god can suffer neither diminution, nor addition, since he is complete [221] and in every respect equal within himself.[222] Wherefore [Scripture] says that no one knows even his grave.[223] For who would be able to comprehend the migration of a perfect soul to him who "is"? Nay, I judge that even the soul that is having the experience is hardly aware of its change to better things, since at that hour it is in a state of inspiration. For God does not consult with those he blesses as to the gifts he means to bestow: he rather is wont to extend his loving-kindness to those who do not suspect its coming.[224]

Philo does not mention the heavenly bodies in this passage, but he does describe the assumption of Moses in terms equaled only in later Christianity. Moses is elevated to sit beside God himself, as himself a deity—deity to the extent that the Parmenidean concept of pure being, complete in itself and incapable of change, now applies to Moses. Where is his grave? The implication is that there was none, that, as Philo says elsewhere,[225] God changed Moses' whole nature, which had been twofold, soul and body, into a single entity consisting of "most sunlike mind." [226] True, Philo could speak of Moses' casting his body like the shell of an oyster as he passed from mortal to immortal nature.[227] But another passage interpreting Moses before God on Sinai seems appropriate to his coming to God at his death:

> When the prophetic mind becomes divinely inspired and filled with God, it becomes like the monad, not being at all mixed with any of these things associated with duality. But he who is resolved into the nature of unity, is said to come near God in a kind of family relation, for having given up and left behind all mortal kinds,[228] he is changed into the divine, so that such men become kin to God and truly divine.[229]

this thinking the king is himself the incarnate Logos. Philo is making Moses this in a scene far beyond political kingship even at its best.

220. Exod. VII, 1.

221. Philo here uses the word "full," *plērē*, as he often does, to describe what in Christian literature became the "fulness," *plērōma*, of God. Cf. Col. II, 9, where God's "fullness" abides in Christ "bodily" just as Philo here says it did in Moses. For Philo see *LA* I, 23; *Heres* 188; *Som.* I, 75; II, 245.

222. Literally "most equal to himself," *isotaitos*. Philo is speaking of the Parmenidean Being as described in Fragment 8: H. Diels, *Die Fragmente der Vorsokratiker*, 6th ed., 1951, I, 235. Parmenides calls the One *oulomeles, homou pan, hen suneches,* and hence incapable of growth or diminution. It is to this that Philo compares Moses. Colson suddenly capitalizes God, apparently because he cannot believe Philo would have said this. "Translation is the tersest commentary."

223. Deut. XXXIV, 6.

224. *Sacr.* 8–10.

225. *Mos.* II, 288.

226. The phrase comes out of the heart of Platonic and Neoplatonic tradition. In the most metaphysical part of the *Republic*, 508B, 509A, Plato uses this adjective for the eye which sees the sun by virtue of being like the sun, in comparison to the intelligence which apprehends the immaterial realities by being like them. Plotinus, I, vi, 9 (ed. R. Volkmann, 1883, 96, line 12), uses it in the same way: "The eye would never see the sun unless it were like the sun, as the soul would not see beauty if it were not beautiful. Let it be first altogether like God and altogether beautiful if it is to see the beautiful and the good." Plotinus goes on at once to speak of the mind. Philo has only condensed what must have been a commonplace simile.

227. *Virt.* 76.

228. Marcus plausibly suggests that *genē* appeared here in the Greek.

229. *QE* II, 29. Marcus' translation of the Armenian. The Greek is lost.

Here is the extreme view, that Moses came *eis to theion*, into the divine, against which we saw Josephus protesting, though Josephus himself would call Moses the "divine man." [230] For a person so deified there could, of course, have been no grave.[231]

The question before us, however, is not how Philo thought but how the worshipers in the synagogue thought, or at least the elders who paid to have these extraordinary paintings on its walls. Thus far we have seen only that under a ceiling decorated with mystic pagan symbolism which was far from being meaningless "cliché," the Jews of Dura had set their holy niche for the Torah with the symbols of Judaism above it. The symbols seem to have been given a mystic interpretation, as shown by the substitution of the sacrifice of Isaac for the shofar. Above this, by a series of repaintings, a design of a tree or vine was worked out in which at the end all Israel was blessed by a Patriarch in the white robe, with the result that the tribes reappeared before the great Three at the top of the vine. Their ascension was aided by a David-Orpheus who tamed the wild beasts to make the transition possible. We saw this to be extraordinarily similar to Philo's long allegory of the tree-vine, but in that allegory a position was given to Moses as the great mediator of the life of the vine which the reredos painting did not suggest.

It is entirely fitting, accordingly, that four portrait panels were put as frames for this painting; and there seems adequate reason to suppose that they represent the hierophant Moses whose character was as unique as his final association *eis to theion*.[232] Only now, with so much before us, do I suggest that the inscription "Moses, son of Levi" beside the first portrait really characterizes all four of the portraits and means that the artist believed, as did Philo, that Moses was the supreme priest of Israel for all time.[233]

To Philo, Levi's importance and the function of Levi's sons lay in the keeping of holy things. The sons of Levi, he says, deemed

> earth and sea and air, yea, moreover, the heavens and all the universe, to be a portion of too little worth. The Creator alone was thought meet for them, since with him they have taken refuge as genuine suppliants and become his attendants.[234]

"The portion of Levi, the lover of God, is God." [235] The Levites "are a ransom [236] for all the others" and as such are "the Logos who has taken refuge with God and become his

---

230. See above, p. 117.

231. If the artist had finished with Moses in panel three, and the fourth hero is Abraham "viewing the stars," the figure would probably still be the mystic one: see the cosmic prayer of Abraham, above, VIII, 206 f.

232. With this went, I am sure, the square haloes of these portraits, as H. Stern still insists: *Theologische Literaturzeitung*, 1958, 251. Stern suggests that such haloes could be shown to represent the " 'magical' significance of portraits in late antiquity," but does not explain or demonstrate this.

Nothing certain seems to me to come out of discussions of them by Grabar, "Le Thème," 176, n. 2, and R. de Vaux in *RB*, XLIX (1940), 139. I cannot go beyond Rostovtzeff, *Dura-Europos and Its Arts*, 1938, 108, who, after agreeing with me that the four figures represent Moses, says: "The semi-divinization of Moses is stressed by the square nimbus which surrounds his head."

233. Philo, *Mos.* ii, 66–186.

234. *Det.* 62.

235. *LA* ii, 52.

236. I quite agree with Colson that the plural *lutra* should be translated as a collective singular.

suppliant." In forsaking the world of created things and taking refuge with God, Levi was the Wise Man (*sophos*), and any wise man is a "ransom for the fool." [237] Indeed the Levite is especially the Minister (*hupēretēs*) of the Beneficent Power of God, "for he undertakes all the rites that belong to that perfect priesthood of God, by which mortality is commended to and recognized by God." This latter interpretation of Levi, Philo says, is "a teaching of the sort that belongs among the secrets." [238] Moses was truly a priest to Philo, a son of Levi, and the character of his priesthood was such as we shall see implicit in the Dura paintings.

For here, expressed in art, is a great unified idea, and only in mystic Judaism do we find this idea at home. The few rabbinic tags that seem to reflect such a conception have no such generic place in the main body of rabbinic thought as to suggest that Jews might have worshiped under such a tree-vine, and with such representation of Moses. Our entire study of the Jewish symbolic vocabulary, both that originally Jewish and that freshly borrowed from the Greco-Roman pagans, has led us steadily to suppose that some such interpretation of the Jewish Bible must have accompanied the universal use of the borrowed vocabulary. We find in Philo a Judaism which precisely fits such a supposititious Judaism, and an elaborate allegory that makes intelligible the reredos and its wing panels. The only probable conclusion is that the Jews (not, I believe the whole congregation) who decorated the synagogue had accepted the symbols because they had come to interpret Judaism much as Philo had done. As we consider the other paintings, it will appear that the men who created them, whether at Dura or elsewhere, had read much apocalyptic literature Philo had not read, and had accepted many haggadic legends Philo probably never heard of. It is not for us to say that the art was "purely Philonic" or "purely rabbinic" or "purely" anything else. The paintings must lead us, as Naomi led Ruth, whither they will. For the time their God must be our God. Thus far, however, the God of Philo and the Judaism of Philo seem more closely to fit the designs than any other one type I know.

For the central reredos painting seems to tell us that the leading Jews of Dura had a burning desire to leave the savagery of bestial desires and follow the leadership of the great hierophants—Jacob at the bottom, David-Orpheus on the way, to the supreme Three at the top of the tree of life. The greatest priest-hierophant of all, for this sort of Judaism, was Moses himself, and that he should be presented in the four crucial aspects of his career was entirely fitting. Philo had himself been "initiated by Moses," [239] and it seems to me quite likely that the Elder Samuel may have been so "initiated" also.

As Samuel and others like him sat before these representations of Moses—not only the four portraits but, as we shall see, Moses the divine baby and Moses saving his people from fleshly Egypt—they might fittingly have repeated to themselves the prayer of Philo to Moses:

237. *Sacr.* 118–121.

238. Ibid. 131–133: *toioutos en aporrētois logos,* one of Philo's most mystic expressions.

239. *Cher.* 49. "I myself have been initiated by the God-blessed Moses into the greater mysteries."

Oh thou hierophant, though the eyes of our soul are closed because we do not desire to see, or cannot do so, still do thou uphold us and help us and not cease to anoint us until thou hast initiated us into the hidden meaning of the sacred words and revealed those locked beauties which are invisible to the uninitiated. This it is meet for thee to do.[240]

Clearly there can be no proof or disproof of such a suggested interpretation of the reredos. It will gain in probability only as it seems to help us to interpret the other paintings in the synagogue, singly and as a whole.

240. *Som.* I, 164.

CHAPTER SEVEN

Symbolism of Dress

THE REREDOS has shown that the costumes may well be crucial for the Dura paintings, a fact recognized by most commentators.[1] The present chapter must address itself directly to the problem, and must try to establish some more methodical approach than seems to have characterized former answers. Clearly we must seek some objective point of view, for to decide by studying the paintings that the Greek costume means this, the Persian that, then to explain the paintings on that basis, and finally to complete the circle by showing that the paintings have in turn explained the dress, has little to commend it.

Only two objective approaches to the problem have occurred to me: to study the textiles found in the ruins of Dura itself, and to trace the history of the costumes as they were used in pagan and Christian art, to see whether the various types of dress in those milieus seem to have had, and kept, stable symbolic values.[2] If these same values consistently clarify the meaning of the Jewish paintings at Dura, we may reasonably suppose the paintings were designed with the values in mind.

We shall use both approaches, but shall find that the textiles in themselves tell us nothing about what sort of people wore them or on what occasions, so that for interpretation we are thrown back chiefly upon the second method. I shall therefore rely on the method that has proved useful throughout this study for evaluating symbols—studying the general development and associations of a symbol, in this case of the forms of dress in the ancient world.

A. THE COSTUMES IN THE DURA PAINTINGS

WOMEN'S COSTUMES can here be quickly dismissed. Apart from the naked woman getting the baby Moses from the Ark in the Nile there seem to be only two sorts of dress on characters recognizable as women. The commonest costume [3] consists of a chiton with loose sleeves to the elbow—that is, the type usually called the colobium or dalmatic; see

---

1. For example, Kraeling, *Synagogue*, 71, 73, 81, 114 f., etc.

2. For "value" in the discussion of symbols, see above, p. 6, and IV, Chap. 2.

3. Kraeling, *Synagogue*, 146, n. 532.

figs. 335, 338.[4] The chiton is sometimes marked with clavi, stripes of color from each shoulder to the bottom. This garment covers the upper part of the body and hangs down to the ankles, as the chitons of the men do not. An himation hangs over the chiton from one shoulder and is wrapped in some strange way round the waist. It nearly covers the chiton from the waist down, but allows a bit of the chiton to show at the bottom. A still more peculiar feature is a fold across the hips. Kraeling[5] seems right when he says that the veil which covers the heads of women in this costume is made of one end of the himation.

The other type of women's dress appears definitely in only two scenes,[6] but very importantly. Here the chiton is a tight-fitting sleeveless garment that again extends to the feet. Over it, as drawn, a skirt hangs from just below the bust; it has a wide flounce that ends at the hips with a stripe of the same color as the chiton. The garment would seem to be a misdrawn peplos. The veil in this case has no relation to the rest of the garment. Bracelets are on the bare arms. Since these costumes can best be discussed in connection with the paintings in which they appear,[7] I shall only say here that both seem misdrawings from originals at whose exact nature we can only guess. The folds as drawn, and in places the structure, will appear quite unreal when we discuss them at greater length.

Men wear armor in the paintings—to indicate, I presume, that they are soldiers. To this obvious conclusion we shall add that the types of armor may prove to be helpful in identifying the origin of the art forms, but armor seems to me to have no special symbolic reference. When the children of Israel come out of Egypt, plate xiv, only some of them are armed, and I take it that their armor represents only that some of the men were thought to constitute a regularly organized fighting force, others not. Armor might well have had a spiritual significance, as does the spear of the St. George type of saints in paganism and Christianity. But in the synagogue I have seen no trace of more than the literal specification that those wearing arms were soldiers.

Other types of masculine dress cannot be dismissed so easily. Actually, apart from the armor, all the costumes of the men fall into two basic categories.

The first of these is the Persian costume of caftan and trousers. When a cape is thrown over these and all are richly ornamented, we have the garb of kings. Aaron and Orpheus are similarly clad, but with the cape fastened by a brooch across the chest. The Persian dress may be dark or light, but I have not been able to see that the shade marks any distinction in meaning for the characters.[8]

In contrast to this costume is the Greek dress of many other figures. This consists first of a long chiton with sleeves, almost always of a light color[9] and ordinarily marked with

4. On these garments see A. Mau in PW, IV, 483, 2025 f.

5. *Synagogue*, 146, n. 532.

6. See figs. 335, 338, and, perhaps, 329.

7. See below, p. 228.

8. For example, in plate xvi four people bear the Ark, two in light Persian dress, two in dark.

The change of shade in Ezekiel's dress may well have meaning, plate xxi, but may only be a concession to the changed color of the background. See below, X, 183.

9. Exceptions are the chitons of two of Elijah's attendants, plate xvi, and the child in the bottom row at the right in plate xiv.

the darker stripes which run like ribbons one from each shoulder down to the hem. The chiton in most cases appears only partially, since it is covered with the himation, but without the himation it can be seen in the Exodus from Egypt, plate XIV, where it is the dress of the lowest row of figures, and still more clearly as worn by the servants of Elijah at the right part of plate XVI. In both of these it is belted up for active motion, an adjustment described in the biblical phrase as having the "loins girded." [10] In a scene of the carrying of the Ark, plate XVI, small figures wear a knee-length chiton as the outer garment, with what Kraeling [11] properly calls an "unidentified garment" underneath it, one which protrudes with exaggerated emphasis over the right knee and shin. Kraeling takes these figures to be children and the dress to be the dress of children, but the only figures certainly children in the synagogue seem to wear the usual belted chiton. [12]

When outstanding figures wear the chiton, only the top and bottom of it can be seen from beneath a large garment worn over it—what the Greeks called the himation, a large rectangular shawl ordinarily draped over the left shoulder, wound round the body just above the right hip, and held by throwing both ends over the left arm. The right arm was thus left free. The himation could, however, for special reasons be pulled over into other positions, as in plates V, VII, and fig. 345. Greek representations of the same garment show similarly occasional departures from the conventional position of the pallium, as the Romans called the himation. This garment must not be confused with the Roman toga, which is a generally similar garment, but much larger and made with one long edge rounded, so that it was folded in quite a different way about the wearer. [13] The himation in the synagogue is always of a light color, with the single exception of the one worn by David as he is anointed by Samuel, plate VII, and we shall find this contrast apparently significant. Most of these himatia—except, conspicuously, that of David—are marked, usually at each of their two corners, with a dark design, ending in squared prongs. [14]

Before the discovery of the Dura synagogue this costume of striped chiton and marked himation as used in Christian art appeared to me to have special significance, and probably to have come to Christianity from Judaism, for its use on Old Testament characters in Christian art seemed originally a Jewish heritage. [15] I have since learned, and pointed out above, that it also appeared in Jewish art apparently worn by a figure in the Sheikh Ibreiq cemetery in Nazareth, [16] by Abraham in the Akedah scene of the synagogue at Beth Alpha, [17] and by a figure on a sarcophagus from the Catacomb Vigna Randanini in Rome. [18] It also appeared on a bust marked "God-fearer" in Rome; [19] it seems to be the

---

10. The chiton thus belted up is often called the "short chiton" in handbooks, mistakenly, I believe.

11. *Synagogue*, 115, n. 391.

12. See the child in the Exodus scene, plate XIV, and Ephraim and Manasseh in the reredos, fig. 323.

13. How different the Roman toga was can be seen at once in handbooks. See, for example, Smith, *GRA*, II, 845–850; F. Courby in DS, V, 347–352. Cf. J. Wilpert, *Die Gewandung der Christen in den ersten Jahrhunderten*, 1898, fig. 6; M. G. Houston,

Ancient Greek, Roman, and Byzantine Costume, 1931, 57–67; L. Heuzey, *Histoire du costume antique*, 1922, 227–279.

14. See above, p. 88, and below, pp. 128, 163 f.

15. See above, I, 24–30.

16. Above, I, 99; cf. III, fig. 55.

17. Above, I, 246; cf. III, fig. 638.

18. Above, II, 27.

19. Ibid., 44.

dress worn by Jonah on a Jewish amulet,[20] perhaps by an angel on another amulet,[21] and by Solomon on still another.[22]

In none of these, however, does the costume appear with such distinctness as in the synagogue paintings. There it is worn by Moses,[23] Elijah,[24] Jacob,[25] Samuel,[26] Ezekiel in his triumph,[27] the twelve heads of tribes at the exodus scene,[28] and figures whose identity in five other scenes is disputed,[29] as well as by the Throne Mates both of Solomon [30] and of the Great King of the reredos.[31] In a few cases [32] three threads hang below the mantle, threads that have usually been identified with the *zizith*, or ceremonial threads required by Jewish law for a prayer shawl.

B. THE TEXTILES OF DURA

Hoping to decipher the meaning of these various types of clothing, one naturally first asks how people in Dura dressed during the third century. We had high hopes of answering this question when a large number of fragments of actual textiles were found in the sand embankment hurriedly thrown up inside the wall at the time of the last siege, as well as other pieces in a cemetery. Those in the embankment, Frank Brown assures me, seemed to be the dumpings of what would correspond to a box of old rags, for many were already patched and mended, and no garment was preserved entire. These have now been well published [33] and show surprising affinities with details of the synagogue paintings, but just as surprising differences. First, there are fragments, some nearly intact, of sixteen tunics (what I am calling chitons), most of them with narrow or broad vertical stripes, or clavi, similar to those on the chitons of the synagogue, fig. 104.[34] Secondly, nineteen fragments show the pronged ornament; and these, by analogy with the synagogue dress, are all supposed by those who published the textiles to have come from himatia. The ornament sometimes takes the form of a stripe ending in an arrow, which also is represented in the synagogue.[35] The accompanying illustrations, text fig. 12,[36] show both types. In addition, however, a number of other stripes appeared, woven into the cloth or sewed onto it, and with very rich decoration and design; these differ strikingly from the simple monotony of ornament on Greek dress in the synagogue. The pieces had a great variety of color also, although here we may well take care, since some of the dyes may have held true, others may have faded. Much of the cloth had apparently not been dyed at all, but was

20. Ibid., 225; cf. III, 1042.

21. Above, III, fig. 1052.

22. Ibid., fig. 1056.

23. See, for example, plate v and figs. 324 f., 330 f.

24. See fig. 335.

25. See fig. 345.

26. See fig. 337.

27. See plate xxi and figs. 348 f.

28. See plate xiv and fig. 330.

29. See figs. 326, 334, 336, 341 f.

30. See fig. 329.

31. See fig. 323.

32. See figs. 324–326, 329–331, 336, 349.

33. R. Pfister and L. Bellinger, *Textiles*, 1945 (The Excavations at Dura-Europos, Final Report, IV, ii).

34. See ibid., plate v; cf. pp. 14 and 17, no. 1.

35. See the dress of the last person on the lower row of fig. 339.

36. From *Textiles*, 5, nos. 3, 11, 14, 19, 23.

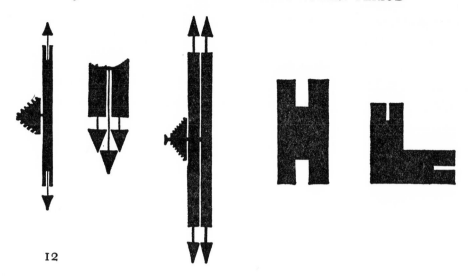

12

what we call "unbleached"; and some of these may originally have been "white," for pure whiteness, as any laundress knows, is extremely hard to preserve. Even in the sand of the desert, garments lying exposed for seventeen centuries could come out really white only by miracle. But the authors point out that a price list of the transactions of the dealer shows that white garments were quite the most expensive,[37] so we may presume that white was rarely worn. I can accordingly see no reason why the authors say: "Pictures, texts, and fragments alike testify to the fact that the clothing of Dura was, for the most part, white." [38]

We have, then, evidence about the clothing from three sources: from the paintings, the price list, and the textile fragments. But all our pictorial representations are from religious art (where the figures are either gods or priests sacrificing) or are pagan, Christian, or Jewish heroes—all, as such, presumably in distinctive dress. Furthermore, the price list shows white dress to have been very expensive, and the fragments of textiles, as the authors say, "are unlike any tunic or mantle in the pictures." [39] We have little evidence, accordingly, from which to conclude either the color or character of ordinary dress at Dura. It seems to me highly unlikely that the ordinary clothing at Dura was either white or ornamented in the way we see it in the paintings or in original textiles. These ornate fragments may well have come from a sacred vestry instead of from a repository of ordinary clothing. It is perplexing that so many of them seem to have been rags when dumped into the embankment, but this in no way indicates that the place where they had been kept was a common or ordinary one. The cloth patches were presumably in much better condition when thrown into the sand in the year 256 than they are now, and it is quite possible that they represent a store of garments, especially of pieces on which were sacral markings, from a ritualistic treasure.[40] This, however, let me repeat, we can no more assert

37. *Textiles*, 12 f. But the meaning of "white" is dubious: see below, pp. 165–168.

38. Ibid.

39. Ibid.

40. As a matter of fact the rags were found not far from the synagogue itself. On the discovery of

the textiles at Dura see also R. Pfister in *Revue des arts asiatiques*, VIII (1934), 86. I find the same danger in discussing the textiles from other cities of the region, such as Palmyra: idem, *Textiles de Palmyre*, I, 1934, 7–9; idem, *Nouveaux Textiles de Palmyre*, 1937, 7–9, 13; idem, *Textiles de Palmyre*, III,

than that they were ordinary rags. The fact is that for evaluating the costumes in the synagogue paintings, the textiles have nothing to tell us unless we beg the question of their origin and character. All the textile fragments tell us is that the ornaments shown on the painted costumes of the synagogue were used on costumes of some sort worn at Dura.

C. THE PERSIAN COSTUME

IF SURVIVING TEXTILES do not tell us when and why people wore a given costume or ornament, we must fall back upon our second possible approach to the costumes in the synagogue paintings and investigate how the sorts of garments and ornaments depicted were used throughout ancient times.

We may well begin with the Persian costume already mentioned, since that is a problem which can be quickly stated but cannot be solved at all. The dress is very often represented in the paintings, yet it still seems on the whole an intrusion into a basically Greek pictorial convention. The persons who wear it do not seem to fit into any classification.[41] Persian dress appears first on the images of the two pagan gods that lie in fragments before the Ark of the Covenant, plate XIII. Here, we shall see, the artists seem to be transferring the incident from the old god of the Philistines to represent the utter futility of the pagan gods in Dura as compared with the God of Israel.[42] The artist seems, that is, to have intended these figures to be recognizable. It will be noticed that the gods have a cape like a chlamys falling behind their caftan and trousers. Basically the same costume appears on Aaron, and, perhaps, on Orpheus, though Aaron's cape is not thrown over the back. In two paintings, plates VI and IX, enthroned kings wear the costume, but the cape has become a coat that has sleeves and a knee-length skirt. In another, a captain wears the Persian costume with the coat when leading his troops on horseback, but Saul has no coat when he sleeps if—as I believe, with most commentators—the upper sleep-

---

1940, 7–9, 11 f.; Pfister assures us that the Palmyrene textiles came only from graves, and we shall see there and elsewhere abundant reason to suppose that burial dress may have had symbolic character. The textiles show indisputable evidence for kinds of cloth people at the time were making, their materials and techniques, but must be treated with great caution as evidence of how people ordinarily dressed. In treating a similar lot of textiles found in a grave in another place in Syria, Pfister follows J. Lauffray in suggesting that the very considerable quantity of textiles at the one place shows that at the final siege people took refuge there and were slaughtered. They accordingly concluded that the fragments represent everyday dress. In view of the great luxury of many of them, this seems an unlikely guess. If the textiles do indeed witness a final slaughter, as is by no means sure, the refugees may have put on sacramental and talismanic clothing for what they knew would be the end. See Pfister, *Textiles de Halabiyeh* (*Zenobia*), 1951, 3, 66 f. (Institut Français d'Archéologie de Beyrouth, Bibliothèque archéologique et historique, XLVIII).

41. As, for example, that of Kraeling, *Synagogue*, 73, who said of the Persian dress that it "is regularly associated with court and temple personnel" in contrast with the " 'lay' group, including patriarchs, prophets, and members of the people not associated with either the religious or the official class." This is a distinction that seems to me not "regularly" made at all.

42. See below, X, 96.

ing figure is he, fig. 344. Such a coat with the trousers appears also on Mordecai, who rides with "royal apparel" by the king's decree,[43] where in contrast with Haman, his coat has become the chlamys again, billowing out behind him as does the coat of Mithra when he kills the bull, and so again is associated with divinity. We know that Mordecai on this occasion wore the royal robe, and that the cloak of the captain, when he is mounted, billows out in the same way. The royal figure is, *eo ipso*, a divine figure, and actually follows a type which appears on Syrian reliefs. To this we shall return.[44]

The Persians, of course, represented their kings in caftan and trousers,[45] but when we have the whole figure on coins, fig. 105,[46] no cape or coat appears. The convention went east for coins of the hellenized Kushans in India, fig. 106,[47] where the kings more resemble the synagogue kings than do the Persian kings themselves. We have no tradition to suggest how or why the Jews of Dura came to think that they could not represent kings unless they clothed them in the oriental dress of royal divinities. In the synagogue the conventional two attendants of the king may be in Persian dress but without the royal cape,[48] or in the full Greek dress.[49] In any case, in these scenes and in the scene with Aaron, whose helpers wear the simple Persian dress, the contrast between the priest or king with the cape or coat and the attendants without it clearly marks an important distinction. This I say in spite of the fact that the greatest king of all in the synagogue, the one at the top of the vine, fig. 323, wears only the caftan and trousers, not the cape or coat, as well as Gute could make out from the remains of the painting. In Jacob's dream, the angels on the ladder have the cape, fig. 345, which strengthens the suggestion of Kraeling that these angels are also kings;[50] they may be indicated as divine kings.

As to the simpler Persian dress, I cannot see that it is put upon characters in any consistent way at all. In the reredos we saw Jacob blessing the thirteen tribes—he in the Greek robe, all the others in Persian dress—and in that dress they appear standing round the great throne above.[51] They also wear this dress as they stand in their little booths receiving the miraculous streams Moses gets for them from the rock, fig. 331. But the same heads of tribes wear the full Greek dress twice in the Exodus scene, plate XIV. It is possible that they wear the Persian dress in the reredos as courtiers when with the king, but they can hardly be called courtiers with their father Jacob. They may, as was sug-

43. Esther VI, 7–11; VIII, 15. The dress in the painting has no resemblance to this description, fig. 336.

44. See below, pp. 180–182.

45. See above, p. 83.

46. From J. de Morgan, *Numismatique de la Perse antique*, 1933, Planches, plate XXI, 5 (E. Babelon, Traité des monnaies grecques et romaines, III, Monnaies orientales, I). It is a bronze coin of Vologeses I, A.D. 51–78. A great number of such representations can be seen in the plates of this volume. The king is sometimes mounted on a horse: ibid., plate XXII, 11 f.

47. From P. Gardner, *The Coins of the Greek and*

Scythic Kings of Bactria and India, 1886, plate XXV, 6; cf. p. 124 (Catalogue of Indian Coins in the British Museum, III). See also R. B. Whitehead, *Catalogue of Coins in the Punjab Museum, Lahore I, Indo-Greek Coins*, 1914, plate XVII, 31; cf. pp. 173 f. It is a coin of Kadphises II, of the first century A.D. The inscription with the king is in Greek and Kharosti. Shiva stands on the other side with a humped bull.

48. See figs. 336 and 338.

49. See figs. 323 and 329.

50. *Synagogue*, 73 f. He calls the cape a chlamys. The original is so damaged that we do not know how it was fastened at the neck.

51. See above, pp. 104 f.

gested above, be servants at the throne.[52] How Solomon was dressed on his throne we do not know, fig. 329, but his two attendants sit on either side in the Greek robe, while a person in Persian dress leads two women forward. The identity of the women is by no means established,[53] and that of the man in Persian dress even less so. With the Throne Mates here again in the Greek robe, we cannot take the Persian dress to be simply the costume of a courtier. Still less can we make it the costume of a priest, for while four men wear it carrying the Ark in fig. 339, the four who carry it in fig. 347 wear the belted Greek chiton with stripes. In this latter scene both of the two men with spears who attack each other on horseback wear the Persian dress, figures which, we shall see, also follow a convention.[54] We recall that the soldiers with Saul had Persian costume with bows and arrows, but no armor, fig. 344. It is hard for me to believe that in the great battle scene the Ark is carried by enemies of Yahweh: in their dignity, and with their military guard of honor, they seem to have quite as much claim to be Levites as the men in Persian dress who carry the Ark in fig. 339. The men in the Esther scene, fig. 336, who wear Persian costume, whether in court or not, are sharply contrasted with the four much larger figures in the center of the picture wearing Greek robes. We felt the same contrast between Jacob and the sons he blessed, and it seems expressed also in fig. 334, where the Ark returns from the temple of the destroyed pagan gods: the oxen (contrary to scripture) are whipped and guided by drivers in the Persian dress, while three majestic figures in the Greek robe walk behind. Even more striking is the contrast made in the Ezekiel scene, figs. 348 f., where Ezekiel himself, instead of the Persian dress, wears the full Greek robe for the final stages of the miracle, but, as I believe, returns to the Persian dress when he is arrested and beheaded.[55]

Only one suggestion seems possible from these examples: the full Persian dress when shown with the cape is extremely sacred and marks a king or heavenly being; but the Persian dress without the cape may be used in almost random exchange with the Greek chiton, and figures thus dressed are shown to be of lesser significance than those in either the full Persian or full Greek costume. We shall watch for the usages of Persian dress as we examine each scene in greater detail, though we shall, I fear, find little to help us in making closer distinctions. But throughout we shall be asking ourselves, without definite answer, why the Persian dress should have intruded itself at all into a convention of art that will seem clearly to have begun with Greek costume only.[56]

D. *THE CHITON AND HIMATION IN THE GRECO-ROMAN WORLD*

THE CONTRAST between the full Persian dress with the cape and the ordinary Persian dress without it has suggested that the full Greek dress with the himation may have some

52. Above, p. 106.
53. See below, X, 103.
54. Below, X, 172–175.
55. Below, X, 183–191.

56. Notably, in Christian tradition the Persian dress appears only for the three kings of the Nativity, and for the three boys in the furnace; see, in general, below, p. 157.

distinctive meaning also.[57] Lack of adequate background in Persian symbolic art makes it impossible to follow this distinction in Iranian tradition. We have, however, much evidence for the use of Greek costume, and can trace a continuity of its tradition that at least suggests meaning behind this distinction as made at Dura.

1. Classical Greece

NOTHING CAN BE FOUND in classical Greece analogous to the emphasis put upon the chiton and himation in the synagogue, and, we shall see, in Christian art. In early times Greeks appeared mainly in a long chiton, but in classical Greece the chiton, rarely with sleeves, was much shortened, and the long chiton put only on gods, priests in official function, actors, musicians, or charioteers—that is, on "persons who came before God or the people on ceremonial occasions." [58] Soldiers and ephebes sometimes wore the chiton under their more typical chlamys, which was a cape fastened at the neck, one that could be spread over the shoulders or could hang directly down the back.[59] Figures with the chlamys and no chiton at all appear everywhere in this period.[60] The large shawl or himation of the Dura paintings was occasionally worn for warmth by older people, and when worn it usually was wrapped about the body as at Dura. But it could still be used as a shawl thrown symmetrically over the shoulders. It actually occurs more commonly on statues without the chiton under it.[61] In contrast to this usual dress, both men and women appear with overwhelming regularity on grave reliefs wearing the chiton and himation, and this, we shall see, persisted into later usage.[62] So it seems appropriate that Dionysus often wears them as he leads Hephaestus on an ithyphallic ass to Olympus,[63] and that king Polydectes and a courtier behind him wear them as Perseus holds the head of Medusa before their freezing eyes, fig. 107.[64]

2. The Hellenistic Period

IN THE HELLENISTIC PERIOD these garments were little changed except to enrich the materials with fine threads, embroidery, and the like, a custom which had begun on garments of the classical period [65] but was elaborated for the clothing of Roman times to make the stripes and marks we are discussing, as well as much richer ornament.[66] The

57. The flying cape often became the Cosmic Cloak on which Eisler, *Weltenmantel und Himmelszelt*, 1910, has uncritically assembled a great deal of material. Nothing indicates such a meaning for the cloak or cape on the synagogue figures, but wearers of the cloak are sufficiently distinguished from those in only the caftan and trousers so that the cloak in itself may have carried such a meaning in the synagogue also. Both the Persian cloak and the himation are essentially coverings over a basic garment.

58. Bieber, *Tracht*, 32.

59. See above, pp. 129 f.

60. Varieties of the chlamys are well illustrated by Bieber, *Kleidung*, plates xxxv–xxxvii. See also Heuzey, *Histoire du costume antique*, 115–141.

61. Cf. Bieber, *Kleidung*, plates xxxviii–xlii.

62. See A. Conze, *Die attischen Grabreliefs*, 1893–1922, passim.

63. See above, VI, figs. 187–190, 192; cf. Reinach, *Vases*, Millin, ii, 66.

64. From Reinach, *Vases*, Millin, ii, 3; cf. p. 45. It is a red-figure calyx-crater by the "Mykonos Painter," at Catania. See Beazley, *ARF*, 355, no. 7.

65. See, for example, above, VI, figs. 192, 206 f., 209, 212.

66. See Bieber, *Tracht*, plates 43, nos. 2 f., 46–48.

chiton by this time often has short sleeves, as in fig. 108,[67] a hellenistic statue at Naples. This sort of dress could appear on people of various sorts, since, as Miss Bieber remarks, the Greeks followed personal taste in dress more than did the class-ridden Romans.[68] So it could appear at Delphi on a child, fig. 110,[69] or on merchants in a shop.[70] Such examples seem relatively rare, however, and the shops may be selling ceremonial wares. Most examples come from memorial statues or grave reliefs and at once raise the question whether the person depicted is wearing his ordinary clothes or a specially recognized holy garb. A statue from Cyrene for example, fig. 109,[71] traditionally called "Hadrian," shows him in this dress instead of the toga. Miss Bieber noticed this antiquarian tendency in such places and concluded: "It must have the meaning that with this dress was connected the conception of some definite (*bestimmten*) divine or heroic personality to whom the living or dead person was in honor assimilated." [72] Although Miss Bieber thinks that the dress recalled originally some "definite" divine personality, she sees people from all over the Roman world using these garments apparently without having any one deity in mind, a usage she calls careless. She thinks it marks the "closing period of hellenic civilization." Therein she may have missed the essential development of later antiquity, in which the "definite" god or goddess came to have little importance in comparison with the sense that Deity is One, and that the Saving Principle should be called by many names. A heroized and divinized mortal, royal or lay, was assimilated not to the ultimate One but to the Saving Principle or Person.

Miss Bieber seems right in saying that no specific deity can be associated with many, or even with most, of such representations in the Roman period,[73] but I cannot see that this would make the robe any less important for the figures wearing it, or for us. For Miss Bieber has, I believe, correctly sensed that this sort of dress, depicted long after it appears to have been commonly worn, had become a sacred robe. We may suggest as a parallel that the costumes of late antiquity and the early middle ages have survived as the sacred garb of priestly ritual, and of monks and nuns: on occasion, however modified, they even give some dignity to academicians. We shall accordingly watch whether usage suggests that the chiton and himation should be thought of as a religious symbol—not one that

67. Courtesy of Soprintendenze alle Antichità della Campania, Naples. See Bieber, *Tracht*, plate 33, no. 1.

68. Ibid., plate 41.

69. Ibid., plate 36, original in the Museum at Delphi, no. 1791.

70. Ibid., plate 43, no. 1. It is a first-century A.D. relief at the Uffizi in Florence. See also the shop of the maker of knives at the Vatican, published by O. Jahn, "Darstellungen antiker Reliefs, welche sich auf Handwerk und Handelsverkehr beziehen," *Berichte, Königliche-Sächsische Gesellschaft der Wissenschaften, philos.-hist. Classe*, XIII (1861), 328–330, plate IX, 9a. The smith may be at the right in ordinary clothes, selling a sacrificial knife to a priest in mantle and chiton. But in a wall painting at Pompeii a baker seems to be in the robe selling bread over a counter: Maiuri, *Roman Painting*, 144.

71. Courtesy of the British Museum: see Bieber, *Tracht*, plate 51, no. 1. Cf. the Egyptian relief of Antoninus Pius and his family, below, fig. 138.

72. Bieber, *Tracht*, 52 f.

73. For a fine collection of hellenistic reliefs see A. Mühsam, "Attic Grave Reliefs from the Roman Period," *Berytus*, X (1952/3), 53–114, with plates VII–XXIV. She speaks only briefly of the garments, but notes, p. 73, that fashion trends do not appear: "Men wear the himation, never the Roman toga."

distinguished a particular religion but one that was part of the lingua franca of symbolism at that time, adaptable to a number of religions.

The earliest robe with striped chiton that I know appears on the strange "vase of the Persians," thought to be of the time of Alexander the Great, fig. 111.[74] It is worn by the man who stands before "Darius" in the middle of the Persian court depicted in the central register.[75] He makes what will appear [76] to be a sacred gesture toward the king, a gesture repeated by the last figure at the left. It is not in point to go into the elaborate discussion which full interpretation of the painting would require, but the Erotes or Victories on Darius' throne, the figures and activities depicted throughout, and the mixture of Greek and Iranian dress and motifs seem to indicate some Greco-Iranian mystic conception. In that case the man before the king would be taken to be a "mystic philosopher." His chiton and himation are Greek, but his hat and shoes may be Persian, and it may be that the stripe for the chiton came from the Orient, where ornament on dress was always more important than for the Greeks, for ornament on dress seems to have had little currency in Greek art.

The chiton-himation appears next a hundred years later, among the Etruscans, but with them so rarely that we have no reason to suppose it represented ordinary Etruscan clothing. Fig. 112,[77] a wall painting from a long-closed tomb near Querciola, shows the garb in the most striking way. The meaning of the scene is disputed, but Messerschmidt seems to me right in seeing in it a father welcoming his son to the lower world, represented by the gate as well as by the demons with their hammers. The dress of both father and son is strikingly the one we are tracing. If van Essen [78] is right in dating it between 230 and 200 B.C., it is the earliest funerary occurrence of the robe with its striping that I know. Notably the younger man's cloak is fringed. The same dress seems also to appear on parents similarly welcoming a son to the lower world on an Etruscan sarcophagus.[79] It reappears on many funerary reliefs, for example fig. 113,[80] where it is worn in full by three men while a fourth wears only the himation. The man on the right thus clothed is parting from his wife; the other three carry the little scrolls that we shall often see with people in this dress.[81]

74. From FR, plate 88; cf. Text, II, 146–149. See also Will, *Le Relief cultuel gréco-romain*, 351–353.

75. Furtwängler's suggestion is quite acceptable that the *Persai* on the little *bema* under him applies to all the group.

76. Though perhaps, as sometimes also appears, it is the gesture of oration.

77. From F. Messerschmidt, "Ein hellenistisches Grabgemälde in Tarquinia," *Studi etruschi*, III (1929), 161–170, plate XXVIII. Further bibliography is reported there. See also G. Q. Giglioli, *L'Arte etrusca*, 1935, plate CCCLXXXVIII, 3. Here the scene, as usual, is reproduced without the gate, and hence misunderstood.

78. C. C. van Essen, *Did Orphic Influence on Etruscan Tomb Painting Exist?* Amsterdam, 1927, 38; cf. 23 f.

79. Messerschmidt, plate XXX, 1; R. Herbig, *Die jüngeretruskischen Steinsarkophage*, 1952, 74, *c*, no. 116; cf. p. 60. On Roman sarcophagi the iconographic tradition may be continued for Oneus standing thus attired before a gate when he quarrels with Meleager about Atalante's taking part in the fatal hunt: see Robert, *Sarkophag-Reliefs*, III, plate LXVII, 225, 226, 228. Oneus as king continues in the same dress on other Meleager sarcophagi: ibid., plate LXXVIII, 230; LXXIX, 231; LXXX, 233, 235; etc.

80. Courtesy of the Soprintendenze alle Antichita, Palermo. Cf. Herbig, plates 55, 57, no. 76; cf. pp. 41 f. It is at the National Museum at Palermo.

81. See below, pp. 146 f.

At the left is again the gate of Hades: we feel that the costume here is used under very much the same conditions as in the other examples. With these in mind it is notable that the incumbents of Etruscan sarcophagi as carved on the lid in almost all cases wear this same garb, with or without the chiton, and that in many scenes where the dead man is in Hades, or on his way there, he is distinguished in the same way.[82] The stripe was probably painted on the tunics, since it appears occasionally—as in fig. 114.[83] In fig. 115,[84] of the second century B.C., the dead person comes to Hades with the stripe again on the chiton. In the "Procession of the Dead" in the Tomba del Tifone, the same robe seems repeatedly used.[85] Most of these examples fall in the hellenistic period; comparison of them with the older wall paintings,[86] suggests that we have here an invasion of the Greek dress to take the place of a similar one original with Etruscans themselves in their funerary art. Indeed Bulard [87] may be right in saying that when the Etruscans took over the Greek chiton and himation for their ceremonial dress, they began making the chiton with the stripes that had long been meaningful to them, stripes which in Rome were soon to be called clavi.

In any case, from this time on, the Greek himation and striped chiton soon becomes the ceremonial dress, the divine dress, and in this form appears throughout the Mediterranean world. So it can be seen on two hellenistic tomb paintings from Cyprus in the British Museum, of which I publish one, fig. 116.[88] Scholars for a century have supposed that this costume was alluded to in the great mystic inscription from Andania, a town in Messenia in lower Peloponnesus.[89] The inscription, definitely dated in the year 92 B.C.,

82. For the portrait figures see Herbig, passim, and for the Hades scenes, or approach thereto, see ibid., plates 12a, 29b, 40b–d, 43a, d, 50, 70a, b, 74b, 80a, 85a, 86a, 108c, 109b, c. One gets the same impression from reliefs on Etruscan vases: see E. Bruun, *I Relievi della urne etrusche*, 1870, passim, esp. plates XVII–XXV, LXXVII f. On plate LXVII, 1 (cf. p. 74), it is worn by king Priam as he receives the Amazons, and so is again the robe of a king.

83. Courtesy of the Louvre Museum, Paris. Cf. Heuzey in DS, I, ii, 1245, fig. 1625, where the stripe, only faintly visible in the photograph, is clearly indicated.

84. From Messerschmidt, *Nekropolen von Vulci*, 1930, 49, fig. 43 (*JDAI*, Ergänzungsheft, XII), a sketch at the Gregorian Museum. See also the urn, ibid., 53, fig. 49.

85. I do not publish this, since the photograph in F. Weege, *Etruskische Malerei*, 1921, plate 49b (republished by Giglioli, plate CCCLXXXIX, 3), shows that it has now almost hopelessly flaked off. A reproduction published in F. Poulsen, *Etruscan Tomb Paintings*, 1922, fig. 45 at p. 58, gives much more detail, and so is from an earlier photograph or has been restored. A still earlier line drawing was published in *Mon. ined.*, II, plate v, from which

J. Martha, *L'Art étrusque*, 1889, redrew it for his fig. 280, p. 415. The earliest reproduction I know is in a quite impressionistic colored plate in Mrs. Hamilton Gray, *Tour to the Sepulchres in Etruria*, 1841, frontispiece. From this perhaps we can get the original color effect. The robes are painted all in soft, light colors, and thereby recall the various tintings of the dress at Dura.

86. See, for example, Messerschmidt, *Nekropolen von Vulci*, plates 4 and 10; Giglioli, *L'Arte etrusca*, plates CVIII, CXI; Martha, *L'Art étrusque*, plate IV at p. 428.

87. M. Bulard, *La Religion domestique dans la colonie italienne de Délos*, 1926, 63–66.

88. Photo courtesy of the British Museum. See R. P. Hinks, *Catalogue of the Greek, Etruscan and Roman Paintings in the British Museum*, 1932, plate III, 8; cf. fig. 6 on the same plate, and pp. 5, no. 6; 6, no. 8. It is of the third century.

89. P. Le Bas, *Voyage archéologique en Grèce et en Asie Mineure*, 1870, Part II (Inscriptions), Vol. II, Section 1, 2 (Explications), 161–176, no. 326a; H. Sauppe, "Die Mysterieninschrift aus Andania," *Abhandlungen der königlichen Gesellschaft der Wissenschaften zu Göttingen*, VIII (1860), 217–274; W. Dittenberger, *Sylloge Inscriptionum Graecarum*, 1900, II,

gives us one of the most important documents about the mystery religions from antiquity. A considerable number of dignitaries are named, and the following is noted about the costume:

> Those [men] to be initiated into the mysteries shall be barefoot and wear white clothing. The women [to be initiated] may not wear transparent dress, nor shall the marks (*sameia*) on their clothing be wider than a half-finger's breadth. Women of ordinary condition shall wear a linen chiton and himation worth not more than a hundred drachmas; young girls shall wear a *kalasēris* [90] or a *sindonitas* [91] with a himation costing not more than a mina. Female slaves shall wear a *kalasēris* or *sindonitas* and a himation worth no more than fifty drachmas. The clothing of the *hierai* [92] shall be as follows: women a *kalasēris* or undergarment (*hupoduma*) without a *skia*,[93] along with a himation, both worth no more than two minas, but the young girls shall wear a *kalasēris* and himation worth no more than a hundred drachmas. In the procession the adult female *hierai* shall wear a woman's undergarment and a woolen himation, on which the marks shall be not more than a half-finger wide; the young girls who are *hierai* shall wear a *kalasēris* and a himation which are not transparent. No one may wear gold, or rouge, or white paint, or a band in the hair, or braids, or any shoes unless made of felt or of skins of animals offered in sacrifice. The *hierai* shall have round wicker seats with white pillows or cushions having on them neither a skia nor a purple stripe.

These statements leave many questions open, but tell us a great deal. For although only the first sentence prescribes the clothing of men who are candidates for the mystic initiation, the elaborate specifications for the women show how important the matter was considered. I should guess that men came barefoot in white garments, and that stripes were on those garments. That was all taken for granted: but the women, apparently, had been getting out of hand, since elaborate prohibitions almost always suggest a practice. They had been coming with gold ornaments, their faces painted red and white, and wearing diaphanous clothing. That is, some of the women had been using the parade as a means of offering themselves,[94] and it is to this that we owe the detailed description. We

---

461–473, no. 653; *IG*, v(i), 1390; F. C. Grant, *Hellenistic Religions: The Age of Syncretism*, 1953, 31 f. (The Library of Religion, II); Kern in PW, I, 1894, 2116–2120; G. Daux, "Note sur le règlement des mystères d'Andanie," *Revue de philologie*, 3d series, XVI (1942), 58–62; also the bibliography in *Supplementum Epigraphicum Graecum*, XI (1954), 172, no. 978. Cf. Pausanias, *Description of Greece*, IV, i, 2, 6, 8; ii, 7, 10; xxvi, 6; xxxiii, 6.

90. A long Egyptian or Persian garment with tassels or fringe: see LS, s.v.

91. Any garment of fine cloth, usually linen.

92. I shall guess that the *hierai* and *hieroi* were called "holy ones" because they had been initiated in former years. We have thus descriptions of the dress for those about to be initiated, and for those already initiated.

93. Literally, a "shadow." This use is unique and its meaning uncertain. It may mean "spotless," but in LS, s.v., it is conjectured that it means without any markings. A few lines below in the inscription the word reappears in contrast with "purple stripes" and so Le Bas guesses it means some kind of dyed pattern other than the *sameia* and "purple."

94. Philo describes how male prostitutes offered themselves as much like women as they could by "braiding and adorning the hair of their heads, painting their faces with red and white paint," a phenomenon especially conspicuous at the celebration of pagan mysteries: *Spec.* III, 37–41. The words seem quite proverbial for prostitutes.

must, however, be cautious how we dissociate this from religion. It is entirely possible that we have here another of the slight traces of ritualistic and orgiastic copulation which was quite accepted in many ancient oriental religions, and tended to reappear, according to pagans, in worship of Dionysus, Aphrodite, and even Christ; according to Christians it was common in Gnosticism.

One wonders whether the *kalasēris*, which was a chiton associated with Egypt, was not the striped chiton that appears so much on Egyptian mummy portraits, and whether the dress was not already by 91 B.C. a standardized symbol to go from one mystery religion to another. Nearly two centuries later Plutarch witnessed the interchangeability of Dionysiac and Egyptian mystic values and ideas,[95] and the references to the dress and stripes in the inscription suggest that this interchange may well have been going on long before him. Be that as it may, the importance of attending mystery rites in a white chiton and himation with stripes has an indisputable witness at Andania.[96]

3. *The Roman World* [97]

IN THE PAINTINGS of Pompeii robes with stripes have not yet been established as a fixed convention, but have importance in many scenes. At the lararia, figs. 117 [98] and 118,[99] the striped garments are togas and tunics; but it is dangerous to infer from these scenes that we have the usual Roman garb with clavi, since the paintings unquestionably represent religious ceremonies. A young priest wears the himation and striped chiton on a fresco from

95. See above, VI, 75–80.

96. It may be worth suggesting that the seats and pillows which were *not* to have a purple stripe may indicate that this was peculiar, and that people ordinarily wanted the stripes on their mystic banqueting cushions. These may be the stripes on such cushions that have been remarked many times. See above, p. 67.

97. The following section was completed some time before the important article appeared by Margarete Bieber, "Roman Men in Greek Himation (Romani Palliati): A Contribution to the History of Copying," *Proceedings of the American Philosophical Society*, CIII (1959), 374–417. I have added to my study a few examples which I learned from her, but little else, since in general only in the last section, pp. 411–417, does she comment on the meaning of the dress. She points out that the many statues in the himation with empty sockets for portrait heads "imply that the figures must have had a definite meaning" (p. 412), but then seems to minimize that meaning. She makes of the scrolls which the figures usually carry only that they indicate educated men (p. 413); she says that the garb expressed piety and modesty, and "*therefore* it

became the prescribed form for funerary, commemorative, and honorary monuments" (ibid.); again "We see it so frequently in art *because* it was a popular costume for everyday wear" (p. 415; in both quotations, italics mine). But she herself points out that the robe is the proper one in which to appear before Pluto and Persephone, and quotes Tertullian that the dress had religious association. It seems to me that the evidence goes farther in this direction than she indicates, and that the monuments, especially the funerary and ritualistic ones, give poor witness indeed to ordinary costume. But the reader will find in her study a rich collection on the dress, and a critical history of its various drapings.

98. National Museum, Naples. Photo Anderson, 25,709. From Pompeii. The figure with the pig recalls similar scenes at Delos from perhaps a century earlier: Bulard, *Description des revêtements peints à sujets religieux*, 1926, plates XVIII, XIX, XXI, XXV (Ecole Française d'Athènes, Délos, IX).

99. Photo Anderson, 24,875. Pompeii, Casa dei Vetti. Cf. Maiuri, *Roman Painting*, 147; Elia in *AAL*, *N*, 1934, 272, fig. 5; and an Isis shrine as published by P. Gusman, *Pompeii* (1900), 83.

Pompeii, fig. 121,[100] and one suspects that the similarly clothed Canace in fig. 119 [101] also has sacerdotal value.[102] Three figures, identified as priests, in a procession of a thiasos of the Magna Mater at Pompeii have the same costume.[103] In the house of Menander at Pompeii a mural shows Cassandra prophesying woe to Troy at the entrance of the wooden horse. As prophetess she is the only figure in the painting who wears the striped chiton and mantle.[104] Figures with the striped chiton and himation bear divine gifts as they float in a heavenly ceiling with cupids and birds, fig. 21.[105]

The striped chiton without the mantle again appears most strikingly upon a row of "slaves" painted in the late second or early third century on the walls of a house in the Via dei Cerchi at Rome, four of whose six figures can be seen in fig. 122.[106] One of these carries a light wand, two have cloths thought to be table napkins (*mappae*), one a garland, and one a dish or basket of fruit. The floor is strewn with undescribed utensils, boxes, vessels, and a pair of sandals. It has been customary to suppose that such a procession indicated that the room in which it was painted was the dining room, and because they are in the dining room the figures have been taken to be table servants. If, however, they are table servants, I suspect that the meal at which they are ideally serving is a sacred meal of some sort. For the cloths and the garland they carry, along with the vessels and closed boxes on the floor (dubiously an accompaniment of elegant banqueting), are much more conspicuous than the single tray of fruit the meal seems to offer. And the sandals removed beside one of the "servants" suggests the bare feet of religious ceremony in the ancient as in the modern East, as well as the bare feet of Moses at Dura, figs. 324 f. Lugli came to the same conclusion, that the room was a sacred chapel, by the obvious route of considering the wall paint-

100. Courtesy of the Soprintendenza alle Antichita della Campagna. Cf. Maiuri, plate facing the table of contents, and pp. 89 f. It is at the National Museum, Naples. The dress seems too short for a woman.

101. Photo Alinari, 29,821. See P. Marconi, *La Pittura dei Romani*, 1929, fig. 137; cf. p. 103. It is at the Vatican Museum, where it was taken from the Roman villa of Tor Marancio. Canace is here represented with the dagger, ready to kill herself, and the artist may well have considered her suicide a sacrifice.

102. See the priest in the robe sacrificing with the three nymphs, fig. 189.

103. Spinazzola, *Pompei*, plate XIV. See also Venus in dark purple with gold clavi, ibid., plate XV.

104. Maiuri, *La Casa del Menandro*, 1932, Tavole, plate V; cf. Text, 44–48.

105. Alinari (Photo Brogi 6534). It is a ceiling from Stabiae at the National Museum, Naples; see Curtius, 412 and 415, fig. 226; Swindler, *Painting*, fig. 619. The quartered design filled with symbols recalls the ceiling of both the early and later synagogues at Dura: see above, p. 42. The striped tunic appears also on two of the famous portraits of Pompeii: Maiuri, *Roman Painting*, 100, 102 f. Maiuri tries to make the second represent a baker and his wife, "obviously unlettered, capable at best of entering up the accounts of their thriving bakery," in spite of the fact that the man holds a scroll, and that the woman holds a tablet while she crosses her lips with the stylus. To an American, such automatic ascription of low intelligence to bakers is quite unintelligible, granted that the man was a baker at all. In a portrait, the stylus to the lips would more obviously refer to secret writings than to perplexity about addition.

106. From a watercolor painting by F. G. Newton, published as plate III by Mrs. Arthur Strong, "Forgotten Fragments of Ancient Wall-Painting in Rome, II," *Papers of the British School at Rome*, VIII (1916), 91–102. Cf. D. Marchetti in *AAL, M,* Ser. IV, Vol. X (1892), 44–48; Wirth, *Römische Wandmalerei*, plates 29–31; cf. pp. 126–128.

ings together with the mosaics on the floor of the same room. Here, fig. 123,[107] are two lines of another procession made up of four men in each line, wearing the same striped chitons and with the high shoes of the Moses figure.[108] In the mosaic procession the figures carry banners and caducei. How the scene could have been more definitely flagged as a religious one, some sort of mystic procession, it is hard to imagine. Since the same strange boxes are on the floor in both processions, the painted and the mosaic, the only possible conclusion seems to be that the two processions mark different episodes in rites of the same cult, and that the room was a mystic chapel (where mystic meals may well have been served).[109] The same problem seems to me presented by a banqueting scene in a Pompeian mural where the servants are similarly dressed, and the banqueters wear a himation over their striped tunics.[110] I should guess that they are a type of religious servitor called *camillus*, of which the Metropolitan Museum has a fine specimen in bronze, fig. 124.[111] Even in bronze, this figure shows the stripe up the left leg and shoulder put in by copper inlay.

Orpheus wears the full costume as he leads Euridice toward the gate of Hades, while an individual seated in front of him wears the striped chiton.[112] The Elysium to which Hermes leads the fortunate wearing the full robe shown in fig. 125 [113] may be a part of the same mystery as that of the house of the Via dei Cerchi. Both designs are of approximately the same date, early third century. It is just possible that the mystery here also was that of Sabazius, since we saw Vibia brought in to judgment by Mercury, and then to an Elysian banquet by the "Good Angel," where again the waiters, and those who were judged "good," wore the striped tunic.[114] Hermes himself wears the stripes on another Pompeian painting.[115]

This dress appears again for the teacher, the philosopher, or the poet, a usage not at all in contrast to the mystic use, for by the second century the word "philosophy" had come

107. From G. Lugli, "La Sede degli araldi pub-lici," *Capitolium*, IX (1933), 451; idem, *I Monumenti antichi de Roma e suburbio*, I, 1930, 405, fig. 88a, cf. pp. 402–406; idem, *Roma Antiqua*, 1946, 614–616. The eight figures were also published separately by M. E. Blake in *Memoirs of the American Academy in Rome*, XVII (1940), plate 18; cf. pp. 96 f.

108. Wirth speaks of their wearing *hosen*, which appears in Miss Blake as "hose." I see on the legs no trousers, but only light-streaks as in the garments. Oriental trousers at this time are always represented as loose and baggy. See A. C. Levi, *Barbarians on Roman Imperial Coins and Sculpture*, 1952 (Numismatic Notes and Monographs, no. 123).

109. Lugli recognized the figures as mystical, which Wirth admitted to be possible, but thought it a room used for the training of slaves as waiters, so that its decorations were a "token of great peda-gogical understanding." This Miss Blake followed: she called the painting "realistic pictures of ancient

waiters pursuing their profession . . . a glimpse into the intimate life of the Romans." That these are "simpler" explanations than the obvious re-ligious one I do not comprehend. I take the room to have been the mystic chapel of the house, as Phyllis Lehmann understood the room she called the Hall of Aphrodite; see her *Roman Wall Paintings from Boscoreale in the Metropolitan Museum of Art*, 1953, 76 f. (Monographs on Archeology and Fine Arts, V).

110. Marconi, fig. 116; cf. p. 82.

111. Courtesy of the Metropolitan Museum of Art, New York: gift of Henry G. Marquand, 1897. For the *camillus* see E. Samter in PW, III, 1431–1433; L. C. Spaulding, *The "Camillus"-Type in Sculpture*, 1911.

112. Marconi, fig. 136, p. 103. It is a fresco from Ostia, perhaps of the late second century.

113. From Wirth, plate 38; cf. pp. 148 f.

114. See above, III, figs. 839, 841 f.; and II, 45 f.

115. Spinazzola, *Pompei*, plate XII.

largely to mean mystic teaching, as it does, for example, in Philo. So when Virgil is put into that costume with a Muse at either side of him, fig. 126,[116] we feel that Virgil is being presented as the religious seer, almost, if not quite, apotheosized. The convention appears in a Vatican manuscript of Virgil of the fourth to the fifth century, fig. 127.[117] We know that in Plato's time poets were thought to be seers, men inspired, and that Plato usually treats them with great respect in spite of his theoretical protests in the *Republic*. Socrates himself was told in a dream to "make music": he had considered his philosophy supreme music, but in prison thought it safe before he died to make some formal verses. The connection of poetry and immortality is obviously assumed throughout,[118] and from Plato's time the works of the poets are cited with the reverence of a Calvinist preacher or an orthodox Jew citing the Scriptures.[119]

Figures in the chiton and himation have long been recognized as poets or philosophers in Pompeii [120] and at Ostia.[121] Indeed, I cannot resist suggesting that the costume means the same in the Baths of Caracalla. Here in mosaic is a large series of representations of boxers and other athletes with amazingly powerful physiques, intermingled with men in the robe, of which fig. 129 [122] gives a good example. In this mosaic most of the figures in the robe gesture with one hand as though teaching. In itself this recalls the Greco-Roman ideal, which we usually use Juvenal's line to express: [123] *orandum est ut sit mens sana in corpore sano.* But we notice that all but one of the men in the robe hold little palm branches in one hand, as do several of the athletes. With the human figures are four plaques where the palm branch seems to be represented with boxers' equipment. When we consider that the Baths of Caracalla were almost a community center,[124] with two large library rooms as well as club rooms, and that a large Mithraeum [125] was beneath it, we may well recall the close connection in the Roman mind, as formerly in the Greek, between athletics and religious philosophy. The Greek gymnasium was a place where both the body and the mind were trained, and we have seen that one of the most widespread conceptions of religion,

116. Courtesy of the Vatican Museum, where it is. Another, almost indistinguishably similar, is at the Musée Alaoui, Le Bardo, Tunisia.

117. Courtesy of the Vatican Library, where it is in Codex Vat. Lat. 3867, fol. 3ᵛ. See Swindler, *Painting*, 409, and fig. 629. The mark on the himation will seem to be highly important, see above, p. 128, and below, pp. 162–164.

118. *Phaedo*, 60D–61B. Plato's rejecting of the poets in the *Republic* is better known than his usual treatment of them as divinely inspired. See esp. the *Ion, Phaedrus*, 244A–245E, and A. E. Taylor, *Plato*, 1929, 38–41.

119. See below, pp. 141–147, for the figure with the scroll.

120. See, for example, Curtius, fig. 162 on p. 273; Maiuri, 64; Spinazzola, plate xxvi.

121. Wirth, plate 26. See the god Silvanus in the same dress at Ostia, ibid., plate 37.

122. Photo Alinari, 29,925. Cf. Blake, 111 f., and plates 28 f. Her plate 28 gives a general impression of the mosaics as they are set up in the Lateran Museum, and plate 29 selects all those wearing the chiton and himation, or only in the himation. Miss Blake describes these as "trainers." The full publication is by B. Nogara, *I Mosaici antichi conservati nei Palazzi Pontifici del Vaticano e del Laterano*, 1919, 1–3, and plates I–IV.

123. *Satires*, IV, x, 356.

124. E. Ghislanzoni in *AAL, N*, 1912, 305–325. Bieber in *Proceedings of the American Philosophical Society*, CIII (1959), figs. 61 f., pp. 413–415, shows two sarcophagi on which a couple wearing the robe appear before Pluto and Persephone, one led in by Hermes.

125. Zeus, Mithra, Helios, and Serapis seem here to unite in the "One": Ghislanzoni, p. 323.

found even in the letters of Paul himself, was that religion is the great *agōn*, or struggle. Victory, symbolized by the crown or palm branch, meant spiritual victory, immortality, quite as much as it did physical victory in the games. It is true that nothing but the contrast between the naked bodies and the robes suggests this here directly, but nothing whatever identifies the robed figures with Miss Blake's "trainers." The combination of the Mithraeum and libraries with the symbolic representation of physical and spiritual achievement at a bath suggests how the baths were adapted to Romans of all sorts, from the cynically Stoic to the members of mystery religions.

We obviously cannot here review all the appearances of the robe in Roman sculpture. I shall accordingly, as I have already done with similar problems, appeal to a "random sample," and take in this case the pieces in the Vatican Museum, and of these only the ones shown in the plates by Amelung and Lippold. In the three volumes of this publication I have noted the robe on only twenty-three people, which means that it is familiar but not common in Roman carving. Five carvings show the funerary couch with a man or woman lying on it in chiton and himation, two of them with cupids.[126] In one instance the cupid [127] sits on the man's leg and plays a lyre. This connects the whole with the hope of immortality which Marrou expounded for such symbolism.[128] Since we have supposed that such a pose assimilates the person to immortality, even though the appurtenances of the funerary banquet are not shown, this high proportion seems significant. The person on the couch occasionally wears a mantle without the chiton, but wears no other kind of dress. On a sarcophagus for a small child a boy wearing both garments holds a large bird and another bird looks up at him from his feet. The birds,[129] like the cupids [130] which have already appeared, suggest that the boy is thought of with reference to the future life. One fragment shows a woman standing in the chiton and himation, but all context is lost.[131] On a cinerary urn a man and woman in the Greek clothing are being married: [132] the reference may be to their eternal union in the urn, or to a mystic marriage that promised immortality.

On another sarcophagus a man and woman sit on either side of what we may call the mystic door or the door of death, fig. 128.[133] Both have scrolls and wear the chiton and himation, and a pair of Muses flank each of them. The Muses are similarly dressed. Under the chair of the woman is a female comic mask, under that of the man a male tragic mask,

126. See Amelung, *Sculp. Vatican.*, I, plate 70, no. 533, pp. 662 f.; plate 103, no. 121, pp. 853 f. (the cupid playing a lyre with this figure hardly indicates to me, as to Amelung, that the man portrayed liked love songs); II, plate 1, no. 1, pp. 3 f. (here again the person, a woman, is accompanied by cupids); plate 19, no. 73, pp. 179 f.; plate 58, no. 404, pp. 615 f.

127. The first listed in the preceding note.

128. Marrou, *MA*.

129. For the symbolism of birds, see above, VIII, 22–70.

130. For the symbolism of cupids, see above, VIII, 3–21. Amelung calls a recumbent female, in his I, plate 31, no. 6, pp. 314 f., a figure of Autumn surrounded by cupids with grapes. She wears the robe, as do four Seasons with cupid, ibid., plate 29, no. 177, pp. 291–293. All wear the robe, and suggest to me the mystic meaning of Seasons: see above, VIII, 190–192.

131. Amelung, I, plate 31, no. 5, pp. 313 f.

132. Ibid., I, plate 22, no. 34, pp. 194 f.

133. Courtesy of the Vatican Museum: see Amelung, II, plate 13, no. 48; cf. pp. 117–120.

while gorgonea and lion masks with rings are on the central doors that stand slightly ajar.[134] Here we have poetry as Music which takes one safely through the door of death. All these motifs—including, as we shall see,[135] the scroll—seem to point to hope of future life. In the Vatican Museum just below this piece is the lid of a sarcophagus with portrait busts of a couple, each in the robe and each portrayed against the curtain that serves on Roman sarcophagi as an alternative for the door.[136] Even more strikingly in another funerary relief a woman in the Greek dress is being trained by a "philosopher" or mystic teacher on either side of a central doorway; [137] apparently on the strength of her mystic knowledge, she goes behind the veil of death carrying her scroll and accompanied by a cupid. On a few pieces Roman dress is worn where we should expect the Greek, as on one sarcophagus where a man in a toga and a woman in a Greek mantle are led through the door together by a cupid,[138] and on another [139] where the man and wife, similarly clothed, stand on either side of the central door of death, each led by a small boy again, a boy whom we probably should take to be a cupid in spite of his wearing a tunic. One of these two boys carries a vase, the other a little casket. Many other figures are on this latter sarcophagus, but not so as to confuse the sense that here we have a very well established convention, in which the man may wear the toga but usually, like the woman, wears the Greek dress as one or both of them go into the future life with mystic tokens and the cupid as psychopomp.

One piece perhaps shows an anomalous use of the Greek dress: a child sarcophagus on which a group of children—many in the full robe, some only in the chiton—play at "castellated nuts." [140] Some of the play is by girls in front of a curtain, which we have just said usually indicates death when on a sarcophagus, so that the whole may well have some eschatological reference.

It is not surprising that the persons clothed in the chiton and himation on funerary reliefs should seem to have tokens of immortality. We are surprised, however, that on only ten pieces other than funerary ones can I find any real indication of this sort of dress. Three of them are statues of enthroned goddesses,[141] while one majestic standing figure probably represents a goddess also.[142] A statue of Dionysus [143] has the full Greek dress, as does a figure of Hera [144] and a woman who stands at an altar sacrificing with a man wearing the

---

134. For the symbolism of masks see above, VII, 202–223.

135. See below, pp. 146 f.

136. Amelung, *Sculp. Vatican.*, II, plate 13, no. 49*a*, p. 126. Cupids at the ends of this lid seem to me to express both death and hope in death.

137. See above, IV, fig. 108, and p. 143. Cf. G. Kaschnitz-Weinberg, *Scultura del Magazzino del Museo Vaticano*, 1936, plate LXXXIII, 520 (Monumenti vaticani di archeologia e d'arte, VI). The two ends of this sarcophagus are also in the Vatican Museum: see Amelung, III, 176 f., nos. 573, 580; plate 66. They each show the same woman, simi-

larly clothed and with a scroll, between two Muses.

138. Amelung, I, plate 29, no. 169, pp. 288 f.

139. Ibid., II, plate 17, no. 60, pp. 153–158.

140. Ibid., I, plate 68, no. 497A, pp. 638 f. For the game see Smith, *GRA*, 247 f.

141. Amelung, I, plate 113, nos. 213, 215, 216, pp. 879–881.

142. Ibid., plate 114, no. 218, pp. 881 f.

143. Ibid., II, plate 4, no. 16, p. 45.

144. Ibid., plate 80, no. 442, pp. 717 f. This frieze has been so much restored, however, that it has little evidential value.

toga.[145] When, finally, a man wears the chiton and himation in a portrait statue,[146] one can accordingly conclude that he has been portrayed in ceremonial garments. For the use of the robe in this random sample has led us too often to monuments of ritualistic dignity, if not to mystical or eschatological associations or to the gods themselves, for us to suppose that this dress was ever used casually, or merely to correspond to what we might call "formal" dress.

4. Greco-Roman Egypt

WHETHER FROM ROME or from its own hellenistic infiltrations, Egypt took over the convention for its mummy portraits in a most striking way.[147] The chiton and himation appear, though not always, on people in the Isis mystery.[148] In one scene from Herculaneum, fig. 131,[149] at the Naples Museum, all are in white except a figure at the front, left, who has the striped chiton with a dark himation, a scene that may represent this person as being initiated. This, if true, would throw considerable light on the scene of the anointing of David at Dura, where the same contrast is represented.[150] Another procession of Egyptian worship in Rome likewise puts the priests in white garments.[151] We know that the changing of robes had long been a highly important matter in Egyptian religion. Even in the age-old Pyramid Texts we read "O, *N.*, take thy garment of light, take thy veil upon

145. Ibid., plate 61, no. 415, p. 647 f. A man wears a toga in what seems a mystic marriage also on another Roman sarcophagus: ibid., III, i, 79–82, no. 522; plate 30. G. Lippold says the carving of the clothing has been entirely recut, so that the man may well originally have worn the himation.

146. Ibid., I, plate 51, no. 286, pp. 498 f.

147. The best collection of these in color that I know is by W. M. Flinders Petrie, *The Hawara Portfolio, Paintings of the Roman Age*, 1913 (British School of Archeology in Egypt and Egyptian Research Account, XIX), and idem, *Roman Portraits and Memphis (IV)*, 1911 (same series, XVII). Some are beautifully reproduced in *EES*, II, ia, plates VI–XI; and in W. de Grüneisen, *Le Portrait: Traditions hellénistiques et influences orientales*, Rome, 1911; D. B. Tanner published several in the *Bulletin of the Fogg Museum*, II (1932), 4–9. Since the publication of the interesting study by P. Buberl, *Die griechisch-ägyptischen Mumienbildnisse der Sammlung Th. Graf*, 1922 (with excellent reproductions), it has been agreed that the portraits date from the first to the fourth century after Christ. H. Drerup, *Die Datierung der Mumienporträts*, 1933 (Studien zur Geschichte und Kultur des Altertums, XIX, i), dates them roughly the same, beginning from Augustus; he

supposes that the Romans introduced such portraits into Egypt, but this seems very doubtful to me, for C. R. Williams has instances of a much earlier use of Greek dress in Egypt: *JEA*, V (1918–19), 282–285; A. Reinach in *RA*, Ser. IV, Vol. XXIV (1914), 32–53; Ser. V, Vol. II (1915), 1–36. Older items are cited there. Interesting material and comment will be found in M. Dimand, *Die Ornamentik der ägyptischen Wollwirkereien*, 1924.

148. See the "Festival in the Isis Temple" from Herculaneum, at the National Museum, Naples, published by Curtius, 315, fig. 180.

149. Courtesy of the Soprintendenza alle Antichità delle Campania; see Marconi, 80, fig. 108.

150. See below, pp. 187–196 and fig. 337.

151. It is the great Palestrina mosaic at the Barberini Palace in Rome. A drawing of the whole mosaic was in *BCA*, XXXII (1904), 260; the procession, in the lower right corner of the mosaic, can best be seen in Société Archéologique d'Alexandrie, *Monuments de L'Egypte gréco-romaine*, I (1926), plate LVI, and in G. Gullini, *I Mosaici di Palestrina*, 1956, plates I and XIX; cf. Rostovtzeff, *MDAI, Röm.*, XXVI (1911) 59–62. See also the Isiac procession in Amelung, *Sculp. Vatican.*, II, plate 7, no. 55, and the sacrifice, ibid., plate 82, no. 19.

thee, clothe thyself with the eye of Horus . . . that it may gain thy respect among the gods. . . . This is a sound garment which Horus has made for his father, Osiris." [152]

In the much later Book of the Dead the garment is said directly to have saving power: "Destroy ye [all] the evil which belongeth unto Åmen-ḥetep by means of this garment of purity. Hold [ye] him guiltless, then, for ever and ever, and destroy ye [all] the evil which belongeth unto him." [153] This "garment of purity" would seem to come to the corpse especially at burial. In the mysteries of Isis in Roman times, Apuleius tells us, the young men in the processions wore robes that were "snowy and festal," probably the Greek himation. The initiates in general wore linen garments, *candore puro luminosi* "pure shining white." [154] It is the shining, light effect that was the real meaning of the garments. Lucius himself got a "crude linen robe" to enter the mysteries,[155] but emerged with twelve stoles and in a religious dress.[156] The dress consisted of a fine linen garb covered with embroidered flowers, and a chlamys that hung down his back embroidered with beasts, dragons, and griffins. So clothed, crowned with a royal crown, and carrying a torch, he was adorned "like the sun." This made him initiated only into the religion of Isis: he had still to go on into Osiris himself. The text does not say that he got the linen robe as culmination of the second initiation, but this is implied in that the priest of Osiris who visited him to encourage his coming into the higher state was thus attired.[157]

Plutarch's testimony is just as direct. The so-called "bearers of the vessels" and "wearers of the sacred robe" (*hierostoloi*) have the secret writings of the gods within them, the outer mark in the "sacred garb" (*hē esthēs hē hiera*). "Wearing a coarse cloak does not make a philosopher," he continues, "nor does dressing in linen and shaving the hair make votaries of Isis." It appears that the linen garment of the priest of Isis could also be a "heavenly blue." [158] Apparently the special garment was widely worn.

It may be presumed that the garment thus described was our "robe." That dress, with stripes, appears on a painted grave stele of the Ptolemaic period in Egypt, fig. 133,[159] in which the attendant wears only the chiton. But many more than half of the people portrayed in mummy portraits of the Roman period wear the robe.[160] One of the most interesting examples I know has been published as fig. 257 in Volume VI,[161] while a fairly common

152. Mercer, *Pyramid Texts*, I, 141 f., lines 737*a–d*, 740.

153. *BD*, 580, (chap. CLXXI, 6).

154. *Metamorphoses*, XI, 10; ibid., 9: *veste nivea et cataclista. Cataclista* is a transliteration of the Greek *katakleiston*, a word applied to the himation when it was folded over, or closed. There were white curtains in the shrine: ibid., 20.

155. Ibid., 23: *linteo rudique*.

156. Ibid., 24.

157. Ibid., 27. Cumont, *L'Egypte des astrologues*, 1937, 118, n. 4, has a large collection of parallel passages.

158. Plutarch, *On Isis*, 3 f. (352B–D). G. Parthey,

Plutarch über Isis und Osiris, 1850, 275, already pointed out that the monuments confirmed Plutarch's statement.

159. From E. Breccia, "Nuovi scavi nelle Necropoli di Hadra," *Bulletin de la Société Royale d'Archéologie d'Alexandrie*, N.S., VII (1930), plate XIV; cf. p. 116.

160. Taking the portraits in Edgar, *Coffins*, as offering a random sample, I found the stripe recognizable on at least fifty portraits as compared to twenty-six without stripes. Nineteen seem to wear the chiton and himation.

161. See also A. Reinach in *RA*, Ser. V, Vol. II (1915), 16, fig. 13; Pagenstecher, *Nekropolis*, 1919,

adaptation of the stripe for an otherwise quite Egyptian dress can be seen in fig. 255 of the same volume.[162] In Volume V, fig. 186, a woman is shown wearing the Greek robe in an Egyptian ceremony getting the divine fluid. Another striking Egyptian representation shows the deceased in the full robe and carrying a scroll, coming into the presence of the gods, fig. 130.[163] We shall discuss the scroll with such figures later, but in this case we would assume he is carrying the Book of the Dead, or a part of it, or a later counterpart used in the Isis mystery. The figure in the robe going into the presence of the gods is not common, but at least two other instances exist; [164] so we may conclude that the mummy portrait busts only abbreviate this event: the people buried are dressed to come into God's presence. Most of the portraits show only the bust, and we cannot say how the dress was finished below the chest; but the presumption is that, especially in the instances when it is white, it went down to form the usual himation and chiton. It is worth suggesting, though no supporting evidence can be brought forward, that such uniform burial costume corresponds to the hints given by Apuleius. Thus the darker robe may be worn by one initiated only into the earlier rites, those of Isis, which Apuleius describes in terms of its rich embroidery, while the white robe may tell us that this person is clothed in the *candore puro luminosi* of the rites of Osiris himself, the robes that mark him "adorned like the sun." Whether the god was called Osiris or Serapis cannot be determined, for Serapis usually appears in the Greek robe in Roman times, as in a stele from Xanthos in Lycia in the British Museum, fig. 134 [165] though of course if stripes originally had been painted on this material, none are now left.[166] The same figure is called Dusaris in Syria.[167]

In Egyptian material the Greek himation and striped chiton again seem to declare that the one who wears them has in some sense transcended ordinary human nature. It is interesting, therefore, to see that in Egypt a new feature appears with this uniform of sanctity, namely the peculiar bar with forked ends, described above as inevitably put on this robe in the Dura synagogue.[168] We shall discuss this mark below,[169] but note its appearance here. It can clearly be seen on the two mummy portraits, of figs. 255 and 257, Volume VI. Fig. 132 [170] of the present volume shows the mark very distinctly, while the stripe on the chiton can be seen just below the grapes. The pronged bar on the cloth beside the lady's cheek is bent into a right angle in fig. 135,[171] and the stripe is clearly in-

44, fig. 29; the painted Roman Egyptian tombstones described in that work, chap. II, repeatedly seem to have had figures in the robe upon them.

162. See also above, VI, 91 f. (with further examples cited in n. 165) and 117.

163. From Musée des Beaux-Arts Alexandre III à Moscou, *Pamiatniki*, n.d., plate xv. It is a shroud in the Golenishchev collection.

164. Ibid., plate xvi; Edgar, *Sculpture*, plate xxiv, 27.541.

165. Courtesy of the British Museum; cf. A. Michaelis, "Serapis Standing on a Xanthian Marble in the British Museum," *JHS*, VI (1885), 287–318, plate LVIII, where many parallels are given.

See also W. Drexler, "Der Isis und Serapis-Cultus in Kleinasien," *Numismatische Zeitschrift*, XXI (1889), plates 1 f.; *EES*, II, ii, plate III, 8.

166. The stripes may well have originally been painted on the little statues of Serapis in Edgar, plate II, 27.436; plate III, 27.438.

167. See above, VI, fig. 245; cf. pp. 68 f.

168. See above, pp. 88, 126.

169. See below, pp. 162–164.

170. Courtesy of the Egyptian Museum, Cairo. See Edgar, *Coffins*, plate xxi, 33.154; cf. plate XLVII, 33.281.

171. Courtesy of the Egyptian Museum, Cairo. See Edgar, plate xxi, 33.155; cf. plate XXIX, 33.209.

dicated in spite of the darkness of the costume in general. Such a darker dress, I suspect, may indicate an initiate into Isis rather than Osiris. When we see that a large swastika could take the place of this pronged bar on a robe,[172] we must suppose that the bar itself carried some significance.

5. Syria

AS WE GO NORTH toward Syria, we find that the chiton and himation continue to be worn by prominent people, such as priests or the dead, though relatively little painting tells us how these garments were marked. Sarcophagi of the East, indeed, remind us of the hellenistic grave stele, in that the people portrayed on them almost always wear the Greek chiton and himation. As they lie on the funerary couch—celebrating, I believe, the eternal banquet of immortality—they usually wear the himation, as in fig. 90, a relief from Smyrna at Leiden, but this seems an abbreviation of the full costume, which does occasionally appear in such representations.[173] Standing figures, however, like those here accompanying the man on the couch, have usually the full dress. Men seem especially to be so attired, and women also, as they are portrayed under shells in niches, fig. 136,[174] or sit as "philosophers" reading scrolls, fig. 137.[175] The philosopher seems to be giving the saving instructions, a mystic knowledge or gnosis to the veiled lady beside him. A similar motif shows the two sitting opposite each other on a sarcophagus from Kolch-hissar at Konia.[176] One need only go through the rich collection of such sarcophagi by Morey [177] to feel the importance of the himation, usually with the chiton, on funerary portraiture.

These figures often carry scrolls, which seems to me by no means to indicate that they are all poets, or philosophers in the usual sense, as has often been suggested, though such people would certainly carry scrolls. Still less does Pfuhl seem right that the dress and scroll simply marked a person as having enough education to read.[178] The convention of robe and scroll carried over to the East, so that the two "magi" who flank the cult scene in the sanc-

172. Ibid., plate xxx, 33.210.

173. As it did on tombstones on the Rhine: J. Klein, "Grabmonumente aus Bonn," *Jahrbücher des Vereins von Alterthumsfreunde im Rheinlande*, LXXXI (1886), 96–100, and plate III.

174. Courtesy of the Istanbul Archeological Museum. The right lateral face of a sarcophagus from Selefkeh: see Morey, *The Sarcophagus of Claudia Antonia Sabina*, 1924, fig. 63; cf. pp. 39 f. (Sardis, V). All three hold scrolls. For women see ibid., fig. 62.

175. Courtesy of the Istanbul Archeological Museum. See ibid., fig. 65; cf. pp. 40 f. It is the front of a sarcophagus from Sidamara at the same museum. On this and the foregoing sarcophagus see also T. Reinach, "Le Sarcophage de Sidamara," *Mon. Piot.*, IX (1902), 189–228, with plates XVII–XIX.

176. G. Mendel in *BCH*, XXVI (1902), 224, fig. 2.

177. *Sarcophagus*. See also E. Michon, "Sarcophages du type d'Asie-Mineure," *Mélanges d'archéologie et d'histoire*, XXVI (1906), 79–89; M. Lawrence, "Additional Asiatic Sarcophagi," *Memoirs of the American Academy in Rome*, XX (1951), 116–166.

178. A rich collection of ancient figures with scrolls was made by T. Birt, *Die Buchrolle in der Kunst*, 1907. To some of his conclusions E. Pfuhl objected: "Zur Darstellung von Buchrollen auf Grabreliefs," *JDAI*, XXII (1907), 113–132; see Birt's reply, *JDAI*, XXIII (1908), 112–124. But see also Marrou, *MA*, 1–153; Cumont, *Symbolisme*, 253–350.

tuary of the Dura Mithraeum wear Persian dress as they sit upon thrones and hold each a scroll, containing, one must suppose, the mystic secrets, fig. 140.[179] In Christian funerary and ecclesiastical art, when the figures who hold it are Christ and the saints, the scroll would seem to refer to the saving Gospel or creed, in whose hope and power the saint has achieved his sanctity. Similarly, we thought that in fig. 130 the Roman-Egyptian would presumably have in the scroll all or part of the Book of the Dead. The figures on pagan monuments must have presented, ordinarily, the rich upper classes, and it is to me unthinkable that such people claimed especial dignity from the fact that they were literate. On the other hand, it was precisely from this class that the initiates of mysteries were largely recruited. My guess is, accordingly, as already indicated, that in paganism the scroll signified the mystic, or eschatological, hope of the people buried or celebrated, and that the Christian scroll similarly represented the message and hope of Christianity. A lady holds the scroll as she goes to the world behind the curtain of death in the central panel of a sarcophagus, while the side panels show her being given the mystic teaching; she seems to tell the story behind figures with the scroll in all funerary monuments, pagan and Christian.[180] What is important for our purpose here is that on this sarcophagus, as on practically every one illustrated by the authors quoted, the scroll is held by a person in the chiton and himation.[181] It is the deified imperial family of Antoninus Pius that has the scroll along with other divine symbols in fig. 138,[182] for in mystic Egypt deification was by no means a post-mortem achievement.

The mosaics of Antioch might well have presented our chitons and himations, but unfortunately the robe rarely appears—because, I dare suggest, the meaning of the decorations rarely called for them. The striped chiton appears in street scenes, but without significance,[183] so far as one can see. A waitress attending a dining and drinking couple wears the same dress, and here symbolism is a greater possibility, since a man and woman on a banqueting couch so commonly represent immortality or mystic achievement.[184] Closely connected with this is a handsome figure of the winged Comus, the patron demon of banquets, in the same striped chiton.[185] Still more direct would seem to be the testimony of a mosaic in a tomb, a mosaic that shows several women at a banquet.[186] Here the most important figure seems to be Mnemosyne, Memory. Levi interpreted this as the funerary or memorial banquet; if he is right, as I believe, the several people at the banquet who wear the striped chiton, if not the himation also, are appropriately clothed. More perplexing,

179. From a copy by H. Gute in the Yale University Art Gallery. Cf. Rostovtzeff, *Dura-Europos*, VII/VIII, plates xvi–xviii. For the place of this figure in the whole design see above, III, fig. 57.

180. See above, IV, fig. 108.

181. If the scroll is taken to represent a poet, we would have the same impression. We have already mentioned, above, pp. 139 f., that the poet was such by divine inspiration.

182. From Edgar, *Sculpture*, plate xxvi; cf. pp.

53–55.

183. Levi, *Antioch*, plate lxxix; pp. 326–336.

184. Ibid., plate xlv*d;* pp. 203 f. For such scenes in general see ibid., 189. Cf. the mystic attendants in the Roman house on the Via dei Cerchi, above, p. 139.

185. Levi, plate cl*b;* pp. 50–54.

186. Ibid., plate lxvi*b;* pp. 296–304. Cf. Frank Brown in Rostovtzeff, *Dura-Europos*, VII/VIII, 156.

again, are two scenes—one of Atalante and Meleager, the other of Hippolytus, the nurse, and Phaedra—in which certain characters wear the striped chiton and others not.[187]

In several Antioch mosaics the robe is quite perplexing, as in a wrestling scene where the naked athletes seem from the fragments to be supervised by people in the striped chiton and himation.[188] What the men dressed in this way are doing cannot be judged from the fragments, but we recall that athletes and persons in the robe were strikingly presented together in the Baths of Caracalla.[189] Accordingly this mosaic cannot be used against the present argument that the robe is a mark of sacred distinction. In a very fragmentary mosaic of the months, "May" (one of the four preserved) is thus dressed; she seems thereby a sort of divinity and is performing some ritualistic act, or bearing divine tokens.[190] In another house King Ninus reclines on a couch looking at the portrait of his beloved Semiramis.[191] The legend of Ninus and Semiramis is not fully enough preserved so that we can judge whether his dress, the full robe, has meaning. Again a mosaic centers in a pair of plaques, in one of which Tryphe, Luxury, appears as a woman, and in the other Bios, Life, a man wearing the full robe.[192] It is impossible to say exactly in what sense Life is here represented, since the Greek word has many applications, including "livelihood." The two together, then, may represent luxury, and Bios the means of prosperity. But as Levi points out, the personal abstractions in these mosaics are usually on a higher philosophic level, and we may presume that Bios here stands for something exalted, as, in fact, Luxury might also do, in spite of her usually pejorative implication.

The full robe appears also in a mosaic of clearly philosophic inspiration, fig. 139,[193] where time and eternity are contrasted. Eternity, Aion, is represented at the left as an old man with a crown, only his head and hand still left. With this hand he holds a wheel.[194] We have no way of knowing how he was dressed, since all the rest of this part of the mosaic was destroyed in antiquity, and the lower part repaired with slabs of marble. To the right of him, however, are the three Chronoi, aspects of time as contrasted with eternity, labeled Past, Present, and Future. The Past, at the right, is an old man with wreath and cup. The Future, at the left, is a young man with only the mantle and a fillet. In one hand he holds the cup, and in the other a crown, which as Future he is apparently not yet ready to put on.

---

187. Levi, plate xia, b; pp. 68–75. Another scene in which three figures have this chiton is of very uncertain meaning, plate xiiia, a scene which Levi, pp. 83 f., with some hesitation, interprets to represent Andromache and Astyanax. The interpretation is warranted only if, as Levi says, the large male is "dragging" the little child. I see no trace of cruelty in what is left of the mosaic.

188. Ibid., plate lxid, e; pp. 256 f.

189. See above, p. 140, where it was suggested that the gymnasium as a place both of wrestling and of philosophic discussion is a tradition that goes back to Plato, and continued throughout the ancient world.

190. Levi, plate vb; p. 37.

191. Ibid., plate xxa, b; pp. 117 f.

192. Ibid., plate lia; p. 224 f. See also plate xliiib, and p. 191 f., for Bios as a female.

193. Courtesy of the Department of Art and Archeology, Princeton University. See Levi, plate xliiid; pp. 197 f.

194. We recall at once the wheel in the strange funerary plaque at the Lateran Museum: see above, IV, fig. 41. Eternity as a wheel is familiar in Indian philosophies, but I always hesitate to go outside the geographical limits of the Greco-Roman world to explain its symbols.

In the center is Present wearing a wreath and a white tunic with red clavi. He extends his right hand along the bolster toward an incense burner in the foreground. Levi reasonably suggests he may be putting incense on the burner, that is, offering sacrifice. It is the Present alone which can act to propitiate the gods, we are told: now is the time. Hence it is the Present who is marked as especially sacred.

The last instance of the robe at Antioch, so far as I know, is in a series of three plaques in each of which are a man and a woman, he each time in the full robe.[195] Since one of the men carries a money bag, Levi believes that the availability of the women as hetairae is indicated. He seems to me too assured on the subject: his explanation is possible, but no more than that. For it will be recalled that Hermes the psychopomp also carries the purse, and the wreath in the other hand of the same man could refer to immortality quite as well as to a banquet with hetairae.[196] The purse itself often has the same implications. Raingeard [197] has a most illuminating discussion of the purse of Hermes, in which he points out how frequent a funerary device it is, and says that it is strange Hermes should have it thus in so many scenes which have no relation with money at all, as when he presents it to Demeter, who certainly did not need to have Hermes enrich her. Raingeard also shows how others carry it in funerary art. It seems then an alternative of the caduceus to show hope of immortality through the help of Hermes. To carry the purse seems to mark one as having Hermetic power or association. I strongly suspect that the man who stands beside a woman in the Antioch mosaic and holds the purse and crown is marked as someone with superhuman prerogatives, whether in this world or the next.

The Antioch mosaics have been given so much attention here because they provide highly important evidence for the art and symbolism of the East, even though we could find little in them that defined significantly the meaning of the robe. We can conclude only that in a considerable number of mosaics a religious interpretation of the robes seems to give point to the scenes in which they appear, while no usage specifically contradicts such a meaning.

At the same time funerary stele in Syria show the deceased wearing the chiton and himation as in other parts of the Greco-Roman world.[198] At Nawa in the Hauran two very interesting helmets have been discovered. The relief on one of these has been sketched as in fig. 141.[199] Abdul-Hak rightly supposes that what is represented is a highly distinguished officer of the Roman army getting a crown from God himself for his services. Victory, the messenger who brings the crown, wears the same dress with the stripes as does the Helios (of whatever local name) above her, which suggested to Abdul-Hak that Victory was "considered to be an emanation of the power of the God." [200] Here, then, we seem to have the

---

195. Levi, plate xlviiia, *b, c;* p. 217.

196. The other mosaics which went with this in no way suggest that the house was itself a brothel.

197. P. Raingeard, *Hermés psychagogue*, 1934, 418–423.

198. M. Meurdrac and L. Albanèse in *Bulletin du Musée de Beyrouth*, III (1939), 50, plate viii.

199. From S. Abdul-Hak, "Les Objets découverts à Nawa," *Les Annales archéologiques de Syrie*," IV/V (1954/55), 168–174, plate iv.

200. Ibid., 170.

meaning of the striped tunic quite literally spelled out. Its wearer was, or shared in, divinity.[201]

6. Palmyra

As we go farther East, the robe is used with much more recognizable consistency than at Antioch, probably because our remains more commonly have funerary or religious reference. On the funerary portraits, of which Palmyra has left us many scores, the person portrayed may add to this dress embroidery or jewels in oriental profusion. But the robe clearly is the basic garb, at least for funerary wear, and usually it appears in simple Greek form. The quite representative bust of fig. 142 [202] only abbreviates the costume of fig. 143,[203] in the same way we saw being done in Egypt. Such figures frequently carry religious tokens in their hands, notably the scroll. But aside from telling us that at least funerary or memorial dress had this form, most of these stones tell little to our purpose.

One stone seems illuminating, fig. 144.[204] Here a man in full Greek dress with a scroll stands beside a pedestal on which is a modius encircled by a wreath, as the headdress ascribed to the kings of Persia was encircled with a diadem.[205] At the left is an assistant in a short belted tunic who carries what is probably a scroll case and what seems to me a box for sacred objects, though, as Ingholt and Simonsen suggest, it may be a tablet of several leaves. Perhaps the relief represents a "philosopher" with his scroll, and a pupil carrying school equipment. In any case I doubt that this is an ordinary man with an ordinary slave. When a man with sword and shield wears the costume,[206] I must admit that the combination seems to me utterly unrealistic and that, if the figure is human at all, the robe shows

201. I do not analyze the figurines of Syria, a fine collection of which was published by M. Chéhab, *Les Terres cuites de Kharayeb*, 1951–54 (Bulletin du Musée de Beyrouth, X and XI). The robe appears here on a few scattered figurines, but since figurines have no context, it is hard to construe their exact implication. On plate LXIII, for example, four figurines sit with boxes in their laps, which may well be portable escritoires, while a fifth stands in the robe holding a book; cf. plate LXIV, 4. The children wrapped in a mantle in plates LXX–LXXIII, LXXXIII, may also represent something more than a *jeu d'esprit*. But this cannot be determined either way.

202. Courtesy of the Istanbul Archeological Museum. See H. Ingholt, *Studier over palmyrensk skulptur*, plate IV, 1; cf. p. 34.

203. Courtesy of the Metropolitan Museum of Art; cf. ibid., plate IV, 3; cf. p. 36. For these busts and figures from Palmyra see also D. Simonsen, *Sculptures et inscriptions de Palmyre à la Glyptotèque de Ny Carlsberg*, 1889; J. B. Chabot, *Choix d'inscriptions de Palmyre*, 1922, esp. plates XXVI–XXXII; R. Amy

and H. Seyrig, "Recherches dans la nécropole de Palmyre," *Syria*, XVII (1936), 229–266; Ingholt, "Inscriptions and Sculptures from Palmyra," *Berytus*, III (1936), 83–125, plates XVIII, XXVI, and V (1938), 93–140, plates XXXVI–L; Seyrig, "Sculptures palmyréniennes archaïques," *Syria*, XXII (1941), 31–44; Abdul-Hak, "L'Hypogée de Taai à Palmyre," *Les Annales archéologiques de Syrie*, II (1952), 193–251; [H. Ingholt], *Palmyrene and Gandharan Sculpture*, Yale University Art Gallery, 1954, plates 1–16; J. Starcky, "Inscriptions palmyréniennes conservées au Musée de Beyrouth," *Bulletin du Musée de Beyrouth*, XII (1955), 29–44, plates XVII–XX.

204. Courtesy of the Ny Carlsberg Glyptotek, Copenhagen; cf. Ingholt in *Berytus*, II (1935), plate XXXIII, 2; cf. pp. 73 f. See also Simonsen, plate I; cf. pp. 7 f. In Simonsen's reproduction the figure at the right has a head with a tiara which Ingholt showed did not belong on this piece at all.

205. Xenophon, *Cyropaedia*, VIII, iii, 13.

206. Seyrig in *Syria*, XXII (1941), 39, fig. 8.

the soldier's happy fate in the future world quite as much as the arms show his occupation on earth. Certainly no soldier ever tried to fight (or to march) while holding the ends of the himation about him. Seyrig is probably right in regarding the figure as a deity. Or perhaps we have another reference to the spiritual *agōn*.

On Palmyrene monuments we meet for the first time as a common phenomenon the interchange of the Greek dress with oriental tunic and caftan. The dead man can be reclining in the typically Greek way in either dress, usually enriched with lavish bands of embroidery.[207] The Greek bolster on which he lies becomes almost incrusted with such decoration. Occasionally the embroidered strips take the place of the simpler western ones on the western costume itself, and in one case the pronged ornament suddenly appears on the himation thus embellished, fig. 145.[208] I know no other instance of this ornament on a Palmyrene monument, but it does appear on at least five pieces of Palmyrene textiles from tombs of the period,[209] so that it was probably often used on funerary dress.

Why some of the funerary figures should have Persian costume and others the Greek robe does not appear. The choice may have been determined by whether the person depicted worshiped in Mithraic terms or in terms of some western rites. Any explanation must be a pure guess. The "duality" of costume perplexed Seyrig, for he was convinced, as am I, that neither the full Greek costume nor the elaborate one with caftan and trousers was commonly worn at Palmyra. He suggested that both were pretentious costumes, because it "seemed more flattering to appear in the style of Antioch or of Seleucia on the Tigris," [210] especially for the rich on festal occasions. The suggestion can hardly be rejected: but it still seems to me less likely than that the costumes had some religious reference. If one supposes that the banquet scenes represent the dead at an earthly symposium, Seyrig's suggestion must indeed be accepted. But since these scenes have so often appeared to reproduce the dead as Dionysus at the eternal banquet, and to imply immortality, I must associate the costumes here, as we have done elsewhere, with religion.

Generalizations, however, are dangerous. In one relief from the temple of Bel two priests clothed only in the long chiton sacrifice at an altar between them, while men behind them wear the full Greek robe.[211] Four figures, which seem to me divine figures with halos in another relief, likewise seem to have only the chiton.[212] The gods Aglibol and Malakbel appear in trousers and halo, with companions in Persian dress in one relief,[213]

207. For illustration of such cloth see Pfister, *Textiles de Palmyre*, I–III, passim.

208. From Seyrig, "Armes et costumes iraniens de Palmyre," *Syria*, XVIII (1937), 25, fig. 16. He says that it is an unpublished relief on a sarcophagus, dated A.D. 260, but does not say where it is preserved. This study of Seyrig gives altogether the best account of Palmyrene dress. The person holds a pine cone, and hence apparently wears mystic garb. See Pfister, III, plate xc; cf. p. 30.

209. Pfister, I, plate v; III, plates A, iiid, ivc; and p. 16, fig. 6.

210. In *Syria*, XVIII (1937), 4 f. He goes on here to describe the local costume from other monuments.

211. Seyrig in *Syria*, XV (1934), plate xviii at p. 156.

212. Ibid., plate xix at p. 158. Seyrig's discussion of these, pp. 160 f., as a group of bystanders with disheveled hair seems quite impossible. Bystanders are never introduced in reliefs or paintings of processions in any ancient piece of art I know. The veiled women in this scene must be part of the procession. For the scene and further discussion see below, fig. 167, and pp. 183 f.

213. Seyrig, 179, fig. 2.

but in another they wear armor beside a female in the Greek costume, who was thought by Seyrig to be a goddess. Two reliefs clarify the problem, if they do not solve it. Fig. 146 [214] shows at the right two gods whom Seyrig here calls Aglibol and Iarhibol wearing the full Greek dress; at the left a haloed goddess also in Greek dress stands beside Heracles. This piece is dated in the first century before Christ. In fig. 147 [215] the same two gods appear again with Baalshamin standing between them. All three wear the dress of warrior kings.[216] This piece is later, of the third century after Christ. Possibly the difference reflects only a greater hellenization on the part of the individual responsible for the earlier relief. More probably, however, the change reflects a shift quite general in Palmyra at the time. For in the centuries between these two reliefs the upper classes of Palmyra, who made the monuments we now find, radically changed. In the first centuries before and after Christ, long under the influence of the Seleucid empire, they were eagerly cooperating with Roman troops against the Parthians, and accepting Roman overlordship. Hellenization must long have been universal. By the third century, however, they were doing all possible to set up Palmyra as queen of the East, independent of Romans and Parthians alike. For this they seem to have sustained themselves from their own Aramaic roots, if their minds were not freshly open to Parthian ideas. It is quite to be understood, then, that the gods should wear the robe of Greek dignity in the earlier period, along with the oriental halos that kept their original character and value, but should appear as oriental kings in armor in the third century. This would not mean that either costume reflected the dress of men on the street: it rather indicates what was thought proper for the gods at each period.

The transition was marked by the confusion we have been noticing. So on a relief from the temple of Bel two pairs of priests sacrifice beside a sacred palm tree with the two bunches of dates.[217] Their costumes are not at all clear, but seem to combine something much like the chiton and himation with Persian trousers. On funerary reliefs [218] a man often lies in the familiar way with the cup in his hand. He usually has the tiara of priest, the pose of Dionysus, the full Persian dress, while behind him are his wife, seated, and two or three standing males, his sons, in the Greek dress. The sons usually have a tiara like the father's, but the Greek dress. In one, the father has a Greek himation with the trousers, but he and the two sons still wear the tiara.[219]

Such confusion, it seems to me, drives us to the conclusion that either the Greek or the

214. From Seyrig in *Syria*, XXIV (1944–45), plate I at p. 64; see pp. 62 f.

215. From Seyrig in *Syria*, XXVI (1949), plate II at p. 25; cf. pp. 29–33. The date of the piece is uncertain. Seyrig dates it on artistic grounds in the first century A.D., but J. Starcky, ibid., 40 f., shows that its dedication is clearly of the date A.D. 228, and I follow Starcky.

216. For their dress see A. Hekler, "Beiträge zur Geschichte der antiken Panzerstatuen," *JÖAI*, XIX–XX (1919), 190–241.

217. Seyrig in *Syria*, XV (1934), plate XXII at p. 182.

218. One is very well published by Seyrig in *Syria*, XV (1934), plate XXIV, 2. For discussion of this see Ingholt, *Studier over palmyrensk Skulptur*, 94–97, with extended bibliography at p. 94, n. 6; For a similar scene see Seyrig in *Syria*, XVIII (1937), 16, plate IV.

219. Amy and Seyrig in *Syria*, XVII (1936), 248, plate XLVII, 1; cf. p. 249.

Persian dress could be used alike by gods and priests or by great men. Yet we return to the fresco of a tomb at Palmyra discussed in a former volume,[220] where a man in the Greek robe with stripes, and two tassels at the end of his himation, stands surrounded by grapes—clearly in the Dionysiac grape arbor.[221] Ingholt says that one of the vine stalks grows from a vase, and this, though not apparent in the reproduction, marks the vine all the more certainly to have religious implications.[222] A woman faces him wearing the himation drawn over her head, a skirt, and a green chiton with the clavus in light brown.[223] She also stands in the vine, so that whatever relation to the Persian costume the Greek one may bear, the striped Greek clothing again impresses itself as religiously meaningful. This same impression is made by the other paintings from Palmyra, those in what is called the Tomb of the Three Brothers, or Magharat el-Djedideh.[224] The portraits in these tombs are in medallions, each held high above the head of a Victory. These portraits have great importance for showing more exactly the dress of most of the funerary busts, and here, in fig. 148,[225] we see that the dress, with the stripes, so much resembles that of the mummy portraits of Egypt at the time that we know we have been right in associating the Greek costume at Palmyra with the western funerary dress. In these portraits the persons hold a symbol of some kind, which, as in similar cases in Egypt, seems to indicate a religious implication in the dress also.

A word must be said about the remains of textiles found in the graves.[226] The corpses were ordinarily wrapped in a linen cloth, with woolen or silk cloth twisted round it, the cloth being strips torn from old but highly decorated mantles and other garments. Nothing indicates that white was much worn in Palmyra, but the fragments were often dyed with expensive imported purple or indigo and may well represent sacred vestments.

Palmyra, then, has by no means solved all our problems. We still do not understand the significance of the Greek as contrasted with the Persian costume; but we do feel that both had deep meaning for the people who wore them, and that as in Egypt the meaning was connected with their hope of divinization, or quasi apotheosis, in the life after death. The costume we are tracing, the striped Greek chiton, which now seems increasingly to have been worn under a himation bearing the pronged ornament, seems to have been much more than ostentation, especially when placed on a funerary or memorial monument.

220. See above, VI, fig. 243, and pp. 67 f.

221. Above, VI, 46–50.

222. The vine growing from the vase or cup seemed very important above, VI, 56–58, 65, 67, and passim. The importance of the vine on Palmyrene funerary remains has been well pointed out by Will, "Le Relief de la tour de Kithot et le banquet funéraire à Palmyre," *Syria*, XXVIII (1951), 70–100. Will sees active Dionysiac symbolism and syncretism. We must never lose sight of the fact that the tree-vine of the synagogue reredos

seems originally to have grown from a vase.

223. Ingholt, plate III; cf. pp. 5 f.

224. For general description, and the inscriptions, with bibliography, see Chabot, 96–111. See also J. Starcky and S. Munajjed, *Palmyra, "The Bride of the Desert,"* 1948, 16–18.

225. From B. Farmakovskii, "Paintings in Palmyra" (In Russian), *Izvestiia Russkago Arkheologicheskago Instituta v Konstantinopole*, VIII (1903), 172–198, plates XXIII, 2; XXV, 1, 2.

226. For bibliography, see above, p. 151, n. 207.

7. Pagan Dura

IN PAGAN DURA eastern and western dress are again so mingled that a clear-cut distinction of their meaning cannot be made. One very important painting in the nave of the temple of Adonis suggests a difference, however, that may help considerably, fig. 149.[227] Brown's clever restoration from a great mass of fragments seems quite reliable, though he himself deplores the complete absence of evidence as to what sort of platform the god stood upon. There can be little doubt that the painting of the god looked very much as his sketch represents it. He wore the typical trousers and caftan of the East, with a cloak something like a chlamys, falling freely behind his back but fastened over the breast by a brooch. The bush of wavy hair is assured, the sword on which his left hand rests is highly probable, and he may well with the right hand have been making the oriental gesture of blessing which Brown has represented. The priests beside him all wear the Greek costume, as often in pagan sacrifices, and this I take to be an instance of the "veneer of Greek artistic influence," which Hopkins rightly says conceals in such cases "neither the fundamentally eastern conception of the godhead, nor the inherent stiffness and convention of the typically eastern rendering of the religious scene."[228]

In the Mithraeum of Dura, however, the god himself can wear the chiton, fig. 150.[229] At the left Ahura Mazda as Zeus wears the Greek robe while he hurls the thunderbolt, and at the right, also in the robe, is a god whom Cumont and Rostovtzeff identify as the god of Time, Chronos.

Probably the god keeps his oriental character and dress in the temple of Adonis. The original white robes of the priests, however—robes shortly to be discussed— were changed into the Greek chiton and himation, even though the artist was so little acquainted with them that he shows the himation held in the right hand instead of the left.[230] The priests also have the large pronged ornament conspicuously splashed across their himation,[231] the mark we saw on burial robes of Egypt and once on a funerary garb at Palmyra, fig. 145.

It is perplexing whether this mark is to be considered Greco-Egyptian or originally from the East, for it seems thoroughly indigenous when it appears on the white himation of Conon, fig. 151,[232] in the Temple of the Palmyrean Gods at Dura. Beside him two priests

227. See Frank Brown in Rostovtzeff, *Dura-Europos*, VII/VIII, 159 f., fig. 44, plates XIX f.

228. C. Hopkins, "Aspects of Parthian Art in the Light of Discoveries from Dura-Europos," *Berytus*, III (1936), 1–30; quoting from p. 28. Hopkins wrote this before Brown had restored the painting we are discussing, but his words fit exactly.

229. Courtesy of my colleague Frank Brown. See du Mesnil du Buisson, "Le Nouveau Mithréum de Doura-Europos en Syrie," *Gazette des Beaux-Arts*, Ser. VI, Vol. XIII (1935), 8; Cumont and Rostovtzeff in Rostovtzeff, *Dura-Europos*, VIII/IX, 105, and plate XVIII, 1.

230. In Palmyra we saw that oriental gods took on the Greek dress with much greater freedom. See above, p. 151. Adonis kept his Persian caftan, though he covered his lap with a Greek himation as he lay on the funerary banquet couch in Palmyra: Seyrig in *Syria*, XXVII (1950), 228–236, plate IX and fig. 1. This still seems to be the garb in spite of the remarks of A. Alföldi, "Gewaltherrscher und Theaterkönig," *Late Classical and Medieval Studies in Honor of A. M. Freund*, 1955, 43.

231. Brown illustrates one of these in Rostovtzeff, *Dura-Europos*, VII/VIII, plate XX, 5.

232. From J. H. Breasted in *Syria*, III (1922), plate XXIX at p. 190; see esp. pp. 191 f. F. Cu-

offer sacrifice in long white robes which, like their conical hats, seem to me entirely oriental. Greek art of the type associated with the Eastern Mediterranean is represented by the colonnade behind these figures, and by what seems to be Conon's utterly misdrawn himation. The splashes of red on his chiton reappear at the bottom as two broad clavi. Similar clavi appear on the chiton of three other men painted as sacrificing in the same temple,[233] but on another painting there, of definitely later date, the white gown of the priests with Conon has disappeared: the sacrificants wear the white (unmarked) chiton and himation.[234] The two assistants on either side, however, wear only the belted chiton with clavi, like many of the assistants in the synagogue.[235]

While Palmyra, then, went farther than Dura in adopting Greek dress for their gods, priests, and apotheosized dead, the tendency in Dura seems to have been in the same direction. No systematic or consistent use of the Greek robe, or of the markings on it, appears, but, as in Palmyra I see no reason to believe that the changes of mode in the dress of gods and priests occurred in response to a change in modes of common dress. In the second century, when the upper classes of Palmyra were returning to their oriental roots and seem to have been reverting to oriental dress for gods and heroes, Dura was held firmly as a Roman camp. Here no kings, queens, or aristocracy aspired to be independent of Rome, so that the white robe of priests, and divine dress in general, could change to the Greek chiton and himation, or, as with Adonis, could remain oriental. If we had sufficient evidence, we should probably see that some gods changed consistently to Greek dress, others did not. But such evidence does not exist.

In all of this, however, nothing really prepares us for the costumes of the heroes of the synagogue. Here suddenly emerges a strong convention which can be compared only with that of the mummy portraits of Egypt for its impressive consistency. Not that we can give a consistent explanation to the robes of either Egypt or the synagogue. But the Jewish painting in the synagogue, while it still shows a perplexing mixture of eastern and western dress, has succumbed to an influence only partly felt by the pagan art of Palmyra and Dura, a tendency to clothe kings in decorated eastern dress, servitors in simple eastern dress or Greek chitons, and great heroes of the Bible and what we shall suspect are heavenly beings in the full Greek dress. The pagan costumes represented in Palmyra and Dura make this sort of clothing seem quite natural in the synagogue paintings. In the synagogue, however, the full Greek robe has become so dominant a convention as to suggest a powerful influence

---

mont, *Fouilles de Doura-Europos (1922–1923)*, I, 1926, 41 f., explains how the painting perished after its discovery. His reproductions of this painting, ibid., plates XXXII–XLII, are not so good as those in *Syria*.

233. One can make it out only by comparing plate XLV in Cumont, *Fouilles* with the description, ibid., pp. 76–81.

234. Ibid., plate LV.

235. See especially fig. 342. Frank Brown in Rostovtzeff, *Dura-Europos*, IX, i, 162, and fig. 87,

shows a god being crowned under a grape arbor, in a strange little wall shrine painted on plaster. He wears the striped chiton. The symbol was so important that it was repainted six times on as many successive layers of plaster. We recall the people under the vine in the robe at Palmyra, above p. 153. The famous scene of the sacrifice of the Roman tribune before the Palmyrene triad, Cumont, plate L, has nothing to our purpose. The tribune and his company wear what may have been their dress for campaigning in the desert.

of some art tradition within Judaism itself, in which the Greek dress played a particularly important part in identifying what I may in general call religious heroes. We have seen the robe and its markings in Egypt, and also in scattered places in paganism from Etruria to Dura. Was the costume ever used anywhere else in the strongly conventionalized way it appears in the synagogue?

E. THE CHITON AND HIMATION IN CHRISTIANITY

THE QUESTION has only to be asked for one to recall the art of early Christianity, including that of the so-called gnostic monuments of Italy,[236] in which exactly this conventional costume does appear everywhere, but always worn only by the great figures, the saints, or by God or Christ. Tertullian tells us explicitly that in adopting it the Christians knew they were taking over a traditionally sacred robe. In his *On the Pallium* he tells how it was used in the mysteries of Demeter, Bellona, Saturn (where there were unusually broad phylacteries), and Aesculapius. Now that Christians have adopted it, he says, it surpasses all the clothing of the gods or priests.[237] He continues to record that scholars and philosophers and others also wear it, but concludes:

> I confer on it likewise a fellowship with a divine sect and discipline. Rejoice, mantle, and exult! A better philosophy has now deigned to honor thee, ever since thou hast begun to be a Christian's vesture.[238]

Christians appear to have used it originally not for their own heroes but for Old Testament figures, which makes it likely that it came into Christianity from a convention that began not with Christianity at all but with Judaism.[239] We can best approach this subject by moving from the known to the unknown—that is, from the assured use of the robe in Christianity back to its less assured use in Old Testament illustration, presumably in copies of, or selections from, the Septuagint.

In contrast to the scattered appearances of the Greek himation and chiton with their marks in paganism, Christian art supplies us with a superabundance. Hence Christian sarcophagi need not be systematically examined, for while the clothing we are investigating appears everywhere on them, the paintings and mosaics of Christianity show us the markings as reliefs do not, and give us in themselves more material than we can discuss. Christian sarcophagi, as we have seen, used much of the old vocabulary of pagan symbolism, but they also continued the pagan custom of showing the dead in their new glory, along

---

236. It will be sufficient for these monuments only to refer to the illustrations in J. Carcopino, *De Pythagore aux apôtres*, 1956, esp. those in the tomb of the Viale Manzoni, at pp. 83–221.

237. Tertullian, *On the Pallium*, IV, 10 (ed. V. Bulhart in *CSEL*, LXXVI, iv, 120). •

238. Ibid., VI, 4 (p. 125).

239. With this I come at last to the observations I made many years ago, which started me out on this line of study. See above, I, 23–30.

with incidents from sacred legends—in their case, of course, Christian legends. That the incidents portrayed by Christians were the raising of Lazarus and the drawing of water from the rock rather than Selene coming to the sleeping Endymion or the boar hunt of Adonis should by no means obscure the basic continuity in symbolism, namely that one should be buried with scenes of the cult stories in which divine power was so manifested among men that they could find hope in it even for life after death.

The paintings and mosaics, however, show us the same scenes with the garments more specifically identified, and show them in exemplars presumably of an earlier date.

In the paintings, dress was largely conventionalized for the various figures. Jonah appears almost always naked in his adventure with the fish, as well as when he lies under the gourd.[240] Daniel likewise usually stands naked between the lions,[241] but may wear a short tunic or chiton.[242] Adam and Eve at the tree are naked, but in contrast to the figures on the Naasene amulet I published elsewhere, they cover their genitals with leaves in shame.[243] The Three Boys in the furnace on the contrary wear a badly drawn Persian dress with cap and trousers;[244] the upper part of this dress can become the striped chiton.[245] The only other figures that wear Persian dress are the magi in scenes of the infancy of Christ.[246]

Several figures appear regularly wearing only the striped chiton: the mysterious quarryman cutting rock with an *ascia;*[247] the paralytic carrying his bed;[248] little David with the sling;[249] a seated figure, which Wilpert, for some reason no doubt, identifies with

---

240. There seems no necessity to give complete references for the following statements. For Jonah, see, for example, Wilpert, *Pitture*, plates 26, 47, 104. He can appear under the gourd in the full Greek dress occasionally, as in plate 44; cf. pp. 338–351. In connection with the Christian use of the pallium, or chiton and himation, it is unfortunate that this volume was already in the press when the new Catacomb Via Latina, Rome, first became available for close study. In this catacomb the use of the Greek robe entirely agrees with my conclusions about its meaning elsewhere, but the new material would greatly have enriched my presentation. See Ferrua, *Via Latina*, passim, and my "Catacomb Art," *JBL*, LXXXI (1962), 113–142.

241. Ibid., plates 62, 103 f., 106, 169 (in one on this plate, and on plate 166, he has a loin cloth).

242. Ibid., plates 5, 25, 73, 89. Wilpert discusses the Daniel scenes, pp. 308–316.

243. Ibid., plates 93, 101, 169, 171, etc.; pp. 298–302. Cf. above, III, fig. 1145, and my "A Jewish-Gnostic Amulet of the Roman Period," *Greek and Byzantine Studies*, I (1958), 71–80. I should add that when being baptized, Christ is usually without clothes.

244. Wilpert, *Pitture*, plates 62, 78, 114.

245. Ibid., plate 196. For the Three Boys see Wilpert, pp. 329–333. In one of the paintings in the newly discovered Catacomb Via Latina the Three Boys wear the flounced female garment which elsewhere in this catacomb appears only on figures of Victory. With the three figures together wearing it, however, the effect is to make them look like the Three Nymphs discussed below, pp. 203 f., and figs. 186, 188 f. See Ferrua, *Via Latina*, 84 and plate LXXXIX, 1; cf. 47 and plate XIII, 2.

246. Ibid., plates 60, 116, 231, 239; cf. pp. 176–181. See also F. Deichmann, *Frühchristliche Bauten und Mosaiken von Ravenna*, 1958, 133.

247. Wilpert, plates 48, 59; the dress of the cutter in plate 69 is indistinguishable. That these are realistic scenes I challenged on good grounds above, II, 28 f. W. H. Gilmore was prompted by this passage to remind me that G. W. Elderkin, *Kantharos*, 1924, 109–114, plate IX, shows and discusses sileni assisting in the resurrection of Dionysus, each using an ascia.

248. Wilpert, plates 27 (without stripes), 69, 98; pp. 201–203, 243–245.

249. Ibid., plate 55; pp. 256 f.

Job;[250] Noah emerging from the sarcophagus-ark;[251] and, most important of all, the Good Shepherd, though he often has a small cloak with his chiton.[252]

The figure of Noah takes us to the striped dalmatic, for Noah usually has the pose of what is called an orant, a praying or adoring saint, and his chiton has often become a dalmatic. This was a full-length garment, or one falling well below the knees, usually with long sleeves and again marked with the vertical stripes. Orants are so familiar as to need no discussion.[253] But the striped dalmatic seems a step in sanctity above the striped chiton, for Mary often wears it as she is enthroned with the child, especially in scenes of the adoration of the Magi.[254] Most of the orants in the dalmatic are females; when, rarely, orants wear the full Greek costume they are usually males.[255]

In all of this we seem to be following a definite series of conventions. The naked Jonah would appear to reflect the naked figures in the marine thiasos, whose value, we have had reason to suppose, Jonah carried over into Christianity.[256] Scriptural story required the naked Adam and Eve, but the naked Daniel is an anomaly. We may reasonably suppose that the type was adopted by Jews[257] and perhaps independently by Christians, from a pagan original without clothes, since nothing in the biblical narrative indicates Daniel's nakedness, and neither Jews nor Christians would presumably have invented the naked figure.[258] Both would have put clothes on him rather than the reverse. The immediate original may have been a figure of Dionysus with lions, since Dionysus so often appears with felines, but I know no such representation of Dionysus in pagan art, and the figure in itself is basically eastern.[259]

The Persian dress of the Magi reflects, I believe, the tradition that they were kings,

250. Ibid., plates 56, 71, 147, 166, 226; pp. 352–354. A pagan original for this figure, also in striped chiton, sits on a pile of rocks or a mountain with the "friends" addressing him in a painting in the Temple of the Palmyrean Gods: Cumont, *Fouilles*, Atlas, plate XLVIII. The newly discovered Catacomb Via Latina rather strengthens this identification, since it shows this figure twice, perhaps three times, with a woman holding out food to him on a stick, while, in one of the scenes that is clear, she holds her nose with her other hand. In this example, she wears a striped dalmatic, and the man has blotches on his leg which Ferrua identifies with his boils. See Ferrua, *Via Latina*, 56 and plate C; cf. pp. 42 and 70, plates VI, 1 and LVIII, 2.

251. Wilpert, plates 56, 60, 67, 186, etc.; pp. 316–322. See above, III, fig. 701; II, 120.

252. Wilpert, plates 63, 66, 69, 266, etc.; p. 81. Cf. H. Leclercq in CL, XIII, ii, 2272–2390.

253. Wilpert, plates 43, 57, 62, etc.; pp. 420–426.

254. Ibid., plates 81, 141, 144; pp. 176–184. She seems to wear it also when faced with a figure in the Greek robe whom Wilpert identifies with Isaiah: pp. 172–175.

255. As ibid., plates 45, 61, 75. But a female orant seems to wear the chiton and himation in plate 25.

256. See above, VIII, 104.

257. For Daniel in Jewish representation, see above, I, 99, 255; VI, 32. He was an orant between confronting lions, as in Christian art, but so little remains of the Jewish figures that we can say nothing of their clothing.

258. A glance at the illustrations in CL, IV, 228–247, shows a wide variety of clothing put upon Daniel: the chiton, Persian dress, even full priestly dress. But the sarcophagi confirm us in thinking that the basic representation was nude: see Wilpert, *Sarcofagi*, plates XCVI; CXXII, 3; CLXXXVIII, 3, 12; CCVII, 3–6, 9 f. I ask the question without prejudice: was the naked Daniel with the lions associated with the lion-taming Heracles?

259. W. Deonna, "Daniel, le 'Maître des Fauves,'" *Artibus Asiae*, XII (1949), 119–140, 347–374; see on Daniel's clothing, 124, n. 38.

fig. 159,[260] and therefore parallels the clothing of kings in the Dura synagogue. One can only surmise why the Three Boys in the furnace wore the same dress. It is obvious to suggest that Christians in the West wanted to represent them as Easterners in Babylon, but such realism is so foreign to the figures in general that we must suppose some idea lay behind the convention. Perhaps they were first drawn in the East, where this Persian dress seems to have had a meaning, difficult as it is to ascertain it.

The paralytic, the boy David, the quarryman, and Job (if Job it be) certainly represent lesser lights by Christian standards, and we suspect that they all wear the chiton for that reason. The Good Shepherd may well have the chiton because it was the simple pastoral dress of the original figure which early Christians borrowed.[261] When, as in the chapel of Galla Placidia in Ravenna, Christians created their own design, in which Christ was seated and surrounded by his flock, he was given the Greek chiton and himation.[262] In baptizing the naked Jesus, John wears now a simple loin cloth,[263] now a chiton,[264] and then the full robe; [265] the difference may express a changing evaluation of John, though I hesitate to draw conclusions from Wilpert's dubious chronology for these paintings.[266]

Why, when Noah emerges from the ark as an orant—that is, represents a soul rising to glory—he usually wears the chiton, I cannot say. His chiton, however, tends to become the dalmatic because his was the pose of an orant, and even the Virgin Mother wears the dalmatic in glory. Although the striped dalmatic came to express the soul's final achievement, the chiton and himation together were used much more commonly to represent the heavenly company. In spite of its appearance on Noah, perhaps the very obvious suggestion should be made that the dalmatic was properly a feminine dress, akin to what seemed to us the garb of an initiate into Isis, while the other was masculine and, originally, Osirian. The latter dress appears more commonly because the figures represented in heaven were ordinarily masculine. Christ, the Apostles, and the great company of saints appear almost exclusively in the chiton and himation, with their stripes and special marks. In what seems to me an important symbolic scene, fig. 152,[267] the soul stands as an orant in the dalmatic before the great throne upon which Christ sits, balanced with his two Throne Mates or

260. On this tradition see P. Benecke in *HDB*, III, 206*a*. Tertullian, *Against Marcion*, III, 13, and *Against the Jews*, IX (ed. A. Kroymann, *CSEL*, XLVII, 398; LXX, 291), says in this connection that the "East generally held the magi to be kings." On the Magi see G. Vezin, *L'Adoration et le cycle des Mages*, 1950; L. Olschki, "The Wise Men of the East in Oriental Traditions," *Semitic and Oriental Studies Presented to William Popper*, 1951, 375–395 (University of California Publications in Semitic Philology, XI).

261. For similar dress on Endymion as shepherd see Leclercq, CL, XIII, ii, 2287, fig. 9862. See A. Veyries, *Les Figures criophores*, 1884 (Bibliothèque des Ecoles françaises d'Athènes et de Rome, XXXIX).

262. C. Diehl, *Ravenne*, 1907, 31; von Berchem and Clouzot, *Mosaïques chrétiennes*, 93, fig. 105; Deichmann, *Frühchristliche Bauten und Mosaiken von Ravenna*, plate 3.

263. Wilpert, *Pitture*, plate 27.

264. Ibid., plate 29.

265. Ibid., plates 29, 58.

266. Even though he estimates the dates too early, as all agree, he may still be right in putting the first two a century earlier than the others.

267. From Wilpert, *Pitture*, plate 247; cf. plates 205, 243, 245. An original photograph sent me from the Vatican shows few of Wilpert's details. Whether he supplied them in his copy or they were there in the original and have since chipped off, I have no way of knowing.

Guards in the ancient convention of royalty. Christ and the Guards wear the full Greek dress. We instantly feel the sense of contrast in the other costume, the sense of a soul come into the divine presence.[268] That this orant, like most others in the catacombs, is a female seems to me to reflect the gender of *pseuchē* or *anima* rather than the sex of the person or persons celebrated.[269] Even Noah coming out of the ark, we may now suggest, has become the soul coming out of the sarcophagus, and so appropriately he comes out wearing the dalmatic. More often, however, Christ sits in judgment alone, or with a number of saints, all in the full robe, fig. 153.[270] A variant representation of eternal bliss was made by adapting the pagan and Jewish eschatological banquet, which seems to have meant in Christianity the heavenly Eucharist, and in these the banqueters usually wear the full Greek dress, though this is not always true of either Christian or pagan banqueters.[271] Again the Christians seem to be adapting a pagan convention. The change of robe has already appeared twice in the Christian-Jewish scenes we have illustrated. Fig. 94 shows Moses the shepherd in a tunic only, Moses on Sinai in the full robe. Fig. 100 shows Abraham seeing the three angels, he in a chiton, they in the full dress, but with Abraham wearing the full dress as he sacrifices Isaac.

It is in the figure of Christ himself, as well as of the saints portrayed with him, that the chiton and himation appear with predictable regularity in the Christian catacombs and mosaics, fig. 70. The assumption would be that for this the Christians had taken over another convention, and here we seem to me to be on firm ground.[272] For in the early representation Christ in the robe repeatedly balances Moses in the same robe. Usually in such a balance Christ holds a rod as he raises Lazarus.[273] He also holds the rod when he multi-

268. The same sense of contrast appears, ibid., plate 267, where Christ in the Greek robe multiplies the loaves (according to Wilpert perhaps he turns water into wine) before a banqueting table, with the banqueters in the same dress, while a female in a dalmatic balances Christ at the left.

269. The dalmatic, even on women, is often short as garments for females would not have been in Roman art.

270. From Wilpert, *Pitture*, plate 170; cf. plates 96, 126, 148, 155, 177, 193, 225, 252; and pp. 360–383.

271. See, for example, ibid., plate 41, no. 3. Most of the scenes are carelessly drawn, like this one, but a study of them all makes it quite clear that the banqueters ordinarily wear the striped chiton, and usually himation as well. See ibid., plates 27, 57, 62, 133, 157, 265, 267. In plates 15, no. 2, and 65, no. 3, the representation is surprisingly like that of the Vibia scenes from the mystery of Sabazius reproduced above in III, figs. 842 f. The same gesture appears in both, and fig. 843 makes a point in the inscription that there are

seven banqueters, a feature reproduced in these and several other Christian scenes. See J. Baum, "Symbolic Representations of the Eucharist," *The Mysteries, Papers from the Eranos Yearbooks,* ed. Joseph Campbell, 1955, 261–273 (Bollingen Series, XXX, 2); originally published in *Eranos Jahrbuch,* XI (1944), 327–346. Only in relatively late catacomb paintings is this form fully adapted to Christianity by changing the seven to Christ with the twelve.

272. An important strand in the fabric of this symbolism is the tradition of the philosopher's robe, mentioned above, pp. 139 f. F. Saxl discussed this: "Der Dialog als Thema der christlichen Kunst," *Wiener Jahrbücher für Kunstgeschichte,* II (1923), 64–77. That for Christianity, as for paganism and hellenized Judaism, the word "philosophy" had come to mean a mystic doctrine for the purgation of souls, Saxl does not suggest.

273. See above, III, figs. 2 and 4; cf. Wilpert, *Pitture*, plates 46, 55, 58, 108, 143, 190, 192, 198, 212, 227, 240, 248.

plies the loaves, fig. 154,[274] and changes the water into wine,[275] or heals a leper, fig. 155.[276] In all of these New Testament scenes the rod has no place, so that Christ with the rod seems to be a Christian adaptation of a figure with whom the rod was meaningful. That is, the Christ figure with robe and staff is an adapted Moses.[277] If, as I believe, the Moses striking a rock on a sarcophagus fragment from the Catacomb Vigna Randanini is Jewish,[278] we would have direct evidence that the Christians found this convention among Jews, and presumably adapted it from them. I should guess that Christians from the first thought of this miracle as a type of the Eucharist, after the anthology of the Jewish teaching that the rock which gave water in the wilderness actually gave the Logos or Sophia.[279] We know from Paul [280] and the Fourth Gospel [281] that this Jewish teaching was taken over directly for Christ and the Eucharist. Christians later came to call the figure striking the rock Peter,[282] but Moses had furnished the prototype of the figure of Christ with the rock giving the eucharistic fluid. Moses at the rock was apparently represented by Jews in two ways, first by Moses with the lifted rod striking the rock, which became the pose of Christ in raising Lazarus; and second by Moses using the rod to touch a spring from the ground

274. Courtesy of the Pontificia Commissione di Archeologia Sacra, Rome. In this miracle Christ always carries Moses' rod: see Wilpert, *Pitture*, plates 45, 54, 68, 74, 105, 115, 120, 196, 228, etc., and pp. 269–278.

275. See above, III, fig. 3.

276. From ibid., plate 68, no. 3. The leper wears only the striped chiton.

277. This was recognized by T. B. L. Webster in *JRS*, XIX (1929), 153 at no. 71. The same figure with robe and rod was painted in an illumination of the Vergilius Vaticanus (Cod. Vat. Lat. 3225, fol. 13), in which Aeneas thus arrayed watches two workmen dig up, apparently, the horse's skull that portended wealth and victory in war: *Aeneid*, I, 441–445. See A. Grabar and C. Nordenfalk, *Early Medieval Painting*, 1957, 94 (The Great Centuries of Painting).

278. See above, III, fig. 804; II, 29 f.

279. Above, VI, 181, 183–187, 193–204.

280. I Cor. x, 1–4.

281. John VI, 41–58, does not equate the blood of Christ with water from the well of the wilderness as it does the body of Christ with the manna, but the implication seems plain to me.

282. The original design simply represented Moses at the rock, as was recognized by G. Stuhlfauth, *Die apokryphen Petrusgeschichten in der altchristlichen Kunst*, 1925, 50–71, esp. p. 52. The design apparently needed new interpretation for most Christians, however, and I should guess that the

hero who brought new salvation from a rock early became Peter the Rock in popular Christian "explanations." Such a new explanation of the image itself, I continue to guess, prompted the Christians to create a new legend, still extant, that Peter struck the side of his prison wall to get water to baptize two guards whom he had converted. Christian artists then soon introduced the guards into the scene, though the artists' form of the legend would have been rather one associated still with the Eucharist than with baptism, since the little characters with Peter usually drink the water rather than plunge into it. The history of the form in Christianity obscures its apparent origin as Moses, and its earliest use as such by Christians. For the legend of the guards, Saints Processus and Martinianus, see *Acta sanctorum*, *July*, I, 1867, 270 f.; Stuhlfauth, 45–50; H. Lietzmann, *Petrus and Paulus in Rom*, 2d ed., 1927, 187–189 (*Arbeiten zur Kirchengeschichte*, I); P. F. de' Cavalieri in *Studi e testi*, XXII (1909), 35–39. E. Dinkler, "Die ersten Petrusdarstellungen," *Marburger Jahrbuch für Kunstwissenschaft*, XI–XII (1938–39), esp. p. 18, ignores the Mosaic origin of the scene altogether. In the new Catacomb Via Latina, Moses strikes the rock as a single figure in one scene, but in another has two men with him, whom Ferrua properly calls Jews. See Ferrua, *Via Latina*, 53 and plate XXXV; 46 and plate XIII, 1. The later "soldiers" with Peter seem an adaptation of these two, one of whom here drinks and the other points toward the miracle.

at his feet. We seem to have examples of Moses in each of these acts at Dura.[283] They both had great importance for Christian art, which used the one to show Moses (or Peter) striking the rock, and the other to represent the multiplication of the loaves and the changing of water into wine.[284] Both poses appear in manuscripts of Cosmas Indicopleustes.[285]

Moses could, of course, be represented by Jews without the rod, as we saw him in the panels flanking the reredos at Dura,[286] and it was the figure without the rod that Christians more usually adapted for Christ. But the convention by which Christians commonly put all angels and saints in this robe corresponds to the convention in the Dura paintings by which, as we have said,[287] it is worn by many prominent figures. The Dura paintings now finally assure us of what the use of the robe in Christian art had made highly likely, that although the convention began in paganism, it came to Christianity through its adoption by Jews for the holy figures of their Bible. The Jewish use itself now appears to have had behind it a long tradition in paganism by which philosophers and mystical saviors or initiates were put into this robe, so that when Jewish and later Christian saints were put into it, their especial Jewish or Christian sanctity seems announced in some way corresponding to that of pagan philosophers, saviors, and mystic saints. "Rejoice, mantle, and exult!"

An artist could use this convention in making his own designs much as he wished, as we have seen in earlier volumes was done with symbol after symbol. We have seen, for example, that the Female Principle was represented by, or with, the shell, and that the Principle or the devotee could appear in almost any design or combination with the shell without altering the symbol's meaning.[288] So the robe symbolizes superhuman sanctity, attained through the mysteries, Christianity, or Philosophy (which here must be capitalized). This statement I have not "proved," but it becomes increasingly probable when we see the material as a whole. It is worth testing as a hypothesis in interpreting the Dura paintings that on Jewish characters it announced their Jewish-mystic sanctity.

F. THE GAMS

WE MAY FURTHER STRENGTHEN the probability that the tradition was consecutively an artistic and symbolic form by examining more closely the peculiar marks that have appeared with astonishing regularity on the himatia, marks which in Christian tradition came later to be called "gammas."[289]

We have already encountered these marks not only on Christian robes,[290] but in hellenized Egypt,[291] Palmyra,[292] and pagan Dura,[293] and they have occurred on the rem-

283. See fig. 331. He holds the rod up as he is about to strike the Red Sea, but down as he closes it, fig. 330.
284. See above, III, figs. 3 f.
285. See the illustrations in Riedin, *Cosmas Indicopleustes*, I, 228–232, figs. 229–236; plate XII.
286. See above, pp. 110–123; plate V.
287. Above, pp. 125–127.
288. Above, VIII, 95–105.

289. The marks were more commonly called *gammadiae:* see Leclercq in CL, VI, 610–614; but *gamma* and *gammadium* were also used: C. Ducange, *Glossarium Mediae et Infimae Latinitas*, 1883–1887, s. vv.
290. See figs. 100, 102, 152–154, 159.
291. Figs. 132, 135; IV, figs. 102, 114.
292. Fig. 145.
293. Fig. 151.

nants of clothing found in Dura.[294] The mark appears (*a*) as a straight bar with two prongs at each end on the mummy portrait of fig. 132, and on the portrait of Virgil, fig. 127. Or (*b*) it could be bent at right angles, still with the prongs, as in fig. 156.[295] It could become a simple angle without the prongs, or remain a straight bar with the prongs apparently at only one end, as in fig. 157.[296] It appears in the latter form on all the "robes" in the paintings of the Dura synagogue, and on a figure on a sarcophagus lid from Palmyra, fig. 145. But the textiles of Dura suggest that prongs belong at both ends of the mark, and that folds of the garments conceal the prongs at the other ends of the bars.[297] Actually I can find no instance of the prongs at one end of the bar in which the other end does not disappear in a fold or bend.

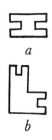

Most conspicuously it appears upon a banner from Roman Egypt, fig. 158,[298] though here also its meaning does not become definite. The banner shows a figure which Rostovtzeff plausibly called Victory, though she has no wings. She stands upon a globe to indicate her deity, and she offers a palm branch in her left hand, a crown in her right. But Rostovtzeff does not mention the four right-angled marks with double-pronged ends which occupy the corners. If only this example existed, one would assume that the four simply framed the central figure. In view of the prominent funerary use of the mark in the period and later, however, this seems a dangerous assumption. What was the banner, and for what was it designed? Unfortunately, one cannot say; its origin is unknown. Rostovtzeff, after reviewing the various uses of such banners, ends by "not hesitating to regard it as a military banner," because of the Victory. He admits that the banner probably had been found in a grave, and hence thinks it was a *donum militare,* a sort of prize, or what we would call a decoration, which some officer wanted with him eternally. But Rostovtzeff does not even allude to the omnipresent funerary Victories which give crowns and palms to the dead. My own feeling is the reverse, that the marks in the corners show that the banner is a religious one, probably carried in the religious procession of some group that hoped for immortality. In fig. 123 we actually saw such a religious procession with banners, and we can now see that the banners which lead both columns there have the identical marks in the corners. Since Victory so commonly appears as a symbol of immortality, and such bars are so artificially emphasized on funerary figures, it seems more likely that the Egyptian banner, which, we assume, came originally from a grave, had had a religious rather than a military use. So we notice that on the two women, twice presented, in the scene of the Infancy of Moses, plate IX, the mark appears on the skirt of one woman in the group at

---

294. Above, p. 128.

295. Photograph by courtesy of the Egyptian Museum, Cairo. Cf. Edgar, *Coffins,* 65 f., no. 33.209, plate XXIX. See the mark also on the Egyptian woman in fig. 135, and on Moses and Jeremiah in fig. 100.

296. Photograph by courtesy of the Greco-Roman Museum, Alexandria.

297. See also the marks in figs. 152–155, 159.

298. From Musée des Beaux-Arts Alexandre III à Moscou, *Pamiatniki,* n.d., plate XXIV: a Roman-Egyptian cloth in the Golenishchev Collection. Cf. Rostovtzeff, ibid., Text, IV, 149–153; idem, "Vexillum and Victory," *JRS,* XXXII (1942), 92–106. In the latter study Rostovtzeff gives interesting examples of such banners used in religious ceremonies.

the right, on both at the left. We assume at once that they were special women indeed.

Such an ancestry of the mark explains for the first time its almost omnipresence on Christian robes, as well as the extreme diversity of its forms. On a mosaic representing Abraham at Santa Maria Maggiore [299] the pronged bar is on his robe, along with *c*, which latter appears also on his robe in the lower register of the same mosaic. In these I see an incomplete rendering of the frequent *d*, which looks like the letter "I," and in this mark itself I see a degeneration of the straight bar with double-forked ends, *a:* the bar has become a simple vertical between two forks. Conspicuously the bar forked on both ends appears on the himation of the holiest of the three "angels" in this mosaic, the figure at the center of the upper group. Both appear, more or less fully, in fig. 159,[300] where the prong-ended angle can be seen along with the "I" in various sorts of misrepresentation. Here distinctions in dress appear carefully indicated, as, I am sure, they are at Dura. The heavenly beings, including the boy Christ with the Magi, have the fully marked dress. Mary at the Annunciation wears what I have called the rich dress of Isis; Joseph, at the right, has only the striped chiton. The mark was often partially shown, I am sure, because it came in the folds of garments. Accordingly, later Christians, to whom the mark, like the robe itself, was probably known only in iconography, often represented it still more partially. Meanwhile the tradition of the original angle was preserved in the word *gamma*, used for the mark in any shape, a term which has perplexed lexicographers who know only the great variety of forms in which the mark could appear.[301] I have seen the band with square-pronged ends on modern goat-skin rugs of the Near East, where the mark seems to be quite traditional and conventional. The great care for its accurate representation in Greco-Roman Egypt,[302] however, and at Dura, along with the examples from Palmyra,[303] suggest strongly that it had not yet lost a direct symbolic reference in those circles. Shall we then assume that the frequency and distinctness of the mark on the Dura and Palmyra textiles [304] is to be evaluated from the religious art, so that the textiles, at least those having the marks, are to be considered as pieces of ceremonial garments; or are we to suppose that the actual textiles can be taken to indicate that the marks on the painted robes were "purely decorative," and without meaning? Again I feel that we must follow the long tradition of the art, rather than the isolated and unidentified scraps of textile evidence, and take it to be the greater probability that the marks had some symbolic force. That symbolic force, if I am right in assuming there was one, neither the paintings nor the textiles, unfortunately, make explicit.

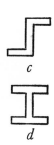

c

d

299. See above, III, fig. 1.

300. The Annunciation and the coming of the Magi: a mosaic at Santa Maria Maggiore, Rome (Photo Alinari, 30,122). See the marks on dress at Ravenna in Deichmann, *Früchristliche Bauten und Mosaiken von Ravenna*, passim, esp. figs. 316–321, and the mosaics in Sant' Apollinare Nuovo. Among these the mosaic representing the kiss of Judas, fig. 187, especially intrigues us, since Christ and the Apostles have the prong-ended angle on the himat-ion, but Judas does not. We can draw no conclusions, however, because the artist may have not shown it with Judas simply because in turning for the kiss Judas hides the part of the garment where the mark would normally have appeared.

301. See above, p. 162, n. 289.

302. Figs. 134, 156 f.

303. Above, pp. 143–146.

304. Above, pp. 128, 153.

G. LITERARY TRADITION ABOUT GRECO-ROMAN DRESS

ONE HAS ONLY to look at the section on "Kinds of clothes" in Pollux [305] to despair of any accurate treatment of the subject.[306] He gives names for so great a variety of articles without adequate distinction between them that we must clearly keep to such general terms as chiton, himation, peplos, chlamys, and dalmatic in discussing the costumes. For because of the inaccuracy of the representations and the confusion of literary terms it seems impossible to reconcile them. Only two points seem worth emphasizing from the literature, one the importance of the philosopher's robe, and the other the ceremonial importance of white or of light-simulating colors.

The philosopher's coat was a himation made of cheap coarse wool, hence scratchy and called *tribōn*, from *tribō*, which primarily means to rub.[307] In later usage the term came to mean a "rubbed," hence shabby, garment. It was early popular as the garb of Spartans, part of their practice of austerity, and was worn, apparently on that basis, by Socrates and Antisthenes. From them it came to be the distinguishing mark of the philosopher, though always used by the poor. It is usually worn as a simple "wrap-around," without a chiton under it, so that any himation worn without a chiton could be said to be worn "as a tribon." Like all terms for clothing, this one lost distinctive meaning, and from the monuments we have seen one would judge that the mystic teachers, or "philosophers," usually wore the Greek chiton and himation.

Literary sources suggest that the color of the garment was much more important than the form; it certainly was much more often mentioned as marking an occasion of dignity or of sanctity.[308] Yet, although the color is usually called *leukos* and translated "white," I am not at all sure that that translation is always right. To be sure, the word is used of snow, but it also describes the color of gray dust; it means white hair but also silver hair; it is used of "white" gold, or gold mixed with silver, which was probably pale yellow. It also means bright or shining, and so can be used of the sun, light, aether, the shining surface of glassy water, and even a "clear" voice and a happy day.[309] The opposite is *melas*, black or dark or dull. When a garment is called leukos, accordingly, we know that it was of a light, bright color, but not at all that it was what we would now call white.[310] The sacred "white linen"

305. *Onomasticon*, VII, 46–61 (ed. Dindorf, 1824, II, 71–75).

306. Amelung, in PW, III, 1899, 2310–2335; 2342–2347; VIII, 1913, 1609–1613, does his best to explain forms of chiton, chlamys, and himation. Miss Bieber (see Abbreviations and above, p. 137, n. 97) cites both literary and representational sources.

307. On the *tribōn* see the articles s.v. by M. Brilliant in DS, V, 414–416, and by E. Schuppe in PW, A XII, 1937, 2415–2419, where detailed evidence is given. The definitions in LS miss the change in meaning which these other scholars demonstrated. That Spartans had worn shabby

and patched clothing as a distinctive form of dress is unlikely, and without evidence.

308. The subject is briefly treated by Karl Mayer, *Die Bedeutung der weissen Farbe im Kultus der Griechen und Römer*, Diss., Freiburg im Breisgau, 1927, 19–28, a section on "Weisse Gewänder."

309. These are the meanings given in LS, with the sense of the bright or shining as primary.

310. My colleague E. L. Bennett told me that the word has still that meaning in Greece. He was asked whether he wanted his brown shoes polished "white or black," and said he wanted the "white," whereupon they were polished a light brown, not dark.

garments, for example, were probably a light yellow. Mayer thinks the light color (which he discusses always as white) actually had its primary value in its being apotropaic, but this his evidence by no means supports. A piece of leukos cloth was said by Plato to be a most suitable votive gift to the gods,[311] where the "light" cloth is definitely contrasted with a dyed cloth and would seem to mean a cloth of the natural color of the wool or linen. The shroud for the chief man of Plato's ideal state must also be "light," [312] presumably in the same sense as in the other passage. The proximity of the two statements suggests that the color symbolism was much the same in both cases, and that the "lightness" expressed divine character, a character into which the deceased leader of the community presumably had come.

This conclusion is much strengthened by a passage in Plutarch, in which I keep the "white" of Rose's translation: [313]

Q. Why do the women, when in mourning, wear white dresses and white kerchiefs? A. (a) Do they, as the Magi are said to do, take sides against Death and darkness by this action, and assimilate themselves to light and brightness? (b) Or do they consider that as the body of the dead is dressed in white, so the relatives should be? They adorn the body in this manner because they cannot do so to the soul, which they desire to dismiss bright and clean, as one that has now come victorious from a great and complex struggle. (c) Or is frugal simplicity most becoming on such occasions, while dyed garments are some of them expensive, some, mere vanities? For we may say of black, just as truly as of purple, "These be cheating garments and cheating colours." Naturally black (wool) is really dyed, not by art but by nature, being mixed with a preponderance of dusky matter. Only natural white therefore is pure and unmixed, neither stained nor imitable by dyes; it is therefore peculiarly fitting to the dead at burial. For a dead man is become simple, unmixed, pure, in short freed from the ingrained dye of the body. In Argos, Socrates records, they wear white garments, washed in water, when in mourning.

The undyed sheep's wool would certainly not be white in our sense, but by its lightness it represented life as against the darkness of death; the lightness of a soul that had finished the *agōn* of this life, about which we have had such frequent occasions to speak; [314] the purity of one freed from contamination with the body—that is, moral purity as it was considered in all Platonic tradition. The newly clothed priests and those who worshiped at the shrine of Asclepius at Pergamum,[315] those who worshiped at Priene [316] and Andania,[317] all wore "white" garments, as did mourners in the procession of Aratus [318] and mourners of the third century before Christ at Gambreion [319] and of Iulis in Ceos of the fifth century.[320]

311. Plato, *Laws*, XII, 956A. Cicero later heartily approved this passage: *De legibus*, II, xvii, 45.

312. Ibid., 947B. Cf. Pausanias, *Description of Greece*, IV, xiii, 3: "The Messenians used to carry out their chiefs for burial wearing crowns and dressed in white himatia."

313. Plutarch, *The Roman Questions*, XXVI, as tr. by H. J. Rose, 1924, 131.

314. See above, VII, 134–171.

315. M. Fränkel, *Die Inschriften von Pergamon*, 1890, I, 36, no. 40 (Königliche Museen zu Berlin: Altertümer von Pergamon, VIII, 1).

316. See above, p. 165, n. 308.

317. Above, pp. 135 f.

318. Plutarch, *Life of Aratus*, 53.

319. W. Dittenberger, *Sylloge Inscriptionum Graecarum*, 3d ed., 1920, III, no. 1219.

320. Ibid., no. 1218. The foregoing references were taken from Mayer, 19–28.

The reader should not misunderstand what I have said about the meaning of leukos: the Egyptian portraits so commonly show really white dress that apparently the Egyptians wanted a costume as near as possible to what we would call white. The Pompeian paintings give the same impression.[321] But any light color would do for contrast with dark clothing. We have seen [322] that the white of Lucius' costume of initiation was *candore puro luminosi*, which seemed to make of his dress an adaptation of the "robe of light" of earlier Egypt.

Such continued to be the significance of the robe in early Christian literature. In the transfiguration story Christ's divine nature was manifested to the disciples by the fact that his face shone like the sun, and his garments became white like light.[323] The "young man" who sat in Jesus' tomb, "dressed in a white robe," as described by Mark XVI, 5, became in Matthew XXVIII, 2 f., the angel of the Lord descended from heaven. "His appearance was like lightning, and his raiment white as snow." In Luke XXIV, 4, the apparition was of two men in garments "like lightning" or "of lightning." John XX, 12, has them simply two angels in white. The "two men in white" who appeared at the ascension, like Mark's young man, have always been taken to be angels. Simply an allusion to the dazzling garments meant at once "garments of light," and revealed the heavenly nature of those who wore them. So in Revelation III, 4 f., 15, those who "conquer" in the great *agōn* will walk with Christ in white garments, while in VII, 9–14, we read of the great multitude of the victors in Christ who stand before his throne, wearing garments which they have made white in the blood of the Lamb. Revelation makes so many references to white [324] that even the white horse [325] and the white throne [326] seem likewise to be this supernal light. Paul spoke directly of this change of vesture on two occasions, and made it specifically our changing the garment or tent of flesh in which we now dwell to don a new garment. In the new garment we shall not be "naked," but will be clothed with incorruptibility (*aphtharsia*) or immortality (*athanasia*), two terms for deification, one from philosophy and the other from popular religious parlance. "Behold I tell you a mystery," Paul says as he gets into the heart of this conception, and I surmise the figure was much closer to the symbolism of the new robes in mystery religions than we can ever document. Paul was sure he had received this "victory" from Jesus Christ, as, I judge, Lucius thought he had had a similar victory through donning the robes of Osiris. The Giver has changed, but not, I suspect, the gift.[327] Probably the same idea lies behind I John III, 2 f.:

321. See above, p. 137.

322. Above, p. 145.

323. Matt. XVII, 2. Mark IX, 3, has the garments a shining white that no fuller could equal; Luke IX, 29, speaks of lightning brilliance in describing garments. All agree that Jesus was changed into a being of light. See Cumont, *Lux*, 429–431.

324. Cf. Rev. IV, 4; VI, 11; XIX, 14.

325. Rev. VI, 2; XIX, 14. See below, X, 172–175, for the contrast of the white and black horses in the Dura synagogue.

326. Rev. XX, 11.

327. I have freely combined I Cor. xv, 42–57, with II Cor. v, 1–4. The body as a tent appears in the Prologue to the Fourth Gospel, where the Logos "became flesh and lived in a tent among us," which I can understand only as a hendiadys meaning that the Logos lived in a fleshly tent among us, or as we live. The idea was probably a common one, for Ecphantus says of the king: "He is like the rest of mankind in his earthly tent (*skanos*), inasmuch as he is formed out of the same material; but he is formed by the supreme Artificer, who in making the king used himself as an archetype." The "king" is obviously different from the material tent in which he lives. See my "The Political Philosophy of Hellenistic Kingship," *Yale Classical Studies*, I (1928), 76.

It does not yet appear what we shall be, but we know that when he appears we shall be like him, for we shall see him as he is. And every one who thus hopes in him purifies himself as he is pure.

With so much on the bright robe of light and purity in the New Testament, the Church inevitably continued the symbolic use of white robes, so that the *Catholic Encyclopedia* in discussing the symbolism of color in vestments, can succinctly say: "White, the symbol of light, typifies innocence and purity, joy and glory." [328] The continuity of this tradition need not here be traced. For example, St. Perpetua in a vision saw the divine pastor "with many thousands of white clad figures standing about him." [329] It may be pointed out, however, that "We shall be like him" is the Christian reinterpretation of the old pagan dream of apotheosis. The pagan value of apotheosis, expressed symbolically in the pagan white robe, was still expressed and affected for Christians by continuing the symbolism of the robe, which was now worn by Christ, God, and his saints alike.

H. JEWISH COSTUME

BEFORE CONCLUDING, even hypothetically, that the costume which has appeared symbolic for pagans and Christians had similar value for Jews, we must look at the records of Jewish costume at the time.

Krauss [330] tells us that the Jews then paid great attention to their clothing, and dressed as richly as their means allowed. [331] In particular, the religious and political aristocracies of Palestine took care to show their social importance by their clothing. For example, Josephus tells that shortly before the fall of Jerusalem the Levites persuaded King Agrippa to call a sanhedrin, with instructions to its members to reverse the former law and grant permission to Levites to wear the same linen garments as priests. [332] It is generally presumed that these were white, or at least "light." Jews distinguished between "white" and "colored" garments, with, I suspect, the general meaning of "light" or "dark." White was the garb of joy, of purity, and of social dignity, while colored clothes were left to women, and to men of the lower classes. [333] God himself, Daniel had said, is clothed in a garment white as snow, [334] while a Psalm says, "Thou coverest thyself with light as with a garment." [335] God appeared to Moses as a flaming bush, and on Sinai as insupportable light and glory, and the light was so transferred to Moses himself that his face also shone. [336] This idea continued in Jewish tradition. God has a face of fire, and the light of the universe at creation

328. *The Catholic Encyclopedia*, 1913, IV, 135*b*.

329. *Passio, SS. Perpetuae et Felicitatis*, IV, 8 (ed. C. van Beek, 1938, 21).

330. S. Krauss, *Talmudische Archäologie*, 1910: "Kleidung und Schmuck," I, 127–207. For this subject see also the rich collection of material in H. Riesenfeld, *Jésus transfiguré*, 1947, 115–129 (Acta Seminarii Neotestamentici Upsaliensis, XVI).

331. Krauss, 130–136.

332. Josephus, *Antiquities*, xx, 216–218 (ix, 6).

333. Krauss, I, 144 f.

334. Dan. VII, 9. Cf. A. Rosenzweig, *Kleidung und Schmuck im biblischen und talmudischen Schriften*, 1905, 38. God has fringes at the corner of his robe: Ginzberg, *Legends*, II, 362.

335. Ps. CIV, 2.

336. Exod. III, 2; XIX, 16–18; XXIV, 17; XXXIII, 18–23; XXXIV, 29.

was kindled from God's light, while Enoch, who saw this, was himself given a robe of light.[337] The risen righteous and elect will have garments of glory and light,[338] in which they will be like the angels.[339] Krauss sees the white-robed angels of the New Testament, whom we have just discussed, to be a part of the tradition, continued in the Talmud, that angels wear white.[340] The garment seems the same as the celestial clothing, that "of light," which the rabbis say Adam originally had, but lost at the Fall, a garment which Gabriel brought to Enoch.[341]

Connected with this, though in what way I cannot say, is the white robe of the rabbi on the Sabbath, for when R. Judah ben Ilai washed himself for the Sabbath and sat in his fringed linen robes he "was like an angel of the Lord of Hosts." [342] Blau said that the rabbis, like the philosophers, had a distinctive mantle, but that we do not know what it was.[343] I strongly suspect that R. Judah ben Ilai has given us the hint: it was a white or light dress much like those we have been discussing, a robe of holiness which the Essenes also took over. For we know that the Essenes gave a white robe to each new member as a mark of his final entry into the order—that is, upon his initiation—and that thereafter he wore white always.[344] Herein the Qumran community probably resembled the Essenes, for members of the community called themselves "sons of light," in anticipation of heaven where, in a life of eternity, they would wear "a crown of glory and a raiment of majesty in everlasting light." [345] The community could also have had no more fitting mark of their dedication and hope than to wear white robes in this life. For their dress we have no such evidence, however, as for the Essenes. But the Jewish tradition that angels wore white is early witnessed by the Testament of Levi,[346] who "saw [in a dream] some men in white raiment saying unto me: Arise, put on the robe of priesthood," etc. He was thus invested by seven heavenly figures, a conception that seems to me reflected in the scene of the anointing of David at Dura, plate VII.

The convention of the sanctity of the white-robed figure may have been very old. We most obviously think of it in connection with the high priest who took off his official garments on the Day of Atonement and went into the Holy of Holies wearing only a white linen ephod,[347] a garment that seems to have been the robe of light, at least in later interpretation.[348] We must also note that Samuel as a boy wore a "linen ephod," [349] as did David when he danced before the ark,[350] in both cases probably the same garment the high priest

337. II Enoch XXII–XXV.

338. I Enoch LXII, 15; CVIII, 12; cf. v, 6 f.; XIV, 18–21.

339. Ibid. LXXI, 1; LXXXVII, 2; XC, 21 f., 31.

340. Krauss, I, 550, n. 212.

341. Ginzberg, *Legends*, I, 79, 135, 139; V, 103, n. 93.

342. *BT, Shabbath*, 25b (ET, 1, 111).

343. L. Blau in *HUCA*, III (1926), 210.

344. Josephus, *Jewish War*, II, 123, 137 (viii, 3 and 7).

345. The Manual of Discipline, as published by

M. Burrows, *The Dead Sea Scrolls*, 1955, 375.

346. Testaments of the Twelve Patriarchs: Levi, VIII, 2. See above, VII, 169.

347. Exod. XXVIII, 4; Lev. XVI, 4.

348. It is to this aspect of the problem that Riesenfeld, 115–129, has made especially rich contribution.

349. I Sam. II, 18 f. See the remarks on the articles of clothing by K. Budde, *Die Bücher Samuel*, 1902, 20 (Kurzer Hand-Commentar zum Alten Testament, VIII).

350. II Sam. VI, 14.

wore when he entered the Holy of Holies. Each year Samuel's mother made for him in addition a little *me'il*.[351] It was in this latter robe that he was still dressed when he appeared from the grave to the witch of Endor.[352] As such he looked like God to her, or a god.[353] Josephus expanded the sentence to say that Samuel appeared to her "distinguished and of divine majesty (*theoprepēs*)," so that she reported that he had a "form like God." [354] The Septuagint reads "gods," and is best expounded in the Biblical Antiquities of Pseudo-Philo: [355]

> "what is his form (*species*)?" And she said: "Thou inquirest of me concerning the gods. For behold his form is not the form of a man. For he is arrayed in a white robe (*stola*), and has a mantle (*diploïs*) wrapped around it, and two angels lead him." And Saul recalled the diploïs [356] that Samuel had rent when Samuel saw him.

Here the Septuagint plural, "gods," is interpreted to mean Samuel accompanied by two angels, and the clothing is distinctly understood to be the "white" chiton and himation. Pseudo-Philo seems to have taken the stola to be the long Greek chiton, for on it he says the *diploïs* is draped; and the *diploïs*, which the Septuagint here uses to translate *me'il*,[357] seems to be an abbreviation of the *tribōn diplous*, a form of the philosopher's *tribōn*.[358]

Whatever the original form and significance of the me'il, therefore, it would appear that by the time the Septuagint translation of I Samuel was made, the garments of Samuel, which made him look like God, or a god, were already associated with the Greek dress of sanctity we are investigating. We may suppose that at least Josephus and Pseudo-Philo envisaged Samuel as wearing this dress. If anyone were to represent the incident in an illumination for the Greek text, he would inevitably have represented Samuel (with or without the two angels) in the Greek robe, and would have done so fully convinced that Samuel actually wore such clothing in life and death. That Samuel should be painted as he is in Dura, plate VII, accordingly, seems not only natural but inevitable. It may be that this passage was the bridge over which the white wardrobe of the Jewish saints was carried from paganism to Jewish art. If Samuel was thus dressed, it is very possible that other Jewish heroes would be put into these garments, and so shown to be "in the form of God."

351. Cf. Exod. xxviii, 4.

352. I Sam. xxviii, 13 f.

353. On how Elohim is to be understood here commentators disagree: see Budde, 181. The AV translates "gods"; ARV "a god"; P. Ketter, *Die Samuelbücher*, 1940, 172; cf. 175 f., "gottähnliches Geistwesen" (Die Heilige Schrift für das Leben erklärt, III, i).

354. Josephus, *Antiquities*, vi, 332 f. (xiv, 2). Marcus properly translates that Samuel looked to the witch as *ho theos*, which can only mean "God."

355. Pseudo-Philo's *Biblical Antiquities*, lxiv, 6; ed. G. Kisch, 1949, 269 (Publications in Medieval Studies, University of Notre Dame, X).

356. I Sam. xv, 27 (LXX).

357. This is true not only here but in I Sam. ii, 19; xv, 27. It also translates the *me'il* as the robe of Saul in I Sam. xxiv, 5, 12. But *me'il* has other translations: I Sam. xviii, 4; Job i, 20; ii, 12.

358. In their studies of the *tribōn* (see above, n. 307) both Brilliant and Schuppe recall that the *tribōn*, the commonest term for the himation of the philosophers, was often worn "doubled over." The Cynics especially wore the *tribōn*, and Diogenes, a Cynic, is the only pagan I can find who wore the *diploïs*: *Greek Anthology*, vii, 65 (Loeb ed., II, 39 f.).

The "bridge," however, may have been less the convenient passages about the dress of Samuel [359] than a general adopting of the robe by Jews other than Essenes. For there is some reason to suppose that this dress was commonly seen in Jerusalem as the garb of Scribes and Pharisees. Our evidence is late, indeed the fourth century; I have not seen Epiphanius' remarks on Palestinian clothing at the time of Jews considered in discussions of the subject. He says in commenting upon Matthew XXIII, 5: [360]

> They [the Scribes] had certain "borders" (*kraspeda*) [361] as tokens of their citizenship (*politeia*), alike to show their pride and to win the commendation of those who saw them. And they put "phylacteries" [362] upon their himations, that is broad purple stripes (or marks, *sēmata*). Now one must not think, because in the Gospel they are given this name, that the reference is to amulets (*periapta*, lit., amulets of the type bound around) since some people are used to understanding "phylacteries" [in the Gospel] as amulets of this kind. The account has no reference to this sort of thing. But since these people dressed in outer garments of the type of *ampechonai* [363] and dalmatics of the type of colobia, adorned with broad stripes [364] of purple made of purple cloth, those who were most accurate were accustomed to call the stripes of purple "phylacteries," and for this reason the Lord called them "phylacteries" as worn by these men. What follows makes clear the meaning of the words, "and the borders of their cloaks." For he [the Lord] said "borders (*kraspeda*) in the definite sense of fringes (*krossoi*), and "phylacteries" in the sense of the stripes of purple, when he said "Ye make broad your phylacteries and deep the fringes on your cloaks." And each of them wore certain tassels at the four corners of the cloak (*tribōn*),[365] attached to the cloak by being extensions of the warp itself,[366] during the time when they were fasting or living as virgins. For as each man appointed for himself a time of holiness or discipline, so these were their tokens to be seen of men by which they made it known that no one should touch them while they were sanctifying themselves.

In the next section Epiphanius says of the dress of the Pharisees:

> They outdid the scribes in the above described dress (*schēma*), that is in the *ampechonē* and other articles of dress and in their effeminate himatia, going beyond them in their broad high boots (*en plateiais tais krēpisin*) and in the lacing of their boots (*hupodēmata*).

Epiphanius seems to have had amazingly detailed information about the dress of the religious aristocracy of Judaism at the time of Jesus. His account tallies so perfectly with

359. The special power of the mantle of the prophet has no such tradition of color and form in the Bible, but that the "virtue" of the prophet was in his mantle appears in Elijah's leaving it for Elisha: II Kings II, 8–14.

360. *Panarion*, XV, i, 3–7; ed. K. Holl, I, 209 (*GCS*, XXV).

361. Cf. Matt. IX, 20, where the woman touches the "border" of Jesus' garment.

362. Epiphanius, *Panarion*, loc. cit.

363. *Ampechone* is a variant of *ampechonon*, which

Mau, PW, I, s.v., describes as a cloak (*periblōma*) of great size: "In the temple inventory of Diana Brauronia it is distinguished from the himation, but the distinction between the two is not known."

364. *Platusēma*, the word most used in Greek for the *latus clavus*.

365. The confusion of the *ampechonē* with the *tribōn* is noteworthy. Sharp distinctions in terms cannot be made.

366. Such tassels, made in exactly this way, are shown in the Dura paintings, figs. 324, 326, etc.

the Dura paintings that if he had had them before him he could not have given a more accurate description of the costume. Perhaps the most striking feature of this passage is Epiphanius' description of the shoes, for the type he mentions, the laced *krēpis* or *hupodēma*, was called by the Romans the *calceus*, and such boots distinguished the Roman patrician or senator, though occasionally they are found in the provinces upon representations of Roman officials of lesser dignity. In the Dura paintings men clothed in the white robe wear sandals, but the boots are twice shown beside Moses as he stands barefoot before the Lord. All the details—*ampechonē, colobium,* himation, stripes, tassels, fringes, and boots, as Epiphanius describes them—correspond perfectly to the dress of the chief figures in the Dura paintings. Epiphanius characterizes the garb as effeminate because the effeminacy of the *ampechonē* was proverbial, and an *ampechonē* with fringes and tassels would all the more merit the scorn of both Greeks and Romans. When he distinguishes the "phylacteries," as stripes or marks of purple cloth appliqué, from the *periapta* with which many were associating the word, it is quite likely that the original meaning of "phylacteries" was already being forgotten, and that the tradition had begun of identifying the "phylacteries" with the tefillin, the little box with scriptural quotations bound to the forehead worn by Jews in prayer, a tradition still reproduced in all commentaries with the confidence of repetition. Epiphanius obviously had definite information, but from what source, and how reliable was it?

Unfortunately we have no way of answering the question. Epiphanius as a historian does not have the standing of Eusebius or Hippolytus, and he not only used poor sources uncritically but seems not to have been averse to filling in gaps from his imagination.[367] His explanation of the phylacteries as stripes rather than tefillin, however, makes sense, since there is a definite limit to the size of tefillin—the limit of the breadth of one's forehead—and that the reference should be to stripes is inherently quite plausible. Still Epiphanius may have been drawing not upon an ancient and reliable source but upon illustrations in some one of the now lost, and so to us still hypothetical, illustrated texts from hellenized Jews. His description of the costumes, even to the shoes, makes it highly unlikely that he was here improvising as he wrote. I should myself guess that he was right, that Jews took over the sacred white costume with its stripes, not only for biblical illustration, as Dura shows, and not only for actual dress in the Dead Sea communities, but also for a mark of their piety by Scribes and Pharisees.

Such a conclusion must, of course, be subject to evidence on dress in rabbinic writings. This was fortunately collected by Krauss, and we find that as with other evidence much

---

367. The best discussions of the sources of Epiphanius are still: R. Lipsius, *Zur Quellenkritik des Epiphanius*, 1865; idem, in *A Dictionary of Christian Biography*, 1880, II, 149–156. Lipsius here, pp. 152 f., calls him "an honest but credulous and narrow minded zealot," and speaks of his collecting "a large but ill-arranged store of historical information." He adds, "His communications concern-ing the various Jewish sects are for the most part worthless," but they seem to me to be like his records of Jewish-Christian and Gnostic sects, in "exhibiting a marvellous mixture of valuable traditions with misunderstandings and fancies of his own." See also A. Hilgenfeld, *Judenthum und Judenchristenthum*, 1886, who discusses the passages on the dress of the Scribes and Pharisees on p. 72.

of it supports our conclusion, and nothing that I can find discredits it, although nothing definitely "proves" it. We have already mentioned the angelic resplendence of Rabbi Judah in his white garments.[368] Rabbinical Hebrew and Aramaic had many words for different sort of clothing, but the influence of Greek civilization was such that the Tannaim themselves borrowed and transliterated the Greek word *colobium*, explaining it as a sort of dalmatic, a word they also transliterated.[369] To these words, which seem to have been used for the undergarment we here ordinarily call the chiton, corresponded an outer garment, called, among other names, the pallium—a word likewise transliterated. This mantle, more usually called the *tallith*, carried the tassels of piety.[370] The Aramaic word for ornament on clothing came to have as a variant a transliteration of the Greek word for purple stripes, or for a garment trimmed with such stripes, *periporphuros*,[371] and Krauss tells us that the rabbis were careful so to arrange their clothing that its ornament would be visible,[372] another detail which recalls the carefully shown ornament on the garments of the Dura synagogue. It then becomes significant that the word for such ornament was also transliterated by the rabbis, and became *gam*, used several times for ornament in clothing. The great Babylonian scholar of the eleventh century, Hai Gaon, explained the *gam* as the Greek gamma, and described it as "a piece of fine stuff, like purple cloth, sewn on a seam." [373]

Only one hypothesis seems to me to account for all these facts: the Jews—not only the Essenes and Qumran sects, but the learned and distinguished rabbinic Jews—borrowed this robe, borrowed it in such a way that it kept its pagan value as the dress of piety, even of divinity; but by adding fringes and tassels, they made it the dress of Jewish piety. Indeed Blaufuss suggested, on the basis of a statement in the Tosefta to the *Abodah Zarah*, that the Jewish white robe of the time not only was the robe of Isis but often still had on it for Jews the moon and stars of Isis symbolism.[374] Without any evidence but his profound knowledge of antiquity, Lidzbarski suggested that the white robe still worn by the head of an orthodox Jewish household on especially festal occasions is a survival of the ancient usage, pagan as well as Jewish, of such garments. A pious Jew will be clothed in that robe when he is buried, "so that he may appear white before God." [375]

In short, the Greek robe seems to have been treated like all the other borrowed symbols we have been considering. Originally the robe of philosophic mystical piety, the robe of Osiris, it was borrowed by Jews, but could no more be the robe of Osiris for them than it was for Christians when they put it on their saints. In Christianity, like the halo, it marked divine, or supernal, holiness in heaven or on earth. For Jews it seems to have

368. See above, p. 169.

369. S. Schemel, *Die Kleidung der Juden im Zeitalter der Mischnah*, Diss., Berlin, 1912, 28, n. 4. The meaning of these words seems to have changed with different times and places.

370. Ibid., 36, n. 2; cf. Krauss, I, 167; Rosenzweig, 64.

371. Krauss, I, 163 f.

372. Ibid., 589, n. 439.

373. Ibid., 596, n. 499.

374. H. Blaufuss, *Götter, Bilder und Symbole nach den Traktaten über fremden Dienst (Aboda zara) in Mischna, Tosefta, Jerusalemer und babylonischem Talmud*, 1910, 30, 44 (Jahresbericht des K. Neuen Gymnasiums in Nürnberg für das Schuljahr 1909–10, Suppl.).

375. M. Lidzbarski, *Auf rauhem Wege*, 1927, 43.

meant much the same in terms of Jewish holiness. When used in the synagogue as the garb of the great heroes, it suggests that the heroes—Moses, Jacob, Elijah, Samuel, to name only a few—by their having this robe in contrast to those beside them are marked as people of a distinctively holy character. When others whom we cannot so easily identify are put into the same dress, we must be careful before concluding that they are merely bystanders, let alone the accursed prophets of Baal.

At this stage I do not draw firm conclusions. But the tradition of symbolic dress in the period has shown new possibilities of interpreting the paintings. The conclusions of this chapter, I repeat, must be taken as only hypotheses. We have, I believe, found an objective approach to the dress of individuals in the paintings of the synagogue, but whether the conclusions from general use in the period can be used as a basis for interpreting the Jewish paintings does not yet appear. As we go into an examination of the paintings, we shall see whether our hypothesis of the meaning of the robe helps consistently to explain their significance.[376]

376. Just as my proofs were released for printing I received a new book, F.-N. Klein, *Die Lichtterminologie bei Philon von Alexandrien und in den hermetischen Schriften, Untersuchungen zur Struktur der religiösen Sprache der hellenistischen Mystik*, Leiden, 1962. On pp. 61–65 Klein discusses "Das Lichtkleid als Symbol des Besitzes göttlichen Lichtes," and comes to much the point of view I have expressed above, but of course on the basis of relatively little material. He does not use archeological sources, has not seen the volumes of this series, and contributes little that is new on the whole subject.

PART XIV

THE BIBLICAL SCENES ON THE WEST WALL

CHAPTER EIGHT

Jewish Royalty

ANY APPROACH to the biblical paintings of the synagogue must begin from some arbitrarily selected point, and I have already indicated that what seems to me the least arbitrary is the center of the west wall, the site of the Torah shrine with the reredos above it and its four portraits of Moses. Still, I believe, interpretation should follow the eye of the observer. Once the full decorations had been completed, a worshiper who made his prayers facing the Torah shrine, and the Holy City behind it, would have his attention caught most often by the scenes that flanked the shrine. These, as plate 1 shows, were first a pair of felines, each with a female mask beside it, and above them two scenes of royalty. The royalty presented, however, is the unique royalty of Israel.

A. THE PURIM TRIUMPH

THE SCENE AT THE LEFT, plates I and VI, and fig. 336, presents basically two incidents from the Book of Esther, but does so in terms of three groups of figures. At the left Haman leads Mordecai in royal splendor; at the right a group centers in Ahasuerus on the throne, with Esther and attendants. The painting has three names inscribed in Aramaic. "Mordecai" stands under the belly of Mordecai's horse, "Ahasuerus" on the third step of the king's throne, and "Esther" under her footstool. Whatever else is in doubt about the painting, there can be none about these three characters.[1] From the viewpoint of composition, however, a central group of four heroic-sized figures in the Greek robe dominates the design, so that, although they have no place in the biblical story of Esther or in extra-biblical tradition, if we are to follow the composition they must be given the central place in interpreting the scene as a whole.[2]

The painting presents a most striking example of the mingling of hellenistic and

1. Torrey in Kraeling, *Synagogue*, 271 f., inscriptions 8–10.

2. Kraeling, *Synagogue*, 157, n. 582, recognizes the "balancing central element," but, as we shall see, tries to explain the figures away as "specta-tors." His interpretation of this scene, accordingly, is an excellent example of the fallacy of approaching the paintings book in hand, so that what is represented seems important only when details can be explained as illustrating some extant portion of the Bible or rabbinic haggadah.

Persian dress.[3] If the central four had been omitted, we should have had a rather straight-forward representation of details that are largely biblical, a design which might seem at first quite suitable to be put into an Aramaic or Hebrew scroll for Purim. The presence of the Greek figures, however, throws the whole, artistically, into another dimension. For these, we feel, we should know the hellenized Jewish interpretations of Purim, but of this little remains. We shall do best to begin with the painting itself.

The group on the right presents, primarily, Ahasuerus on his throne, with Esther beside him on a chair; a man in Persian costume hurries to the king at the foot of the throne and holds to him what Kraeling takes to be a scroll. Behind Esther is a small feminine figure, her servant: Kraeling was probably right in calling her Esther's personal maid, "what was proper for a queen."[4] Beside and behind the king stand two men in Persian costume, his Throne Guards, the proper companions of a king.

Kraeling's description of the costumes in this group need not be repeated in detail. The king wears a red "Persian" hat and a red cloak over a blue underdress of long smock and trousers. All his garments are decorated with golden bands which Kraeling says are marked as though woven with continuous scrollwork designs.[5] The king's left hand rests lightly on the hilt of the sword, his right is extended as though to greet the man before him, or to accept the proffered document. His yellow throne, probably of gold, stands upon a dais approached by four steps, the two ends of each step marked alternately with the royal eagle or lion.[6] A pair of lions support the seat, and a red cloth is thrown over the back of the throne. Like other such figures, he holds his legs in the peculiar position in which Sassanian kings, fig. 79,[7] are often represented. The Persian king, that is, is presented for Jews as he would have been presented for Persians, with the symbols that indicated his divine character as king.

Esther sits on a throne of the sort usually occupied by kings in the synagogue paintings, a chair with turned legs. She wears a tight blue bodice with a long pink skirt from beneath the breast to her feet, plate VI.[8] A drape is wrapped round her legs, reddish brown, but with clusters of spots on it that make little rosettes, another mark of divinity or royalty, or both.[9] They probably represent jewels. Esther's hair curls softly on her shoulders in a way to recall the headdress of the female figures in the tiles, figs. 24, 25, quite unlike the hair of the females in fig. 338 or of the dado, or of Esther's own maid. She wears pendant earrings, a necklace, a brooch, arm bands and bracelets, and perhaps a ring.

3. Esther scrolls, and the medieval tradition in general, though often reproducing similar incidents, seem to have no connection with the Dura paintings. See, for example, those published by R. Wischnitzer-Bernstein in *EJ*, VI, 810–814, and Kraeling, 164.

4. *Synagogue*, 160.

5. Ibid., 158.

6. See above, VIII, 33. Kraeling, 158 f., cites interesting midrashic material that connects this throne with the throne of Solomon, and hence sug-

gests why it may resemble the throne of Solomon in WA2, fig. 329.

7. See above, p. 83.

8. See the drawing in Kraeling, *Synagogue*, 159, fig. 44, and for all details, fig. 336.

9. See the robe of Khusrau II, above, VII, fig. 211; cf. ibid., figs. 167, 170, 189, 197, 199 f., 203. See also the lining of the mantle of the god Iarhibol at Dura: Rostovtzeff, *Dura-Europos*, V, plate XXXVI, 3; and the garment of Aphlad at Dura: ibid., plate XIII.

From her head a long white veil falls behind her shoulders to the waist,[10] and in accordance with Scripture [11] she wears a crown, though an unusual one. It consists of three rectangular-topped pegs which go down not to a round gold base but, if correctly reported, to a wreath on her hair. The crown must be supposed a variant of the turreted mural crown most commonly associated with Tyche. Fig. 160 [12] shows a crown near in form to the one on Esther. It consists of a "wall with three projecting towers" which broaden out at the top. In this case it is worn by Atargatis-Astarte, *paredros* of Adonis, from whose temple it comes. The mural crown took many forms, and was commonly put upon gods, goddesses, and royalty. We have seen it on Gē, fig. 58. The form on the head of Esther, my colleague Alfred Bellinger tells me, is also closely to be compared to the crown on a coin of Elagabalus of Bostra, where it is worn by the Tyche of the city.[13] Esther, as she sits on her throne wearing the wreath-crown, and the cloak with rosettes, has clearly been given the pagan tokens of full royalty. Her throne has no steps of lions and eagles, but she sits a bit higher than the king, and with her appurtenances seems marked as having royal divinity even more definitely than the king himself.[14]

The conventional two companions of the king have interest only insofar as they, like the companions of Pharaoh in fig. 338 but unlike those in figs. 74 and 329, wear Persian dress. Kraeling's guess is good that the companion behind Ahasuerus holds a book, but his suggestion that the strange object in the left hand of the companion beside the king is a "key" is not so convincing.[15]

We recognize the attributes of royal divinity given to both king and queen, but what incident is represented? Who is the vigorous young man in Persian dress who holds up the scroll to the king? And what is on the scroll? Kraeling points out that prostration before a king does not appear in the synagogue, and he thinks this reflects Jewish reluctance to give divine honors to a human king.[16] I quite agree that the purpose of the scene is to represent someone, apparently of great standing because of his jeweled arm band, who brings the king important news, and Kraeling seems on the whole plausible in sug-

10. Cf. the veils on the women in WC4, fig. 338. I should imagine that these veils ordinarily covered the women's faces. Kraeling, 159, n. 593, has an interesting collection of material on women's veils.

11. Esther II, 17.

12. Courtesy of the Yale University Art Gallery; cf. Frank Brown in Rostovtzeff, *Dura-Europos*, VII, 163–165, and plate XXXI.

13. G. Hill, *Catalogue of the Greek Coins of Arabia, Mesopotamia, Persia*, 1922, plate IV, 2 (*CBM*). He also called to my attention as parallels: coins of Troas in W. Wroth, *Troas, Aeolis, Lesbos*, 1894, plates IV, 8–12, VI, 17, XXIV, 3, 5 (*CBM*); of Gaza in G. F. Hill, *Coins of Palestine*, 1914, plate XV, 17 f. (*CBM*); of various places in Galatia in Wroth, *Ga-*

latia, Cappadocia, and Syria, 1899, plates XXIX, 2–4, 8, XXX, 1 f., 6, XXXI, 12 f., XXXII, 6–10, XXXIV, 8–10 (*CBM*); of Alexandria in R. Poole, *Alexandria and the Nomes*, 1892, plate VIII, 192, 961, 1620 (*CBM*).

14. Compare the queen standing behind the throne of David, while Nathan denounces him, in a Chludoff Psalter illumination: J. J. Tikkanen, "Die Psalterillustration im Mittelalter," *Acta Societatis Scientiarum Fennice*, XXXI (1903), 27, fig. 34.

15. Kraeling, 161, fig. 45, publishes a detail drawing of it. I have no idea what the object is: it still seems to me to be more probably the hilt of a sword, in spite of Kraeling's pertinent objections. See also his remarks in 172, n. 657.

16. *Synagogue*, 161 f., esp. n. 604. Refusal to bow before the king or his emissary is an essential part of the tradition of Mordecai in the story.

gesting that the news is of the destruction by thousands of those who had opposed the Jews.[17] To this we shall return after considering the other incidents in the painting.

The scene of Mordecai on the horse led by Haman [18] at the left of the panel is more striking than that of the king and his court. As he should, according to Scripture, Mordecai wears the full royal apparel, consisting of the red hat,[19] blue caftan and trousers, and red coat with gold bands flowing out behind him, such as Ahasuerus wears. A quiver of arrows hangs beside him. The figure especially recalls the royal horseman of plate XVII, except that there the front legs of the horse show much more motion. In contrast, while Mordecai's horse steps out bravely with the hind legs, he plants the two front feet in rigid opposition. Hopkins has clearly shown that such a figure, one especially who rides with flying chlamys on a horse standing in this position, is that of a divinity, used also for the divine king.[20] In Syria it was widely used, almost always with a quiver of arrows, for a god Genneas,[21] actually called by many names (now, among others, the "Cavalier god"). One without the chlamys can be seen in fig. 161,[22] from Dura, and we shall discuss others shortly.[23] Mordecai is thus deliberately presented as the Cavalier god, a figure instantly recognizable by any person at Dura, and as such, the divine king. Mordecai's royalty is also marked by another detail: he wears the royal diadem, slightly indicated as a white line under his cap, but with the end strings in white zigzag prominently on either side of his neck.[24] The diadem was so much the mark of divinity that even when this painting was made, no Roman emperor (with the possible exception of the mad Gaius) had yet dared to assume it for himself. Sixty years later Constantine for the first time wore one.[25]

17. I cannot agree, however, that the small figure before the throne is Mordecai himself, in view of his heroic presentation on the horse.

18. Kraeling, 152, quite rightly says of this that there can be no doubt the scene represented is described in Esther VI, 1–11.

19. It is conspicuous that neither the king nor Mordecai wears the golden crown mentioned in Esther VI, 8, though Mordecai does so in *MR*, *Esther*, X, 12 (ET, 121), and Esther herself does so in the painting.

20. I follow Hopkins rather than Kraeling in believing that Mordecai's horse has this position familiar in eastern art: C. Hopkins in *Berytus*, III (1936), 20 f.; idem in Rostovtzeff, *Dura-Europos*, VI, 228–238. Hopkins has assembled excellent material, but does not mention the apparently unique position of the feet of the king's horse in the synagogue. Hopkins' articles are confusing in that he has throughout interchanged "off" (properly "right") with "near" (properly "left"). See also Widengren, "Juifs et Iraniens," 209; "Iranische Religionsgeschichte," *Numen*, II (1955), 95.

21. See H. Seyrig and J. Starcky, "Genneas,"

Syria, XXVI (1949), 230–257, for additional examples.

22. Courtesy of the Yale University Art Gallery; see Hopkins, *Berytus*, plate VI, 1, at p. 20. Cf. another in Rostovtzeff, *Dura-Europos*, IX, ii, plate XLVIII. It was found in the debris thrown together to make the great ramp behind the city wall, and may have come from any part of the city.

23. See below, p. 181.

24. It is perhaps worth pointing out in passing that the horse's mane at the forehead bristles in a way which suggests the whorls of Arkell's horse: see above, VII, 71. In midrashic tradition the horse was a black one: Ginzberg, *Legends*, IV, 435; cf. VI, 476, n. 169. The change to white in this painting is interesting in view of the duel between riders on black and white horses in fig. 347; see below, X, 172. The diadem is conspicuous on either side of the head of the central person in fig. 147.

25. The material is adequately collected in Smith, *GRA*, I, 619 f. See esp. Sextus Aurelius Victor, *De caesaribus*, XLI, 14 (ed. F. Pichmayer, 1911, 167).

When the artist put one on Mordecai in so conspicuous a way, he distinguished Mordecai as the divine king. His much greater size would suggest greater significance than that of Ahasuerus.

The figure of Haman, as Kraeling points out, is presented in degradation.[26] He wears only a belted caftan whose short skirt barely covers his genitals: even his feet are bare. In utter contrast to the splendor of Mordecai he leads the horse like a slave groom, one hand on the horse's bridle, the other loosely holding the halter rope.[27]

Kraeling and Hopkins both recognize that the scene of Mordecai and Haman together has been adapted from representations of the eastern cavalier deity, though they do not consider this fact in interpreting the scene as a whole. They seem to me to be underestimating the resemblance and its significance. In a relief from Hama, fig. 162,[28] the deity is clothed exactly as is Mordecai in the synagogue. In the great Sassanian rock reliefs the king and Ohrmazd face each other, each mounted and each with the same cloak and diadem streaming behind him. The only difference is that the god offers the king a crown (of divine royalty). The Cavalier god, that is, could be Ohrmazd himself, or the king.[29] The "cavalier" is often hailed by a person standing before him, probably a lesser divinity, and offered a crown: see figs. 163 [30] and 164.[31] Or, as in fig. 165,[32] the figure in front may seem to be simply leading the god's horse. On amulets of the St. George type the mounted figure, either alone or led by a Victory or angel, and properly shown with the flying chlamys, is identified with various superhuman persons as he spears the snake or woman.[33]

26. He cites (p. 156) midrashic stories to show how tradition liked to anticipate the ultimate humiliation of Haman by having him forced on this occasion to do Mordecai the most degrading services. See also Ginzberg, *Legends*, IV, 438; VI, 477, n. 174; *JE*, IX, 8 f.; and esp. *BT, Megillah*, 16a (ET, 94 f.).

27. The halter rope is a presumption from what looks like the frayed end of a rope in Haman's hand. It is not connected with the horse, but may well be all that is left of the tether by which animals were commonly led at the time. See figs. 166 f.

28. Courtesy of the Direction des Antiquités, Lebanon. See Rostovtzeff, "Dura and the Problem of Parthian Art," *Yale Classical Studies*, V (1935), 225, and fig. 42; Hopkins in Rostovtzeff, *Dura-Europos*, VI, 228–238; S. Ronzevalle in *MSJ*, XXI (1937–38), plate XVII, 1.

29. L. van den Berghe, *Archéologie de l'Iran ancien*, 1959, plates 27, 129, pp. 23 f. Herzfeld in *Revue des arts asiatiques*, V (1928), 132, and plate XXVII, fig. 5; idem, *Iran in the Ancient East*, 1941, 314 and plates CXII–CXXV. In the latter work Herzfeld says that the king and god face each other on their horses while two storms blow their gar-

ments, one left and one right. One can get into absurdity when trying to see realism in a symbol. For some reason which I do not know, this representation required the garments to fly out behind the rider, realism or no, which makes the garment of Mordecai all the more recognizably symbolic.

30. From Rostovtzeff, *Dura-Europos*, VI, plate XXX, 1. It is a relief dedicated to Ashadu and Shadai. See Hopkins, ibid., 228–238.

31. From the same plate, no. 3. It is a relief from Khirbet-el-Hamam: see Hopkins, ibid., 233–238.

32. Courtesy of the Direction des Antiquités, Lebanon. It is a relief from Ferzol. See Seyrig in *Syria*, XIX (1938), 364; Ronzevalle in *MSJ*, plates VI–VIII, pp. 29–40. See also the three reliefs in Rostovtzeff, *Dura-Europos*, VI, plate XXX, one of which is from Dura itself.

33. See above III, figs. 1048–1050, 1052, 1054, 1063, 1067; cf. E. Kantorowicz in *Art Bulletin*, XXVI (1944), 218 f., and figs. 31–33, 35. The flying chlamys appears also with classical horsemen, of course, as on the Parthenon: see Bieber, *Kleidung*, plate XXVII; Heuzey, *Histoire du costume antique*, 131–134.

In fig. 166 [34] I should guess that the empty saddle awaits the soul of the person buried in the grave, Maqqai, and that Ingholt is right in recognizing him as the central one of the three who stand beside the horse. He seems destined for deification by the horse waiting for him,[35] as he seems deified on the couch above.[36]

The synagogue artist is apparently composing the scene directly in terms of the lingua franca of the symbols about him, but he is using that lingua franca freely to give a Jewish message. Mordecai on the horse has with obvious intent been presented as the equivalent of what pagans saw in their Cavalier god. The diadem he wears only emphasizes the artist's conception. Before him Haman stands as the familiar figure before that god, but degraded to show the humiliation of the heathen.[37]

If symbols are thus being adapted, we should expect to find real significance in the four men who dominate the entire design at the center. Much larger than any other figures in the painting, they stand in the Greek himation and chiton exaggeratedly marked with broad stripes and prongs, as they hail Mordecai, or perhaps both incidents, with uplifted right hands. But only three hands are raised. The colors have presumably dulled, but there appears to be a group of three, two in light pink and one in light yellow, led by a man in what was probably painted as white. The man in the white robe has very broad stripes on his chiton, the man just behind him in yellow has less broad stripes, the man in pink at the right, who seems to be third, has only narrow stripes, and none appear at all on what little can be seen of the fourth figure. Gute apparently saw the two central faces intact before they were moved to Damascus. The dominant white-robed figure followed by three to make a group of four form a group that balances with the scene of the anointing of David, plate VII, where the dominant white-robed figure is accompanied by six others to make a group of seven into which David comes, see plate I. In this there seems some meaningful intent.

Who are these men? Kraeling calls them "bystanders," a "static mass . . . least plastic and most lifeless" of all figures in this painting: their gestures are stilted, they have only seven instead of eight feet to stand on; they are given "neutral rendering." But these four persons, standing thus rigidly in the dress which we have seen much reason to suppose was highly significant, make upon me an entirely different impression. The very formal-

34. From *Syria*, XVIII (1937), plate IV at p. 16. Cf. Ingholt in *Berytus*, II (1935), 63–67, and plates XXVI, XXVII.

35. Cf. F. Benoit, *L'Héroïsation équestre*, 1954, 62 f. Seyrig, "Le Repas des morts et le 'banquet funèbre' à Palmyre," *Les Annales archéologiques de Syrie*, I (1951), 32–40, esp. 39 f., discusses this relief, with the banquet above it. He sees in it a representation of a rich man about to leave for a hunt, and concludes that since this is a rather important moment, the whole, with the funerary banquet above it, is of a "caractère hautement mondain." Increasingly it appears that those of us who look for religious significance on funerary monuments will see different things from those who want earnestly to see casual, and "mondain," incidents. With material whose interpretation cannot be rigorously demonstrated, one's conclusions must largely be determined by one's premonitions. For connection of the horse with deification or heroization, see S. Eitrem in PW, VIII, 1144 f.

36. See below, pp. 227–232. For another Cavalier god relief, see above, VII, fig. 125.

37. One is not surprised that in this scene it is precisely Mordecai's and Haman's eyes which have been scratched out, after the Jewish manner of annulling a pagan image which might be used as an idol. See above, pp. 23 f.

ity of their representation, their lack of realism, recalls rather the rigidity of the gods than carelessly represented human beings. I have never seen an ancient composition in which bystanders as such are represented: always the figures in some way participate importantly in the action, if only as part of an army or company of hunters.

Seyrig, in fact, seems to me to have made the same mistake in discussing a relief from the temple of Bel at Palmyra, fig. 167.[38] Here again we have a procession of people and animals. The first animal is a horse, and behind it a man leads a camel with a closed canopy as saddle on its back, in which presumably some god or important person is concealed. The camel is led by a rope, and veiled women precede and follow. But the center of the fragment as we now have it is occupied by four figures in Greek, or Greco-Parthian robes, who with uplifted hands hail the procession. The resemblance to the composition of the Dura painting is striking. Seyrig called these four figures "bystanders," but did not notice that each of them has a halo, which, in addition to their dress, indicates that they are divine figures. "Bystanders," accordingly, in the ordinary sense they cannot be.

I see something similar in the synagogue painting. Indeed the four central figures seem to me heavenly beings (the Jews would probably have called them "angels"), marked as such by their size and dress and by their being unrealistic and stiff—that is, hieratic—as angels, saints, and other heavenly beings were to become in Byzantine art. We shall see such figures intruding in scene after scene at Dura, and notice the same rigidity in almost all of them, especially as they stand together in groups. True, the midrashic tradition does say that "27,000 youths, sent for the purpose from the royal palace, each holding in one hand a golden jar and in the other a golden cup," marched before Mordecai on this occasion.[39] Our four figures in the synagogue painting do not attempt to illustrate such a procession, for they have no gifts, but only stand with three uplifted hands, which may represent, as I think, divine blessing rather than the adulation of subjects. I see no reason why their eight feet should have become seven, or why the twelve feet which should have been drawn with the six figures behind David in fig. 337 should have become nine. But the three hands for the four figures seem much more significant when we see that for the six figures of the other scene only three hands again are held up in blessing. In two other scenes, figs. 334 and 342, men comparable to these are presented in threes. The number three seems important, though here presented by four men in the robe, and presented by seven, including Samuel, when David is anointed. We shall return to this.[40]

What, then, would the scene indicate? The picture seems to present Mordecai, not only as Jewish royalty in terms of the midrash,[41] but as much more. He far surpasses gentile rulership, and he comes into this supremacy through heavenly intervention. The scene on the right where Esther sits higher than Ahasuerus, and wears the crown of divinity, appears to represent the coming of the messenger anouncing that the Jews had destroyed "seventy-five thousand of those who hated them." [42] The Jews had indeed "done as they

38. From *Syria*, XV (1934), plate xix; see pp. 159–165.

39. *JE*, IX, 8 f.

40. See below, X, 91–96.

41. Ginzberg, *Legends*, IV, 383; VI, 459, n. 64.

42. Esther ix, 16; cf. verses 6 and 15.

pleased to those who hated them." [43] That the scroll given the king actually had this report is pure supposition, but a reasonable one from the literary tradition and from the
nature of the painting itself.[44]

Purim has always meant to Jews a foretaste of their ultimate supremacy over their
enemies. Ginzberg quotes from a midrash that in the time to come only Purim and the
Day of Atonement will be celebrated. He also cites the Jerusalem Talmud that at that
time all the books of Scripture will lose their value except the Pentateuch and the Book
of Esther.[45]

As has been said, we have no hellenistic midrash telling the story of Esther. But if
the meaning of the scene is as has been said, its essential points of interpreting the story
of Esther and Mordecai could as well have come from hellenistic as from rabbinic sources.
It is well known that in the canonical Hebrew Book of Esther, God is never mentioned,
and that the Jews are saved by the heroism and sagacity of Esther and Mordecai themselves. The whole tone of the book, however, is altered in the Septuagint by additions put
into the text.[46] For by these additions the salvation of the Jews from Haman and the Persians generally becomes the intervention of God in answer to the prayers of Mordecai and
Esther.

Mordecai prays in part:

> I did this [refuse to bow to Haman] that I might not set the glory of man above the glory
> of God; and I will bow before no one but thee, my Lord, and I will not do these things
> in pride. And now Lord, who art God and King, the God of Abraham, spare thy people:
> for they [our enemies] look at us for destruction, and desire to blot out what was thy
> heritage from the beginning. Despise not thy portion, which thou didst redeem for thy-
> self from the land of Egypt. Hear my prayer, and have mercy upon thy allotted [people],
> and turn our sorrow into festivity, that we may live to sing thy name. O Lord, destroy
> not the mouth of those who praise thee.[47]

Esther seems to feel that the conflict is really one between the gods of the Persians
and the God of Israel. She prays in part:

> Lord, do not surrender thy scepter to those who are not [gods], and let them not make
> merry at our downfall. But turn their counsel against themselves, and make an example

---

43. Ibid., verse 5.

44. Kraeling, *Synagogue*, 162 f., made the same
interpretation: but I see no reason to suppose that
the messenger is Mordecai himself. Du Mesnil, *RB*,
XLIII (1934), 553, suggested that the scroll being
given the king is the "record" of Mordecai's re-
porting a plot against the king's life. He did not
repeat this in his *Peintures*, and Kraeling rejects the
suggestion (ibid.) because the king is not shown in
bed. I still regard it as the only possible alternative
to the one in which Kraeling and I are agreed,
since it was a favorite subject in later Esther cycles.

45. *Legends*, VI, 481, n. 194.

46. The longer additions, and indeed the repeated paraphrases and glosses in the Greek, really
make it into a hellenistic midrash. See E. Bickerman, "Notes on the Greek Book of Esther," *Proceedings, American Academy for Jewish Research*, XX
(1951), 101–133. On p. 123 Bickerman says of the
Dura painting of Esther with the king that it represents an incident "which seems to be unknown in
the extant written sources."

47. Esther IV, 17*e–h* (LXX) (ed. A. Rahlfs, I,
960).

of him who has taken the initiative against us. Remember us, O Lord, and make thyself known at the hour of our tribulation. Give me courage, O King of gods who dominates every relationship.[48]

"Make thyself known at the hour of our tribulation" might have been the title of the painting, which seems to illustrate the answer to this prayer quite as much as any details in the haggadic tradition of the rabbinic schools, for here heavenly intervention appears to establish the royal supremacy of the Jewish people. The Jews of Dura, as they looked at the painting of Mordecai, might well have said, "Blessed is he that cometh in the name of the Lord." [49] I suspect that the strange way of indicating divine intervention, the four hieratic figures in the robe lifting three hands in benediction, also had meaning.

The conclusion of the story of Esther in the Additions of the Septuagint might also be quoted as an actual caption for the painting: "God remembered his people and vindicated (*edikaiōsen*) his inheritance." [50] The Greek word was probably used originally by the author as I have translated it,[51] but the various forms of *dikaios*, "just," had in Greek too many connotations for the allegorizers to let it pass. With the Pythagoreans the number four was the symbol of justice,[52] and Philo knew this very well.[53] To the three in Deity we shall return, but in the language of the day the four figures could well have been saying that God was intervening to bring justice to his people. Such a conclusion brings us back to the Pahlavi dipinto on the design mentioned above.[54] "Judgment is near" seems now indeed an appropriate caption to indicate the judgment by divine intervention which would finally vindicate the Jews, and allow their Messiah to take over all the trappings that were so pretentious when on gentile royalty.

Whether the tradition that lay behind the painting came to Dura in Aramaic like the inscriptions in the painting, in Pahlavi like the dipinto upon it, or in Greek cannot be determined. The painting expresses all aspects of royalty in oriental terms; but the divine intervention, if I am right in interpreting the central figures, is expressed in the

---

48. Ibid., verses 17*q–r*. Two smaller details in the additions may show a hellenizing attitude on the part of the one who made them. First Ahasuerus describes the Jewish God as *hupsistos, megistos, zōn*, "highest, greatest, living" (ibid. VIII, 12*q*, ed. Rahlfs, I, 968), and he attributes it to the Jewish God that his own kingly rule (*basileia*) and that of his ancestors, was brought into the fairest (*kallistē*) order (ibid.). But while Philo could have made capital of both details, they cannot in themselves be traced to Hellenism. The account of the incident in Josephus, *Antiquities*, XI, 184–296, seems based upon the LXX with these additions. See esp. sections 229–233 (prayer of Mordecai and Esther); 237 (the king changes his mind, I suppose, by the will of God); 259, 280, 282 (God of Jews made the king do as he did); and 279 (the royal rule, and

that of the king's ancestors, given by the God of the Jews).

49. Ps. cxviii, 26.

50. Esther x, 3*i* (ed. Rahlfs, I, 973).

51. As in Exod. xxiii, 7.

52. Anatolius makes this the meaning of the number, *apud* Iamblichus, *Theologoumena arithmeticae*, 23 (ed. V. de Falco, 1922, 29, lines 5–10).

53. *Opif.* 51. Here the number four equals justice because it is the first square (*isakis isos*). Since Aristotle says that justice has a definite number with the Pythagoreans (*Metaphysics*, 985B29), and again (*Magna moralia*, 1182A14) says that the Pythagoreans are wrong in making justice the number that is *isakis isos*, it is fairly certain that the identification was one of the earliest and most persistent parts of the Pythagorean tradition.

54. See above, p. 12.

convention of men in the Greek robe with its markings. Somewhere the two conventions, Greek and oriental, came together, each, apparently, vitally symbolic. A creative symbolist, whether at Dura or elsewhere, has asserted himself to make a new type of design, to say a new thing, at least new for art. Here what is said is that the Jews will, by divine intervention, surpass gentile royalty. It is Mordecai who rides the horse as the cavalier god, Esther who wears the crown of Gē or Astarte, the great central figures in the robe who seem to bring it all to pass. According to the canonical account and later midrashim, Mordecai's triumph on the royal horse was short-lived. He returned to his sack cloth, and Haman resumed his place beside the king. The fall of Haman had no immediate connection with this incident. The man who designed the painting did not heed this. He used biblical narrative in both the throne and the cavalier groups with the same freedom as he did the pagan symbolism, not to illustrate biblical incidents but to express an idea of his own. Here is allegory in art as clearly as Philo's writings give us allegory in pagan language.

Where was this creativity going on, a creativity using the language of pagan symbolism to represent the culminating of pagan hopes in Jewish tradition? I strongly suspect that as this and the other paintings are considered together, we shall conclude that the creative designer was at Dura itself, perhaps Samuel the Elder, the donor. Some person at Dura apparently corresponded to the "philosophers" who directed the craftsmen at the stone-cutting establishment where Diocletian traded.[55] We have watched him directing that the reredos be worked over and over until it satisfied him symbolically. Such a person (in later times, for the symbolism of a cathedral, he would have been the bishop) created the plan, selected the ideas to be executed, and then hired craftsmen to execute them. The Dura designer had pagan symbolism of clothing with which to interpret biblical incidents, but he is presumably saying in detail on the walls what he said in essence in the reredos—what, indeed, the Torah in its shrine and the Jewish symbols above it meant to him.

If I am right, we shall understand what he is saying not by looking for exact parallels elsewhere but by understanding the symbolic vocabulary, and seeing how the designer freshly used it in the paintings. Indeed, I suspect that the history of art has been altogether too much concerned with finding archetypes, after the mistaken analogy of families of manuscript tradition from an ultimate original autograph of an author.[56] That there were standard reproductions of a few hellenistic original statues must not obscure the fact that, generally in antiquity, individual artists, or the designers directing them, worked with a vocabulary of symbols somewhat, again, after the analogy of medieval workers. Ancient artists, I am sure, made their designs by combining recognized symbols. Each artist, or directing bishop, or "philosopher," instructed the craftsmen in the design or, if he was a miniaturist, himself predesigned it, and in the design, in spite of his established vocabulary of symbols, he expressed his own creative impulses. It has often been remarked that the

55. See above, pp. 21–23.

56. For example, that there was a common original of the Octateuchs seems as clear as that the other early illuminated mss., the Ashburnham Pentateuch, Vienna Genesis, etc. are, immediately or originally, creations of quite distinct people. We shall understand what all of them are doing only in terms of their common symbolic vocabulary.

execution of the synagogue paintings falls quite below their design or composition, from which it has been concluded that the artists were making poor copies of models, presumably from manuscript illuminations. As we saw the composition of the reredos being altered again and again to bring out an idea, and as we shall see that the designs in the synagogue balance and complement one another, we shall, I believe, increasingly feel that here at Dura was a creative designer, a philosopher indeed, who was expressing for the congregation and for the good of his own soul the deepest meanings he saw in Judaism. The poor execution meant a poor craftsman, not a poor designer.

This scene, that is, has sharpened our hypothesis for interpreting the scenes of the entire synagogue.[57] We must follow the symbolic vocabulary and the composition closely to see whether such an interpretation illuminates the pictures, so that the pictures illuminate the Judaism of the congregation, or at least of their leaders.

B. SAMUEL ANOINTS DAVID

To balance the Esther scene portraying the triumph of Judaism in terms of pagan and divine royalty, the Elder Samuel had an extraordinary painting executed, one in which his namesake, Samuel the Prophet, anoints David, plate VII and fig. 337. Identification of the scene is made certain by the Aramaic titulus, which reads "Samuel anointing David."[58] The Prophet, wearing a white Greek robe fully marked, stands head and shoulders taller than the other figures. He holds toward David's head a large horn, through whose smaller end, we understand, the oil is dripping upon the new king. David wears the robe also, but in an unusual way. Like the elder Moses in fig. 102 he has the himation over both shoulders as one today wears a shawl; his hands are wrapped in its folds across his body like the hands of Moses. This position of the hands appears only in these two instances in the synagogue, and must be interpreted in a similar way in both scenes. In strong contrast to the Moses figure, however, David's chiton shows no stripes either above or below the himation, and the himation, with no pronged marks upon it, is a dark purple with pink high lights. Behind him stand a row of six figures, all in the fully marked robe. The colors of their garments are white, light yellow, or pink—colors the artist used when he wanted to present a row of figures in "light" garments without the monotony of putting all the figures in pure white.[59] It is notable that in this group only the figure at the left has, like Samuel, a beard. Of this Kraeling properly says: "In the rendering of the beard short vertical black and white strokes are used, and of these the latter recur in the treatment of the hair. The purpose of these details is undoubtedly to represent him as older than the others."[60] He also notices that the six figures at the back have only nine legs and feet between them, and

57. See above, p. 174.

58. Torrey in Kraeling, *Synagogue*, 272, inscription 11.

59. In the scene of the Purim Triumph balancing this, four men have appeared. The one at their head is in white and the other three wear light pink and yellow like the men with Samuel; they also stand with their hands raised, three hands for the four men. Both the similarities and the differences suggest meaning. See above, p. 182.

60. *Synagogue*, 167.

that only three raise their hands. The reasons for these two abbreviations seem quite different to me. Legs and feet in these paintings had apparently little significance; to have crowded all fourteen feet under David and his companions would indeed have made a meaningless clutter.[61] Kraeling explains as similarly meaningless the three raised hands of the six men. But here there was ample space for at least two more hands, and we recall that three hands had answered for the four similar men of fig. 336. We shall have to inquire whether the three might not have been significant for the meaning of both groups.

If such a scene, with no biblical identification, had been found in Pompeii or Alexandria, we should at once have supposed that the artist was representing the initiation of a neophyte into a mystic cult. His dark dress, the humbly covered hands, would seem to illustrate the novitiate before he had received the new garments of the cult, as Lucius received them on his initiation into Isis. In Samuel we should have recognized a supreme hierophant, and in the men with him members of the mystic thiasos. That with the hierophant the thiasos presented itself as a group of seven would have been taken seriously, as well as that by the three hands the group presented also the mysterious values of the triad.

Clearly as the composition in itself suggests such an interpretation in a synagogue painting, we cannot forget its Jewish association. Whatever else may be implied in the scene, it basically represents Samuel anointing David, as the titulus assures us. We start in an attempt to explain the meaning of the painting, then, with two facts: one, that artistically it represents initiation into a mystery religion, and, two, that at the same time it represents the historical anointing. I do not see how we can ignore either of these.

The double impression is increased as we see parallels in later Christian illuminations. For David could be anointed alone by Samuel, still in the robe, as in fig. 168,[62] from the Vatican Psalter of the eleventh century. Here his exaltation to divine prerogative is indicated, as L'Orange points out, by his elevation on a shield.[63] When his brothers are with him, however, they are always led by the father, Jesse. Fig. 170,[64] from the Paris Psalter, presumably of the tenth century, shows Samuel, again in a late echo of the Greek robe, anointing David in the presence of a large Jesse and five smaller brothers. Jesse may well be wearing a survival of the Greek robe, but the brothers and David seem to be medieval shepherds, though David is still distinguished by stripes. The background is architectural, which suggested an Alexandrian prototype to Morey,[65] while Hellenism survives in the figure of *Praotēs*, "Gentleness," the "Personification"—that is, divine counterpart—of that

61. Seven legs and feet sufficed for the four similar figures in fig. 336, and, I believe, for the same reason. See above, p. 183.

62. Courtesy of the Vatican Library, Rome; cod. vat. gr. 752, fol. 82, Psalm xxvi. Cf. H. L'Orange, *Studies on the Iconography of Cosmic Kingship in the Ancient World*, 1953, 104, fig. 76; see his pp. 103–109 (Instituttet for Sammenlignende Kulturforskning, Oslo, Ser. A, XXIII).

63. David has become the medieval king, although Samuel retains the old Greek robe. Cf.

Weitzmann, *Roll and Codex*, 178–180, figs. 183–188.

64. Courtesy of the Bibliothèque Nationale, Paris. Psalter, ms. gr. 139, fol. 3ᵛ.

65. Morey, *Early Christian Art*, 194 f.; J. Gutmann, "Jewish Elements in the Paris Psalter," *Marsyas*, VI (1954), 42–49; H. Buchthal, *The Miniatures of the Paris Psalter*, 1938, 18–21 and plate III (Studies of the Warburg Institute, II); C. R. Morey in *Speculum*, XIV (1939), 143, figs. *1a, b.*

virtue. A very similar painting is preserved in the Vatican Bible of the same century.[66] It is probably the same personification which appears in fig. 169,[67] a twelfth-century version of the tradition, where Samuel and Jesse still have the robe, Praotes and the architecture are preserved, but there are seven brothers, who, like David, are not in the Greek dress. In spite of the variety in the number of brothers, these three illustrations have a common archetype. The miniature in the Homilies of Gregory Nazianzenus, fig. 171,[68] has been thought by Morey to have derived from the Paris Psalter, chiefly because the number of brothers is the same and because the architectural feature of the one seems to survive in the other. But Praotes does not appear, and the flat line of brothers is actually more like the Dura presentation than any other, so that I am more inclined to agree with Buchthal that the "Gregory miniature represents an earlier stage of composition." [69] In a fourteenth-century Psalter in the Chludov collection, fig. 172,[70] Jesse and the brothers have disappeared entirely, the architecture has become quite Christian and eastern, Praotes is replaced by a Christian angel, and the robes are Christian. Even the horn now pours from its broad end. Yet descent from a common archetype seems obvious.[71] A miniature which came ultimately from the same original, but not by the line of the manuscripts we have been considering, is presented in fig. 173,[72] where seven brothers crowd behind Jesse.

The miniatures in the Paris Psalter seemed so Alexandrian that Morey,[73] who rarely admitted such a possibility, said it might have come from an archetype originally designed for Jews.

Different as are the Christian representations from the Dura paintings they still present such resemblances to it that some common tradition seems inevitable. All have Samuel in the Greek robe, all but one show him anointing David from the narrow end of the horn, and when they show the brothers at all, show Jesse with them. But in the synagogue an altogether new arrangement appears, apparently to permit some new interpretation of the incident. Dura shows the six brothers in a hieratic pose that no other representation attempts to give. Jesse seems gone.[74] The architecture has disappeared, and the scene has

66. It is ms. vat. reg. gr. 1, fol. 263, reproduced by Buchthal, plate xvii, fig. 27. Whether this is more like the common original than the painting in the Paris Psalter has caused a dispute which need not concern us.

67. Courtesy of the Vatican Library, Rome; cod. vat. gr. 333, fol. 22ᵛ. See Gutmann, fig. 4; Buchthal, fig. 71.

68. Courtesy of the Bibliothèque Nationale, Paris; ms. gr. 510, fol. 174ᵛ. Morey, 194, calls it of the ninth century; cf. Buchthal, 56.

69. Buchthal, 19, in this agrees with K. Weitzmann, *Die byzantinische Buchmalerei des IX und X Jahrhunderts*, 1935, 45.

70. From Arkhimandrit Amfilokhii, "Izsleolovaniia o slovianskoi psaltiri, XIII–XIV v. biblioteki A. I. Khludova," *Drevnosti. Trudy imparatorskogo moskovskago arkheologicheskago obshchestva,* III (1873), fig. 3.

71. Another adaptation of the tradition seems to me to appear on the Byzantine plate from Cyprus in the J. P. Morgan Collection, now at the Metropolitan Museum in New York: O. M. Dalton, *The Burlington Magazine*, X (1906–07), plate ii, fig. 4, at p. 361.

72. From ms. gr. 17, fol. 4ᵛ, at the Biblioteca Marciana, Venice.

73. Dalton, p. 71. L. Bréhier, "Les Origines et l'évolution de la peinture byzantine," *RA*, Ser. V, Vol. XXX (1929), 220–243, esp. 222 f., points out that allegorical figures indicate that the painting represents an allegorization of a biblical scene, and he connects this with Philo and Alexandria.

74. In figs. 169 f. and 173 there are bearded brothers, so that Kraeling's argument, p. 168, seems justified that the figure with the beard in the Dura

become an abstraction without setting or realism. We shall see the process of hieratic abstraction illustrated in the scene immediately above this one, fig. 333. Here the temple, which in another painting is shown realistically with Aaron, is flattened out to become a pure hieratic symbol. In abstracting the scene of anointing, the artist has made Samuel tower above the brothers, though they wear the same robe. The artist presents not two great figures, Samuel and Jesse, but only one, and David is no longer a "boy." No Praotes or angel blesses the scene, and David is not elevated upon a shield to indicate divine-royal character; but the impression is given just as strongly that the anointing of David marks a great event for him. It would seem that at Dura the original representation was reinterpreted in mystic terms. Someone, whether the Elder Samuel of Dura or another before him, conceived that the fluid which came to David from the hierophant of the Seven took David into a heavenly company, and probably a heavenly nature. The seven, originally derived from an illustration of the historical incident, have become the mystical Seven. Hence, just as it has been generally supposed that the fourth panel portrait, fig. 102, shows a man coming reverently into the presence of God, since his hands are covered, we can only suppose that David similarly stands in divine presence. The six brothers, like Samuel, show no comparable humility before the divine power coming to David, but only hail it with the three uplifted hands, as do the great robed personages in figs. 336 and 337. In the language of mystic iconography, accordingly, we should judge from the painting itself that the Seven represented the manifestation of Deity, and that before it David covered his hands. So much the history of the painting would suggest to us. Is there any Jewish literary account of Samuel and David that would throw light upon such a sophisticated representation of the scene?

Certainly the rabbinic tradition of David, unless Ginzberg [75] has made serious omissions, gives no such suggestion. In the rabbinic stories David was the shepherd and mighty hunter and his selection by God for the kingship was indicated in the fact that the oil would not flow out of the horn when Samuel tried to anoint the brothers but at the approach of David gushed out of its own accord and flowed all over him, its drops changing into jewels, while the horn remained as full as before. The anointing was kept secret for a time, according to the story, but became manifest when David developed prophetic gifts.[76] The only passage from such Judaism I can find remotely applicable to the scene as depicted is one in the *Biblical Antiquities* of Pseudo-Philo, LIX, 4, where, after his anointing, David begins to sing a psalm: [77]

> From the ends of the earth will I begin to glorify [him], and from everlasting days will I utter a hymn. At the beginning when Abel pastured sheep, his sacrifice was acceptable

---

painting is the oldest brother Eliab. In the Bible of St. Etienne Harding, III, fol. 13, Jesse is an old man, bent and with a long beard. He leans on a crutch, and seven brothers stand behind him: C. Oursel, *La Miniature du XIIᵉ siècle à l'Abbaye de Cîteaux*, 1926, plate v. That is, Jesse, when represented, is so much distinguished from his sons that he may not be in the Dura scene at all.

75. *Legends*, IV, 80–85.

76. For David as prophet see the references, ibid., VI, 249, n. 24. The most important of these, however, is Josephus, *Antiquities*, VI, 166.

77. Ed. G. Kisch, 1949, 260. See the translation of M. R. James, 1917, 231 f.

rather than his brother's, and his brother killed him in envy. But it was not so with me since God kept me, and because he gave me to his angels and guardians to keep me. For my brothers envied me, and my father and mother neglected me. When the prophet came they did not call me, and when the Messiah (*Christus*) was named they forgot me. But with his right hand and mercy God drew close to me; wherefore I shall not cease to sing hymns [to him] all the days of my life.

This passage has been quoted because its reference to David in the care of angels and guardians is the only one I know from what I am in general calling rabbinic sources that might explain David's standing with the holy Seven.

Philo, however, has much that is directly to our purpose. He in general makes little comment on biblical passages or incidents outside the Pentateuch, but he does allude to Samuel and David several times, and in doing so, like the painting we are analyzing, talks simultaneously in biblical and mystical language. The painting itself seemed to tell us that the anointing of David meant his reception into the company of Seven of whom Samuel was the chief, and that at such reception David covered his hands as being in the presence of God. We may then properly begin with Philo's remarks about Samuel himself, for the dominant figure of the painting is not David, but Samuel.

Here the protracted nature of the present series of volumes shows its great disadvantage. Its first volume was really my *By Light, Light*, in which was set forth the "Mystic Gospel of Hellenistic Judaism," a gospel constructed largely, but by no means entirely, from the pages of Philo. The passages in which Philo speaks of Samuel are among his most cryptic, and cannot be understood unless one can see their relevance to his deeply hellenized Judaism as a whole. I must accordingly digress for a moment to epitomize that Judaism.

Philo, deeply loyal to the one God of his People, was still so much influenced by the budding Neoplatonism of his day that he conceived of God as the One who revealed himself and had relations with all creation, including man, through a great radiation of the divine nature.[78] After the analogy of the sun, that radiation could be called God's Light; after the analogy of speech, his Logos or Utterance; after the analogy of kingship, his Law. These terms, along with his Mind, Wisdom, Spirit, Virtue, Son, and a number of others, Philo uses with little discrimination. Another term for this radiation, one of great importance, is Form, for the coming of this Stream to matter introduced form into it. It also comes into the material body as Soul to give it life. Philo liked to play with these terms: he had no system for their relation to one another, indeed freely quoted people who were obviously using the terms differently from what he preferred in a given association, because he lived before a Church had begun to base its existence upon detailed orthodox creeds and specifically defined terms.

Metaphysically, Philo suggested stages by which the one radiation broke itself up into manifestations, so that the totality of the one God actually presented itself as seven descending stages.[79] There was first the Ultimate, and then a group of three, with another

78. For the "God of the Mystery" see esp. *By Light, Light*, chap. 2.

79. See the diagrams, ibid., 24 and 29.

group of three beneath it. These divisions in no sense modified Philo's monotheism, for they represented Godhead only as man sees it from below. God reveals himself, that is, as seven, then more highly as two sets of three, but to a man who can see God's reality as it is, the seven, the three,[80] are ontologically the One.[81]

Spiritual experience, Philo believed, takes one above the welter of material confusion, until one can actually transport oneself in spirit into the immaterial world which these Seven represent. This change of orientation meant really a change from the world of flux to the world of permanence, from time to eternity. Philo almost always described it either in terms of allegorized biblical passages, incidents, or language, or in terms from the mystery religions. In the allegories the terms from both were treated as quite interchangeable. So when the Dura artist turns the incident of David's anointing into a scene of mystic initiation, he is doing in art exactly what Philo did in his allegory, as we shall see now in considering what he says of Samuel and David.

We may begin with a treatise of Philo, which opens with a discussion of how the "angels of God went in unto the daughters of men," [82] and so considers the whole problem of divine begetting on human women.[83] The angels, mentioned in the Bible, he says were of course wicked ones, and through their activity with the daughters of men they begat vices (*kakiai*). In contrast the "wise man" is "illuminated by the bright and pure rays of understanding," and thereby he "sees God and his Powers," Philo's usual way of referring to the Seven.[84] In this way the mind learns to beget (sexes are a bit confused) not for itself but for God. Actually it is this Light-Stream which begat Isaac in Sarah, and the child was only attributed to Abraham. Philo merely alludes to this in the passage, though he makes the idea clear elsewhere.[85] Here he says that such a child is not kept for oneself, but is dedicated, given back, to God.[86] Samuel, Philo continues, was similarly begotten. Hannah, like Sarah, was Sophia and Grace,[87] and she "received the divine seed and became pregnant," and the child that was brought forth she named Samuel. For the allegory Philo has apparently ignored his onomasticon and gives a mistranslation of the name Samuel. In the Hebrew (and correctly in the Septuagint) the name is associated with the root *sha'al*, meaning to "ask": [88] Hannah "asked Yahweh for him." Philo says that the name means *tetagmenos theōi*, whose translation, by no means secure, may be given with Colson, "appointed to God." Philo cryptically expands this to mean that "his type of existence (*tropos*) had its appointed place in the order (*taxis*) of God." [89] (Philo obviously knew the tradi-

80. One recognizes the kind of thinking about the Radiation which later, as Modalism, orthodox Christians rejected.

81. Philo's use of the three as a figure for the One in extension is parallel to a statement in Iamblichus, *Theologoumena arithmeticae*, 14 (ed. de Falco, 16): "The triad makes the power of the Monad extend into activity and evolution."

82. Gen. VI, 4.

83. *Immut.* 1-19.

84. Ibid. 3.

85. See my *By Light, Light*, 154 f.

86. *Immut.* 4. An allusion, of course, to the sacrifice of Isaac, the Akedah.

87. The name Hannah in Hebrew means grace or graciousness, but when translated into the Greek *charis* took on a more technical meaning. Philo makes it mean "her grace" (*charis autēs*). He probably had this from some onomasticon.

88. I Sam. I, 20; *Immut.* 5.

89. Cf. *Migr.* 196, where Samuel is the *tropos* appointed by God to the highest *taxis*.

tional interpretation of the name, for he says that Samuel, having been asked for by Hannah, was a gift from God.) His *tropos* connects him with Isaac, and, like Abraham, Hannah had to give her child back to God.[90]

After a digression on the propriety of returning God's gifts, Philo continues with the hymn of Hannah,[91] in which she says "The barren [woman] has borne seven." Samuel is then himself the Seven, Philo explains, which number is, actually, the same as the One.[92] With this, he returns to the name Samuel as "appointed to God," and explains Samuel's relation to the cryptic *taxis* of God, though, after his manner, he uses all possible synonyms for *taxis:*

> For Samuel, the one 'appointed to God' alone, holds no company at all with any other, but is put in order (*kekosmētai*) with respect to the One, the Monad, the Truly Existent (*to ontōs on*). This order (*katastasis*) is that of the Seven, soul at rest in God.[93] It toils no more at mortal works, since it has left the Six behind. For [God] has appointed the Six to the [rank of those] things which cannot receive the Primal Realities, but is of necessity restricted to sharing in the secondary ones.[94]

Philo shortly says that the child of Hannah, as the Seven, "has the same value (*isotimos*) as the Monad."

Philo has said all he wishes at this point and in his baffling way wanders off to other things. Taken by itself, the passage gives the impression that what Philo has been saying is pure *jeu d'esprit*. I suspect, however, that in such apparently passing fancies Philo deliberately refers to a teaching which was quite intelligible to his mystic readers, and which he purposely left unexplained for ordinary people. For this interpretation of Samuel recurs, in the same allusory way, in other treatises. For example, in commenting on Hannah, the "barren" woman who "brought forth seven" in bearing Samuel, he says that the word "barren" means:

> the mind which is sterile in that it cannot receive mental seed as a fertilizing agent, but which aborts and miscarries the copulations and intercourses of wicked things. It clings, however, to the embraces of the Seven and of the supreme principle of Peace akin to it. For she [Hannah or the soul] wants to become impregnated by this, and to be called its mother.[95]

Here we are deep in that most difficult of all concepts, the concept of the mother who bears the God who impregnated her. In Ancient Egypt we found the idea expressed in the phrase that the supreme God was "the bull of his own mother," and that the ultimate property of God lay in this power and origin. The birth of Samuel through Hannah merely released to men the Seven who, or which, is the One. Hannah, of course, gives him back to God. Her

---

90. I Sam. i, 28; *Immut.* 5. But Philo may have also in mind the real meaning of Samuel, as explained in I Sam. i, 20.

91. I Sam. ii, 5; *Immut.* 10.

92. *Immut.* 11, 13; cf. *Post.* 64.

93. One cannot say whether this is a reference to the individual soul of Samuel, or to Samuel's soul as being the cosmic Psyche soon to be made famous by Plotinus. I strongly suspect the latter.

94. *Immut.* 11–13.

95. *Mut.* 144.

son was "appointed to the *taxis* of God," the same phrase we met in the other passages.

This, it would seem, we ourselves re-enact when we are filled with God in an ecstatic madness. What Hannah gave back to God was not a "human being." [96] Samuel's *taxis* was well set in the order of the divine army, Philo tells us in quite another treatise. Indeed, while:

> Samuel did perhaps exist as a human being, yet the tradition has come down to us that he existed not as an animate being compounded [of soul and body], but that he was Mind, and rejoiced only in the worship and service of God.[97]

When Philo speaks of the values of the six and seven more abstractly, he of course gives "Holy Logos" as the supreme name for the metaphysical Seventh.[98] The conception of the unique sanctity of the Seven occurs constantly in Philo's writings, and is joined in allegory with a host of other associations.[99] We have had enough, however, to show that Philo associated the six with the created world and its objects. The great principle that made a unity was the metaphysical reality, the Logos, which came in to dominate the welter of the six by introducing into it the unique character of the One. The Six plus the One making the Seven represented, then, that metaphysical order to which Philo ultimately hoped to come. The Seven was the One made available to man. At the highest vision, as I have said, this Seven actually became the One. But to man, Philo is saying, God's supreme gift is that the One make itself available for man's salvation in a child born of a woman. Could one so born be considered a human being? Is Philo speaking of an historical Samuel? He is perplexed to answer, as were many Christian theologians for several centuries thereafter with a similar problem. Philo, however, has in several distinct passages given us Hannah as the Mother of God, and Samuel, by being the Seventh or the Seven, as the manifestation of God to men. In discussing the idea we feel that Philo, for all his Torah, is less committed to the historical event than were Christians to the historical incarnation. But like them, Philo's great hope was to get beyond the world of the six into the world where the Light and Life of the Logos manifested the unity of God as the Seven.

Philo read all this allegory into the simple and lovely story of Hannah and Samuel. Similarly, I believe, the "philosopher" who designed the scenes at Dura (or the scenes the Dura artist was copying from somewhere else) has reinterpreted the naturalistic incident of the anointing of David as preserved in the Christian illuminations. However many brothers appeared with Jesse originally, that group is here turned into six hieratical figures, with no architectural setting. They are six, carefully subordinated to Samuel the great Seventh. The historical king David, in his dark robe, had his greatness, the painting is telling us, as he got his royal commission, his royal nature, from the fluid of the Seventh, who could be represented as such in a painting only as he towered over the other Six. It is no wonder that

---

96. *Som.* I, 254.

97. *Ebr.* 143 f. In 145–152, Philo goes on to discuss Samuel's refraining from strong drink and Hannah's "sober drunkenness," in a way that is valuable but not immediately to our point here.

98. *LA* I, 16; cf. 2–16.

99. We cannot stop to review the subject. See the rich collection of passages in Leisegang, *Index*, 216 f.

David has piously covered his hands. Philo has so much to say about the sacred three that the three raised hands, here and in the Esther panel, seem definitely to be intentional, but I feel that in reconstructing the language of these paintings it is best to go a step at a time. Perhaps the three was there as a parallel representation, as it was with Philo, of the One in relationship.[100] Perhaps it went with the Seven to create the perfect Decade, another equivalent of the One. Perhaps the three had more specific reference to the Logos and the two primary Powers, a conception repeatedly emphasized by Philo, and one which we have seen and shall often meet again in the Dura paintings. But nothing in this painting of David with Samuel suggests a choice between these. Perhaps, like Philo, we should feel all of these simultaneously. A digression to discuss this would only detract from the "plain meaning" of the painting as a whole, that David was the supreme king of Israel, and still its ultimate hope, because he had received the holy oil from Samuel the Seventh, he who was "appointed to the *taxis* of God." David was not the hope in this scene of such earthly Jewish supremacy as we saw in the Esther painting. Rather David was the type of one initiated by Samuel, as, Philo says, he himself was initiated by Moses—that is, was brought to the metaphysically real world to which Philo said Judaism and the Jewish Patriarchs were the supreme guides.

Philo does not stand alone in the tradition of a Seven in white garments who gave men special gifts from God. The Testament of Levi, VIII, 2–17, tells how Levi dreamed that he (through Aaron) would get the priestly powers:

> And I saw seven men in white raiment saying unto me: Arise, put on the robe of the priesthood, and the crown of righteousness, and the breastplate of understanding, and the garment of truth, and the plate of faith, and the turban of the head, and the ephod of prophecy. And they severally carried [these things] and put [them] on me, and said unto me: From henceforth become a priest of the Lord, thou and thy seed for ever. And the first anointed me with holy oil, and gave to me the staff of judgment. The second washed me with pure water, and fed me with bread and wine [even] the most holy things, and clad me with a holy and glorious robe. The third clothed me with a linen vestment like an ephod. The fourth put around me a girdle like unto purple. The fifth gave me a branch of rich olive. The sixth placed a crown on my head. The seventh placed on my head a diadem of priesthood, and filled my hands with incense, that I might serve as priest to the Lord God. And they said to me: Levi, thy seed shall be divided into three offices, for a sign of the glory of the Lord who is to come. And the first portion shall be great; yea, greater than it shall none be. The second shall be in the priesthood. The third shall be called by a new name, because a king shall arise in Judah, and shall establish a new priesthood, after the fashion of the Gentiles [to all the Gentiles]. And his presence is beloved, as a prophet of the Most High, of the seed of Abraham our father.

> Therefore, every desirable thing in Israel shall be for thee and for
> thy seed,
> And ye shall eat everything fair to look upon,
> And the table of the Lord shall thy seed apportion.

100. See my *By Light, Light*, 33–36.

And some of them shall be high priests, and judges, and scribes;
For by their mouth shall the holy place be guarded.[101]

The investiture is here thoroughly hellenized. Many of the traditional appurtenances from the Old Testament are mentioned, but Aaron is fed bread and wine, which to Charles suggests Christian influence but which will not go beyond Judaism for those who have read Volumes V and VI of this work; he gets a purple girdle, a branch of olive, and a "diadem of priesthood." His line will produce three great masters: first, the supreme of all men, whom Charles plausibly takes to be Moses; second, the priesthood, or Aaron; and third, a new king-priest. This last may indeed have been intended, as Charles supposes, to indicate "the Maccabees, in particular John Hyrcanus," but by the third century after Christ the hopes of this kingship, if that was the original reference, had completely vanished. Hopes of a permanent king-priest may well have changed into mystical hopes for many.

This ordination or investiture of Levi by the Seven, and the association with Moses and a great king, would seem a frame of thinking that had some relation to both Philo's allegory of the *taxis* of Samuel and the painting at Dura. Reference to the bread and wine, and to the "table of the Lord" which the priesthood will administer, again suggests, but by no means demonstrates, the possibility that ritual was associated with such kingship or priesthood.

In this painting and the Esther scene we have encountered our first balance of compositions flanking the Torah shrine. On the left, with Esther, the Jews certainly triumph, but in a much more mundane way than they do on the right. There, by what has seemed to be divine intervention manifested in the four central figures, Jewish supremacy proclaims itself in Mordecai's riding in the accouterments of the Cavalier god, led by the chief gentile in almost naked humility. At the same time a messenger reports to the pagan king the destruction (gratifyingly thorough) of the enemies of the Jews, and Esther sits enthroned higher, and her crown makes her more dignified, than the king himself. Balancing this on the right, the true supremacy of Israel shows itself in David's metaphysical kingship. I believe that the "philosopher" who designed this wall will appear to have represented such a contrast throughout, the double message I have so long felt in Philo. In their life, law, and cultus, Jews are quite supreme, he felt, and this will show itself in their ultimate rulership of all men. The "philosopher" at Dura seems to have accepted this Judaism, but to have added to it another in which, I suspect, he, like Philo, was much more interested: a Judaism in which Israel, meaning the "man who sees God," gets the metaphysical vision that gives escape from the material world of the Six altogether, and a life now and forever centered in the Seven who is the One. Had we only these two scenes, again, such an interpretation would seem an overinterpretation. It will seem less so as we examine the details in the other paintings of the synagogue.

101. From Charles, *Apoc. and Pseud.*, II, 308 f. The supernal Seven appears often in early Chris-   tian symbolism, as in fig. 153.

CHAPTER NINE

The Miraculous Babies: The Infancy of Moses

W E HAVE BEEN FOLLOWING the eye of the observer as our guide to the relation of the paintings and their meaning. In doing so we have found that on the lowest register, above the Dionysiac symbols of the dado, two scenes of Jewish royalty, but with utterly different implications, flanked the central Torah shrine. Our impression that such a balance had not occurred by chance seems confirmed when we see that on either side of these two paintings, in turn, stands a scene of infants, fig. 335, and fig. 338. At the extreme left, beside the Esther scene, Elijah restores the widow's baby to life, and at the extreme right the princess, or some female, takes the baby Moses from the ark in the river. Similarities of details in conception and execution will appear as we discuss the two designs. In antiquity, true royalty and the wonder child always stood close together in men's minds, whether the royalty was that of such a king as Alexander, or as the child of Virgil's Fourth Eclogue,[1] or as the Christ. It may well seem to be in continuation of the master designer's symbolic plan that royalty and baby scenes were thus put together. The answer to this will depend upon whether or not the two scenes seem to make the babies into *Wunderkinder*.

In the long painting we are here considering, plates I and IX and fig. 338, at least two episodes are presented.[2] Interpretations of the painting as a whole have varied, but no one has doubted that the naked woman in the river, who takes a baby from a gabled box, is taking the baby Moses from his little ark in the Nile. With her are five other figures: two women at the left hold a baby between them, and three others above her and at the right have objects in their hands. At the right of this scene a second group shows the court of Pharaoh. He sits enthroned between two Throne Guards with his back to a gate, which opens in a crenellated wall.[3] Pharaoh wears the royal Persian dress, quite similar to that of

1. One recalls at once the classic study of E. Norden, *Die Geburt des Kindes*, 1924 (Studien der Bibliothek Warburg, III).

2. Some of the material in this section was briefly presented at the International Congress of Jewish Studies, Jerusalem, 1957, and published as "The Paintings at the Dura-Europos Synagogue: Method and an Application," *IEJ*, VIII (1958),

69–79. As I have since continued with the study of the other paintings, I have seen reason to change several details of interpretation.

3. The wall with its gate is given so much space in the painting that, if the rest of the design is symbolic, one would naturally look for symbolism in the wall and gate also. A doorway has already appeared to have deep symbolic meaning: above,

Ahasuerus in fig. 336, and, like him, has the diadem. A curtain above their heads marks this royal group. Facing them stand the same two women who appeared with the baby at the extreme left; they are marked to be the same by the color of their dresses. At their feet stoops a clothed woman whose hair resembles that of the naked woman discovering Moses in the adjoining group. What she originally bent over was destroyed by a seepage of water in the wall soon after it was painted. Traces of the bulrushes right along to the throne of Pharaoh, however, make it apparent that the river continued the whole length of the painting, and that she was stooping over something in it, apparently the ark again. She may actually have had the baby in the ark before Pharaoh, though such a situation, so far as I know, has no parallel in literature or art.

A. THE GROUP WITH PHARAOH

THE TRADITION of the infancy of Moses in the Octateuchs presents the story as a succession of scenes, figs. 174 and 175.[4] In the first, Moses is born, attended by three women, two of whom bring gifts while a third washes the baby in a basin beside the water pitcher; a house and a crenelated wall form the background. In the upper register of the second of these scenes the daughter of Pharaoh, nimbed and in a priestly robe, discovers the ark and the baby, while Miriam watches at the bank. The princess is led forward by a woman whose cap may be intended to identify her with the woman washing Moses in the previous scene. Architecture is again in the background. In the lower register two women, one with a cap again, watch the nimbed princess present Moses as a young boy to Pharaoh, who sits enthroned and nimbed with his two attendants.

I formerly assumed [5] that the Dura painting likewise illustrates the traditional story in making Pharaoh's acceptance of the boy follow his discovery. It is true that in this part of the Dura painting the two women as well as Pharaoh and his two attendants so much resemble the figures in the Octateuchs as to suggest a common archetype. But we have seen the "philosopher" at Dura use elements from various sources to express his own ideas, and freely alter the archetype to present his interpretation of an incident, so that common details by no means indicate identical meanings in the compositions as a whole. Parts of one of the miniatures in the Ashburnham Pentateuch of the seventh century, fig. 176, in fact

---

IV, 103, n. 111. See E. B. Smith, *Architectural Symbolism of Imperial Rome and the Middle Ages*, 1956, 12 f., 38-40, 43, 181 (Princeton Monographs in Art and Archeology, XXX), where rich material is collected to show that a gate with a king indicates his divine royalty. The king again sits with the open legs of Iranian royalty: see above, p. 83. The assimilation of this into biblical tradition appears in the special treatment demanded for the "king's gate" in Esther IV, 2; see also C. Warren in *HDB*, II, 113a. What if any of this symbolism was implied in the painting cannot be said. The wall perhaps only represents Egypt, as it may do

in fig. 330.

4. From *Const. Octateuch*, plate XIX, figs. 92-94 (fol. 156ʳ), of the twelfth century. Cf. *Smyrna Octateuch*, figs. 152 f., which adds a masculine figure, presumably Moses' father, to the group; see also *Rome Octateuch* (vat. gr. 746), fols. 72ᵛ, 153ᵛ, which have not been published to my knowledge: cf. Weitzmann, *Joshua*, 6 f. Moses is similarly presented to Pharaoh as a young boy in the mosaics at Santa Maria Maggiore.

5. The paper for the Congress in Israel already cited.

resemble the Dura composition more than the Octateuchs do.[6] Here a general scene of Pharaoh giving orders to his servants balances a group in which he commands the two midwives, Siphrah and Puah, to destroy all Jewish boys as they are born.[7] On this folio various scenes from the life of Moses follow, but at the bottom, fig. 177,[8] the princess and her attendants find the baby at the river, and Moses' mother and sister hold him between them.

In the Dura painting Kraeling[9] associated the group in which Pharaoh sits at the right with the same incident of the midwives, and he considered the two women holding out their hands toward Pharaoh to be those midwives whom many Jewish legends identified with Jochebed and Miriam, the mother and sister of Moses.[10] They wear exactly the same dress as the two women holding the baby at the extreme left, who, all agree, are the mother and sister, and I see no reason to doubt that the two pairs represent the same two women. The woman at their feet bending over a lost object in the river defies identification. That the object before her was another representation of the ark, and that she is either putting the baby in or discovering it, seems the only possible supposition. Since it was Jochebed, the mother, who put Moses into the ark, and it seems most likely that Jochebed is one of the two midwives who stand above the stooping figure, we may have in the long-haired woman the princess herself, this time clothed and in the act of discovering the child in its little boat. Or the figure may be someone else launching it. I should agree with Kraeling, however, that the baby is being put into the ark.[11] The ark itself, in that case, presumably looked like the ark as drawn in the scene where the "princess" takes Moses out of it. To that we shall return. On the whole, then, we suppose that the group at the right shows Pharaoh with his attendants giving orders to midwives to kill the Israelite boys, and, if we have properly guessed at what the stooping woman was doing in the river, the baby she is leaving in his ark there represents the despair of the parents—the fact that he was left to die.

B. *THE DISCOVERY OF MOSES*

THE GROUP at the left throws us into quite another mood. Here what is apparently the same young woman stands naked in the river, its water reaching only a little above her knees. With her right hand she seems to gesture toward the "midwives," Moses' mother and sister, who hold the baby. But the gesture may not concern them at all, for she faces full front, and may be indicating the wonderful character of the baby whom she holds in

6. From *Ashburnham Pentateuch*, plate XIV, fol. 56[r].

7. Exod. I, 15–21.

8. From *Ashburnham Pentateuch*, plate XIV, fol. 56[r].

9. *Prelim.*, 360; *Synagogue*, 173. He thinks that one of the midwives in the Dura painting holds an obstetrical instrument in her hand. See his drawing, *Synagogue*, 173, fig. 46. He may be right, although it appears to me that the "instrument" may be a loop in her garment. Cf. Sonne, "Paintings," 314.

10. Kraeling, *Synagogue*, 177 f.; see his references in n. 684. Ginzberg, *Legends*, II, 265–269.

11. *Synagogue*, 174. The figure is so unlike the other two identified that I cannot agree with him that it is she, specifically, who does so.

her other arm. Or it may be a characteristic gesture of this figure. Whether she is the princess herself or the slave girl whom the biblical narrative says the princess sent into the river to bring the baby to shore,[12] or neither, cannot be specifically determined. We shall see that she is really much more than any of these.

Even this baby, however, is secondary to the baby held by the mother at the left, for Gute, fig. 338, has shown that the baby held by the "princess" originally was painted without any features on his blank face. Not until the mother has him did the artist paint eyes, nose, and mouth on the baby.[13] This will seem important as we continue.

1. The "Princess"

THE WOMAN who finds and exalts the baby can be clearly identified as a goddess or divine figure. A glance at representations of the goddess Anahita and her female attendants shows that the "philosopher" has used this divinity in directly recognizable form to be the one who should save the baby from the waters. Fig. 178 shows the "princess" in detail from an early photograph. She stands in the water only deep enough to mark herself as a water figure, and yet to leave exposed her pudendum, whose vertical line is clear in the original. The conventions of the time suggest that such a figure would have been a goddess, and I think she can definitely be identified. Beside a wrist band and arm band on the right arm, she wears two necklaces, one apparently a string of pearls, but below it a flat band from which hangs a round medallion. The band appears quite clearly in Gute's painting, fig. 338, but the medallion is unmistakable on her chest in the original photograph. Fig. 179 [14] shows what I take to be Anahita in the Sassanian form. In the Hermitage Museum alone, little vases depict fourteen of these figures,[15] and another such vase is reported as being in Teheran.[16] The publishers call these women servants or priestesses of Anahita,[17] but I suspect that they at least sometimes represent Anahita herself, since, as in this instance, they often have haloes. They take many poses, but usually hold their hands gracefully out to the side, and present some symbolic object: dove, basket of fruit, lotus (or poppy), a covered box, perhaps a pomegranate, once, as in fig. 180,[18] a baby. An older representation of Anahita shows her clothed, but bringing similar tokens in a similar pose, fig. 181.[19] These figures always have the necklace in the form of a band with a pendant, but the pendant may be a cluster of three jewels, as in fig. 182.[20] In all of them the pudendum is sharply emphasized, as was the age-old custom with female deities of the East.

The "princess" who takes Moses from the ark has exactly this necklace with the medallion, had obviously the same emphasis upon the pudendum, and holds out her arms

12. Exod. II, 6.

13. The features shown in plate IX were apparently added for the "restoration" of the scenes at Damascus.

14. From J. Orbeli and C. Trever, Orfèvrerie sasanide, Moscow-Leningrad, 1935 (Musée de l'Ermitage), plate 44.

15. Ibid., plates 44–47.

16. K. Erdmann, Die Kunst Irans zur Zeit der Sasaniden, 1943, 102. F. Sarre, Die Kunst des alten Persien, 1923, 72, n. to plate 129 (Die Kunst des Ostens, V), calls them dancers under arcades.

17. Erdmann, 132, n. to p. 101. Orbeli and Trever, p. XLIII.

18. From Orbeli and Trever, plate 47.

19. From Sarre, 46, fig. 12.

20. From Orbeli and Trever, plate 45. See the necklace very clearly, above, VII, fig. 151.

in the same characteristic fashion. Whether she still holds something in her right hand I cannot say, since the paint suffered considerable flaking here. But from what survived of the paint she may possibly have held a small pomegranate. The dignified baby in her arms, who seems giving a blessing, little resembles the scrawny infant of fig. 180, but looks not unlike the Seleucid-Bactrian baby in its mother's arms on a silver plate from the region, fig. 184.[21]

Anahita was by no means a mere iconographic "cliché" taken at random.[22] During the Sassanian period she was the most popular deity of Iran, says Nyberg. She was the fire goddess, but she was recognized as the angel of waters, or the divine stream flowing from a sacred mountain at the behest of Ohrmazd, and she herself was the "holy water-spring Anahita." [23] This seems indicated by the ripples in the robe when held before her as in fig. 182. Ohrmazd himself offered sacrifice to her "by the good river Daitya." She purifies the seed of males and the wombs of females, helps them in delivery, and fills their breasts with milk.[24] She was generally a "saving" goddess.[25] An amateur uses the Zend Avesta, or the Pahlavi translations,[26] with caution, but it seems agreed on all sides that though Anahita had many other functions, she was so much the Mother Goddess that the Greeks identified her with the Great Mother and Aphrodite (as well as with the Athena and Artemis of war).

21. Courtesy of the Smithsonian Institution, Freer Gallery of Art, Washington, D. C. Cf. K. Weitzmann, "Three 'Bactrian' Silver Vessels with Illustrations from Euripides," *The Art Bulletin*, XXV (1943), fig. 21; cf. his fig. 13, and A. U. Pope, *Masterpieces of Persian Art*, 1945, 49, plate 33. Weitzmann's suggestion that the figures on this bowl represent *personae* from the plays of Euripides would be more convincing if to make his point he did not have to ignore a bullfight prominently in action under a tree, and the spread eagle which occupies the center of the bowl, and which, far from serving "only a decorative purpose," and with "no significance with regard to the frieze," would seem to me to set the tone of the bowl as a whole. He thinks the woman and child represent Hypsipyle and Opheltes of the *Hypsipyle*. He may be right, though he admits that she does not carry the stage properties which the lines describing her demand, and I see no warrant for saying that she is "rocking" the child. Whoever she or the baby may be, she seems rather to be holding him out as a Wunderkind. But even if Weitzmann is right, the baby Opheltes, as Weitzmann himself recalls (pp. 314 f.), was the son of Euridice, a child of such importance that he became a favorite motif on monuments, including sarcophagi.

22. For Anahita, see H. S. Nyberg, *Die Religionen des alten Iran*, 1938, 260–263 (Mitteilungen der Vorderasiatisch-Aegyptischen Gesellschaft, XLIII); S. Wikander, *Feuerpriester in Kleinasien und Iran*, 1946, chaps. III, IV, and VII (Skrifter utgivna av Kungl. Humanistiska Vetenskapssamfundet i Lund, XL). On this latter see Widengren, "Iranische Religionsgeschichte," *Numen*, II (1955), 92, 122 f. See also Cumont in *HERE*, I, 414 f.; E. Meyer in Roscher, *Lex. Myth.*, I, 330–334. Wikander, 61 f., suggests that three little images of the Parthian period, published by Pope, *Persian Art*, IV, plate 134D, E, F, represent Anahita. They have nothing in common with the images we are discussing except the emphasized pudendum of one of them. But I see no reason that Anahita should always have been represented in one way. See also Wikander, 93; Widengren, *Numen*, I (1954), 72; ibid., II, 92, 122 f.

23. Zend Avesta, II, Aban Yasht, 1883, tr. J. Darmesteter (SBE, XXIII), 53 f., 84.

24. Ibid., Aban Yasht, 1, 2 and 5, pp. 54 f.

25. Widengren, "Der iranische Hintergrund des Gnosis," *Zeitschrift für Religions- und Geistesgeschichte*, IV (1952), 102.

26. See the notes by E. West in his translations of *Pahlavi Texts*, I, 1880, 67, n. 4, 336, n. 4; II, 1882, 65, n. 6 (SBE, V, XXVIII).

One has only to mention Aphrodite to recognize that the female in the Nile of the synagogue painting is very much the Aphrodite type, and that actually the same can be said of the Anahitas on the Sassanian vases, remote as they are from the classical goddess. We have not far to go from the synagogue to discover her. Fig. 185 is the fragment of a wall painting of Aphrodite found in the vestibule of a house only two doors away from the synagogue on the same street.[27] It probably came from an upper story, the archeologists thought, and so we have no way to guess its setting. The figure is unquestionably that of Aphrodite, with Cupid or Eros beside her. She is nude, but a drape is behind her which Baur thought she could not herself be holding. Gute, who made the painting, clearly thought she did hold it, as she does in the plinth from Les Fontaines which Baur himself cites.[28] Baur was inclined to think that in the synagogue painting the two fully clothed figures, one on either side of Aphrodite, are the Horae who clothe Aphrodite in flowery robes as she floats to Cyprus on the sea. What I see in this and in the plinth at Brussels, as well as in the later Anahitas on the vases, is indeed an Aphrodite-Anadyomene figure, in which she holds the robe loosely behind her or, if in front, draped low to show her groin. As such, the figure was ideally suited to represent Anahita in the East, who took the place of numberless old mother goddesses. In the Dura painting of fig. 185 a cupid stands beside her, a proper accompaniment of her birth from the sea, as in the shell of the Brussels plinth. Fig. 183 [29] shows Anahita as Aphrodite with the cupids on a Sassanian ewer. Not only in general Sassanian tradition, then, but in a house practically adjacent to the synagogue, we have a figure of Aphrodite-Anahita who in general outline, hair, and the position of her hands startlingly resembles the figure who takes the baby from the ark. For the synagogue artist the drooping garment became water only to the thighs. The baby himself just as startlingly resembles the Eros beside Aphrodite in the position of his hands. I see no possibility, therefore, that a contemporary observer could have missed the resemblance, or have failed to recognize that the artist painted Aphrodite-Anahita as the one who finds the baby Moses.[30]

Connection with the Aphrodite-Anahita painting in the neighboring house seems finally established by the clothing of her two female companions, which closely resemble the clothing of the mother and sister of Moses in the synagogue painting. I have said that I doubt these were Horae in the pagan painting, but I may be wrong, and have no alternative to suggest. Of only one thing am I certain, that to paint the Moses scene the artist drew upon some painting of Aphrodite, who in Dura was probably often called Anahita, with the baby, and with female attendants in their peculiar dress. So startling an invasion into the Moses story, for representation in a synagogue, would hardly have occurred as the mere borrowing of a form. The infant is indeed Moses coming out from the ark in the

---

27. See P. Baur in Rostovtzeff, *Dura-Europos*, VI, 279–282, and plate XLIII. A photograph of the central part of this painting is published there, but the painting is so defective that I publish only the reconstruction by Gute. The original is in the Damascus Museum, no. 8439.

28. Cook, *Zeus*, II, 68, fig. 27b.

29. From Pope, *Persian Art*, I, 735, fig. 252. A silver ewer, formerly in the Stroganoff Collection.

30. Baur recognized the similarity of the two figures but made no inferences.

Nile, but he comes out to divine company in the arms of the goddess, herself quite as recognizable as though flagged with a written label.[31]

2. The Three Nymphs in Iconography

THE SIGNIFICANCE of all this for the baby, whose meaning must be the central interest of the scene, is further indicated by the three women on the bank, who identify themselves as clearly with Greek figures as does the naked "princess" with Aphrodite-Anahita. They have generally been called the maidens who "walked beside the river" with the daughter of Pharaoh.[32] The biblical passage, I agree, has suggested the form of representation.[33] But a glance at the dress of the three and at the tokens they conspicuously carry shows indisputably that they have been represented as the three Nymphs of western paganism. The one on the right carries what Kraeling describes as a "fluted gold dish," markedly the design of a shell, as shown in *a* of text fig. 13.[34] She holds this, as we shall see

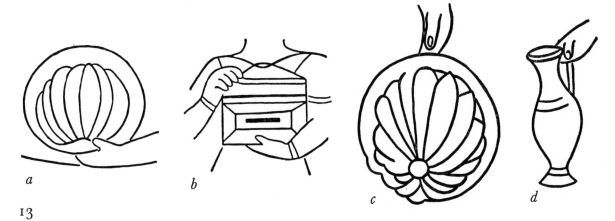

a   *b*   *c*   *d*

13

was proper, close to her body. The central one carries a casket of some sort, *b*, presumably filled with gifts. The Nymph on the left has in one hand a fluted bowl, *c*, so shown that the flutings again associate themselves with the shell, and in the other hand a water pitcher, *d*, tipped slightly as for pouring. The dress of each of the three gives the effect of a tight-fitting bodice ending in a peplum that falls as a short skirt over a long skirt. The veils over their heads seem to be a local orientalization, but their dress otherwise varies only slightly from one commonly put upon the Nymphs, when they were clothed at all. The dress distinguishes them, as du Mesnil says, from any other woman in the painting,[35] and he recalled

31. How widespread was the use of the Aphrodite figure by Jews we do not know. There may be more behind the story of Gamaliel and the statue of Aphrodite than we can now say (see above, IV, 17); she appeared on a lamp in a Jewish grave in Rome (above, II, 104; III, fig. 943). After this material had gone to the press, I received the excellent study by Gutmann, "The Haggadic Motif in Jewish Iconography," *Eretz-Israel*, VI (1960), 16*–22*. On pp. 17* f. he has a very valuable note with a rich collection of references to Christian and

Jewish representations of the scene in which the woman or women discovering Moses are naked. He does not, however, discuss the pagan background of the figures.

32. Exod. II, 6.

33. The maidens, five of them, really walk with the princess in the scene depicted in the *Ashburnham Pentateuch*, fig. 178.

34. See Kraeling, *Synagogue*, 175.

35. The nearest to it appears on the Psyches in fig. 348.

the similarity to the dress of the Nymphs.[36] He did not recognize their tokens, however, and so made little of their presence in the painting.

Like Anahita-Aphrodite, the three Nymphs present so striking an invasion of a pagan element into the biblical scene that we must stop to go thoroughly into the matter to demonstrate that these actually are the Nymphs, and to ascertain what their presence would have implied for the interpretation of the biblical incident.

Fig. 186 [37] shows a votive relief found in southern Bulgaria dedicated to the *numphai aenaoi*, the "eternal," in the sense of "everflowing" Nymphs, "for the security (*sōtēria*) of the house." With it was found a very similar plaque, also dedicated to the Nymphs but showing them in the familiar pose of the Graces.[38] The form of fig. 186, however, is by far the commonest. The function of the Nymphs and Graces in paganism,[39] like their representation, was by no means generally distinguished, but the Nymphs were ordinarily associated with water. The best literary account of this is given by Pausanias,[40] describing the carving on a table at Megalopolis in Arcadia:

> Nymphs were also carved on the table. Neda bears Zeus as an infant child; Anthracia, who is the Nymph of the Arcadians, bears a torch; Hagno has in one hand a water pitcher, and a bowl in the other.[41] The tokens carried by Anchiroë and Myrtoesse are water pitchers, from which evidently water flows down.

Accordingly, flowing vases appear at the two lower corners of fig. 186. Figures that look like the three Graces, but which are again called "Nymphs" in the inscriptions, often appear accompanied by such vases in other parts of Thrace, as for example in fig. 187,[42] but they may also carry the shell pressed to the body, and a flowing pitcher, as in fig. 188.[43] The three women at Dura dressed in the overhanging peplos, with shell basins, shell, and water pitcher, could be only the three Nymphs.[44] Indeed, a group of three women in this

36. Du Mesnil, *Peintures*, 125. Their presence in the scene meant nothing to him; it has only been mentioned, if that, by later commentators.

37. From C. M. Danov, "Antike Denkmäler in Bulgarien," *Bulletin de l'Institut Archéologique Bulgare*, XI (1937), 200, fig. 178. Mentioned by du Mesnil, *Peintures*, 125. Danov says of it: "Jetzt ins Ausland verkauft."

38. Danov, fig. 179.

39. The most important study of the Nymphs is the article "Nymphai" in PW, XVII, 1527–1599, where the Greek Nymphs are described by H. Herter and the Roman by F. Heichelheim, with bibliographies in columns 1581, 1599. For the Nymphs in Thrace see G. Kazarow in PW, VIA, 509–512. See also P. Monceaux in DS, IV, 124–132; L. Bloch in Roscher, *Lex. Myth.*, III, 500–567.

40. *Description of Greece*, VIII, xxxi, 4.

41. See H. Stoll in Roscher, *Lex. Myth.*, I, 1818, s.v. Hagno.

42. From V. Dobrusky, "Inscriptions et monu-

ments figurés," *BCH*, XXI (1897), 124, fig. 5. He lists a large number of such objects.

43. From ibid., 128, fig. 10. Dobrusky says that the Nymph at the right originally held a flowing pitcher like the one at the left.

44. The veil that hangs to the shoulders, and thereby suggests Hathor more than any other form I know, seems to be represented ibid., 129, fig. 11. An interesting study could be made of these figures and of various symbols they present: sometimes cupids take the place of the vases in the corners of the plaques, surely with meaning, ibid., 126, fig. 7, Danov, 200, fig. 179; sometimes they lead the Thracian horseman, Dobrusky, 122, fig. 4. Sometimes they carry what looks like a round fruit, ibid., 124, figs. 5 f., 130, fig. 12 (see my fig. 191), but which may be a sponge, another rather obvious symbol of bathing; sometimes perhaps a snake, but more likely a strigil, ibid., 137, fig. 16; they stand beside Zeus and Hera making libations, ibid., 138 f., figs. 17 f., in which case the idea of eternal pour-

garb, even without the tokens, must be identified as the Nymphs. So they stand beside a sacrificing priest in fig. 189,[45] where without tokens or inscription their identity is clear.

In Italy the Nymphs are more often represented nude, or clothed only from the waist down. The most famous single western instance of their appearance is the votive plaque found in Rome, and now at the Vatican Museum,[46] where, as usual, they carry the shell in such a way as to identify it with the vulva. The identification becomes explicit in the Nymph of Madrid, fig. 190.[47] This shows that with the Nymphs the shell has the same meaning as with Aphrodite,[48] and explains why at Dura and in fig. 188 it is held to the body.[49] Amelung[50] published a beautiful example of a Nymph with the shell, and recognized the identity of the shell with that of Aphrodite, where it meant fertility as the source of life. This symbolism is emphasized when, as in fig. 191[51]—a figurine from Pompeii— the shell is filled with a spray of grapevine, bearing grapes, along with other fruits. Little channels lead back from the angular edges of the shell to pipes, so that originally water flowed out from the shell. Similar figurines were found in Byblos, Syria.[52]

The Nymphs in all this are the source of the divine fluid, of fruitfulness; that is, as we saw with the divine fluid, they offer life, divine life.[53] So in a painting at Pompeii they could hold a bubbling basin at either side of a spouting fountain, with a river god taking the place of the third Nymph and the dove and peacock drinking from the fountain, which, not by chance, still has the fluting of the shell.[54] An alternative presentation shows them bringing the basin, which may or may not be fluted or gadrooned, and may or may not have itself served as a fountain. One of the important ways of getting the fluid was to be washed in the Nymphs' basin.[55]

Since we saw that milk was one of the divine fluids, the Nymphs of course give the

---

ing may have taken a new form of representation. In other cases the dress with peplos identifies them sufficiently, and they carry no tokens at all: ibid., 129, fig. 11. See also E. Espérandieu, *Recueil général des bas-reliefs, statues et bustes de la Germanie romaine*, 1931, no. 199 on p. 131.

45. From Dobrusky, 137, fig. 16.

46. See above, VIII, fig. 71.

47. Courtesy of the Prado Museum, Madrid. Cf. Reinach, *Statuaire*, II, 405, no. 6.

48. See above, VIII, fig. 67.

49. Cf. the Nymph with shell at Herculaneum, Reinach, *Peintures*, 48, no. 4. See also idem, *Reliefs*, II, 124, no. I, and 492, no. 3; III, 36, no. 5, and 79, no. 4; idem, *Statuaire*, I, 97, no. 5, and 436; II, 405; F. de Clarac, *Musée de la sculpture*, 1836–37, IV, plates 750, 754. Other instances are listed by M. Bratschkova, "Die Muschel in der antiken Kunst," *Bulletin de l'Institut Archéologique Bulgare*, XII (1938), pp. 80–128, nos. 211 f., 215, 217–221, 266 f., 326, 720–722, 724, 783, 787, 920.

50. *Sculp. Vatican.*, II, plate 8, no. 77; cf. Text, 213.

51. Courtesy of the Soprintendenza alle Antichita della Campania, Naples; cf. *AAL, N,* 1927, 70, fig. 32. Maiuri, who published it, says that this is an "unnatural and illogical contamination" of the motifs, but the whole seems to me directly meaningful.

52. J. Lauffray in *Bulletin du Musée de Beyrouth*, IV (1940), 28 f., fig. 15.

53. By such symbolism they also associated themselves with human fertility, and played a large part in weddings: H. Herter in PW, XVII, 1549 f.

54. Reinach, *Peintures*, 48, no. 3; similar Nymphs flank a river god on a Pompeian painting at the Louvre: see ibid., 46, no. 1, and 48, nos. 1 f.

55. Pausanias, *Description of Greece*, VII, xxxi, 4 (ed. W. K. S. Jones, Loeb Series, IV, 58), mentions the Nymphs carrying water pitchers (*hudriai*) and basins (*phialai*). They were carved upon a table in the shrine of Demeter and Kore at Megalopolis in Arcadia.

fluid to divine infants by nursing them at the breast. An offering was made to them in that character (*tropheia paidōn*), and Herter [56] has an interesting collection of material on such a popular cult. They nursed most of the divine babies: Zeus,[57] Dionysus,[58] Adonis,[59] Hera, Kore, Angelos, Hecate, Hermes, Pan, and such heroes as Achilles, Aeneas, Rhesos, Hippolytus, and others.[60] Ordinarily, we take representations of the Nymphs as nurses in pagan art to be scenes of their nursing the infant Dionysus, often with entire justification from the context, as in fig. 193.[61] Here one Nymph nurses him, a second stands at his right, and a third pours water from a pitcher into a basin.[62] In many cases the baby cannot be identified. For example, a striking relief fragment, fig. 192,[63] at the Vatican shows the Nymph herself emerging from the basin and nursing a female infant. When the Nymphs appear with the baby on funerary monuments, which is not common apart from representations of Dionysus, the individual in the grave would seem himself to be coming into divine life. We saw such a scene from a presumably pagan tomb in Palestine near Ascalon.[64]

Indeed, in what was ancient Thrace, not far from where the votive plaques with Nymphs were discovered, a number of plaques were found dedicated "To the Nurses," *Nutricibus*.[65] Often only a single "nurse" with the baby appears on the plaque, but this single one seems collectively to represent the three Nymphs, for all dedications address her in the plural, and she appears on other plaques with her two companions, as in fig. 194,[66] where they carry their distinctive attributes.[67] Again we have evidence of the active

56. PW, XVII, 1550.

57. The infant Zeus, variously called locally, was nursed by the Nymphs: Pausanias, *Description of Greece*, IV, xxxiii, 1, VIII, xxxviii, 3, xlvii, 3; Apollodorus, *Bibliotheca*, I, i, 6 f.; Callimachus, *Hymn to Jove*, lines 32–41; Diodorus Siculus, *Historical Library*, v, lxx, 3.

58. See the references by O. Kern in PW, V, 1035 f.; A. Maiuri, *La Casa del Menandro*, 1932, 339, fig. 131; plate XXXIX. By taking various human beings, even young adults like Hylas, into the water, the Nymphs turned them into gods or heroes. On this see Cumont, *Lux*, 325–328.

59. Ovid, *Metamorphoses*, x, 514; Servius, *Eclogues*, x, 18; see below, p. 212.

60. This is Herter's list in PW, XVII, 1551, where he gives references for each. For Adonis see also Reinach, *Peintures*, 64, no. 1; G. E. Rizzo, *La Pittura ellenistico-romana*, 1929, plate cxx.

61. Courtesy of the Walters Art Gallery, Baltimore. Cf. Lehmann, *Baltimore*, fig. 2. On p. 11 he identifies the three as a Nymph and two maenads, with which I cannot agree. Cf. his fig. 7, and pp. 14 f., 37. See also Reinach, *Reliefs*, III, 106, no. 3, 136, no. 1; idem, *Peintures*, 105, nos. 2 f.; H. Sitte, "Fragment eines Sarkophagreliefs," *JÖAI*, XII

(1909), 215–223.

62. Cumont, *Symbolisme*, 85, seems drawing only on his imagination in saying that a Nymph pouring out from a pitcher represents the origin of rain from the heavens. Nymphs were occasionally connected with rain: Roscher, *Lex. Myth.*, III, 75 f. But on a sarcophagus this association would be highly unlikely.

63. Courtesy of the Vatican Museum. Cf. Amelung, *Sculp. Vatican.*, II, 731; plate 82, no. 8.

64. See above, V, fig. 70; cf. p. 60. Cumont has two child sarcophagi in which a female takes an infant to bathe him as the first step in his mystic advance to apotheosis: *Symbolisme*, 334–343, with plate XXXVI. I am sure the female with the infant and basin is a Nymph. See also Marrou, *MA*, 30–32.

65. K. Wigand, "Die Nutrices Augustae von Poetavio," *JÖAI*, XVIII (1915), Beiblatt, 188–215. Why they are called Augustae is not clear.

66. Ibid., 206, fig. 114. The Nymph on the right carries the bathing basin by handles: see Amelung, *Sculp. Vatican.*, II, plate 58; Reinach, *Statuaire*, II, 405, no. 1. In carrying the basin she recalls the Dura scene again.

67. In ibid., 207, fig. 115, a Nymph carries a

value of the figures of the Nymphs with babies, whether to nurse or bathe them.

The convention of the Nymphs with the divine baby was used to show the divine origin of the king. Fig. 195 [68] shows a mosaic recently published by M. Chéhab, from the Villa de Soueidié, Baalbek. It tells the story of the birth and enthronement of Alexander. Olympias is named as she lies on the birth couch, with a "servant" beside her. Below, "Alexander" is being bathed in an elaborately fluted basin by a "Nymph." In what was originally the center of the scene, "Alexander" sits enthroned with "Olympias" and "Philip."

We have seen that the Nymphs, whether they nurse the baby at the breast, or bathe him, or both, seem clearly to mark the divine baby. Fig. 174 shows the baby Moses as represented in the Octateuchs. The tradition of the origin of the saintly or divine baby went over, obviously, into Christianity, especially in the form of the bathing.[69] Fig. 196 [70] uses the traditional form to indicate that Mary herself, as born of Anna, was the Wunderkind: here the three Nymphs have become women bringing gifts, while a fourth bathes the little saint. A ninth-century Christian casket at Rome is decorated with scenes from the life of king David, fig. 197,[71] where David's divine royalty is indicated as we saw done for Alexander. In the upper left of the front face a Nymph bathes the new-born king in a basin, which, like the ewer, is conspicuously marked for shell value by its fluting. Nymphs bathe the infant John the Baptist in a fourteenth-century illustrated manuscript of the Gospels,[72] but he, from conception, was a Wunderkind. They often bathe the infant Christ, as on a twelfth-century bronze door in Benevento, fig. 198.[73] Such a convention for the Christ child is so common [74] that the basin and ewer of the Nativity of Ugolino at the

shell: she was recognized as a Nymph by A. Conze, *Römische Bildwerke einheimischen Fundorts in Österreich*, 1875, II, 13 (Denkschriften der Kaiserlichen Akademie der Wissenschaften, Wien, philos.-hist. Klasse, XXIV). In the figure here shown, and in Wigand, 208, fig. 116, she carries a pitcher and a spherical object which Wigand plausibly suggests may be a bathing sponge. These objects appear in our fig. 187.

68. Courtesy of M. Chéhab, Director of the Archeological Museum, Beirut. It is in the Museum of Beirut. See his *Mosaïques du Liban*, 1958, 46–50, and plates XXII–XXV (*Bulletin du Musée de Beyrouth*, XIV and XV).

69. It seems to me clear that when Mary nurses the divine Christ she carries over, with other motifs, the value of the nursing Nymph.

70. From the *Menolog. Basil II*, II, plate 22, at the Vatican; tenth century.

71. Photo Alinari. Cf. Weitzmann, *Roll and Codex*, fig. 141; cf. p. 151. See also the birth of David in which the three Nymphs stand behind the mother's bed and a fourth has the baby beside

the basin: Mt. Athos Pantocratoros, cod. 49, fol. 5ᵛ, published by Weitzmann, ibid., fig. 140.

72. B. D. Filow, *Les Miniatures de l'Evangile du roi Jean Alexandre à Londres*, Sofia, 1934, plate 68, no. 3, fol. 140 (Monumenta artis Bulgariae, III).

73. Photo Alinari. Cf. Weitzmann, *The Fresco Cycle of S. Maria di Castelseprio*, 1951, plate XXVII, fig. 63 (Princeton Monographs in Art and Archeology, XXVI). He shows two ivories with the same scene, ibid., figs. 61 f.

74. See also ibid., figs. 5, 54, and cf. pp. 37 f. A similar scene is in a ninth-century fresco, now destroyed, at the Chapel of San Lorenzo at the source of the Volturne: E. Bertaux, *L'Art dans l'Italie méridionale*, 1907, I, 96, fig. 33. The Nymphs bathe Christ on a twelfth-century mosaic in the Palatine Chapel at Palermo; and in the Greek Gospel, Bibl. Natl. gr. 43, fol. 13ᵛ: G. Vezin, *L'Adoration et le cycle des Mages*, 1950, 44, fig. 5; plate XIVb. See also Filow, plate 8, fol. 10, and the fresco in the Cemetery of S. Valentino, Rome, in Weitzmann, plate XXIV, fig. 54. Here one of the Nymphs has become Salome, probably the woman in the

Fogg Art Museum, Harvard University, fig. 199,[75] can now be seen directly to have symbolized the infant's divinity.

We saw in fig. 196 that the Nymphs could also bring a box of gifts, and that is what the central Nymph at Dura seems to be doing. Such boxes often contained jewels, in antiquity as still today, but by no means always. In the Middle Ages boxes of this sort could be used for saints' relics or other holy objects.[76] While the magi bring their gifts to Jesus ordinarily on round trays,[77] in two instances shown by Leclercq one of the three carries a box.[78] Without going into detail, a study of boxes in several typical collections of ancient art [79] has led me to conclude that in classical art such a box is also usually a jewel box, but is often a box of offerings for sacrifice, or an object in a Dionysiac procession. One can by no means safely assume it is always a woman's jewel box. In this case, since the other two Nymphs obviously bring the symbols of the Wunderkind to Moses in the water, we presume the central Nymph has some divine endowment for him in the box. It seems no coincidence that the Anahita in fig. 182 has a very similar covered box. Anahita and the three Nymphs have closely assimilated meanings for the man who designed the paintings in the synagogue.

The Nymphs who washed a baby, then, in pagan and Christian usage, indicated that the baby was a god in the pagan sense, or the Christian Christ child, or an especially

---

Protevangelium of James XIX, 3–XX, 4 (M. R. James, *The Apocryphal New Testament*, 1924, 46 f.), who made trial of Mary and certified her virginity; cf. Weitzmann, 55. The motif frequently appears in the mural paintings of the ninth- to eleventh-century churches of Cappadocia: Guillaume de Jerphanion, *Une Nouvelle Province de l'art byzantin: Les Eglises rupestres de Cappadoce*, 1925–1942, plates 100, 179, 190, 198 (Bibliothèque archéologique et historique, V, VI). In these paintings when two women bathe the child, one is labeled "Salome," the other "Mea": when only one, she is called "Mea." Jerphanion did not recognize these women as the midwives, but in his Text, II, 442, he says that the design itself is that of the infancy of pagan heroes. Weitzmann, 55, says that *emea* is equivalent to *hē maia*, which is used here as a proper name. The word means primarily a nurse or foster mother, apparently, but could also mean a midwife, so that it applied to the figure in either capacity. It was the proper name for the mother of Hermes, and Porphyry equates Maia with both Proserpina and Demeter, as the universal *trophos*, or nurse: *De abstinentia*, IV, 16, 1 (ed. J. de Rhoer, 1767, 312 f.). Such adaptation of old symbols to new mythology is the constant phenomenon in symbolic transition.

75. Courtesy of the Fogg Art Museum, Harvard University.

76. Strzygowski, *Kopt.*, 171. For boxes of this type, presumably covered with bone, as Strzygowski here points out, were commonly made in Alexandria, but imitated elsewhere. See esp. the box discussed ibid., 172–175, with plates XI–XIII, where one of the women carved on the box carries a shell. M. H. Longhurst, *Catalogue of Carvings in Ivory*, I, 1927, plate XXIX (Victoria and Albert Museum), publishes two boxes inscribed with women's names, presumably toilet boxes; cf. plates XIV, XXXII, XXXV f., LXXI. See also O. Pelka, *Elfenbein*, 1920, 75 f. (Bibliothek für Kunst- und Antiquitatensammler, XVII). But definitely with sacred associations are the boxes in Longhurst, plates XXXIV, XXXVIII, LXXIV, LXXV, and in Pelka, pp. 31, 33, 108, 120 f., 132.

77. These are to be associated with an offering of gifts as old as the Greek lecythus vases: see, for example, Pfuhl, *Malerei*, III, figs. 529 f., 532, 534, 540 f., 544, 547, 551.

78. See the collection of instances by Leclercq in CL, X, 1931, 980–1067. The two with the box are p. 994, fig. 7458, from a very early catacomb, and p. 1043, fig. 7489, probably of the eleventh century.

79. Reinach, *Peintures;* idem, *Reliefs;* idem, *Statuaire;* FR; Pfuhl, *Malerei;* E. Gerhard, *Etruskische Spiegel*, 1840–97.

sacred saint, or a person of kingly state, which meant, in ancient tradition, a person "hedged" with divinity. Used on a sarcophagus, the device seems a wishful symbol that the deceased would also be born into a new and heavenly existence. I do not know an instance from either pagan or Christian usage in which the Nymphs with their washing did not indicate that they were endowing the baby with superhuman character or proclaiming him as having it. No instance parallels the design of the symbol as presented in the synagogue painting, but the elements are all so clearly traditional and recognizable that I see no reason to doubt that following a Jewish tradition, or originally with himself, the master designer at Dura introduced the Nymphs deliberately and skillfully into the scene of the infant Moses, and did so in order to intensify the notion that Anahita-Aphrodite was drawing from the water a Wunderkind with royal nature at least "hedged" with divinity.

Somehow related to the Moses scene is the extraordinary limestone relief at the Coptic Museum in Old Cairo, fig. 200,[80] a piece which presents so many interesting features that I must digress a little to discuss it. It shows two women in striped chitons (perhaps dalmatics), the one on the left seated, the other advancing left. As at Dura their faces are frontally presented. The hair is the heavy curly type familiar at Palmyra (fig. 148) and on Parthian coins (fig. 105), and the pointed cap of the East sits high upon it. The seated woman on the left bathes a baby whose hair is similarly drawn, bathes him in a fluted basin on a stand, and with a large bail that arches over the baby's head. The woman at the right carries a smaller bucket by its bail in her right hand, a wreath in her left. This group seems to present a thoroughly orientalized version of the Nymphs with the child, one in which the pitcher of the second Nymph has become a bucket of water.

Other symbols in the relief are important. Between the baby's bath and the woman at the right is the end of a box with a gabled top, which reminds us both of a sarcophagus and of the little ark in the river for Moses at Dura. Above the hand that carries the little bucket stands a peculiar symbol which recalls the so-called Fravashi sign to be discussed below,[81] a form here elaborated, and with rosettes at either side to take the place of what I may call the little "arms." The form is almost certainly not of Egyptian origin.[82]

Perhaps the most interesting symbol in the relief is the large comb above the bail of the baby's bath. It has the usual form of Coptic combs—fine and coarse teeth above and below a solid center.[83] The comb is a most unusual feature in such a scene. I can hardly agree with Munier[84] that it was put here for the toilet of the infant; both he and Cramer seem to me to take the bath altogether too literally. The comb is presented with the bath in the gadrooned vase, the little bucket, the wreath, the gable-roofed sarcophagus, the

80. From H. Munier, "Une Scène de la Nativité sur un bas-relief copte," *ASAE*, XXIV (1924), plate xxiv, see pp. 128–132; cf. M. Cramer, "Eine koptische Reliefdarstellung und ihre byzantinischen Parallelen," *Akten des vierundzwanzigsten Internationalen Orientalisten-Kongresses, München,* 1957, pp. 234–237.

81. See below, X, 151.

82. The spreading double "legs" make the form quite different from the ankh. Munier, 129, calls it a vase of flowers on a tripod, but I cannot agree.

83. For a collection of them see Strzygowski, *Kopt.*, 144, plate viii.

84. Munier, 129, n. 2.

Fravashi symbol, and the rosettes, all symbols of the new divine life the child was being given by the Nymphs, and one would suppose the comb was put with them to reinforce this idea. The comb here recalls the great number of combs found on the breasts of mummies, as if talismans for their future life. One of these showed a horseman apotheosized in a wreath between Victories on one side, and Christ raising Lazarus and healing the blind man on the other, a too heavily iterated presentation of the hope of immortality to be put on a toilet article.[85] When we now look again at the collection of combs on Strzygowski's other plate, and at the large collection of H. Leclercq,[86] and Peter Lasko,[87] we see that unrecognizable as many of the scenes, figures, and symbols on them are, they seem for the most part to have religious reference.

The comb survived as a cult instrument in the Church.[88] In the middle ages, before a priest or bishop went to the altar to celebrate the mass, he would use a comb especially designated for the purpose, and pray. One prescribed prayer is: "May thy kindly Spirit, Lord, cleanse and purify me within and without, my head, all my body, and my mind."[89] The comb is still used in this way after the anointing of a bishop-elect. In the sense of a "visible sign of an invisible grace," the comb became a sacramental (the Church prefers to say "liturgical") object to bring about the answer to this petition. Combs were often put into Christian tombs, also, as in those of St. Cuthbert, with, to me, the same hope of renewing a right life for the person buried. So fig. 201[90] shows a Coptic tombstone with the omnipresent gateway—its entrance marked by what may well be the Fravashi sign, and the comb, put there, presumably, to intensify the symbolism of the gate as the entrance to new life.[91] These two monumental usages seem to me to make almost impossible the pronouncement of Lasko that the combs of Coptic Egypt, found in large numbers, "could not have been more than rather fine articles of daily use," and that the early Christian usage may have come from combs that were "purely practical and hygienic."[92] The early Christian usage seems, like so much of the symbolism we are tracing, to have been the Christianization of a traditional symbol from paganism.

The comb in the gateway, however, makes us recall that normally it was a shell which stood over the gateway.[93] Here we suddenly have our explanation of the whole. For both this kind of shell and the comb were in Greek called *kteis*. We have just been

85. Strzygowski, *Kopt.*, 194, plate XVII, 7117. Cf. the interesting fragment of a comb, no. 7116 on the same plate, with a banqueting scene on one side, and two naked women, one leading a naked child, on the other. The ladies very much recall our Aphrodite-Anahita figure, but nothing identifies them with it.

86. CL, XIII, 2932–2959.

87. "The Comb of St. Cuthbert," in C. S. Battiscombe, *The Relics of Saint Cuthbert*, 1956, 336–355.

88. CL, XIII, 2934 f.; Lasko, 342–349.

89. *Spiritus almus*, the "nourishing" or "nursing" adjective especially applied to the female divinities,

Cybele, Ceres, Venus, etc., and still used for our universities as alma mater. It is quite appropriate that the comb should be the vehicle of the *Spiritus almus*.

90. From A. E. Crum, *Coptic Monuments*, 1902, plate XXXVIII, 8626 (Catalogue général des antiquités égyptiennes du Musée du Caire).

91. On this symbolism of the gate see above, IV, 99–144.

92. Lasko, 344. The word "hygienic" is a modernism quite foreign to ancient or medieval thought.

93. See above, IV, figs. 91, 96, 100, 110, 115; VIII, 95–105, esp. 97.

seeing that the shell as the *kteis* was frequently used with its third meaning directly implied: the vagina, as fig. 190 of this volume shows at once. It seems to me rather obvious that the comb was used on these monuments only as another way of saying *kteis*, saying that one comes into the greater life through the new birth which the Nymphs offer with their shells or with their washing in the shell-fluted basin, but also through the comb, because one has the new life not literally through the shell or comb or basin or Nymph, but through a merciful conferring of divine or heavenly life, which the word *kteis* had come to represent. Just as the shell kept its value and is still used in baptism, so the church still uses the comb for purity of soul and body, along with the oil of the Spirit, to confer new episcopal powers. Such a digression in discussing the Nymphs has been justified only if it strengthens the impression that in the ancient world symbolism was much more active and conscious than today, when the Church can use the shell in baptism, the comb in consecrating a bishop, with no awareness of the original meaning of the object it is using. We cannot project our insensitivity to these forms back upon antiquity.[94]

The impact of this group of symbols is made stronger by comparing the gable-topped sarcophagus of the Coptic monument with the little ark in the Dura painting, to which we now return. Far from trying to represent it as made of bulrushes daubed with pitch, the artist has made it a little sarcophagus with a gabled lid whose top has disappeared, a most obvious symbol of resurrection. The sarcophagus with gabled lid was very popular with Jews at this period, as the photograph of a cave at Sheikh Ibreiq (Beth She'arim) clearly shows, fig. 204.[95] Earlier Jewish ossuaries frequently had this form, [96] and by their smallness and lack of acroteria recall the form of Moses' ark in the painting even more strikingly than do the large sarcophagi. We shall return to this when we have said a few words about the two female figures at the extreme left of the painting.

They wear exactly the same clothing as the two women before Pharaoh, and no one has doubted that the two pairs represent the same two women, but it is to be noted that while only one of the two on the right has the pronged gam, both of those at the left are marked with it. The knee of the woman at the right of the pair with the baby is bent, and Kraeling takes this to indicate that she is advancing toward the ark at her feet. It could as well indicate that she was rising after having received the child from the ark or the "princess." The two women hold up the baby between them, as they do in the *Ashburnham*

94. Like Cramer, I quite despair of identifying the child in the Coptic relief. The crosses on the comb and on the hat of the Nymph at the left obviously suggest Christianity, although if the eastern influence is as strong as I feel it to be, the crosses may have been the familiar Parthian or Sassanian ones. Several of the details, such as the wreath, are to be found in no Christian representation of the birth of Christ, and the little sarcophagus recalls Moses. On the whole I take the baby to be probably Christ, but would not say so more positively.

95. Courtesy of the Department of Archeology, Hebrew University, Jerusalem, Israel. Cf. Avigad in *IEJ*, VII (1957), 77–82, plate 19A, and fig. 4. It is a view of Room XI of Catacomb 20. Avigad says, p. 82: "The shape of the cover is the same in nearly all sarcophagi; it is that of a saddle-roof with acroteria in the four corners."

96. See above, III, figs. 106, 109, 123, 126, 128, 139, 142, etc. Such a sarcophagus, open but with gabled end, awaits the body of Sarah in *Const. Octateuch*, plate xv, 48.

Pentateuch, fig. 177, and instead of disputing which one is handing the child to the other we may say (what is actually represented) that they are holding him up between them as for adoration, or, if the term be too strong, for admiration, as does the woman in the scene from Elijah, fig. 335. Since they wear the same clothing as the women beside Anahita-Aphrodite in the neighboring house, fig. 185, we must assume that the artist considered them to have had analogous functions, though the vagueness of that function for the women with Aphrodite makes it impossible to discuss the analogy further.

The scene on the left half of the Dura painting, accordingly, itself consists of two parts: first, taking the baby out of the sarcophagus-ark, along with the presentation to the Nymphs; and second, his mother and sister, who are the midwives triumphant, holding him up in glory. We ask in what connection babies are associated with death and with the Nymphs, but also are held up as Wunderkinder for admiration and adoration.[97]

Several divine babies are held up for adoration in ancient art, but on the whole surprisingly few. The Greeks and Romans liked to depict gods as Wunderkinder, such as Zeus,[98] Heracles,[99] Telephus the heroic son of Hercules and Auge,[100] Perseus the son of Zeus and Danaë,[101] Apollo and Artemis,[102] Iachus,[103] Adonis,[104] and later Harpocrates.[105] The most important single divine baby of antiquity was, of course, Dionysus.[106] He is shown born from the thigh of Zeus and being given to the Nymphs by Zeus directly, or

97. Babies often appear on tombstones, but their significance, when they do not represent the dead child being memorialized, is beyond our present inquiry. Adequate specimens can be seen in Reinach, *Reliefs*, II, 187, no. 2; 217, no. 4; III, 153, no. 1; 212, no. 1; 269, no. 2.

98. F. Imhoof-Blumer, *Kleinasiatische Münzen,* 1902, II, 484; plate XVIII, 21. This is on a bronze coin of Caracalla from Cilicia (Seleucia on the Calycadnus).

99. For example, three paintings from Pompeii of him as an infant strangling the snakes: Reinach, *Peintures*, 186, nos. 3–5. Cf. Heracles in a *liknon* on a red-figured cylix in the Museo Georgiano of the Vatican, shown and discussed by J. Harrison, *Prolegomena*, 523.

100. For example, two paintings, one from Herculaneum and one from Pompeii: Reinach, *Peintures*, 192, nos. 4, 6.

101. Two Pompeian paintings: ibid., p. 10, no. 5, and p. 11, no. 2.

102. See them as children presented to Zeus on a sarcophagus lid: Reinach, *Reliefs*, III, 167, nos. 1–3.

103. See the essays of E. Gerhard, *Gesammelte Akademische Abhandlungen*, 1868, II, 148–196, 314–389; plate LXXX. Gerhard shows that Iachus was

an alternative for the young Dionysus.

104. A painting from Pompeii shows him tended by the Nymphs, and held over a stream of water (see above, p. 206), and one from Rome shows him presented to Aphrodite: Reinach, *Peintures*, 64, nos. 1, 3. On his being nursed by the Nymphs see Servius, *In Vergilii carmina commentarii Aeneid*, v, 72; *Eclogues*, x, 18 (ed. G. Thil, 1881, 600); Roscher, *Lex. Myth.*, I, 71.

105. See above, VIII, 9 f. I cannot identify the baby in the *ex voto* plaque to Artemis: Reinach, *Reliefs*, III, 174, no. 4. Other unidentified babies can be seen in E. Gerhard, *Antike Bilderwerke*, 1827, plates II, III, and XX; cf. comments in his *Prodromus mythologischer Kunsterklärung*, 1828, 45–49.

106. Still the most important study for this is H. Heydemann, *Dionysos' Geburt und Kindheit*, 1885 (Hallisches Winckelmannsprogram, X), where the literary and monumental material is collected. The references given here can be greatly enriched from this study. Much of interest will be found in the chapters on "The Myth of the Divine Child," by C. G. Jung and C. Kerényi, *Essays on a Science of Mythology*, 1949 (Bollingen Series, XXII): the title in the British publication was *Introduction to a Science of Mythology*.

taken to them by Hermes; [107] or he is presented by Gaia rising from the earth.[108] The symbol can be complicated by Gaia's holding up a cornucopia from which he is born, as on a vase at the Museum of Istanbul,[109] or the baby pouring a libation can simply emerge from the horn, itself filled with grapes, as on a bronze coin of Nysa in Caria (Lydia?), fig. 202.[110] The baby Dionysus often appears in the *liknon*, the cultic cradle-basket, as in fig. 205.[111] He is held up for admiration or reverence by Silenus before the Nymphs, Pan, and Hermes; [112] by a Silenus who makes of his faun skin a sort of *liknon* with fruit, fig. 207; [113] by Pan, fig. 203; [114] by Zeus; [115] by Hermes.[116] He often appears as a glorified baby on a goat or a feline, figs. 206 [117] and 208.[118] He can be the divine baby quite alone, as in fig. 209,[119] or as the center of a triumphant procession, fig. 210.[120]

We have seen that while the Nymphs nursed or bathed many babies, the one most commonly with them was Dionysus. A series of reliefs shows how this nursing or bathing led to the glorification of the child—his existence, really, as a divine person. Fig. 211 [121]

107. See MW, 1856, II, plate xxxiv, 391–399; F. Imhoof-Blumer, *Monnaies grecques*, 1883, 173 f., 339, 387, 407 f. (Verhandelingen der Koninklijke Akademie von Wetenschappen, XIV).

108. MW, nos. 400 f. It is probably the baby Dionysus being born from the horn held by Heracles in the beautiful relief at the Vatican: Amelung, *Sculp. Vatican.*, II, plate 21.

109. See above, VIII, fig. 103; cf. p. 109, n. 333· The baby may be Erichthonius: see Reinach, *Reliefs*, II, 14, no. 2.

110. From MW, II, plate xxxv, 416; cf. p. 22 of the Fortsetzung. Like many of the late imperial coins of the East, this coin does not yet appear in modern catalogues, so far as I can discover, but there seems no reason to doubt its genuineness. The authors say that it is a coin of Maximinus, struck at Nysa in Caria (Lydia?). The occasionally used convention of the children of the Emperor emerging from a cornucopia seems similarly to indicate their divinity: see above, VIII, fig. 101; cf. p. 110 f. Nysa, reputed birthplace of Dionysus and the name also of a Nymph, most appropriately has on its coins this token of the god's birth and nursing by Nysa. For similar coins in the East see Imhoof-Blumer, *Monnaies grecques*, 68 f., 403 f.

111. Courtesy of the British Museum. See T. Combe, *Ancient Terracottas in the British Museum*, 1810, plate xxiv, 44. Cf. MW, II, plate xxxv, 414, and Roscher, *Lex. Myth.*, II, 2046, s.v. *liknites*.

112. A Pompeian wall painting: Reinach, *Peintures*, 105, no. 3; cf. ibid., no. 4, and MW, II, plate xxxv, 406.

113. Courtesy British Museum. A marble statue: see A. Furtwängler, *Der Satyr aus Pergamon*, 1880,

plate iii, 1; on p. 20, n. 4, he lists a large number of parallels (Winckelmann Programm, XL).

114. From MW, II, fig. 410. A photograph, but not clear, is in P. Gardner, *Peloponnesus*, 1887, 103, no. 93, plate xxi, 2 (CBM). It is a bronze coin of M. Aurelius from Zacynthus.

115. See MW, II, fig. 409, who say only that it is a bronze coin of Laodicea in Phrygia.

116. As in the famous statue by Praxiteles: see G. E. Rizzo, *Prassitele*, 1932, plate xcix, statue in the Olympia Museum. See also plates I, iv–vii, xii f., cv–cvii. A coin of Pheneus in Arcadia, Gardner, 194, no. 13; plate xxxvi, 7, is taken as showing Hermes carrying Arcas, since the name Arcas appears on the coin. But since Arcas was also a name for Hermes himself (Lucan, *Civil War*, ix, 661; Martial, *Epigrams*, ix, 24), it would seem more likely that Hermes as "Arcas" is carrying Dionysus on this coin also. See Roscher, *Lex. Myth.*, I, 2413.

117. Courtesy of the British Museum, London.

118. Courtesy National Museum, Naples. Cf. MW, II, plate xxxv, 404 (on the plate, misnumbered 414); see also ibid., 405.

119. From O. Rubensohn in *JDAI*, XX (1905), plate 3; cf. 23. It is a painting on wood from Fayum, now in the Cairo Museum. See Reinach, *Peintures*, 105, no. 5; cf. MW, II, plate xxxv, 415.

120. From W. Zahn, *Die schönsten Ornamente und merkwürdigsten Gemälde aus Pompeji, Herculaneum und Stabiae*, 1852, III, plate 83, no. 1; cf. Reinach, *Peintures*, 106, no. 3.

121. From Gerhard in *AZ*, IV (1846), plate xxxviii; cf. pp. 217–221. It was last reported as being in a private collection.

represents the relief on an ivory pyxis at Milan. The myth notwithstanding, the pyxis shows the mother, Semele, with the shell basin beside her bed, while her baby is taken from her by the Nymphs, with the result that in the next scene he is shown royally glorified on a throne, which is identified with the *liknon*.[122] His divine character is further presented when he next appears on a goat and, as an ephebe, mounts the chariot pulled by felines.

Such a sequence of double birth, the second birth resulting in the glorified baby, has survived on two sarcophagi, while a fragment of a third showing the glorified baby [123] clearly belongs in the same sequence. These sarcophagi greatly illuminate the real function of the Nymphs, as well as the two baby scenes of the Dura Synagogue we are considering in this chapter. The sarcophagi omit the birth scene with Semele that we just saw on the Milan pyxis, and begin with the baby being washed by the Nymphs, as in fig. 212.[124] But though the first birth does not appear, the artist recorded its incompleteness by showing the baby in the central group apparently born dead, with an arm that dangles quite as does the arm of the little dead child whom, we shall see, the mourning mother presents to Elijah. In contrast, as a result of the bath which the Nymphs give him, the child becomes vibrantly alive, and is held up in triumph in the group at the right. One of the Nymphs has turned from the central group to connect the scene of the triumphant baby ideologically with the scene of the washing. A satyr elevates the child, or, as we see by analogy with the other examples, sets him up on a pedestal. Silenus sits at the right of the baby and another Nymph stands behind him. Silenus seems to be giving the grapevine to the young god. The scene at the left of the sarcophagus shows a satyr carrying a thyrsus and leading a ram on which the child Dionysus rides; the little god carries the *liknon*, or mystic basket, on his shoulder. A Nymph, and a man whom Sitte calls the aged Priapus, accompany the young god in the background. The sarcophagus as a whole, therefore, presents the young god glorified, the young god as the mystic savior, and explains the whole by the Nymphs bathing and nursing the lifeless infant and endowing him with divine life and power. The scene is really one of resurrection.

Another sarcophagus, fig. 213,[125] depicts the three Nymphs bathing the baby on the right, with three other female attendants, and at the left essentially the same scene of the elevation of the baby Dionysus, here upon a low rock between a satyr and Silenus. Between these scenes a Bacchic dance, the *ascoliasmus*, is being celebrated.[126] The dance was a sort of bucolic sport, in which the revelers tried to leap on a full wineskin. Here an older man seems beating a young fellow who has fallen off, while a wrapt menad dances at the back. The order has now changed, and the cult scene, or riot scene, has taken the place of the

122. Gerhard calls it a shield, but Roscher in his *Lex. Myth.*, II, 2046 (bottom), calls it the *liknon* with more probability: cf. col. 1617 f.

123. For these sarcophagi see H. Sitte in *JÖAI*, XII (1909), 215–223, and plate IX.

124. Courtesy of Antikensammlungen, Munich. A child sarcophagus in Munich. Sitte, 218, dates it in the period of Hadrian.

125. Courtesy of the Deutsches Archäologisches Institut, Rome. It is in the Capitoline Museum, Rome; Sitte, 221, fig. 112, dates it toward the end of the second century A.D. See also W. Helbig, *Führer durch die öffentlichen Sammlungen klassischer Altertümer in Rom*, 3d ed., 1912, I, 434, no. 786.

126. On the ascoliasmus see E. Reisch in PW, II, 1698–1700.

mystic god with the *cista* riding the ram, but there can be no doubt that this is a variation of the earlier design, wherein the baby's bath culminated in the glorified child. Here again the baby is in the peculiar inert position of the Munich sarcophagus, and its arm dangles in the same lifeless way.[127] Sitte's careful analysis led him to conclude that these scenes all derived from a widely known hellenistic original, and his argument seems quite convincing. He does not recognize, however, that the idea had become so familiar as really to have been abstracted in symbolic language. For example, a Pompeian wall painting shows the three Nymphs with the infant Dionysus, and a pedestal empty in the foreground ready for the glorified child who was to result from their care.[128]

We can at last see also what was depicted in a painting, now destroyed, in the Baths of Titus, fig. 214,[129] where Hermes is with the Nymphs, who receive the baby inert, but by nursing make him vividly alive. We feel a strong analogy in symbolism here, or in the order of events, to the dead child and living child with its mother in the Elijah painting at Dura. The Nymphs appear as the nurse in the Homeric Hymns, and it was Hermes who brought the baby to them.[130]

Double birth was especially appropriate for Dionysus, to whom it was ascribed in terms of several myths. The second birth from Zeus' thigh, in its various forms, comes at once to mind. That the second birth should occur through the nursing of the Nymphs, who, we saw, were essentially nurses, is explained to us by Philo, who said that *hoi polloi* about him considered that an infant which had not yet partaken of human food—that is, had not yet been nursed—was not to be regarded as a human being. Though the Jews did not agree, apparently Greeks justified exposing infants on this basis.[131] A basic rationale seems to run beneath the varieties of myths and representations, that the divine baby who was to bring salvation had become such by a divine nursing or washing, which creates the saving divine child of the mystery religion, or of royalty. The contrast between the religious value of the infant Dionysus and that of the adult Dionysus may well have corresponded to the contrast in value between Christian representations of the infant Jesus and those of the adult Christ. In the infant Jesus the believer feels the ultimate values of salvation through the loving incarnation, quite apart from the future agonies of the savior. Here is the beginning and ending, the love of God manifest in Jesus. In pagan scenes, the baby seems to have had much the same value when Eros or Cupid [132] takes the place of Dionysus in the same poses; or rather when the baby Dionysus is represented as a cupid. It is often hard to say whether an infant held or confronted by a satyr and offered a bunch of grapes is

127. Sitte discusses the fragment of a third sarcophagus which preserves only the incident of the elevation of the child onto, here, a pedestal.

128. *Mon. ined.*, XII (1884–85), plate XVIII. A wall painting in the Villa of the Transtevera, which Reinach, *Peintures*, 328, says is too damaged to reproduce otherwise. See also Curtius, figs. 64 f.

129. From N. Ponce, *Description des Bains de Titus*, 1786, plate 16. The birth of the god with

the Nymphs to wash him in the usual way appeared directly under this painting.

130. Hymn XXVI. The Nymphs prepared Aeneas to reign among the Trojans by bringing him up after he was born of Aphrodite and Anchises: ibid. v, lines 195–199, 256–279.

131. *Mos.* I, 11; cf. *Spec.* III, 109, 117. See my *The Jurisprudence of the Jewish Courts in Egypt*, 1929, 116.

132. On the cupid see above, VIII, 3–21.

Dionysus as a cupid, or Cupid as Dionysus.[133] It really makes no difference, for the two have clearly been identified. The same notion of an offering of love is indicated, apparently, when Venus holds out a divine baby.[134] We remind ourselves again that it is Venus or Anahita-Aphrodite who holds out the baby Moses in the synagogue.

Two elements in the symbolism take us even deeper into mystical thinking. For we have noticed that the little ark is by no means the clumsy basket of bulrushes daubed with pitch mentioned in the Bible, but is a little sarcophagus with a peaked gable, and there is good reason to believe that such a version of the ark was a widespread convention.[135] The baby taken out of such an ark would accordingly be rising from the dead into a new life. With this goes the extraordinary fact that as originally painted, the baby's face had no features, was simply a blank oval, at the time when Anahita-Aphrodite takes him out and gives him to the Nymphs. So Gute represented the child, fig. 338, but in restoring the painting to set it up in the Damascus Museum features were added, as in plate IX. Not until the baby is in his mother's arms at the left does he have his eyes, nose, and mouth. To this I should have paid no attention, except that in the corresponding baby scene with Elijah, as we shall see, fig. 335, the dead baby presented by the widow and the same baby when being restored by Elijah also has a blank oval for a face, while he gets features when, fully restored, his mother holds him in her arms at the right. Anderegg's color photograph, plate VIII, shows these two blank faces untouched. In the case of the baby with Elijah we know that the scene presents a resurrection, a coming into a new life, and the change in presentation has real meaning as it indicates three stages—one with the baby totally dead, one partially restored, and one fully so in his mother's arms. For Moses the same triple stage seems indicated first by the little coffin, then by the baby partially restored, then fully restored in his mother's arms.[136]

That the new birth should involve death, especially in mystic ritual, will surprise no Christian who knows that at baptism he is "buried with Christ," and rises to a "newness of life" which is associated with "glory." [137] In the Church this experience is now properly that of babies, who experience "baptismal regeneration" when, at a basin, water is poured over them from a shell. The new life involves the death of the old.

When the new life, however, begins fully only in the mother's arms a new dimension appears. For here we have the Wunderkind really as a mother-and-child complex, a phenomenon with which we are indeed familiar in Christianity. Such a pattern or such a symbol would in itself imply a world of Jewish thinking for which I know no literary justification whatever. When presented thus so clearly twice at Dura, however, I find it impossible to dismiss the notion that "mother-and-child," like so much of the virgin-birth

133. Cf. Furtwängler, *Der Satyr aus Pergamon*, plate III, 6; cf. pp. 20–22. See Helbig, *Wandgemälde der vom Vesuv verschütteten Städte Campaniens*, 1868, p. 98, no. 373; Reinach, *Pierres*, plate 42, no. 88.

134. As on coins of Julia Mamaea: H. Mattingly, E. Sydenham, C. Sutherland, *Roman Imperial Coinage*, IV, ii, 1938, plate IX, 4–7, 12 (CBM).

135. See fig. 200. Moses is found in such an ark

(covered) in the *Menolog. Basil II*; see M. Uspenskii, *Litsevoĭ mĭesĭatseslov grecheskago imperatora Vasiliĭa II: Mĭesĭats sentĭabr'*, I, 1902, 13.

136. On the possibility that such a convention existed for the infant Dionysus see the discussion of figs. 212 f., above, p. 214.

137. Rom. VI, 3 f.

pattern,[138] may have come into Christianity as an object of hope and reverence from some Jewish original, however far removed from what we think of as talmudic Judaism.

Whatever more the Dura artist may have been saying, at least he seems to be telling us clearly that what Greeks hoped from divine kings or the mystic savior Dionysus, what the Orient associated with the baby Tammuz who was raised from the dead to divinity, all this (and we suppose much more) God had made available to men, pre-eminently to Jews, in the person of Moses. The age-old succession of a mystery, and of religions of the East long before we would call them "mysteries," is here presented: a scene of the death of the saving person, triumphantly followed by his resurrection and glorification. In the synagogue painting the idea is woven into the Old Testament incident as cleverly as any allegory of Philo, and quite as explicitly. Greek and Iranian notions are adopted, only to show that Judaism, when properly understood, presents all religious values, even the pagan values, better than the pagans themselves.

3. The Nymphs in Literary Tradition

BEFORE LOOKING at literary references to such a character in Moses himself, we may well recall not only that the Christians welcomed the figure of the Nymphs to indicate the special character of Christ and the Christian and Jewish saints, but that late antiquity itself transformed the Nymphs and their gifts into metaphysical conceptions which enabled at least some Jews, as we know from Philo, to take them, or the ideas they now symbolized, into their Judaism.

Porphyry gives us most important information about this new interpretation. He, like the Dura paintings, is later than Philo, but some such ideas as Porphyry expresses seem to lie behind what we shall see Philo said much earlier on the subject, and what may well have been in the mind of the "philosopher" who designed the scene at Dura. Porphyry's passage is in his *Cave of the Nymphs*,[139] which allegorizes the cave at Ithaca as described in the *Odyssey*, XIII, 102–112. With an elaboration of detail and indifference to consistency quite worthy of allegory at its best, Porphyry makes the passage present simultaneously a variety of Neoplatonic ideas.

Into all of these we need not go, but among many details Porphyry enlarges upon Homer's having described a stream of water in the cave that was "everflowing," an epithet we have seen popularly transferred to the Nymphs themselves. To Porphyry, the cave symbolizes both "intelligible reality" (*hē noētē ousia*) and the reality perceived by the senses (*aisthētē*). Both ideas seem to him presented together when Homer calls the persons in the cave at once Naiades and Nymphs. The Naiades, who represent flowing water (matter), he says, are to be distinguished from the "powers (*dunameis*) who preside over the waters," the Nymphs. When a soul is to fall, and be born in matter, it becomes moist, and so souls are called Nymphs because the soul is the nymphlike concomitant to material water. In birth, that is, souls are "joined to water, which itself has with it the spirit (or breath) of God

138. *By Light, Light*, 154–158, 164, 171, 173.
139. *De antro nympharum* (ed. A. Nauck, *Porphyrii*

Opuscula, 53–81). The work was translated by T. Taylor, *Select Works of Porphyry*, 1823, 171–200.

(*theopnoos*)." Porphyry says that all this is traditional, and that he had the statement first quoted from Numenius; he adds that Numenius in this connection referred to "the prophet's having said that the spirit of God was upon the water." [140] To Porphyry, and to Numenius,[141] then, the Nymphs are only personal representations of a primal fluid charged with the spirit of God,[142] a fluid that enters into souls as they become incarnate. From the drawings we have seen it becomes clear that this spirit water was especially given to young gods and to divine heroes or kings. The Baalbek representation of Alexander, not far from Dura, was done in the same atmosphere that produced Numenius, and at about the same time.

Numenius himself probably had this conception from a hellenized Jew, or shared the idea with him, since he parallels the spirit-charged primal fluid of the Nymphs with that in Genesis. Numenius, it will be recalled, not only classed the Jews with the Brahmans, Magi, and Egyptians as having "mystic rites, teachings, and institutions arranged in harmony with Plato"; [143] he also spoke of Moses (whom he called Musaeus), as "a man most powerful in prayer to God." [144] True, he says here that the Egyptian sorcerers had such skill that they could disperse the most violent of the plagues Moses brought upon the Egyptians, so that he must have learned about Jewish legends not entirely from loyal Jews. But he had such respect for the Jews that, though an ardent Platonist, he was rumored to have said: "What else is Plato than Moses speaking Attic Greek?" [145] It is tempting to think that Numenius learned about Moses from Artapanus, who said that the Greeks called Moses Musaeus. Artapanus wrote that Moses was the adopted son of the princess; she, being barren, presented him to her husband Chenephus, "king of the regions above Memphis," [146] and so implied Moses' royal character. But Artapanus himself gives Musaeus as a common name for Moses among Greek-speaking people, so that we cannot claim him as the source of Numenius. It is Ezekiel, "the tragic poet," who tells the story of how the princess not only taught Moses about his birth, kindred, and ancestral God, but then, like a son of her own womb, brought him up in royal state and learning.[147]

We have good reason to suppose, therefore, that a Platonic allegory of the Nymphs flourished in Syria and Egypt, one that made them collectively the ideal mother, source of the special material-divine fluid, an idea that was expressed by their shell, by their pouring out water for the infant's bath from the pitcher to the basin, or by their nursing the infant

---

140. *De antro nympharum*, 10 (ed. Nauck, p. 63, lines 10–13).

141. The best introduction to Numenius is by R. Bentler, PW, Supplementband VII, 1940, 663–678.

142. The honey made by the bees in the cave comes to have the same meaning, and this honey is in jars: *De antro nympharum*, 15–19 (ed. Nauck, 66–70). Honey has often appeared as the divine fluid: see above, VI, 237, s.v. honey; also A. Rowe, "A Contribution to the Archaeology of the Western Desert: III," *Bulletin of the John Rylands Library*, XXXVIII (1955–56), 160 f.

143. *Apud* Eusebius, *Praeparatio Evangelica*, IX, 7.

144. Ibid., 8.

145. Ibid., XI, 10. Eusebius, one of the master historians of all time, quotes this as a common saying, but takes no responsibility for its accuracy. I would not be less cautious in using it than Eusebius himself.

146. Ibid., IX, 27.

147. Ibid., 28; cf. *By Light, Light*, 290.

at the breast. In Numenius the allegory appears a century earlier than the Dura paintings, and shows itself to be a part of the hellenized Jewish tradition. The fragments quoted reveal a tradition that Moses was an extraordinary child, a king. Philo goes much farther in appropriating the tradition of the Nymphs, and hellenizing the boy Moses who became king. These writers must occupy us for a few pages.

First, Philo very often used the figure of the heavenly female, who personalizes the flow of benefits, spirit, and divine life to men from God. In view of the pagan representations, it is not surprising that Philo preferred to call them the "Graces" rather than the "Nymphs," since grace, *charis*, was a word he could fit into his metaphysical and religious thinking. He uses the word of course often as the plural of *charis* in the general sense of a kind deed or gift.[148] But clearly the Graces are for him more than "gifts," and must still be spelled in upper case. God "rains down his virgin and immortal Graces." [149] When God promised to be with Abraham, this meant he was accompanied by the "Graces, his virgin daughters, whom the Father that begat them rears up uncorrupted and undefiled"; [150] the same "virginal Graces" accompanied God when God was with Moses.[151] The Graces are then personalities that can be "rained down." No better definition of the Nymphs could be given. But Philo more usually refers to them as "the everflowing sources (*aenaoi pēgai*) of the Graces of God," which meant to Philo "the everflowing sources, the Graces." In a thoroughly gnostic passage Philo describes how God the Father begat the universe from Knowledge (*Epistēmē*), whom God inseminated, though not, Philo hastens to add, after the manner of men. Knowledge is thus the universal mother and nurse, and the world is "the only and beloved son." This son is constantly nourished, and "like a shallow bowl receives from the mighty gushing spring of God's Graces and is straightway filled, so that it spurts up and overflows." [152] No contemporary reader could have missed this allusion to the spouting basins of the Nymphs or Graces. Colson seems entirely right in saying that Philo describes the Logos as the true cup-bearer of God when he says that it is "he who pours the libation, the truly great high priest; he takes the drinks of the everflowing Graces and responds by pouring out the full libation of undiluted intoxicating liquid, that is, the libation of himself." [153] The eternal flow from the fountain of the Graces represents God's limitless bounty, how he always gives without ever being repaid.[154] The eternal fire on the altar symbolizes man's response of undying gratitude for the eternally flowing Graces of God,[155] though they are not for all men but only for suppliants.[156] God keeps this flow free from all evil,[157] to the point that as a result of the fall it was withdrawn from Adam and Eve.[158] But

148. As in *LA* III, 10; *Decal.* 115, 167; *Virt.* 145; *Legat.* 85, 147; *Jos.* 46, 157; *Abr.* 144; *Mos.* II, 222; *Post.* 142.

149. *Post.* 32. Here and elsewhere Colson translates *charites* as "boons," "gifts," or the like. It is a pity to translate it at all.

150. *Migr.* 31.

151. *Fug.* 140 f.

152. *Ebr.* 30–32.

153. *Som.* II, 183. We recall the great figure of

Egypt who similarly receives the flow and gives it out: above, V, figs. 170, 173.

154. *Cher.* 123; cf. *Heres.* 31; *QG* IV, 231.

155. *Spec.* I, 285.

156. *Virt.* 80.

157. *Conf.* 182.

158. *Opif.* 168; cf. *QG* I, 23 (end). In a passage that Marcus confesses he does not understand, *QG* IV, 102, the flow seems to be too high for man. Perhaps one who now recognizes the figure of the

Philo generally thought the flow represented the Stream by which God was connected with the world, the relation of the Unrelated.[159] We have already seen how the world as God's son by Knowledge is constantly flooded from the springs of the Graces; [160] it, or he, is never left without a share in them.[161] Everything that is fair is to be attributed to the "divine Graces." [162]

Although Philo compares the flow to manna, the manna is the *logoi*, collectively the Logos, poured out from the "pure nature called 'heaven'," and this flow will continue for man always: it, too, is called the flow of God's Graces.[163] The Stream of God's Graces is always immaterial, of course,[164] but is sometimes ministered through material things, the essential philosophy of all sacramentalism.[165] It can come to us, actually, as the great Flood came to the world, and destroy all the unworthy (material) elements in our constitution, wash them away like fresh water.[166]

In his one definitely Messianic passage Philo makes that era a fresh flow from the everflowing springs of the Graces,[167] but more typically sees it as the real nature of the Covenant between God and Israel. He mentions this briefly in two treatises [168] but expounds it at length in another, where God's covenant is filled with his Graces [169] and the gracious gift is God's unchangeableness, stability. Stability can fully exist only in God (*to on*): it exists secondarily in the Logos, the Covenant, "thirdly in the Sage, and fourthly in the man of gradual progress." [170] The Logos is of course the Stream to cosmos and to man, and as it comes to the Sage he automatically becomes a ruler and king.[171] He holds out his own cup to this streaming Logos, and the Logos pours himself into it.[172]

The Graces have led us to the ideal Sage, one of Philo's several terms for the man of perfection who may have reached supreme eminence, like Abraham and Jacob, by toil and trouble, "gradual progress," but who, properly, is born to this estate, and is marked off from other men by his having from birth, like Isaac and Moses, an especial allowance of the flow of the Graces. To such a man the gracious God gives a certain additional inheritance or part in the covenant.[173]

Isaac received this at his birth and in his relations with Rebeccah. It appears that in his own person Isaac brought the stream of the Graces to Abraham, who was to go to the land of the Logos or Wisdom and there find awaiting him a "nature which is its own pupil, its own teacher, that needs not be fed on milk as children are fed. . . . That nature is Isaac." A variant figure for this is that on his journey Abraham will be accompanied by

---

Nymphs will be able to make more sense of the Armenian than Marcus did at this point.

159. See my *Introduction*, 127–137.

160. *Ebr.* 30–32.

161. *Post.* 145; cf. *Plant.* 89, 93.

162. *Post.* 42.

163. *LA* III, 162–164. The same conception appears where the manna "comes from the ether and heaven like a spring": *QG* IV, 102; also in *Fug.* 137, where it is the Logos flowing in "perpetual stream," the *aennaoi* of the Nymphs.

164. *LA* II, 80.

165. *Ebr.* 107.

166. *QG* II, 15.

167. *Praem.* 168.

168. *Sacr.* 57; *Mut.* 52 f., 58.

169. *Som.* II, 223 f.

170. Ibid., 237.

171. Ibid., 243 f.

172. Ibid., 245–249.

173. *QG* II, 10.

God along with God's virgin daughters, the Graces.[174] So when Abraham begat Isaac, he received the flow of the Graces through his son. But Isaac himself was given more of this flow by marrying Rebeccah, who was the Constancy or Stability that we saw was the prime element of the Covenant, itself the flow of the Graces. God "wished that his Graces should abide eternally" with Isaac, and so gave him Constancy as his wife.[175] Rebeccah seems herself to be the Graces, or one of them (we saw in pagan art that one was as good as three), and so she is elaborately allegorized in the incident of the well. Here [176] she has a pitcher (*hudria*) which Philo makes represent what Stoics call man's "ruling part" (*hēgemonikon*), the highest mind, in contrast to Hagar, who got water in a water-skin—a symbol of the bodily senses. With this pitcher she goes to the divine spring, Wisdom, and as she gives Isaac's servant to drink, she calls him Sir, thereby indicating the rulership inherent in the Sage.[177] In giving him to drink she was "manifesting the divine abundance that has been poured forth for all to enjoy who are worthy and able to do so." [178] Even in this she does not flood him with the entire abundance, for in this, as in rain (it is amazing how the figure of heavenly water persists), all the divine supply poured down at once would utterly destroy man and creation.[179] In going on to water the camels, Rebeccah is shown strengthening memory, for, after Orphic precedent, the well means memory to Philo.[180] What Philo is saying is quite clear. He has had in mind all along the analogy of the Graces, indeed mentions them once specifically.[181] Rebeccah, like them, pours God's Stream from a pitcher, and he calls the Stream again specifically the sacred Logos,[182] makes it available to men, at first to the servant, then, a fortiori, we conclude, to Isaac himself, who himself as a Wunderkind was the source of grace even for his father. The avidity with which Philo seizes upon Rebeccah's pitcher recalls sharply the flowing pitcher of the Nymphs.

Philo does not use the figure for all the biblical heroes, since he has other figures, and keeps this for those with whom the text associates water or fluid. So Hannah, her very name meaning Grace,[183] seems drunk, for she has drunk deeply of the cup of perfect virtue, and is inflamed by its potency.[184] Moses is of course another recipient of this flow, as we saw, for God came to meet him bringing along his Virgin Graces,[185] and at his death Moses thanked God for the Graces given him from his birth to his old age, Graces extraordinary that were not given to ordinary men.[186]

A literal translation of the "Graces" usually misrepresents to modern minds what Philo meant by the word. Philo no more believed in the personal "Graces, virgin daughters of God," for all his talking of them, than do we. The pagan origin and counterpart of the phrase, however, must have been quite clear in his mind. The Graces of God had become to him what we call the "grace" of God, the everflowing torrent of God's nature and bene-

174. *Migr.* 28–33. Cf. *Mut.* 155; *QG* iv, 19.
175. *Cong.* 37 f.
176. *Post.* 137.
177. Ibid. 138. The Greek *Kurios* is more than Sir. See fig. 70, from Catacomb Via Latina.
178. Ibid. 139.
179. Ibid. 142–145.

180. Ibid. 148–153.
181. Ibid. 145.
182. Ibid. 153.
183. *Ebr.* 145.
184. Ibid. 147 f., 151 f.
185. *Fug.* 140 f.
186. *Virt.* 72.

faction.[187] We can see how the mythological persons as Nymphs and Graces blended in art and literature, while Numenius shows us that the Pythagorean-Platonic school on which Philo rested had spiritualized, immaterialized, them, until their eternal flow was the great Stream of God's nature and benefaction. In this form the idea of God's grace could freely be used in literature, and when represented in art could appear as the Nymphs, the Graces, the Nurses with the babe; they might carry shells, basins, pitchers, boxes of gifts, or simply stand as the three, in their recognizable garments or nude. It was often felt unnecessary to represent the three: one of them, having a shell, or nursing, served the same purpose.

The three Nymphs at Dura now take their place as a device which hellenized Jews would have felt as little compunction at representing as Philo felt in referring to them as God's virginal daughters. I believe that Philo would himself have disliked representing them graphically. But granted the obvious fact that the Jews in Dura were saying what they had to say in the language of paintings, and granted the equally obvious fact that they painted the three Nymphs beside the infant Moses, it seems inevitable that they were talking of God's flowing Grace, and saying that it came to the baby in the special way that made him into a royal figure. Actually the phrase most expressive of the scene is that of the pre-Philonic Jewish poet Aristobulus, who said of Moses that he was "in water born." For here his higher birth is depicted through Aphrodite and the Nymphs—with the water.[188]

Secondly, we have seen frequent allusions to the gift of the Graces which made a person utterly beyond ordinary humans, a Sage whose basic quality was royalty. To this special aspect of the work of the Graces we must pay a little more attention, especially in the matter of Moses, the Wunderkind with regal nature.

In what is known as the *Life of Moses*, Philo wrote for gentiles a description of Moses.[189] He shows how Moses was the true philosopher king described by the political theorists,[190] and the ideal lawgiver, priest, and prophet. The first book of the treatise demonstrates Moses' royal character,[191] and begins at once to indicate how his royalty appeared in the incidents of his birth. Philo warns the reader that he is enriching the biblical account of Moses with oral traditions he has received from the "elders of the People." [192] He says that Moses, born of a distinguished Jewish family, from his birth "struck the eye as having more beauty than goes with a private station." [193] In political theory of the day, beauty beyond

187. This is not the place to go into the history of the doctrine of grace. But Luke clearly had in mind the idea we are expounding when he told the story of Jesus' amazing precocity in the Temple as an illustration of the fact that the "grace of God" was upon the lad. To make sure the reader understood, he put this before the story, II, 40, as well as after, verse 52. In the second passage grace is paralleled with Sophia. If Luke had I Sam. II, 26, in mind for the second statement, he has expanded it and allegorized it, in Philonic manner and matter.

188. See above, pp. 199–217.

189. For this see my *By Light, Light*, 180–198.

190. *Mos.* II, 1 f.

191. He summarizes the book by saying that he has now recalled "Moses' actions in his capacity of king." *Mos.* I, 334.

192. Ibid., 4.

193. Ibid., 9. So Philo has blown up the LXX at Exod. II, 2 (*idontes auto asteion*), into *euthus opsin enephainen asteioteran ē kat' idiōtēn*. Josephus has the child attract the Princess by his "large size and beauty": *Antiquities*, II, 224; cf. 231 (ix, 4, 6).

that of *hoi polloi* characterized royalty.[194] Such was the child found by Pharaoh's daughter, a young woman whom Philo also represents as being married but barren, and eager to have a son to succeed her father. She named the infant Moses, Philo explains, because she had taken him out of the water," for the Egyptians call water *Mōu*." [195] Philo may be abbreviating a tradition found later in Josephus, where "Moses" means "saved from water," [196] but if that is true he seems to be doing so deliberately. For to Philo, Moses was the water-baby, a term which, in view of the graphic representations we have seen, must have meant the Wunderkind.

At this point Philo's story of young Moses ceases to agree with the painting, for it seems likely that in the painting Moses was represented as having been put into the ark in the presence of Pharaoh.[197] Philo's account is much more that of the Octateuch miniature, fig. 175, for Philo has the child early weaned, and brought in to Pharaoh, aristocratic, precocious, and handsome. The princess passed him off as her own child, and so he received a royal education.[198] Teachers at once assembled, some unbidden, some summoned from Greece and Mesopotamia. But all they did was stimulate his recollection. He was shortly far beyond them, "for great natures carve out much that is new in the way of knowledge." [199] Philo clearly is thinking in Platonic terms.

These incidents only begin Philo's demonstration of Moses' supreme royal character, but we need not follow his argument further. Echoes of the concept of the Wunderkind appear in rabbinic legends, all much later than Philo, of course. Like Isaac, Moses was born, the rabbis tell us, of an old woman whose youth had been restored for the purpose,[200] and

194. See the fragments of Diotogenes quoted in my "Political Philosophy of Hellenistic Kingship," *Yale Classical Studies*, I (1928), 69–72.

195. *Mos.* I, 17.

196. Josephus adds the "Egyptian" *esēs*, saved, so that the name means "saved from water": *Antiquities*, II, 228 (ix, 6); *Against Apion*, I, 286 (xxxi). Philo and Josephus both seem to reflect a legendary treatment of the infancy story which originated in hellenistic Egypt, for in Coptic *mō* does mean "water," and *uše* "rescued," an etymology substituted by readers of the Septuagint, who also spoke Coptic, because the original Hebrew etymology became meaningless in Greek translation. The etymology in the Hebrew text was in turn a misunderstanding of Old Egyptian. See G. Beer, *Exodus*, 1939, 20, notes to Exod. II, 10 f. (Handbuch zum Alten Testament, I, iii).

197. This does not do justice to Sonne's ingenuity, "Paintings," 315 f., in suggesting that the two women are midwives, and that the woman at their feet is giving birth to a Jewish child under Pharaoh's own eyes.

198. *Mos.* I, 20. The Octateuchs represent him haloed like Pharaoh and the princess, while Miriam and Jochebed have no such distinction. The Octateuchs represent a mixed tradition of halos, the original pre-Christian one which showed the glory and light of the divine king by giving him what seems originally to have been the disk of solar deities; and the later Christian tradition of the saint in the Christian sense. In this scene the halo on the three seems to indicate their royal character.

199. For Philo's story of Moses' education see *Mos.* I, 21–24.

200. For the material in general see Ginzberg, *Legends*, II, 258–273; this account must be used carefully, however, since his notes to this section in V, 396–403, show he drew on Philo or the rabbis indiscriminately to construct it. The restoration of Jochebed's youth in *BT, Baba Bathra*, 120a (ET, II, 491), was a matter of "straightening out her wrinkles and restoring her youthful beauty," but in *BT, Sotah*, 12a (ET, 61), it meant the restoration of her "signs of Maidenhood," which could only mean her hymen.

we at once recall the hellenistic idea of the virgin birth that Philo explicitly introduces with Isaac, for whose conception Sarah was changed back into a virgin and impregnated by God.[201] At his birth the house was filled with light,[202] a detail hard to reconcile with the rabbi's story that he was concealed in the house three months undiscovered, while two Egyptian women kept constant guard lest a son be born. The effulgent child, a sign of a heavenly father,[203] or of the divine child, the Wunderkind, seems to me an invasion into rabbinic thinking from hellenism through hellenized Jews. In the biblical account Moses had such radiance only after talking with God on Sinai, so that a child of this divine origin seems quite an anomaly from the biblical point of view. Indeed many of my rabbinical friends tell me that throughout rabbinic literature there is a marked tendency to play Moses down rather than up—a tendency, they tell me, which has always perplexed them but which makes sense as a reaction against a tendency of hellenized Jews to go too far in glorifying him.

C. CONCLUSION

THE EVIDENCE seems to lead to the following conclusion. In hellenized Jewish tradition the great biblical heroes began as Wunderkinder, extraordinary in their conception, effulgence, beauty, and precocity.[204] These perquisites of the Wunderkinder were given them by the Nymphs or Graces, the flowing Grace of God. Some of these elements appear in rabbinic allusions to Moses, but with no consistent rationale. In hellenistic tradition a Wunderkind becomes normally a god or king, or both, and the symbolic tradition for representing this was by having him washed by the spirit-filled water of the Nymphs, or by their bringing him spiritual gifts. The tradition went over into the hellenized Jewish art where it was used for both Moses and David, and later adopted by Christians for the births of Mary and Christ. The same tradition explicitly appears in the Dura painting of the infancy of Moses, though adopted more skillfully to the biblical narrative than in the Octateuchs.

There is no reason to assume that this Greek tradition, so skillfully and directly presented at Dura, went from its hellenistic origin to some scattered rabbinic proof texts, and then re-emerged in the clear hellenistic symbolism of the painter. I do not remotely suppose, on the other hand, that the painter, or the directors of the synagogue who may have prescribed the design, worked directly from the pages of Philo. But the painting tells us of a

201. *Cher.* 50 f. Cf. my *By Light, Light*, 154 f., and above, p. 192.

202. *BT, Sotah*, 12a (ET, 61), ascribed to the "Sages"; *BT, Megillah*, 14a (ET, 82), ascribed to Rab. This phenomenon also occurred at the birth of Noah (Ginzberg, *Legends*, I, 145) and Abraham (see above, II, 271 f.).

203. Cain, born of Eve and the serpent Satan-Samael, had divine effulgence at his birth: Ginzberg, *Legends*, I, 105 f. The origin of the effulgence

here becomes apparent.

204. See my *By Light, Light*, 182. This appears also most strikingly in *MR, Deut.*, xi, 10 (ET, 185), where Moses did not even suck his mother's milk: cf. Ginzberg, *Legends*, II, 264. Such self-sufficiency recalls the child Horus, nursing himself from his own finger rather than anything indigenous to rabbinic thinking, although a late Midrash has Abraham nourish himself in exactly that way: see above, II, 269–272.

hellenized Jewish idea which had been clear to Philo, the idea that Moses was the Wunder-kind, one of whose prerogatives was that he had the truly royal nature, and as such could do what he is presented in the Dura wing panels as doing so dramatically: he could go to Sinai, get the Law from the hand of God, and come down to give it to the People.[205] As we shall see in the Dura painting of the Exodus, he could be their mystic leader and savior. Nothing in pictorial design could have proclaimed his character more specifically than to have him drawn from water by Aphrodite and presented by her to the Nymphs, and finally held up for adoration in his own right.

Perhaps one other detail not yet mentioned was designed to announce the same idea. Across the skirt of the last lady at the left, a running or leaping lion is painted, as in the ac-companying illustration, text fig. 14. It is well drawn in outline, quite as good as the draw-

14

ing of the paintings, so that the best guess is that it was put there by the painters themselves as a label of meaning, like the Orpheus, the Ares and Victories, and the figures on the doors of the Closed Temple.[206] We have seen that the lion was much used in Jewish sym-bolism, indeed appeared frequently in the dado itself, as well as in exaggerated importance with Orpheus.[207] It has recently recurred on three sarcophagi at Sheikh Ibreiq (Beth She'arim), figs. 215, 216, and 217.[208] These show that the lion in this position implies a victim, even when it is not depicted beneath his front feet. The arch which covers him in one case bespeaks his sanctity. Since the lion was at this time a proverbial symbol of roy-alty, it may well have been painted over the Moses scene to emphasize the notion we have seen expressed throughout the design, that the little baby king celebrated was the ideal king.

However much of this idea of royalty lay behind the Wunderkind of Isaiah,[209] and so

205. We saw that this too was a "second birth" for Moses: above, pp. 118 f. Apparently, as there were several early explanations of the divinity of Jesus, there were several also for Moses.

206. See figs. 323, 330, 332, and 333.

207. See above, VII, 33, and, in this volume,

pp. 60 and 92.

208. Courtesy of the Department of Archeology, Hebrew University, Jerusalem, Israel.

209. Is. VII, 14–17; IX, 1–7; XI, 1–12. R. Kittel, "Die hellenistische Mysterienreligion und das Alte Testament," *ZDMG*, LXXVIII (1924), 88–101.

would have been an old idea in Judaism, the painter obviously presents it to us here in hellenized symbolism. We return finally to see that the baby Moses, whose story is to be read from right to left toward the reredos, leads properly to the divine or mystic kingship of the painting in which Samuel anoints David. Both present the ideal kingship of Israel without any of the earthly success of Mordecai in the Esther panel. We now turn to the other scene of the baby, the one which accompanies the Esther scene.

Only after the foregoing was fully in type did I have an opportunity to study the scene of taking Moses from the ark in the river as painted in the newly discovered catacomb in the Via Latina at Rome, fig. 350.[210] Here the river again flows directly across the bottom of the painting as a band of water, and Moses lies in the little ark, which has a gabled end as at Dura. Three women stand on the bank to correspond to the Three Nymphs at Dura, but they have quite a different dress. The one at the left, presumably the princess, wears a richly embroidered white gown; the other two, smaller in size, wear striped dalmatics. Beside these three at the left sits a very large figure surrounded with reeds; Ferrua says she wraps herself in her *palla* or cloak. When one compares the two paintings, it appears at once that the compositions are basically similar: the horizontal river at the bottom of the panel, the peculiar opened ark with its gabled end, the three women on the further bank, and the woman with bent knees at the left—all these appear in both paintings. At Dura, however, the princess and her two attendants have become the Three Nymphs, Aphrodite-Anahita has been added rescuing the child, and the female at the left has become two figures. It seems obvious that either the Dura artist or one of his predecessors in the tradition had had a design very similar to the one in the catacomb, but had deliberately changed it to have the baby taken out of the sarcophagus-ark by Aphrodite-Anahita and held up without features to the Nymphs, while the figure at the left, still with bent knees, holds up the fully formed infant. It is possible, to be sure, that the catacomb gives us a simplified version of the more complicated design. But we are trying to go beyond possibilities to probabilities, and here, with what we shall see in the dream of Jacob,[211] it seems more likely that the design began as a simpler representation of the incident described in the Bible, and was complicated by the details added later. If that is so, I cannot see how the specific Aphrodite-Anahita and the Three Nymphs with their tokens could have been introduced for any but symbolic and interpretative reasons. We certainly cannot say any longer that the Three Nymphs were taken over to represent the princess and her servants simply as a handy artistic cliché.

210. Courtesy of the Pontificia Commissione di Archeologia Sacra, Rome. See Ferrua, *Via* *Latina*, 51, plate xciv.

211. See below, X, 166–169.

CHAPTER TEN

The Miraculous Babies: Elijah
Revives the Widow's Son

BALANCING THE SCENE of the Infancy of Moses on the west wall, we see the prophet Elijah restoring the widow's child to life, fig. 335, plate VIII. The two, as we have already observed, have features in common; the balancing of the two therefore appears to be intentional and, accordingly, meaningful.

If one looks to biblical cycles as the basis for interpreting the Dura paintings, this scene would have no place on the west wall. Immediately adjoining on the south wall is a series of four paintings, the first of which apparently shows Elijah meeting the widow,[1] the second, the scene of the futility of sacrifice to Baal,[2] and the third, the divinely granted success of Elijah's sacrifice to Yahweh.[3] From the viewpoint of narrative sequence, the reviving of the widow's son [4] should have come on the south wall as the second scene immediately after Elijah's meeting the widow. The disruption of biblical order must have had some reason, and the most likely seems to be that the incident of the revival (and presentation) of the child was taken to balance the baby Moses, with which we have already seen it has important points in common, and that the plan of designs for the south wall was made later, when other incidents of Elijah were put beside this scene. With this goes the presumption that important as were the other incidents in Elijah's career, from the point of view of the "philosopher" who designed the wall paintings the reviving of the widow's son had independent significance, and this led him to incorporate it into the ideology of the west wall, rather than make it part of a sequence round the room.[5]

1. I Kings XVII, 8–16.
2. Ibid. XVIII, 25–29.
3. Ibid., 30–38.
4. Ibid. XVII, 17–24.
5. Kraeling is aware of the displacement of this scene in the cycle, *Synagogue*, 147–149, and makes several suggestions. He does not see its special relevance to the general decoration of the west wall, and is entirely concerned with how the story of Elijah can be reorganized to make the reviving of the child its culminating incident. No ancient texts support his fanciful rearrangement. In interpreting it seems best to me to follow the design of scenes as a whole rather than biblical incidents whose order and content the artist patently disrupts. Sonne, "Paintings," 324, and R. Wischnitzer, *The Messianic Theme in the Paintings of the Dura Synagogue*, 1948, 20–29, have some good suggestions, but are so committed to making everything messianic that here as in so many places I feel Kraeling is justified in rejecting their interpretations. Wischnitzer, however, did see that in the scene's being on the west wall and in its details, it "had a symbolic quality which went beyond its face value" (p. 29).

The painting itself consists of three groups, each of an adult with the infant. On the left the widow holds out the limp and apparently lifeless child at arm's length toward the prophet. As already noted, the baby's face is a blank oval without features. The widow wears a dark skirt or himation whose end goes over her head like a veil. Her feet are bare, and the upper part of her body has been thought by all observers to be naked, in token of her mourning for the dead child.[6] In the center a man in the light robe, with pink clavi and gams, reclines on a magnificent couch with lions for legs, and holds a baby out before him toward the audience; apparently it is the dead baby now restored to life.[7] The child is badly preserved, but it sits erect, naked, in the man's extended hands, and its face likewise has no features. It holds out both arms as in invitation, much like the right hand of the woman beside it. Above this man and child are two loops of a curtain, and at the right the right hand of God,[8] a convention indicating a miracle, as we shall see in the course of examining the paintings.[9] The miracle, of course, is the reviving of the child. At the right of this group stands the third, a woman now in yellow himation and nearly white striped chiton. She holds the child in her left hand and gestures out with her right, perhaps gesturing to the prophet, perhaps in invitation and demonstration to the observer. The woman's himation is arranged like the dark himation of the other woman in the painting. The child wears only a light pink chiton, but holds up his right hand, apparently in blessing, and holds out his left, apparently in invitation, just the position of the hands of the baby Moses in fig. 338, and of Cupid with Aphrodite in fig. 185. In themselves the mother and child strikingly resemble the later Madonna and Christ child. All have agreed that this is the widow with her restored baby. Notably, the child's face at last has its proper features.

The heroic central figure is identified by an inscription, "Elijah," [10] written on the edge of his bed. The biblical narrative tells how the child was revived on Elijah's bed, so that no one can doubt the incident depicted.[11] But the splendid bed in the painting in no way suggests the cot in the upper chamber mentioned in the biblical narrative.[12] It is the bed, we shall see, of the funerary banquet, or of the deceased, deified or heroized in the

---

6. Kraeling, *Synagogue*, 144, speaks of the "bare left breast of the widow, clearly outlined above her left arm." But the body line below the arm dubiously suggests a bare breast. Also, two lines round her body above the dark skirt, if not an error of the artist, must be either a roll of fat or the bottom of an upper garment. Yet the torso is clearly in the flesh color of the face, feet, and child.

7. Kraeling, *Synagogue*, 145, describes the details here with great care. The long bench under or before the bed seems to me not a footstool but a mounting bench. See the one under the table of Phineus, above, VII, fig. 86. Cf. Reinach, *Reliefs*, III, 444, no. 2; also II, 45, no. 1; 205, no. 1, 240, no. 5. A footstool is smaller and seems indicated only for the woman who sits on the bed in such

scenes: ibid., II, 43; 163, nos. 1, 4; III, 57, no. 1. G. Richter, *Ancient Furniture*, 1926, distinguishes between a rectangular stool, pp. 44 f., and a footstool, p. 72.

8. Kraeling notes a nail on the thumb, but none on the fingers, which, we shall see in fig. 348, would mean the right hand with palm outward.

9. See below, X, 129.

10. See Torrey in Kraeling, *Synagogue*, 271, inscription 7.

11. Without the inscription the figure could have been that of Elisha, for a similar miracle is told of him: II Kings IV, 18–37.

12. Kraeling, *Synagogue*, 149, noticed this discrepancy, but not that the couch was specifically the banqueting couch of funerary association.

next world, on the tops of sarcophagi. If we are to continue to use the history of art and symbolic forms, and at the same time to identify the scene from the Bible or from Jewish legends, as a starting point for recovering the meaning of the Dura paintings, clearly we must begin by examining the implications of such a figure in such a position on such a couch.[13]

It will probably be objected that the couch and the figure on it at Dura had no implications whatever: that the artist wanted to show a great man performing a miracle on a bed, and could use this particular bed the more easily in Judaism because the form had become a meaningless artistic convention in paganism itself. But we cannot assert as a major premise that the form had become meaningless without examining the actual appearances of the bed in paganism with this question in mind. Assuredly, the form was widely used. But wide use of a symbol by no means certifies its loss of symbolic vitality, else certain "holy pictures" in Roman Catholicism, or icons in Eastern Europe, or images of Buddha in the Far East, would have to be considered "dead symbols," which they most certainly are not. On the other hand, wide use in itself cannot be taken to establish living symbolic value, else the egg and dart molding, or roses in wall paper, would have to be treated as living symbols. Before we can begin to judge what was probably in the mind of the Dura "philosopher" in representing Elijah upon this couch, we must continue our laborious method of seeing under what circumstances the symbol was actually used. The "philosopher" did not draw the bed or couch as he did for lack of artistic imagination or technique, since the sleeping person in fig. 344 has no bed at all; and in fig. 345, while the stones of Jacob's bed are clearly presented, the bands of the cushion also appear, to equate the bed with the sacred funerary couch.[14] On the occasions when the "philosopher" puts the Old Testament hero on this couch, therefore, we have every right to take the couch seriously.

In the paintings thus far considered we have come to see that the "philosopher" freely used recognizable pagan conventions as a device for interpreting, evaluating, or allegorizing the biblical incident represented. There is, accordingly, a strong possibility that he also used the convention of the bed to represent in painting what Elijah's miracle meant to him.

So far as I can discover, no one has collected the evidence for a connected history of the symbol of a person partially erect upon a couch, and I can here give only samples from the great mass of material. The figure of a man in such a position on a couch, usually holding a patera, drinking horn, or cantharus, and often with a table of food before him, is a commonplace on tombstones of the hellenistic and Roman periods.[15] Sometimes the banqueter is alone, sometimes he is accompanied by a woman who usually sits at his feet, sometimes there are other attendants. A man in such a partially erect position strikingly

13. We noted such a bed for Jacob blessing the tribes in the reredos painting: see above, p. 105. It is now proper to examine this bed more closely.

14. See above, p. 67.

15. See above, figs. 90, 133, 145, 166. No one could mistake the similarity of this couch to the birth couch, as in figs. 174, 195 f. While their forms have distinctive patterns, both seem to mean that the person is coming into, or producing, new life.

differs from a corpse. Fig. 218 [16] shows a corpse being crowned; on the vase materials are being brought to him for the funerary meal. To my knowledge the earliest such representations come from Etruria. For example, fig. 219 [17] shows the deceased presumably as he was laid out in the sarcophagus, one hand on his breast, the other touching the edge of a patera resting on his body. Even the open eyes do not alter the impression that the man is dead. At a later stage the figure begins to be represented as just awakening, lifting his head slightly from the pillow, as in fig. 220.[18] It is as though the same person as in the previous figure had lifted his head slightly and grasped the patera. He is now certainly not dead. Fig. 221[19] shows the figure vividly alive in the position of people at a banquet. This position had been represented in Etruria on sarcophagi and urns from the sixth century B.C., fig. 222,[20] and had often been used for banqueting scenes in the tomb paintings, as in fig. 223,[21] and on grave reliefs,[22] as well as in little bronze figures.[23] The burial urns and sarcophagi were probably arranged in the tombs to make a great banquet setting.[24] The developing convention for sarcophagi, by which the dead person became represented as being revived and at a banquet, is extremely important. Banquets had been eaten on couches for many centuries,[25] and banquets for the dead, or meals for the dead, are famous in antiquity.[26]

We do not know definitely whether the banquets shown in the tomb paintings, which are presumably the banquets we have watched the dead being revived to share, are ritual banquets of the survivors, or represent eschatological banquets, themselves symbols of the after life; whether the persons at the banquet are the dead, now immortalized, or the living, banqueting in their honor. My own feeling, however, is that while the convention itself shows the way living people ate at formal banquets, both the literary and iconographic evidence make it probable that when such banquets are represented in connection

---

16. Courtesy of the Soprintendenza alle Antichità della Campania, Naples. See E. Gerhard, *Gesammelte Akademische Abhandlungen*, 1866, Atlas, I, plate 1; cf. Text, pp. 3 f., 14. An Apulian vase now in Naples Museum; cf. many representations of the corpse in DS, II, 1371–1392, figs. 3332–3361.

17. Photo Alinari, no. 35,606; it is in the Vatican Museum. Cf. R. Herbig, *Die jüngeretruskischen Steinsarkophage*, 1952, plate 1; cf. pp. 46 f. and 123 f. (Die antiken Sarkophagreliefs, VII). He thinks the date cannot be later than 450 B.C. See also his plates 3 f., 7, 9 f., 11 f., 13–18, 21–26, 33, 38, 40, 45 f.

18. Courtesy of the Deutsches Archäologisches Institut, Rome. Cf. Herbig, plate 44*b*, and p. 41, no. 74. Dated at the end of the fourth to the beginning of the third century. See also his plates 8 f., 19, 26*a*, 27, 44*a*, *c*, 46 f.

19. Photo Alinari, no. 3456. Herbig, plate 53; cf. p. 21, no. 20. First half of the second century B.C.

See also many of the plates of Herbig, 48*a*–87*a*, and O. W. von Vacano, *Die Etrusker*, 1955, plates 34, 36.

20. Photo Alinari, no. 41,088. G. Q. Giglioli, *L'Arte etrusca*, 1935, plate CXVII; cf. p. 24 and plate CXVI; see also plates CXXXVI f., CXXXIX f.

21. Photo Alinari, no. 26,091; see Giglioli, plate CCIII; cf. plate CCXLIV, CCCLXXXVI f. The paintings have often been reproduced, most beautifully in color by M. Pallottino, *Etruscan Painting*, 48, 67, 81, 105 (The Great Centuries of Painting, Skira).

22. Vacano, plate 47.

23. Ibid., plates 68, 73, 76. For a Greek banquet on such a couch see Reinach, *Vases*, plate Millin II, 76.

24. As restored in Giglioli, plate CCCXCV.

25. See Phineus at a banquet on the Phineus vase of Athens: above, VII, fig. 86.

26. The material is conveniently assembled by E. Cuq in DS, II, 1384–1386.

with the dead, the participants are themselves the deceased, or the gods, or both at the same time.

Nilsson [27] sums up the material very well. In classical Greece, he concludes, while Greeks had a funerary banquet, as is practised in almost all civilizations, nothing indicates that the deceased were thought to be present, as the Romans thought at their corresponding feasts. On many graves of the Roman period banqueting couches were represented, but the evidence for this among the Greeks is very late. He thinks there are no banqueting couches on Greek graves, but that the custom came into Greece during the hellenistic period, and then in connection with the new tendency to make the dead into heroes, or minor deities. S. Eitrem says that some three hundred reliefs of this kind exist from various parts of hellenistic and Roman Greece,[28] but while the food before the banqueters shows that they are at a meal for the dead, they seem to be not the living celebrating the funerary banquet for the dead, but the dead themselves now become heroes. The earliest of such reliefs known, fig. 224,[29] is dated, however, in the fifth century, and on it the relative smallness of the man behind the two banqueters suggests that the banqueters themselves were divine. Small human beings very commonly accompany the large figures on the couch. A great many such plaques were dedicated to divine figures, as to Asclepius, Dionysus, and the Dioscuri,[30] or "every possible god," [31] and indeed in those with a funerary inscription the form of the banquet may represent either the deceased or a divinity at the celestial banquet, or both by identification of the deceased with the divinity or hero. The point in which we are interested is that the form itself had early come to indicate the heroic or divine character of the person, or couple, on the couch. Since we saw the symbolic scene so much earlier, and so persistently, with the Etruscans, I suspect that they had much to do with its acceptance, if not its creation, as a symbol of immortality and deification for the whole hellenistic and Roman world.

The convention was eagerly received in the East, and appears frequently in Palmyra. In a wall painting a haloed deity is thus represented, as usual holding up the patera.[32] In discussing the painting I, like Ingholt,[33] called it a Dionysus figure, though I agree that the god probably had another name in Palmyra. The form was as popular among the Palmyrenes for commemorating the dead as among the Etruscans themselves. We have already seen several of these, as in figs. 145 and 166. In the second the cushion is more

27. *Griech. Rel.*, I, 165, 172 f.; cf. II, 222, 522–525.

28. In PW, VIII, 1143 f.

29. Courtesy of the National Museum, Athens. See J. N. Svoronos, *Das Athener Nationalmuseum*, Athens, 1908, I, plate LXXXIII; see also Text, pp. 528–533. Svoronos thinks the naked cupbearer to be a young god or daimon, in contrast to the adoring human on the right. Cf. F. Deneken in Roscher, *Lex. Myth.*, I, 2574. The piece came from the Piraeus, and is dated in the fifth century. See the Italian plaque in Reinach, *Reliefs*, III, 266. In a plaque from Hierapolis in Asia Minor a dancing maenad entertains the divinized banqueters: ibid., II, 104.

30. For the list and references see Eitrem, 1144.

31. Svoronos, 529. He gives an excellent collection of them in his plates LXXXI–XCIV.

32. See above, VI, fig. 240; cf. pp. 67 f.

33. "Quelques fresques recémment découvertes à Palmyre," *Acta Archaeologica*, III (1932), 15 f. That so much grapevine was painted with the figure makes such an identification here highly probable.

elaborately decorated than the cushion of Elijah, but one feels that Elijah's cushion belongs in the same category. The bands on his cushion are also common on Palmyrean couches.[34]

The lions of Elijah's couch are unusual, and, I suspect, eastern. The Egyptians usually made the bed of apotheosis into a lion bed [35]—though this particular design is not Egyptian, but seems rather to be from the East, for fig. 225 [36] shows Adonis on a bed, attended by a mortal woman with disordered hair, who brings him a cup and pitcher. Seyrig thinks that R. Amy, who made the sketch, correctly restored the lifted hand, and that what is shown is Adonis rising from the dead and being offered by the woman "the vases of the funeral meal, or perhaps she has poured out the drink of life." [37] With this, then, very properly go the lions holding victims, a device which in no sense detracts from the general notion that the figure is that of a god or hero rising from the dead.[38] Lesser figures often attend the greater figures on the couches in such scenes, but a design rather similar to the one of Elijah does appear in fig. 226,[39] although here the woman and child are at the foot of the husband's bed.

From the viewpoint of the tradition of art and symbolism in the ancient world, and especially in the East, the great figure of Elijah in the white robe on the couch must accordingly be regarded as that of a heroized being, as, we may now repeat, was the similar figure in the reredos of Jacob twice represented blessing his sons.[40] In such an environment the symbolic form could not have been used inadvertently by the "philosopher." Elijah more resembles Adonis, Dionysus, or another god who can give life than simply a human being whose own heroization is being celebrated. He himself gives the baby life, through the ultimate power represented by the hand of God beside him. The baby itself, finally held up by his mother as for adoration, with its face now fully formed, recalls the exalted baby Moses.

The man who designed this scene seems clearly still to have had in mind the same sort of sarcophagus design as that in figs. 212 and 213. Here the Nymphs, naked from the waist up, hold the dead baby Dionysus, who shows that he is dead in both examples by the way in which the arm dangles, exactly the device borrowed by the "philosopher" for the widow's child.[41] We have, then, the idea of the dead and restored child of the Jewish incident depicted in the convention of a divine or heroized baby, who dies and comes to

34. See fig. 145. Cf. J. B. Chabot, *Choix d'inscriptions de Palmyre*, 1922, plates XXVII, 12; XXXII, 12 f. Such bands are rare in the West; but see an example in the Torlonia Museum of Rome, Reinach, *Reliefs*, III, 341, no. 1.

35. See above, V, 14, and figs. 9, 11, 184; VI, fig. 247. It seems to have had much the same value as the ships of the dead.

36. From a drawing by Amy published by Seyrig in *Syria*, XXVII (1950), 230, fig. 1; cf. pp. 229–236. The piece is from Palmyra, now at the Museum in Damascus.

37. Ibid., 233.

38. See above, VII, 37 f., 40, 43 f., 50, 58. For the lion symbols on Jewish objects: ibid., 31–37.

39. Photo courtesy of Caisse Nationale des Monuments Historiques, Paris. Cf. E. Espérandieu, *Recueil général des bas-reliefs de la Gaule romaine*, 1907, I, no. 76, pp. 66 f.

40. See above, p. 105.

41. In both these cases the baby when dead seems to have no, or unformed, features, but I cannot press the matter from the evidence of a photograph.

life by special miracle. The Moses scene reads from right to left, and culminates as the women hold up the Wunderkind who has been restored to life by the Nymphs, and present him beside the ideal kingship of David and the Seven. In the Elijah scene the action again moves toward the center, this time from left to right. Another Old Testament incident is allegorized to make it mean the same thing—that the power of the Jewish God is manifest through his hero, who offers men the true dying and rising baby. When Moses in the ark in the river was to be allegorized, the Nymphs were ready at hand as the ones who through water gave new divine life to babies. They intervene in the tragedy of Pharaoh's decree to bring to Jews the Wunderkind who is to become their saving lawgiver, hierophant, and king. To balance this, the kingly Mordecai, who had become the Cavalier god and wore the true diadem of royalty, is now certified as having also a divine character. The "philosopher" has such extraordinary ingenuity that he could turn Elijah's pallet in the attic into the funerary banqueting couch of pagan divinity, and endow the baby he restored to life with the prerogatives of the dying and rising Dionysus and Tammuz or Adonis of paganism. So much the combination of pagan elements with Old Testament incidents would seem to imply. We mention again that in both the baby scenes the child's face has fully formed features only when presented in the arms of his mother after his resurrection.[42] No one can look at the widow holding up the baby in this painting without recalling the Madonna of Christianity. I repeat that I know nothing in Jewish literature to justify a supposition that such a figure would have had a religious value for Jews. But I still cannot believe that the symbolism of the dead and restored baby stopped short for the Jewish painter, and did not culminate in the unit of mother and child.

Jewish literature does, however, tell us some interesting things about Elijah and the child. Elijah himself was from very early times associated with the Messiah. The tradition goes back at least to Malachi, whose words close the canonical Old Testament:

> Behold I will send you Elijah the prophet before the great and terrible day of the Lord comes. And he will turn the hearts of fathers to their children, and the hearts of children to their fathers, lest I come and smite the land with a curse.[43]

In the Septuagint [44] the translation of this passage was really a paraphrase. The "terrible" day has become only the "manifest" day, or day of manifestation; Elijah will turn the heart of the father (singular) to his son, of man to his neighbor; and a new verse is added calling upon Israel to obey the law of Moses.

Sirach, with clear reference to this passage, goes much beyond it. According to its Greek text, Elijah

> rose up like fire, and his logos burned like a torch. . . . By [the] logos of [the] Lord he shut up the heavens; thus he brought down fire three times. How glorified art thou, Elijah, in thy miracles, and who is like thee in boasting? Thou hast raised a corpse from death and Hades by [the] logos of [the] Most High. Thou hast brought down kings to destruction, those who were in high esteem from [their] couch.

42. See above, p. 228.   43. Mal. IV, 5 f.   44. Ibid. III, 22–24.

After telling how Elijah himself has anointed kings, and ascended to heaven in a whirlwind of fire, a team of fiery horses, the passage goes on to explain Elijah's permanent value:

> Thou art written down as a reproof [45] for [the] due times, to pacify anger before [it break forth in] wrath, to turn [the] heart of [the] father to the son, and to establish [the] tribes of Jacob. Blessed are those who have seen thee, and those who have died in love, for even we shall live in Life. [46]

Here Elijah has become not simply a messenger of God who averts the wrath of God from Israel, but a cosmic figure, a present hope for the righteous. In spite of the obscurity of the first lines of the second part of the quotation above, there seems to be no doubt that the passage as it now stands gives him the function of the recording angel and the mitigator of divine wrath. The Greek Sirach follows the Septuagint of Malachi in changing "fathers to their children" to "a father to his son," but substitutes for "a man to his neighbor" the new idea that by Elijah the tribes of Jacob will be established. That is, the fathers, whose wrath is softened, have become God himself, who is mollified by Elijah toward Jacob. Even more, like the virtuous men of old who have seen the prophet and died in love, we too through him may come into eternal life Elijah, who revived a corpse and ascended to heaven, can still, apparently, be "seen," and in that vision we have the hope of eternity. We recall that "Israel" for Philo meant "the man who sees God," and how completely the divine vision was for him the basis and process of salvation. The passage of Sirach does not identify Elijah with the Logos, and what the translator intended to imply by the reference to the burning logos of Elijah himself, and his power to use the Logos of God to shut the heavens, and raise the dead, we cannot say with confidence. A Greek reader of these lines who had any acquaintance with hellenistic religious thought, however, would have understood it to say that Elijah, as one of those who brought the Logos of God to men, had himself thereby miraculous power, and having ascended to heaven continued to soften the wrath of God against men and give them hope of eternal life. This passage shows what sort of thinking may have prompted the "philosopher" to have Elijah, the divinized hero, represented as lying on that "couch" which ordinary people were unworthy to occupy, and as holding up the revived baby for the hope of man. As over against this hope Sirach contrasts the collapse of kings and those (obviously gentiles) in high esteem, exactly what is depicted in the Esther scene.

Later rabbinical traditions show Elijah long glorified, though in less mystical vein. [47]

---

45. Reading *elegmos* with ms. A. The reference is to the passage in Malachi just quoted. The obscure "due times," *kairous*, refers to the "great day of the Lord" in Malachi.

46. Sir. XLVIII, 1–11. The last line with its repetition of "life" probably represents a Hebrew infinitive absolute, such as "die the death," merely a form of emphasis. I have translated the Greek as it would have been understood by a Greek reader of the text as it stands.

47. True, Elijah was a patron and revealer of Cabbala: Ginzberg, *Legends*, IV, 229–233. But I have often expressed the idea that Cabbala was largely a continuation and development of the sort of Judaism which seems to me to lie behind the symbols we are studying on Jewish remains. I do not, accordingly, include this in what I am here calling the "rabbinic" tradition, though I am fully aware that many of the most famous rabbis were mystics and, later, Cabbalists.

The stories are altogether too rich and varied to be discussed here. Ginzberg [48] has assembled the material, which tells how Elijah lives on for all time in heaven, is the heavenly recorder, as well as the Psychopomp who guides the righteous to their appointed places in Paradise, and leads sinners first to Gehenna and later, when they have atoned for their sins, to Heaven. In their own way the rabbis had much the same idea as Sirach and the painting, viz. that their hope of immortality largely lay in Elijah. Indeed, according to the rabbinic haggadah, Elijah was a heavenly king—as a man, the incarnation of one of the chief angels, and in some respects superior to the angels. [49] So without Philonic allegory it is quite natural that the hellenized "philosopher" should have put Elijah in the robe of glory on the couch of heroization or divinity. The rabbis also had suggestive traditions about the child who was revived. The boy, it was said, was actually the prophet Jonah, and his revival as a boy taught the general resurrection of the dead, but the boy in these traditions seems to have been old enough at least to eat with his mother and Elijah. [50] Another rabbinic tradition told that the boy was to be the "Messiah of the tribe of Joseph." [51] R. Dosa as early as A.D. 250 mentioned this peculiar figure (suspect by Jewish scholars as a Christian invasion because of his name), and his tradition was elaborated in later rabbinical apocalyptic literature. He will come immediately before the Messiah, son of David (the tradition tells), gather the children of Israel together, and re-establish them in Jerusalem with the Temple worship. But Armilus, or Gog and Magog, will come with their forces and kill him, whereupon the Messiah, son of David, will appear.

That the "philosopher" actually had this specific legend in mind it would be rash to assert. But some such legend is needed to account for the paintings themselves, in which he shows us the baby restored by Elijah and held up for the admiration of the audience, as the double of Dionysus-Tammuz, while he represents Mordecai as the Cavalier god, whose coming seems to promise the earthly restoration of Jewish glory. [52]

Symbolic paintings, symbols in general, as we have seen, always carry more than one

48. *Legends*, IV, 201–235; VI, 322–342.

49. See the passages in *Legends*, IV, 201 f.

50. *PRE*, XXXIII (ET, 240); cf. Ginzberg, *Legends*, VI, 318, n. 9; 351, n. 38. Kraeling, *Synagogue*, 150, n. 546, refers to these legends. See also Sonne, "Paintings," 324–330; Hempel, "Problem," 117, n. 62.

51. Ginzberg, loc. cit. For this Messiah see M. Buttenweiser in *JE*, VIII, 511. The most important passage is *BT, Sukkah*, 52a (ET, 246). I can see no way to connect this with the tradition of two Messiahs in the Qumran literature. See the translation of the Manual of Discipline in M. Burrows, *The Dead Sea Scrolls*, 1955, 383; cf. ibid., 264 f., and 355. These are the "Messiahs of Aaron and Israel." If we could give these a Philonic interpretation, the contrast would be between what I call the Mystery of Aaron (see below, X, 21) and the Mystery of Moses or of the true Israel, since Philo's interpretation of "Israel" as the "man who sees God" would go well with it. Indeed he constantly uses the name in that sense to characterize the inner and true Judaism. But I should not dare seriously suggest from any present evidence that the two Messiahs meant all this in Qumran. Whatever lies behind the two, Israel, like Aaron, must be the person, not the People as a whole, as Burrows suggests.

52. A possible connection of these two scenes may be found in a Jewish legend that Elijah intervened in the crisis in the Persian court, and "assuming the guise of the courtier Harbonah, in a favorable moment incited the king against Haman": cf. Ginzberg, *Legends*, IV, 202; VI, 325, notes 44 f. The courtier in the painting before the king may, then, be Elijah himself, but I cannot support the suggestion in any way.

meaning. Elijah as himself the hierophant and giver of immortality certainly stands forth in the design as its central motif. It does not surprise us, then, that on this scene the writers of the Pahlavi graffiti [53] should have written relatively intelligible notes. One was put upon the foot of Elijah, and reads, in Geiger's translation:

. . . .
When Hormazd the scribe came
and by him this [picture] was looked at: 'Living
the child(?) that had been dead.'[54]

A second inscription, written on the neighboring scene of the sacrifice of Elijah on the south wall, clearly refers to the painting we are discussing.

Month [*Urt-vahišt* ?], day Hormazd,
when Artāv, the scribe, came
and by him this picture was looked at and by him
the child(?) was looked at thus: 'living the dead
(be)came.' [55]

Thirdly, in the scene itself of Elijah with the child, two lines of Pahlavi were written above Elijah's right thigh:

Praise to God, praise! For life,
life eternally he gives (. .?).[56]

The inscriptions rarely interpret the scenes at Dura, but if Geiger's translation is correct, they do so directly in this case, and indicate that the dead child who became living is a type, which represents how God gives eternal life. If the Greeks and Orientals hoped for immortality through their twice-born divine babies, the Jews hoped for eternal life also, and by the painting declared that they had their own twice-born baby, and the great figure who revived him, to justify that hope.

A word should be said in summary of our analysis of the lowest register of biblical paintings of the west wall. We have seen reason to believe that Judaism is being presented simultaneously in two levels or approaches. On the left is Jewish kingship in the mundane sense. Divine intervention brings in a very real Mordecai to triumph over the equally real kingdoms of the earth represented by Ahasuerus and Haman. Beside him the miracle of Elijah symbolizes the divine power to raise men from the dead, and the belief that the Messiah, whose portent will be both Elijah and the miraculous baby he provides, will indeed come from God. In contrast, the two paintings on the other side of the Torah niche present the miracle of the baby who conquers death for a divine life, but this time the baby is Moses himself. This miracle culminates in the purely hieratic kingship of

53. In Kraeling, *Synagogue*, 309.
54. Ibid., 309, inscription 49.

55. Ibid., 311, inscription 51.
56. Ibid., 315, inscription 55.